Secession and Statehood

This book analyses the complex phenomenon of secession as a form of creation of States from the perspective of international law. As opposed to other approaches based on the analysis of the political foundation of the secessionist processes or on the construction of a legal basis that justifies the existing practice, the aim is to provide an explanation of secession as a practice covered neither by the legal regime of the United Nations for the self-determination of colonial peoples nor by the regulations and guidelines relating to the human rights of minorities and indigenous populations, both in the UN and in regional organisations (Organization of American States, Council of Europe or African Union).

It is stated that secession is a practice that does not comply with international peremptory norms – such as those that prohibit going against the territorial integrity of the States, the use of force or intervention in the internal affairs of other States. Even being aware of the inevitable consequences of the effective creation of States and other *de facto* entities on trade relations, communications and the rights of individuals, among other matters, secession is a practice that should lead to an obligation of nonrecognition by States and by international organisations. As an example of this practice, the secessionist process in Catalonia since 2014 is explained and studied.

Ana Gemma López Martín is Professor of Public International Law at the Complutense University of Madrid, Spain.

José Antonio Perea Unceta is Professor of Public International Law at the Complutense University of Madrid, Spain.

Routledge Research in International Law

The Responsibility to Protect in International Law
Philosophical Investigations
Natalie Oman

The Responsibility to Protect in Libya and Syria
Mass Atrocities, Human Protection, and International Law
Yasmine Nahlawi

Public Private Partnership Contracts
The Middle East and North Africa
Mohamed Ismail

WTO Jurisprudence
Governments, Private Rights, and International Trade
Wenwei Guan

State Territory and International Law
Josephat Ezenwajiaku

Territorial Disputes and State Sovereignty
International Law and Politics
Jorge E. Núñez

Indigenous-Industry Agreements, Natural Resources and the Law
Edited by Ibironke T. Odumosu-Ayanu and Dwight Newman

Secession and Statehood
Lessons from Spain and Catalonia
Edited by Ana Gemma López Martín and José Antonio Perea Unceta

For more information about this series, please visit www.routledge.com/Routledge-Research-in-International-Law/book-series/INTNLLAW

Secession and Statehood

Lessons from Spain and Catalonia

Ana Gemma López Martín and
José Antonio Perea Unceta

Routledge
Taylor & Francis Group
LONDON AND NEW YORK

First published 2022
by Routledge
2 Park Square, Milton Park, Abingdon, Oxon OX14 4RN

and by Routledge
605 Third Avenue, New York, NY 10158

Routledge is an imprint of the Taylor & Francis Group, an informa business

British Library Cataloguing-in-Publication Data
A catalogue record for this book is available from the British Library

Library of Congress Cataloging-in-Publication Data
A catalog record has been requested for this book

ISBN: 978-0-367-77420-2 (hbk)
ISBN: 978-1-032-06113-9 (pbk)
ISBN: 978-1-003-20077-2 (ebk)

DOI: 10.4324/9781003200772

Typeset in Bembo
by Taylor & Francis Books

Contents

List of abbreviations

AIP	Aeronautical Information Publications
AMHS	Aeronautical Message Handling System
AU	African Union
BOE	Boletín Oficial del Estado (Official Gazette of the Spanish State)
CIS	Commonwealth of Independent States
DIPLOCAT	Consejo de Diplomacia Pública de Cataluña (Council of Public Diplomacy of Catalonia)
EC	European Community
ECHR	European Court of Human Rights
ECOWAS	Economic Community of West African States
EEC	European Economic Community
EU	European Union
GAOR	General Assembly Official Records
GDP	Gross Domestic Product
HRC	Human Rights Committee
ICAO	International Civil Aviation Organization
ICCPR	International Covenant on Civil and Political Rights
ICJ	International Court of Justice
IDI	Institut de Droit International (Institute of International Law)
IHLADI	Instituto Hispano Luso Americano de Derecho Internacional (Hispanic-Portuguese-American Institute of International Law)
IIL	International Institute for Learning, Inc.
ILA	International Law Association
ILC	International Law Commission
ILO	International Labour Organization
IMF	International Monetary Fund
ISIS	Islamic State of Iraq and Syria
ISO	International Organization for Standardization
ITU	International Telecommunication Union
NATO	North Atlantic Treaty Organization
NOTAMs	Notices to Airmen
OAS	Organization of American States
OAU	Organization for African Unity

OSCE	Organization for Security and Co-operation in Europe
SFRY	Socialist Federal Republic of Yugoslavia
SSR	Soviet Socialist Republics
TRNC	Turkish Republic of Northern Cyprus
UCM	Universidad Complutense de Madrid (Complutense University of Madrid)
UK	United Kingdom
UN	United Nations
UNCIO	United Nations Conference on International Organization
UNCRO	United Nations Confidence Restoration Operation in Croatia
UNESCO	United Nations Educational, Scientific and Cultural Organization
UNGA	United Nations General Assembly
UNMIK	United Nations Interim Administration Mission in Kosovo
UPU	Universal Postal Union
USA	United States of America
USSR	Union of Soviet Socialist Republics

Introduction

The armed conflicts that occurred in the 1960s in places such as Biafra (Nigeria) and Katanga (Congo) highlighted the existence of a political problem of the utmost importance for national and regional security in relation to the creation of States, in these cases by means of secession, the solution to which was not provided for in the general international law that recognised and developed the right of self-determination of peoples under colonial domination. One would have to wait until the Bangladesh War of Independence in 1971 to find an incipient discussion on the subject, just a few months after the United Nations General Assembly had added a final paragraph to the section on self-determination of peoples in its Resolution 2625 (XXV) of 24 October 1970, which contains the "Declaration on Principles of International Law concerning Friendly Relations and Co-operation among States in accordance with the Charter of the United Nations". This new paragraph declared as an exception to the peremptory norm demanding respect for the territorial integrity of independent States that said States conduct themselves in a non-discriminatory manner in respect of the peoples belonging to their territory. In the absence of conventional norms developing this declaration, subsequent explanatory resolutions or conclusive international jurisprudence, the debate about a possible international right of secession has intensified with the passing of time and, above all, with the succession of secessionist movements and processes, some peaceful – be they social or political – and others violent, in the context of serious internal armed conflicts, and some involving the intervention of other States.

One of these secessionist processes has been initiated, so far without success, by a part of Catalan society, some of the regional political parties and the Government (*Generalitat*) and Parliament of the Autonomous Community. The process began to take shape in 2006, as a result of disagreements between this regional parliamentary body and the Parliament of Spain over the new Statute of Autonomy. From then on, the Catalan institutions would insistently issue resolutions on their right of self-determination that would subsequently be declared null and void by Spain's Constitutional Court. After holding two illegal referendums, the first in 2014 and the second in 2017, on 27 October, they would declare their independence, provoking a serious confrontation with the institutions of the State.

DOI: 10.4324/9781003200772-1

These internal tensions and the international insecurity caused by secessionism require a study from an international law perspective to complement those based on an analysis of domestic legal systems. Without underestimating the importance of studying the ever-increasing number of political theories surrounding this issue, the fact of the matter is that one can only do what the rules and regulations allow, and that these are drafted, approved and amended according to set procedures. In our opinion, the worst enemy of level-headed and thorough study of this phenomenon of secessionism is, without a doubt, political voluntarism, meaning a construct of values, ideas and arguments that are disconnected, isolated and even knowingly contrary to the rights and obligations legally established as basic and indispensable norms for peaceful, predictable and orderly coexistence. Although international law may seem slow and wary of normative changes, these occur continually in all areas; it is just that the changes affecting peaceful coexistence between States and the structural principles that inform and govern it, such as protection of the sovereignty and territorial integrity of States, prohibition of use of force and the self-determination of peoples, are determined, fleshed out and amended through a heavily reinforced procedure that requires the consensus of all States. One rung below these peremptory or *jus cogens* norms it is also possible to create conventional or customary norms, among others. It is the latter context that gives rise to – or should give rise to – the debate about whether or not international norms protecting secessionist processes exist, including a thorough analysis of general international practice and the sense of obligation regarding this practice.

In this respect, secessionist practice is not very extensive, if we compare it with State creation by decolonisation or observe the territories where this remains pending, but it generates – as already mentioned – huge legal controversy, serious political tensions and even, in many cases, armed conflicts. The secession of Panama in 1903 and that of Ireland in 1922 were as traumatic for Colombia and the United Kingdom, respectively, and as far-reaching in their regional and international impact as those successfully completed in 1991 in the Soviet context (Estonia, Latvia and Lithuania) or in the Yugoslav context (Slovenia, Croatia, Macedonia, and Bosnia and Herzegovina); as were the attempted secessions, eventually thwarted by the respective States involved, of Chechnya (Russia), Krajina (Croatia), Bougainville (Papua New Guinea), Tamil Eelam (Sri Lanka) and Anjouan (Comoros). And much the same can be said of the *de facto* entities that currently continue to exist, either independently, such as Somaliland (Somalia), or thanks to the decisive support of another State, such as the Turkish Republic of Northern Cyprus, Nagorno-Karabakh (Azerbaijan), and Transnistria (Moldova), South Ossetia and Abkhazia (Georgia), supported by Turkey, Armenia and Russia, respectively.

Each type of secession generates specific problems, but in general they have certain aspects in common, mainly within the framework of the dialectic between effectiveness and legality, since although we understand that – in accordance with current international law – the creation of States by secession is not covered by the regime of self-determination of colonial peoples or by a secession regime of its own, it is plain that some States are indeed created in this way, with subsequent full recognition given by the parent State and the international community, and that certain entities subsist or have done so temporarily without such recognition.

The social importance of these legal questions has increased in recent years as a result of various independence movements, secession attempts and even self-determination referendums outside the colonial context. The Supreme Court of Canada's decision of 30 September 1996 on a possible referendum on self-determination for Quebec, and its subsequent acceptance, under strict conditions, in the Clarity Act of 2000, have reopened the debate on the existence of this possible international right of secession, in that although the decision does not deny this right in general, it does for the specific case in question. This possible and regulated 'separation', which conceptually would no longer be secession for having been consented to by the parent State, was effectively proposed, but not completed, with parliamentary authorisation – by the Scottish Independence Referendum Act 2013 – and an eventual referendum in Scotland on 18 September 2014 (with a negative result). This consensual process raised the expectations of other secessionist movements, which have not been able to distinguish between what is permitted or agreed upon (separation) and what is unilateral (secession). One such movement began in the same year in Catalonia, leading to referendums on 10 November 2014 and 1 October 2017 that failed to meet certain minimum standards and were in any case unconstitutional, and culminating in the regional parliament's declaration of independence on 27 October 2017. It should be added, as a milestone in this context of media and political attention, that the absence of a clear and coherent response from the International Court of Justice (ICJ) in its Advisory Opinion in accordance with international law of the unilateral declaration of independence in respect of Kosovo, of 22 July 2010, has also contributed to the confusion in the legal discussion about these international legal concepts and phenomena.

The general aim of this book is to offer scholars of international law a thorough analysis of the problems posed in this field by the complex phenomenon of secession as an attempt at State creation or an effective form thereof. It particularly focuses on aspects as varied as definition, classification and rationale, the absence of positive law in relation to self-determination of peoples, and the lack of evidence of an emerging international custom to support an alleged 'corrective secession' or 'remedial secession', as well as the necessary correlation between effectiveness and legality, the consequent obligation of non-recognition when an international peremptory norm is violated and, as a specific example, the secessionism promoted by some of the political parties and a part of society in Catalonia. The book provides a more legal positivist than voluntarist view, based on the study of general and specific positive law relating to State creation and of international practice – in general, the various examples it has provided in recent times, and in particular, Spain and Catalonia – and it makes wide-ranging reference to the opposing views of scholars, judges and governments.

Consequently, this work analyses the complex phenomenon of secession as a form of State creation from the perspective of international law and with particular reference to the example of Catalonia and other cases of international and domestic practice. As opposed to other approaches based on analysing the political rationale behind secessionist processes or on building a legal argument to justify existing practice, our aim is to explain the phenomenon of secession as a practice covered neither by the United Nations legal regime for the self-determination of colonial peoples nor by the regulations and guidelines relating to the human rights of minorities and indigenous populations, both in the UN and in regional organisations (Organization of American States, Council of Europe, and the African Union). Indeed, we believe that it is a practice that violates international peremptory norms – such as those prohibiting violation of the territorial integrity of States, use of force and intervention in the internal affairs of other States – and that, while we are aware of the inevitable consequences of the effective creation of States and other *de facto* entities for trade relations, communications and the rights of individuals, among other matters, it should lead to an obligation of non-recognition by States and international organisations.

Chapter 1 addresses the phenomenon of secession as an attempt at State creation or an effective form thereof, from an international law perspective. It outlines the importance of secession as a means of acceding to statehood in the context of the different forms of State creation, and also as an influence on the political tensions and armed conflicts of the past 150 years. It provides a definition of secession, determining its main characteristics and distinguishing it from other concepts. It also includes a classification of secessionist processes by degree of eventual success, plus a brief discussion of the political rationale behind these processes. In order to distinguish them from other cases that constitute separation (consented to or legally provided for) and not secession, we take a look at the possibility of territorial separation in the constitutions or legislation of certain States, such as Canada, or at internally agreed processes, such as that of Scotland.

The first chapter also outlines the complex legal problems that secession poses for international law, issues that the following chapters will focus on in more detail, and which mainly concern the declaration of independence, ascertaining the effectiveness of the constituent elements of the State, the intervention of third States, the recognition of the international community and the effects on matters such as succession in relation to: membership of international organisations, relations with other international subjects, nationality, human rights, treatment of new minorities, etc. All of these issues generate numerous complex problems due to the absence of specific rules, the indeterminate nature of evolving customs and the resulting need, in international law as it currently stands, to resort exclusively to its general and structural principles. The first consideration concerns the unit of self-determination, as there are different types of peoples (colonial, indigenous and ethnic minorities) with different legal regimes, which gives rise to the initial difficulty of classifying certain groups as one of these types, as is the case with the specific community for which the separatist leaders of the Basque Country and Catalonia in Spain claim independence. In the Catalan case, the political theories put forward regarding ethnic identity, recovery of statehood and reparation for historical injustices are discussed in comparison with other secessionist processes.

Chapter 2 explains the impossible basis of secession in the right of self-determination of peoples designed by the United Nations, starting with a review of international practice, specifically in the League of Nations and the UN. It refutes the view of some authors that secession has its foundation in the right to self-determination of peoples as devised by the UN. Indeed, neither the UN Charter of 1945, nor General Assembly resolutions such as 1514 (1960) or 2625 (1970), nor treaties or other UN-sponsored non-legislative texts in the field of human rights (such as the 1966 New York Covenants or declarations concerning minorities or indigenous peoples) regulate a right of self-determination outside the colonial context. By contrast, the regulations and guidelines laid down by the UN and regional organisations recognise the rights of minorities and indigenous people as being individual rather than collective, and so neither do they provide for a right to independence under any circumstances. Nor is there a customary law based on remedial secession – despite the defence of an increasing number of scholars – because, as we argue, there being no explicit positive law, it is necessary to prove both consolidated legal opinion and uniform international practice. International practice, the facts, could not be more negative, vis-à-vis the voluntarism of certain governments and scholars, even taking into account a broad interpretation of Resolution 2625 of 1970, the decision on Quebec, a self-serving interpretation of the ICJ's Advisory Opinion on Kosovo of 2010, or some of the statements in the Spanish Constitutional Court's 2017 Judgment on the Catalan Referendum.

Still in this second chapter, we outline the Catalan secessionist process and characterise the claims and arguments put forward by its sponsors, firstly in relation to the alleged precedents of Quebec, Kosovo and Scotland, and then with respect to the doctrine of remedial secession. After dismissing the purported similarities with the Canadian legal provision and the United Kingdom experience, we analyse the situation of the Catalans as compared with other peoples that have initiated or completed secessionist processes and, based on this analysis, explain the impossibility of applying remedial secession to the case of Catalonia.

Chapter 3 is devoted to State creation through secession in international law, starting with the definition of 'State' and the prescriptions of the 'Montevideo criteria' as the first parameter of statehood (permanent population, defined territory and government) and concluding with the need for sovereignty and independence as conditions of statehood. The study of this subject requires considering the need for effectiveness in relation to the material elements that a State must possess in order for it to exist, as well as examining the legality of State creation – an aspect rarely addressed by academic studies and even less so in international practice – through a review of the international practice that underpins the requirement of respect for legality in accession to statehood, the legal limits that must be observed and the legal effects arising from the violation of international legality in the creation of a State. As will be demonstrated, the theory of eventual success is an insurmountable obstacle for Catalan secessionism, as yet incapable of accumulating the elements of effectiveness that might possibly garner a favourable international response.

Chapter 4 focuses on another fundamental aspect, that of the role of recognition in accession to statehood and the obligation not to recognise a secessionist entity as a State. First, it presents the concept of recognition in international law and its role in accession to statehood, determining the legal nature of State recognition, explaining the eclectic model operating in practice, and reflecting on validity and legality as factors limiting the discretionary nature of the act of recognising new States. Second, it analyses the international obligation not to recognise entities that fail to respect legality in accession to statehood. After refuting the arguments against the existence of an obligation of non-recognition, we look at the international practice that vouches for the existence of an obligation not to recognise entities that have emerged in breach of international legality, confirm that the serious violation of a peremptory norm of general international law undoubtedly forms the basis of the obligation of non-recognition, and specify the content of the obligation not to recognise entities aspiring to statehood that have failed to comply with the principle of prohibition of use of force or the principle of non-intervention in internal affairs. We also highlight the decisive value of institutional non-recognition on the part of international organisations as a means of curbing the state aspirations of secessionist entities, and which is reflected mainly in resolutions calling on Member States not to recognise such entities and to refuse them admission as Member States. The chapter concludes with an analysis of the situation in Catalonia from the perspective of actual events and a possible *de facto* independence, not accepted by Spain.

The book ends with a Conclusions section that summarises the main arguments for the non-existence of a right of secession under current international law, drawing on the milestones and claims that have shaped the process and rationale of Catalan separatism since 2014, erroneously based on inconclusive practice and a fictitious 'right to decide' based on non-existent international norms.

Chapters 3 and 4 were written by Ana Gemma López Martín, PhD, Professor of Public International Law and International Relations, and Chapters 1, 2 and Conclusions by José Antonio Perea Unceta, PhD, Associate Professor of Public International Law, both of whom lecture and carry out research at the Faculty of Law of the Complutense University of Madrid (Spain). Both authors, separately or together, have been investigating these subjects – such as effectiveness in international law or the self-determination of peoples – over the last 20 years. This research has resulted in jount studies such as *Creación de Estados, secesión y reconocimiento* (Valencia: Tirant Lo Blanch, 2018); "El intento secesionista en Cataluña a la luz del Derecho internacional", in *Agenda Internacional*, 25, 36 (Lima, Perú, 2018); and "Los efectos en los derechos humanos de las secesiones de Estados y entidades no aceptadas por la comunidad internacional", en *Foro*, 21, 1 (Madrid, 2018). By Ana Gemma López Martín: "Los requisitos de efectividad y legalidad en el acceso a la estatalidad de las entidades secesionistas", *Icade. Revista cuatrimestral de las Facultades de Derecho y Ciencias Económicas y Empresariales*, 101 (Madrid, 2017); "Creación de Estados en el Derecho internacional contemporáneo en casos de secesión", *Anuario Hispano Luso Americano de Derecho Internacional*, 23 (Madrid, 2018); and "Las minorías en el contexto actual. Una aproximación a su marco jurídico internacional", in *Las minorías en el contexto actual*, (Madrid: Dykinson, 2020). And by José Antonio Perea Unceta: *El derecho internacional de secesión* (Madrid: UCM, 2000); "El derecho de autodeterminación de los pueblos integrados en Estados independientes", in *Anuario Jurídico y Económico Escurialense*, 34 (San Lorenzo del Escorial, Madrid), 2001; "Las cuestiones sobre Kosovo que no quiso responder el Tribunal de La Haya", in *Anuario Jurídico y Económico Escurialense*, 44 (San Lorenzo del Escorial, Madrid, 2011); "El secesionismo catalán en el contexto del Derecho internacional", in Foro, 17, 2 (Madrid, 2014); "La ausencia de fundamentación de la secesión en el derecho de libre determinación de los pueblos y en la violación grave de los derechos humanos", in Carlos Fernández de Casadevante (ed.), *Consecuencias jurídicas de la secesión de entidades territoriales. Una visión para España* (Pamplona: Aranzadi, 2020); and "Los derechos de las minorías nacionales en las entidades secesionadas no reconocidas: jurisdicción del Tribunal Europeo de Derechos Humanos y atribución de la responsabilidad en su efectiva protección", in Ana Gemma López Martín and Carmen Otero García-Castrillón (eds.), *Las minorías en el contexto actual* (Madrid: Dykinson, 2020).

1 Secessionist processes

Concept, classification and rationale. Political bases of Catalan secessionism

The importance of secession as a form of accession to statehood

In the international community, made up of international subjects of differing nature, States play, in any case, an indisputable leading role, as they are the only entities endowed with sovereignty and it is on their foundational nature that the creation, functioning and potentiality of international organisations depend. The political history of humanity is also, therefore, the history of States, of their creation, their development in different spheres, their international relations – whether peaceful or troubled – as well as their transformations and even their disappearance. If each historical period is a universal, regional or local atlas, the first picture shows the States existing at that time. Thus, the image of 1914 differs notably from that of six years later, the First World War having ended and the Austro-Hungarian, Russian and Ottoman empires having been diminished or completely dismembered; just as the image of this interwar period bears very little relation to the one we see in 1960 or 1975, at the outset or towards the end of the decolonisation process, respectively.

Although States are created in many different ways, be it through merger or separation, secession or decolonisation, some ways are more traumatic than others as regards national coexistence and also, of course, in terms of international peace and security, because of the tension or conflict they generate. World history over the last one hundred years has been regularly punctuated by decolonising, separatist and secessionist tensions, unlike other periods, some of which were characterised by the opposite phenomenon, that is, by the creation and expansion of continental and colonial empires. Decolonisation has undoubtedly been the characteristic phenomenon in the creation of States since 1945, just as union, in some cases (Italy, Germany), and secession, in others (Ottoman Balkans), were during the preceding 70 years.

In the same way, the history of Spain over the last century is made up of different stages and episodes of social conflicts, wars, dictatorships, periods of democracy, etc. In all of them, the centrifugal movements of certain sectors of Basque and Catalan society have played a more or less significant role: in the turbulent early years of the twentieth century, during the short-lived Second Republic (1931–1939), throughout the Spanish Civil War (1936–1939) and in

DOI: 10.4324/9781003200772-2

the latest decade of the lengthy period of social peace and democracy that Spain has experienced since 1977. Although Catalan nationalism, in particular, is of unquestionable interest from the point of view of domestic policy concerning constitutional law, it cannot be separated from a phenomenon that is international in scope and should also be regulated and analysed from the perspective of international law.

In order to understand the importance of secession as a form of State creation, it is necessary to distinguish between secession as a political phenomenon and secession as a legal problem. With regard to the former, it is remarkable how this phenomenon, despite the relatively small percentage of States it gives rise to, has still managed to generate so much social and political tension in the States that undergo these secessionist processes, and engender so many threats to peaceful coexistence between States and even a significant proportion of the domestic and international armed conflicts of the last one hundred years.

In fact, although we will clarify the distinction between different forms of State creation later on, and always bearing in mind that certain situations are difficult to classify, of the 156 State creation processes that took place between 1877 (Romania's independence from the Ottoman Empire through secession) and 2011 (secession of South Sudan from the former integral state of Sudan)[1], most of them (67%) occurred in a colonial context, either due to termination of League of Nations mandates (five cases)[2], ceasing to be a protectorate in situations of colonial rule (16 cases, including Morocco and Brunei) or directly through the independence of former colonies (83 cases). Of the remaining cases, one ceased to be a protectorate in a non-colonial context (Andorra), four are unions (such as Yemen or Tanzania), 21 are separations with or without dissolution of the pre-existing State (such as Senegal and Mali in the former case, or Iceland in the latter) and 25 are secessions, representing 16% of the total.

Their relative importance is therefore comparable to separations – characterised by the consent of the parent State – and much lower than the independences produced in the colonial context. However, there are periods in which secession has enjoyed a certain prominence. Between 1877 and 1949, for instance, it accounts for 63.6% of the cases of accession to statehood (14 out of 22), as a consequence of the decline of the Russian, Ottoman and Austro-Hungarian

1 See Appendix for a list of States created between 1877 and 2011.

2 We are referring to the territories that were detached from the Ottoman Empire as a result of the peace treaties (Treaty of Sèvres of 1920 and Treaty of Lausanne of 1923) imposed on it at the end of the First World War and converted by the League of Nations into type A mandates entrusted to France (Syria and Lebanon) and the United Kingdom (Iraq, Jordan and Palestine, which effectively became the State of Israel, and not, for the time being, that of Arab Palestine). In their origins they are examples of secession of territories, since they were imposed on this militarily defeated power, despite the fact that when these nations became independent, between 1932 and 1948, they did so in a quasi-colonial context, in that even though they were not strictly colonies, they nevertheless depended on colonial empires and shared many of the characteristics of actual colonies.

empires after the Balkan wars of 1912 and 1913, the First World War and the Russian Civil War (Romania in 1877, Serbia in 1882, Bulgaria in 1908, Albania in 1912, Finland, Estonia, Latvia, Lithuania, Poland, Czechoslovakia and North Yemen in 1918 and Mongolia in 1921), plus a few other cases (Panama in 1903 and Ireland in 1922). From then on, there is no successful secessionist process until Bangladesh in 1971; just one case out of a total of 64 new States, during a period (1949 to 1971) characterised by the overwhelming predominance of decolonisation (with 56 cases; 87.5%). This scenario continues until 1990, with no independence by secession and 22 in the colonial context (out of 23; 95.7%). Since 1991, however, there have been nine successful secessions, mainly as a result of the dismemberment of the Socialist Federal Republic of Yugoslavia following the wars waged between 1991 and 1995 (Slovenia, Croatia, Macedonia, and Bosnia and Herzegovina), the Baltic republics' recovery of statehood without the initial approval of Moscow in the Soviet Union dismemberment process (Estonia, Latvia and Lithuania in 1991) – before the separations of 11 other new States agreed in the Treaty of Belovheza of 8 December 1991 –, and the end of the civil wars in Ethiopia (Eritrea in 1993), Indonesia (East Timor in 2002) and Sudan (South Sudan in 2011), which account for 30.3% of the States created in a period characterised by separations (15 cases out of 33; 45.5%), by the processes indicated earlier, and others such as the dissolution of Czechoslovakia and the separation of Montenegro.

Secessionism does have, however, a significance in national and international political life that the previous figures and percentages do not reflect, and there are three reasons for this. The first is that all the secessionist processes that have eventually resulted in accession to statehood have – as is typically the case in this form of State creation – gone against the will of the parent State and been fraught with the social and political tensions and humanitarian and economic consequences that usually derive from territorial partitions, generally with resultant minorities that are systematically discriminated against by the new State, either because of their affinity with the State they originate from (the Russians of Estonia, for instance) or because they do not share the mobilised identity of the new majority (e.g. the Albanians of Macedonia).

The second reason is that most of these ultimately successful secessions since Ireland in 1922 have been preceded by serious public disturbances, insurrectionary situations or armed conflicts of varying duration and severity depending on the regional insecurity and casualties involved. The pre-1922 secessions were mainly a consequence of successive Ottoman defeats in the Balkan or Russian wars in the context of the First World War and the civil conflict following the Bolshevik revolution, and therefore they stemmed more from international efforts to undermine the dominance of these waning powers than from nationalist movements. However, in the aforementioned case of Ireland, as well as in Bangladesh, Slovenia, Croatia, Bosnia and Herzegovina, Eritrea, East Timor and South Sudan, secession was preceded by armed confrontations of differing duration and severity and resolved by generally decisive international pressure imposed in one form or another by the international community, be it simply political or, in some cases, embodied in peace agreements. This is the case, for example, of South Sudan[3], a territory that had belonged partly (before Sudan gained independence in 1956) to the British Protectorate of Uganda and even to the Congo Free State, and which, once Anglo-Egyptian domination had been resolved, was forcibly integrated, despite the existing ethnic and religious differences among its population, into the new Sudanese state. The subsequent discrimination of the southern Sudanese minority (Christian and animist) by the Muslim and Arabised majority in the north led to the First Sudanese Civil War (1955–1972), a conflict that resumed and worsened with the establishment of an Islamist regime in 1982 and the Second Civil War (1983–2005). The Comprehensive Peace Agreement (Naivasha, 2005) was promoted by the African Union (AU), with the help of the UN and the mediation of countries in the region such as South Africa, putting an end to a conflict that had caused two million deaths in its final stage alone. The southern territory became, with the new Interim Constitution of 2005, an autonomous region with self-determining powers that it used in the referendum of 2011, the result of which was practically unanimous acceptance of the independence option. The new State, officially known as the Republic of South Sudan, was made possible by a referendum provided for in the constitutional agreement that formed part of the peace agreement; it was not a product of the initiative and desire of Omar Hassan al-Bashir's government, but instead was imposed by the existing conflict and diplomatic circumstances. In other words, it was an inevitable acceptance on the part of the parent State to end a long and bloody domestic armed conflict in which Al-Bashir[4] was unable to prevail.

And third, those 25 cases of creation by secession do not show the true significance of secessionism in the international arena, since many secessionist processes that have undermined international peace and security for decades are missing from that list, either because they were thwarted or because even though they gave rise to *de facto* entities, they have not received international support. We are referring to such major armed conflicts as those of Biafra, Katanga, Chechnya, Bougainville, Abkhazia, South Ossetia and Nagorno-Karabakh, or to situations of tension and violence, even terrorism and rebellion, such as in Northern Ireland, the Basque Country, Cabinda, Tamil Ealam and Mindanao. Equally, no one can doubt the importance of secessionism in the political and legal debate surrounding such contrastingly peaceful matters as the Canadian Supreme Court's decision on the right to self-determination of Quebec (1998), Kosovo's declaration of independence (2008) and the subsequent ICJ advisory opinion (2010), the Scottish independence referendum (2014), and the secession of Crimea and its integration into Russia (2014), to cite just a few of the milestones that have given rise to a substantial amount of international debate as well as specialist literature in recent years. In this context, much of the political agenda in Spain since 2006 has been

3 Regarding this process, see Lokosang, Laila. *South Sudan: The Case for Independence & Learning from Mistakes*. Xlibris, 2010.

4 See Christopher, Anthony J. "Secession and South Sudan: An African Precedent for the Future?". *South African Geographical Journal*, vol. 93, no. 2, 2011, pp. 125–132.

conditioned by the Catalan question, but even more so since the first referendum, illegally called in 2014, which precipitated the confrontation between the authorities and institutions of the Spanish State and those of the Autonomous Community of Catalonia. The political and legal tension between the two reached its climax in 2017 with the second illegal referendum and the subsequent declaration of independence.

The map of issues related to secessionism speaks volumes about the importance of this phenomenon, although it must be said that they vary greatly in nature and significance. Thus, in the Americas, aside from the irredentist claims of certain islands and Central American border zones[5], most of the claims are limited to the sphere of indigenous populations, albeit in a social and legal context specific to these peoples that we will refer to later on. Nevertheless, there are some cases of secessionist movements, the most important being, because of its international impact, the Quebec question, which is clearly a secessionist claim by a minority, specifically the linguistically and culturally French population that formed part of France's colonial possessions until the end of the eighteenth century, before becoming part of Great Britain's Canadian colony. Although the second half of the twentieth century saw a continuous political struggle led by pro-independence parties, with inconclusive illegal referendums, its leap into the international arena took place in 1998 when the Supreme Court of Canada was challenged on the international laws relating to a hypothetical international right of secession for Quebec, which would eventually lead to Parliament passing the Clarity Act in 2000. But Quebec is not the only case. In 1998, the island of Nevis – the smallest of the islands that make up the Caribbean State officially known as the Federation of Saint Kitts and Nevis – held a referendum, provided for in its Constitution, in which 62% of voters opted for independence; as a two-thirds (66%) majority is required for an independence referendum to succeed, this issue will undoubtedly be raised again at the ballot box.

In Europe there are scenarios with a history of tension as a result of non-belligerent secessionist movements (although not always free from terrorism or public disorder) and others in which domestic and international armed conflicts are still being played out directly. Among the former we can point to, among others, Ulster and Scotland (in the United Kingdom), the Basque Country and Catalonia (Spain), Corsica (France), Padania and South Tyrol (Italy) and Flanders (Belgium); and among the latter, Northern Cyprus, Turkish Kurdistan, the territories with a majority Serbian population in Croatia and in Bosnia and Herzegovina, Kosovo (Serbia), Transnistria (Moldova), Crimea and the parts of Eastern Ukraine with a significant Russian population, Chechnya, Abkhazia and South Ossetia (Georgia) and Nagorno-Karabakh (Azerbaijan). Some of

5 This is the case, for example, of the Miskito population – similar in culture to their Nicaraguan affinity group – of the Archipelago de San Andrés, under the sovereignty of Colombia. Aside from the territorial and maritime dispute between Nicaragua and Colombia, settled by the ICJ in its Judgment of 19 November 2012, the Miskito minority on the islands wishes to secede from Colombia and join Nicaragua.

these processes are of an irredentist nature, since the aim is for a minority to secede from a State in order to become part of another more like-minded State (as is the case of Flemish nationalism in Belgium, part of which advocates joining the Netherlands; or the Armenians of Nagorno-Karabakh, currently *de facto* integrated in Armenia as a consequence of the 1988–1994 war), while others simply seek to create a new national State (such as the Catalan or Scottish nationalists, with respect to Spain and the United Kingdom, respectively). In any case, they all aspire to fit – some with more difficulty than others – into the category of ethnic or national minorities, which we will define later on.

In Africa, these processes concern the Tuareg Azawad (Mali and Libya), Casamance (Senegal), English-speaking southern Cameroon, Cabinda (Angola), Somaliland, Puntland and Jubaland (Somalia), Logone (Central African Republic) and Anjouan (Comoros); and in Asia and Oceania, Kurdistan (Syria and Iraq), the Houthis of Yemen, Jammu and Kashmir (India and Pakistan), Tibet (China), Naga and Gorkhaland (India), Tamil Ealam (Sri Lanka), Aceh (Indonesia), the Karenni (Myanmar), Mindanao (Philippines) and Bougainville (Papua New Guinea).

As can be seen, secessionism is the main cause of the conflicts that have taken place in the last three decades in the Balkans and the Caucasus, as well as in other places such as Cyprus, Sri Lanka, Comoros, Sudan and Ethiopia, and it is one of the factors that has triggered other conflicts in other areas of Africa, such as the Maghreb, the Great Lakes and the Horn of Africa. Therefore, it is not only a topic of domestic social and political debate, but also a major problem for international peace and security.

Searching for a concept of secession: distinguishing secession from other legal concepts

By State creation through secession we mean the effective separation of one part of the territory – and its population – from what we call a 'parent State', and which persists as such, without the consent of the latter, but always outside the context of decolonisation and in order to constitute a new State, not to join one that already exists.

The first distinctive feature is *separation*, inasmuch as it distinguishes this form of State creation or modification from merger or union, as regards creating States, and from accession or cession of territory, as regards modifying its territorial and population elements. What occurs is the loss of a part of the territory of a State as well as the population connected to it, which becomes the sovereign territory of a new State or part of the territory of another existing State. In contrast, what occurs in a merger or union is the disappearance of the States that merge or unite to create a new one, as is the case of the Republic of Yemen, constituted as a new State in 1990 through the union of the Arab Republic of Yemen (known as North Yemen, which initially seceded from the Ottoman Empire in 1918 but which was not definitively independent until 1932, first as a kingdom and then as a republic) and the People's Democratic Republic of Yemen (also commonly referred to as South Yemen, which emerged from British decolonisation in 1967).

This separation must be *effective*, otherwise the secession would not have been consummated. To this end, it is necessary to verify both that the parent State has ceased to effectively govern the territory and that no other international subject has taken its place. Practical evidence of the former is, for example, the factual account and demonstration of dependence carried out by the European Court of Human Rights (ECHR) in relation to Transnistria or Nagorno-Karabakh, to rule out Moldovan and Azerbaijani administration, respectively, and to propose Russian control in the first case, and practical integration into Armenia in the second (among others, the case of *Chiragov and Others v Armenia*, with Judgment of June 16, 2015)[6]. In the same way, and for the same reasons, we consider Kosovo as an entity fully seceded from Serbia, but not as a new State, since international representation and both defence and internal security fall within the remit of the Special Representative of the UN Secretary-General for Kosovo and the United Nations Interim Administration Mission in Kosovo (UNMIK), created by UN Security Council Resolution 1244 of 10 June 1999, and, therefore, by the United Nations[7]. Although it has been recognised, for reasons of strict political discretion, by a significant number of States, this is generally the view of international organisations, such as the International Labour Organization, which makes clear on its website that "Kosovo should not be treated as a country. This territory is under an interim civil administration (UNMIK) upon decision of the Security Council on 10 June 1999"[8].

6 See Perea Unceta, José Antonio. "Los derechos de las minorías nacionales en las entidades secesionadas no reconocidas: jurisdicción del Tribunal Europeo de Derechos Humanos y atribución de la responsabilidad en su efectiva protección". In *Las minorías en el contexto actual,* edited by López Martín, Ana Gemma and Carmen Otero García-Castrillón. Madrid: Dykinson, 2020, pp. 27–57.

7 For Goodwin, Morag. "From Province to Protectorate to State? Speculation on the Impact of Kosovo's Genesis upon the Doctrines of International Law". *German Law Journal*, vol. 8, no. 1, 2007, p. 7, since 1999 there has been a loss of effective administration on the part of Serbia, but no new State inasmuch as Kosovo is under international administration. Regarding this question, see Lirola Delgado, Isabel. "El ejercicio de las relaciones exteriores de Kosovo por la UNMIK. ¿Una nueva manera de crear un 'frankenstein' en Derecho Internacional?". *Revista Académica de Relaciones Internacionales*, vol. 10, 2009, pp. 5 et seq. Therefore, for Sterio, Milena. *Secession in International Law: A New Framework.* Cheltenham: Elgar, 2018, p. 20, it merits consideration as a 'protectorate'. As regards the numerous recognitions received, in the opinion of Gutiérrez Espada, Cesáreo and Romualdo Bermejo García. "*Kosovo de nuevo: apuntes críticos sobre su declaración de independencia, su constitución y otras reflexiones*". Real Instituto Elcano, Working Document no. 41, 2008, p. 17, recognising as a State an entity that does not meet all the criteria required by international law constitutes a violation of the principle that prohibits abuse of law. This argument is countered by other authors such as Anderson, Glen. "A Post-Millennial Inquiry into the United Nations Law of Self-Determination: A Right to Unilateral Non-Colonial Secession". *Vanderbilt Journal of Transnational Law*, vol. 49, no. 5, 2016, p. 1185, or Martínez Jiménez, Aitor. *El derecho de autodeterminación de los pueblos en el siglo XXI.* Pamplona: Aranzadi, 2015, pp. 251 and 314.

8 Consulted on 30 October 2017 at www.ilo.org/public/spanish/standards/relm/ctry-ndx.htm.

Second, this separation *does not cause the parent State to disappear*, because if that were the case, we would be talking about a dissolution of the State. An example of this is Eritrea's independence in 1993, which does not prevent the survival of Ethiopia, whose territory and population are reduced but which does not disappear. A case of dissolution (by separation with consent) is that of Czechoslovakia in 1990, since the creation of the new States – the Czech Republic and Slovakia – entails the disappearance of the pre-existing State. A particularly complex case is that of the States that emerged from the wars in Yugoslavia (1991–1995), which we regard as secession, as there was a separation without consent of all the constituent parts of the Socialist Federal Republic of Yugoslavia (SFRY)[9], a State which had been created voluntarily by different peoples and countries after the First World War, and which became quasi-confederal according to the constitutional text amended in 1978. This lack of consensus is particularly evident in Slovenia's independence, since the brief conflict known as the Ten-Day War (27 June–6 July 1991) was fought between the Slovenian territorial militia and the Yugoslav People's Army (JNA, *Jugoslovenska Narodna Armija*) and the disappearance of the SFRY was not certified until 27 April 1992, the date of proclamation of the Federal Republic of Yugoslavia, composed of the Yugoslav federal republics (namely, Serbia and Montenegro) that did not agree to the separation of the other territories.

Third, it is essential that this independence occur *without the consent* of the parent State, because otherwise it would be a case of simple 'separation'[10]. It should be made clear that there is no need for such lack of consent to persist throughout the generally long, complex and troubled process of succession[11], but merely for it to be a subjective feature of the relationship between the

9 In the same vein, Crawford, James. *The Creation of States in International Law*. Oxford: Oxford University Press, 2nd. ed., 2006, pp. 390–391.

10 Ibid., p. 330. As Crawford asserts in his report of 19 February 1997 on "State Practice and International Law in Relation to Unilateral Secession", in the framework of the Supreme Court of Canada proceedings concerning the Quebec question,

> secession is the process by which a particular group seeks to separate itself from the state to which it belongs, and to create a new state on part of the territory of that state. It is to be distinguished from a consensual process by which a state confers independence on a particular territory and people by legislative or other means, a process which may be referred to as devolution or the grant of independence. The key difference between secession and devolution is that the former is essentially a unilateral process, whereas the latter is bilateral and consensual. For the sake of clarity I will use the term 'unilateral secession' throughout.
>
> (Crawford, James. *State Practice and International Law in Relation to Unilateral Secession: Report*. Canada: Department of Justice, 1997. Consulted in https://is.muni.cz/el/1422/jaro2006/MP803Z/um/1393966/INTERNATIONAL_LAW_AND_UNILATERAL_SECESSION.pdf?lang=en)

11 As Kohen points out, "secession is not an instant fact. It always implies a complex series of claims and decisions, negotiations and/or struggle, which may -or may not- lead to the creation of a new State". Kohen, Marcelo G. "Introduction". In *Secession. International Law Perspectives*, edited by Kohen. Cambridge: Cambridge University Press, 2006, p. 11.

parent State and the new entity that seeks and, as the case may be, achieves secession. This is important, first, because the success of this form of accession to statehood ultimately depends in large part on the subsequent acceptance of the parent State, so that what dispels the international community's understandable misgivings about recognising a new State that has stemmed from an obvious violation of the territorial integrity of the parent State is, without a doubt, the parent State's eventual acknowledgement of that factual situation. This is what happened *a posteriori* with Bangladesh (recognised by Pakistan three years after its declaration of independence on 26 March 1971), and with Lithuania (11 March 1990), Latvia (4 May 1990) and Estonia (8 May 1990), all three recognised by the USSR (Union of Soviet Socialist Republics) on 6 September 1991; and *a priori* with Eritrea (referendum on self-determination accepted by Ethiopia in the London Agreement of 1991, held on 23–25 April 1993, independence declared on 27 May), with East Timor (New York Agreement of 5 May 1999, referendum on 30 August of the same year, independence on 20 May 2002 after international mediation and intervention) and with South Sudan (Navaisha Agreement of 9 January 2005, referendum on 15 January 2011 and independence on 9 July of the same year).

Second, in relation to consent, it is also important to bear in mind that a stormy secessionist process may end in an agreement between the separatist movement and the State government or between the latter and other States, generally with the participation of an international organisation, such as the UN or a regional body, but usually after a long period of unrest, repression, guerrilla violence or domestic or international armed conflicts, which prove the dissent inherent in this form of State creation. This occurred in some of the aforementioned cases, such as East Timor, a former Portuguese colony that declared itself independent on 28 November 1975 but nine days later found itself occupied by Indonesia, which formally annexed it seven months later. After more than 20 years of repression (some 20,000 killed out of a population of approximately 600,000) and violence exerted by FRETILIN (Revolutionary Front for an Independent East Timor), the Indonesian Government, under pressure from the international community, held a referendum in August 1999, whose result in favour of independence could only be applied effectively with further pressure from the international community through the UN, whose Secretary General acted as mediator in the talks held between March and May 1999, and which implemented the agreements reached through its peacekeeping operations (UNAMET, United Nations Mission in East Timor, UN Security Council Resolution 1246; and UNTAET, United Nations Transitional Administration in East Timor, UN Security Council Resolution 1272) and the military intervention of INTERFET (International Force for East Timor, UN Security Council Resolution 1264), comprising Australian armed forces. As this case shows, for 27 years Indonesia refused to allow the independence of East Timor, preventing it by brutally repressing its inhabitants, and only agreed to it under pressure from the international community, whereby although the new State was born out of an international agreement, the preceding secessionist process was long and bloody as a result of Indonesia's opposition. Similar situations occur in other cases, such as Ethiopia and Sudan.

In some of these cases, although the new State emerges in an initially colonial context, the process is not one of decolonisation but of secession. It should be borne in mind that the territory of East Timor was a Portuguese colony until 1975 and then an annexed Indonesian territory until 2002, since when it has been an independent State. As Vidmar points out, this is a case of secession rather than decolonisation because East Timor gained independence from Indonesia and not from Portugal[12].

Finally, the two *forms in which secession manifests itself*, i.e. creation of a new State or modification of the territorial and population elements of existing countries, whether by increase or by reduction, are important in legal and political terms, and even though they have certain things in common, they raise particular considerations and pose specific problems[13]. An example of initial secession and subsequent integration into another State is that of Crimea, which declared itself independent from Ukraine on 11 March 2014, proclaiming "an independent and sovereign state" and subsequently, after a referendum, asking the Russian Federation to accept it into the Federation on the basis of an international treaty. Although reference has previously been made to all secessionist processes, the subject matter of this book is secession as a form of State creation, notwithstanding the relevance of some of the points we will make about secessions involving integration into an existing State. This will be the case, for example, with regard to the international unlawfulness of violating territorial integrity, but not necessarily with some of the effects related to subjectivity and

12 Vidmar, Jure. "South Sudan and the International Legal Framework Governing the Emergence and Delimitation of New States". *Texas International Law Journal*, vol. 47, no. 3, Summer 2012, pp. 545–546. The same can be said of Eritrea, since according to Ahmed, Dirdeiry M. *Boundaries and Secession in Africa and International Law: Challenging Uti Possidetis*. Cambridge University Press, 2015, pp. 172–176, the Eritreans considered it as a decolonisation denied in 1950 and reactivated in 1993, although the author maintains that this claim is unfounded, because in the first instance it accepted a solution other than independence – specifically, integration – and by 1993 it was no longer a colony.

13 Both forms are admitted by other authors, such as Kohen, op. cit., p. 3, or Heraclides, who calls 'secession strictu sensu' that which leads to statehood. See Heraclides, Alexis. *The Self-Determination of Minorities in International Politics*. New York: Routledge, 1991, p. 1; but not by Brilmayer, for whom it is indispensable to want to be a subject of international law on a certain territory, since "what distinguishes separatist from the other minority claims is the fact that the group wishes to establish a new state on a particular piece of land", given that, as the author argues, many cases of irredentism are actually just territorial disputes in which the international actors involved claim a particular territory, usually with the complicity of the like-minded minority but sometimes even without it. Brilmayer, Lea. "Secession and Self-Determination: A Territorial Interpretation". *Yale Journal of International Law*, vol. 16, no. 1, Winter 1991, p. 193.

international responsibility, inasmuch as there is an unlawful change in State possession of a territory and its population with respect to an existing subject[14].

This concept of secession or, more accurately, State creation through secession, allows us – as we have pointed out – to distinguish it from other forms of accession to statehood, such as separation or union, and also from another form of State creation, that of *decolonisation, situated in a different context.* The illegality of the act of secession is an integral element, given that it takes place without the consent of the parent State and therefore violates, at least, its territorial integrity. On the international plane, this illegality can be circumvented, obviously, when it is provided for or permitted by a State's domestic legal system, as in the ultimately unsuccessful self-determination process in Scotland in 2014, which would not have been a case of secession but rather of 'separation'. However, a common form of legal territorial separation is the independence of peoples under colonial rule. In these cases, which are not so much separation as territorial 'disintegration', there is no illegality because it is protected by the right to self-determination of peoples.

In our opinion, decolonisation cannot be likened to secession[15] for two reasons. First, because it is carried out in a lawful manner, that is, by exercising a right established in international laws and therefore in accordance with an obligation to which the State is bound, having given its consent in whatever form, and not wishing to provide it being legally irrelevant in a specific self-determination process. And second, because the colonial territory is conceived of as being legally separate from the metropolitan territory[16], as prescribed in

14 The territory of Crimea has a population of two million, of which 59% are Russians, 24% Ukrainians and 12% Tatars. Absorbed into Russia in 1783, during the civil war of 1917–1921 it became the Independent State of the Crimean Tatars, which later joined the Russian Soviet Federative Socialist Republic as an Autonomous Republic, transferred in 1954 to Ukraine. In August 1991, it declared itself independent following a referendum in January and requested the assistance of Russia, which cancelled the 1954 transfer to Kiev. On 5 May 1992, Crimea proclaimed its independence again and the Ukrainian government, in an act of appeasement, made it an Autonomous Republic, although this autonomy was revoked three years later. On 11 March 2014, it declared its independence once again and, after a referendum held five days later (with an 83% turnout and 97% voting in favour), decided to join Russia, a move that was formalised on 18 March 2014 in the Treaty on the Accession of the Republic of Crimea and Sevastopol, condemned by the UN through Resolution 68/262 of the General Assembly, adopted on 27 March 2014.

15 Some authors widen the possibility of secession to include colonial territories; among others, Anderson, Glen. "Unilateral Non-Colonial Secession and the Use of Force: Effect on Claims to Statehood in International Law". *Connecticut Journal of International Law*, vol. 28, no. 2, Spring 2013, pp. 216 et seq.; and Radan, Peter. "Secession: A Word in Search of Meaning". In *On the Way to Statehood: Secession and Globalisation*, edited by Aleksandar Pavkovic and Peter Radan. Aldershot: Ashgate, 2008, p. 18.

16 To the same effect, Musgrave, Thomas D. *Self-Determination and National Minorities*. New York: Oxford University Press, 2000, p. xiii, and Pons Rafols, Xavier. *Cataluña: Derecho a decidir y Derecho internacional*. Madrid: Reus, 2015, pp. 113–114. To the contrary, Pavkovic, Aleksandar and Peter Radan. *Creating New States. Theory and Practice of Secession*. Aldershot: Ashgate, 2007, p. 22.

the customary rules and regulations that make up the international legal regime of the self-determination of peoples. This is expressed in United Nations General Assembly Resolution 2625 (XXV) of 24 October 1970:

> The territory of a colony or other Non-Self-Governing Territory has, under the Charter, a status separate and distinct from the territory of the State administering it; and such separate and distinct status under the Charter shall exist until the people of the colony or Non-Self-Governing Territory have exercised their right of self-determination in accordance with the Charter, and particularly its purposes and principles.

Nevertheless, full exercise of the right to self-determination of peoples is recognised – following its proclamation in the Charter of the United Nations signed at the San Francisco Conference in 1945 – in General Assembly Resolution 1514 (XV) of 14 December 1960; therefore, it is not unreasonable to include within the scope of the phenomenon of secession – as do some authors, such as Crawford[17] – cases of decolonisation that took place prior to this date, since given that self-determination of 'non-self-governing territories' was not permitted and promoted by international law, events such as the independence of Vietnam (1954) can be regarded as secession in the strict sense, insofar as it was achieved through a violent act, whereas others, such as the independence of the British South African colonies, forming the Union of South Africa, with the South Africa Act of 1909 and the Statute of Westminster of 1931, had the full consent of the colonial power, and are, in strict terms, cases of separation[18].

Classification of secessionist processes by degree of success

Classifying secessionist processes according to their eventual success allows us, in our opinion, to complete their distinctive elements, because, as we have pointed out, State creation through secession is typically a long and complex process, from its more or less controversial emergence in the domestic sphere to its arrival in the international arena. In fact, there are processes that are merely a domestic proposal, sometimes based only on a minority cultural, social or political claim, and sometimes with broad support that results in a strong presence in political bodies or mass mobilisation. If they go beyond this national stage it is because there has been a unilateral declaration of independence, in some cases solely with claims before international institutions, demands for recognition or for diplomatic and economic support from other States, and in

17 Crawford, op. cit., pp. 384–388.

18 In the colonial context prior to full exercise of the right to self-determination of peoples, we can consider the creation of India and Pakistan (1947), Indonesia (1949) and Vietnam (1954) as secessions, and the creation of Australia (1901), the Philippines (1946), Libya (1947), the two Koreas, Burma and Ceylon (1948), Laos (1953), Ghana and Malaysia (1957), and Guinea and the Mali Federation (1958) as separations.

others triggering civil unrest, terrorist acts or even internal and occasionally international armed conflicts due to the intervention of like-minded or affected countries. In its international phase, the success of the secessionist process depends on a matter of fact, that is, on there being an effective and exclusive administration of a given territory and its population by a political organisation. However, such effectiveness is usually linked to recognition, first by the parent State, and then by other international subjects, or at least – in both cases – to a toleration of its existence, the most common situation being that general international recognition (including admission to regional organisations and to the UN) does not occur until the State in which it has originated recognises it.

Taking these circumstances into account, we can distinguish between proposed secessions and secessions undertaken, and, within the latter category, between those thwarted over time without international consolidation, those currently existing but rejected by the international community and, third, those fully realised and consolidated, that is, with what we call 'eventual success'. In addition, there are a few special cases of *de facto* independence, but certainly ignored and in any case neither rejected nor accepted, as has occurred with Somaliland.

Proposed secessions

Proposed secessions include, in our immediate setting, the one put forward by certain political forces and sectors of society in the Spanish region of Catalonia in 2014, which we will discuss at the end of this chapter. Another example is Kurdistan, although in this case, in the wake of a historical demand for self-determination, first there was a period of broad self-government between 1991 and 2017, in which year it proclaimed its independence only to be frustrated subsequently by government action. In this regard it is worth remembering that the Kurdish people have claimed their independence throughout recent history, initially vis-à-vis the Ottoman Empire and during the negotiations for its dismemberment, and subsequently in conflict with the various States it has formed part of, especially Turkey, Syria and Iraq[19]. Although a century ago this proposed secession in some way entered the international arena through the peace treaties imposed on the Ottoman Empire, at present it manifests itself in acts of protest – sometimes violent – crushed by the Turkish Government, which have given rise to extensive ECHR jurisprudence, a certain prominence in the civil war that has been ongoing in Syria since 2011 and, most especially, the self-management of Iraqi Kurdistan. Indeed, the air blockade measures imposed by the Security Council in the northern third of the country in 1991 allowed the Iraqi Kurds to exercise autonomous administration of that territory, which was formalised in the federal system established by the 2005 Constitution. In reality, both the Kurdish military support for the military intervention of the United States and its allies in 2003 and, as from 2014, their struggle against the militias of the Islamic State of Iraq (later the Islamic

19 See Kreyenbroek, Philip G. and Stefan Sperl (eds.). *The Kurds. A Contemporary Overview*. New York: Routledge, 1992.

State of Iraq and the Levant), together with the serious problems constantly hindering effective administration of the country, have permitted a certain degree of self-government in Iraqi Kurdistan. This situation led to an attempt to formalise its independence by the then President of the Regional Government of Kurdistan, Massud Barzani, who called a referendum on 25 September 2017 in which the independence option was supported by 92.73% of voters, with a turnout of nearly three and a half million in a territory of barely six million inhabitants. The Iraqi Government began fighting against the Kurdish forces (Peshmerga), eventually defeating them at the battle of Kirkuk in October 2017.

There are other cases with fewer international repercussions, such as the proclamation of the Republic of Logone by one of the Muslim factions in the civil war that has been fought in the Central African Republic since 2103. The Union for Peace in the Central African Republic (UPC), led by Ex-Séléka Noureddine Adam, declared the independence of the predominantly Muslim northern region of the (mostly Christian) country on 14 December 2015. The move was initially supported by the municipalities in the area, but not by the other Muslim militias, who were more in favour of a genuine federalisation of the State than of partition. It has had virtually no international impact, nor even the support of Chad – which props up the former 'Coalition' (Séléka) – and both the French military intervention force and the Blue Helmets operation in the area, the MINUSCA (United Nations Multidimensional Integrated Stabilization Mission in the Central African Republic), established by Security Council Resolution 2149 (2014) of 14 April, have repressed any secessionist action or symbols, in their mandate to support the government and maintain law and order.

Thwarted secessions

Other peoples have managed not only to proclaim their independence but also to endure for some time as entities with exclusive control over a given territory and population until that national project was thwarted by the parent State. Among such thwarted secessions we have, in Africa, Katanga (from the Democratic Republic of Congo, 1960–1963), Biafra (from Nigeria, 1967–1970), Anjouan (from Comoros, 1997–2008) and Azawad (from Mali, 2012–2013).

The Republic of Katanga was proclaimed on 11 June 1960 and lasted until 15 January 1963 in the southernmost territory of the Democratic Republic of Congo, but its secession was frustrated by the government with the help of *Opération des Nations Unies au Congo* (ONUC). Thus, Resolution 169 (1961), of 24 November, reaffirms the Security Council's intention "to maintain the territorial integrity and the political independence of the Republic of the Congo", condemns "specifically secessionist activities" and rejects "the claim that Katanga is a sovereign independent nation", extending the mandate of the Blue Helmets mission to assist the government in restoring constitutional order.

Another similar example is that of the Republic of Biafra, proclaimed on 30 May 1967 and which existed in the south-eastern region of Nigeria until 12 January 1970. Although the differentiation between Hausa, Yoruba and Ibo communities was maintained during the period of British colonial rule in Nigeria, there even being two protectorates until 1912, six years after the arrival of independence in 1960, the new military dictatorship suppressed the federal system and severely repressed the Ibos in the southeast, a territory with important mineral and hydrocarbon resources. In the Biafran War (1967–1970) the civilian population suffered terrible massacres[20], with nearly a million deaths[21]. The Republic of Biafra was formally recognised by a handful of countries (Tanzania, Gabon, Ivory Coast, Zambia and Haiti), but it did not win the backing of the international community in general or of international organisations such as the UN and the Organization for African Unity (OAU)[22].

In 1997, the island of Anjouan, formerly a Sultanate (together with the island of Moheli), declared itself independent from the Federal Islamic Republic of Comoros (subsequently, in 2001, Union of Comoros), a situation which lasted until it was invaded, on 26 March 2008, by a multinational force (Operation Democracy in Comoros) driven by the AU and made up of Senegalese, Libyan and Tanzanian troops, with the backing of Libya and France. Much more short-lived was the Independent State of Azawad, proclaimed on 6 Abril 2012 by the National Movement for the Liberation of Azawad, made up of Tuareg militias at war with the Government of Mali, and which was rejected by regional organisations, the AU and the Economic Community of West African States (ECOWAS) after controlling the northern cities of Gao, Kidal and Timbuktu for a year[23].

We also find examples of thwarted secessions in Asia and Oceania: Aceh (from Indonesia, 1976–2003), Tamil Ealam (from Sri Lanka, 1990–2009), Chechnya (1991–2009) and Bougainville (from Papua New Guinea, 1990–2001). The former sultanate of Aceh proclaimed its independence on 4 December 1976, sparking an armed conflict that was not settled until the 2005 peace agreement between the Free Aceh Movement and the Indonesian Government. As for the island of Sri Lanka, home to the Tamil ethnic minority, mostly Hindu and with its

20 See Nanda, Ved P. "Self-Determination under International Law: Validity of Claims to Secede". *Case Western Journal of International Law*, vol. 13, no. 2, 1981, p. 273.

21 Regarding this secessionist process, see Okoronkwo, Pius L. "Self-Determination and the Legality of Biafra's Secession under International Law". *Loyola of Los Angeles International and Comparative Law Review*, vol. 25, no. 1, Winter 2002, pp. 63–116.

22 The Assembly of Heads of State and Government of the Organization of African Unity meeting in its Fourth Ordinary Session in Kinshasa, Congo, from 11 to 14 September 1967, solemnly re-affirming their adherence to the principle of respect for the sovereignty and territorial integrity of Member States, reiterating their condemnation of secession in any Member States....

OAU, AHG/Res. 51 (IV)

23 See Oraison, André. "L'obligation n de non-reconnaissance de l'État d'Anjouan: les problèmes posés par la nouvelle balkanisation de la République fédérale islamique des Comores", *Annuaire des pays de l'océan Indien*, vol. 15, 1997, pp. 143–164.

own language, the 1960s saw concerted efforts to eradicate ethnic differences to the benefit of the Sinhalese majority, who speak Sinhala and are predominantly Buddhist. Pro-independence movements provoked a civil war between 1983 and 2009, during which, at least from 1990 onwards, they maintained a *de facto* independence[24], which was eventually frustrated when they were defeated by the Sri Lankan army. A similar conflict occurred on the island of Bougainville in Papua New Guinea, which on 1 September 1975 declared itself independent under the name of the Republic of the North Solomons, albeit without any federal agreement being reached with the rest of the neighbouring islands. However, a dispute over mining operations caused public resentment that led to the proclamation, on 17 May 1990, of the Republic of Bougainville, later called Meekamui[25]. The subsequent civil war, between 1990 and 1997, was resolved through the deployment of a multinational Peace Monitoring Group that helped bring about the 2001 peace agreement, which established provisional autonomy, extended in 2005, and allowed for a future referendum on self-determination. Chechnya, for its part, a territory with a predominantly Muslim population that was forcibly incorporated into Russia in 1859, proclaimed the Chechen Republic of Ichkeria in 1991, and remained a *de facto* State from the withdrawal of Russian troops in 1992 until the fall of Grozny in 2000, after two wars between 1994 and 1996 and between 1999 and 2009, when the last insurgency was defeated[26].

The most controversial case from the point of view of international legal analysis is that of ISIS (Islamic State of Iraq and Syria, or Daesh, *al Dawla al Islamiya fi al Iraq wa al Sham*), since this legal analysis is strongly conditioned by political factors that lead many governments and scholars to prioritise the terrorist objectives and tactics of this organisation[27] rather than study it as a militia in an internal armed conflict, a government in a territory embroiled in civil war or – as in the cases we will see later on – as *de facto* entities, these being secessionist processes that failed to reach fruition due to lack of international and parent State acceptance and, in most cases,

24 Stokke, Kristian. "Building the Tamil Eelam State: Emerging State Institutions and Forms of Governance in LTTE-Controlled Areas in Sri Lanka". *Third World Quarterly*, vol. 27, no. 6, 2006, pp. 1021–1040.

25 See Islam, M. Rafiqul. "Secession Crisis in Papua New Guinea: The Proclaimed Republic of Bougainville in International Law". *University of Hawaii Law Review*, vol. 13, no. 2, 1991, pp. 453–476.

26 The Chechen Republic received tentative recognition from the Kremlin at the end of the first war, in which Russia had failed to secure its reintegration. Thus, the Agreement of 31 August 1996 sets out the "Principles for Determining the Basis of Mutual Relations between the Russian Federation and the Chechen Republic", and that of 12 May 1997 establishes the Peace Treaty and the "Principles of Relations between Russia and the Chechen Republic of Ichkeria", with other subsequent agreements on economic cooperation, food production (5 June), oil transportation (13 June and 9 September, which led to the signing of a trilateral agreement with Azerbaijan on 11 July), communications (16 June), banking and customs cooperation, and security services (15 July).

27 See, for example, Bellew, Chelsea Elizabeth. "Secession in International Law: Could ISIS Become a Legally Recognized State?". *Ohio Northern University Law Review*, vol. 42, no. 1, 2015, pp. 239–266.

because the statehood criterion of exclusive administration without dependence on or control by other international subjects is not fulfilled. In contrast, Tomuschat analyses the possible fulfilment of the requirements set out in Article 1 of the Convention of Montevideo on the Rights and Duties of States of 1933, and, although he acknowledges some doubts about ascertaining all of them, he considers that

> nothing is said in this definition about the necessary moral qualities of an entity that purports to be a State. At first glance, it seems as if the accumulation of these elements is sufficient to mechanically elevate the entity concerned to the rank of a State[28].

In Iraq, some of the most radical Sunni groups that had been fighting against the United States and its allied forces since 2003 decided, in 2006, to form the Islamic State of Iraq, which in 2011 controlled the westernmost part of Iraq and extended its area of operation to neighbouring Syria with the start of civil war that pitted several opposition groups against the Government of Bashar al-Assad. In April 2013, its leader, Abu-Baker al-Baghdadi, unified both forces, creating the Islamic State of Iraq and Syria and, on 29 June 2014, proclaiming the Caliphate. Although it had territorial control in Iraq from January 2006 to June 2016, and in Syria from April 2013 to December 2017, its territorial expansion peaked in late 2015, after it had taken key cities such as Fallujah, Mosul, Ramada, Tikrit and Raqqa[29]. What is most relevant for the purposes of this study is that this may be an example of thwarted secession, inasmuch as ISIS, at its apogee, controlled around six million people and a territory larger than many States[30], without any external dependence following al-Baghdadi's proclamation of the Caliphate in 2014, and so it should at least be considered a 'local government' in the civil wars of those States, with the aim – certainly more so in Iraq than in Syria – of becoming an independent State unlike those from which it hailed. It had its own political structure in which the main institutions were the Caliph, the *Shura* and *Sharia* Councils, a Cabinet with half a dozen ministers, and an effective provincial administration – comprising 18 provinces at the height of its territorial expansion, with provincial governors (*walí*) and an emir in charge of each municipality – that provided public services (schools, hospitals, courts, etc.), collected taxes (such as a personal tax for non-Muslims, road transport tolls, wage tax, etc.) and managed resources (mainly

28 Tomuschat, Christian. "The Status of the 'Islamic State' under International Law". *Die Friedens-Warte*, vol. 90, no. 3–4, 2015, p. 227.

29 On the conflict and the terrorist activity of ISIS: Hortal, Cervell, María José and Césareo Gutiérrez Espada (eds.). *El Estado Islámico (DAESH), ¿aprenderemos la lección?*. Valencia: Tirant, 2018.

30 Regarding its territorial control and economic resources, see Ariel Bonfanti, Fernando. "Estado Islámico: Amenaza para el mundo o el surgimiento de un nuevo Estado". *Revista Geográfica Digital IGUNNE, Facultad de Humanidades*, vol. 25, 2016.

water, oil, natural gas, phosphates and cement) as well as other activities, including those more readily associated with a criminal organisation (murder, extortion, kidnapping, looting of antiquities, etc.). It should be emphasised that in addition to the jihadist militias – some 30,000 combatants – it also had its own internal security forces, such as the political police (*Hisba*) or the secret service (*Amniyat*)[31].

Other processes in Asia have not resulted in territorial control and therefore have gone no further than being proposals, as is the case of the Indian region of Kashmir, where there have been pro-Pakistani groups and pro-independence groups, both Muslim, since the Partition of India in 1947; and also, since 1986, of the Gurkhas in the Darjeeling district of the Indian state of West Bengal; or, much more violently, of the Muslims on the Philippine island of Mindanao, who on 12 August 2013 declared themselves independent of the United States as the Bangsamoro Republik, with hardly any consequences.

In Europe there have been some similar cases in recent decades. In the Yugoslavian conflicts which began in 1991, the Serbian communities in the new States of Croatia and Bosnia and Herzegovina tried to achieve their own national States, their ultimate goal being to form a 'Greater Serbia'. In 1991, Croatia's Serbs in the regions of Eastern Slavonia and Krajina declared themselves self-governing and, subsequently, on 19 December, independent, remaining so thanks to the military support of the Republic of Serbia until military defeat at the hands of the Croatian army in August 1995. Likewise, Bosnian Serbs proclaimed the independence of the Sprska Republic on 9 January 1992, which acted accordingly until it was recognised as one of the two entities that make up the federal republic of Bosnia and Herzegovina in the Dayton Accords of 1995[32].

De facto *entities*

Other self-proclaimed independent entities, however, have managed to remain seceded from their respective parent States, despite having been rejected generally by the international community and, on occasions, expressly by the Security Council. This is the case, among what we call *de facto entities*[33], of the Turkish Republic of Northern Cyprus (TRNC, since 1983, seceded from Cyprus),

31 Regarding its administrative organisation, Servitja, Xavier. "El Estado Islámico y la organización administrativa del Califato a nivel provincial". *Revista de Estudios en Seguridad Internacional*, vol. 18, 2015; Caris, Charles and Samuel Reynolds. "ISIS Governance in Syria", *Institute for the Study of War*, July 2014; and Quivooij, Romain. "The Islamic State". *Policy Report*. 2015.

32 On these entities and the UN position, see Perea Unceta, José Antonio. *La actuación de las Naciones Unidas en el conflicto de la Antigua Yugoslavia*. Madrid: UCM, 2000, pp. 139 et seq.

33 On their characterisation, see Cullen, Anthony and Steven Wheatley. "The Human Rights of Individuals in De Facto Regimes under the European Convention on Human Rights". *Human Rights Law Review*, vol. 13, no. 4, 2013, pp.

Transnistria (1990, from Moldavia), Nagorno-Karabakh (1991, from Azerbaijan), and South Ossetia and Abkhazia (1992, from Georgia), as well as, more recently but more unstably, Donetsk and Luhansk (2014, from Ukraine). This is because they all have in common – besides international rejection – the ongoing economic, diplomatic and military support of their 'sponsor' States, in these cases Turkey, Armenia or Russia, as recognised by the ECHR in its jurisprudence[34].

The TRNC was declared on 15 November 1983, nine years after Turkey invaded the northern part of this island with the alleged aim of maintaining the independence of Cyprus and the recognition and participation of its two communities – Greek and Turkish – and of preventing its 'union' (*enosis*) with Greece as had been enshrined in the Treaty of Alliance and the Treaty of Guarantee of 1960 and the resultant Constitution, agreed to by the colonial power, the United Kingdom, and both communities. Operation Attila, carried out by the Turkish Government, resulted in the division of the island, and its economic and military support led to the possibility of creating, in 1983, and maintaining thereafter, a *de facto* entity, which in the opinion of the ECHR is an extension of Turkey[35] and which, however, is not so categorical in the day-to-day reality of the country[36]. In any case, the Security Council has expressly condemned this secession by State military intervention and has urged the international community not to recognise it[37].

As far as the former Soviet territories are concerned, what they have in common is the military intervention of neighbouring States to prevent actual or alleged discrimination – political, cultural, religious, etc. – against their respective minority communities in these States which emerged from the breakup of the Soviet Union in 1990. Said neighbouring States, Russia and Armenia, have been indispensable in maintaining these secessionist entities vis-à-vis the parent States ever since, with their military, economic and diplomatic assistance, despite the rejection of the international community. Thus, the Moldovan Republic of Transnistria was proclaimed on 2 September 1990, Russians and Ukrainians having considered that their cultural identity was threatened in the new State of Moldova and by its decision to make Moldovan (Romanian) the only official language and use of the Latin alphabet mandatory.

691–728; and Pegg, Scott. *International Society and the De Facto State*. Aldershot: Ashgate, 1998.

34 See *Ilaşcu and Others v Moldova and Russia* (Appl. No. 48787/99), Judgment of 8 July 2004; *Catan and Others v Moldova and Russia* (Appl. No. 43370/04, 8252/05 and 18454/06), Judgment of 19 October 2012; and *Chiragov and Others v Armenia* (Appl. No. 13216/05), Judgment of 16 June 2015.

35 Among others, in *Loizidou v Turkey* (Appl. No.15318/89), Judgment of 18 December 1996.

36 On the TRNC, see Rodríguez Villena, Alejandro. "Análisis de la situación de la minoría grecochipriota en la República Turca de Norte de Chipre desde el Derecho internacional". In *Las minorías en el contexto actual*, edited by Ana G. López Martín and Carmen Otero García-Castrillón. Madrid: Dykinson, 2020, pp. 59–72.

37 Resolution 541 (1983), of 18 November, of the Security Council.

By the end of the civil war that lasted from March to July 1992, the *de facto* independence of the new Transnistrian entity had been preserved thanks to the assistance provided by the Soviet 14th Guards Army, established in that territory in 1956.

The situation in the Caucasus is much more complex, since the most disputed and contested borders of the new States arising from the agreement reached in 1991 to reconfigure the former USSR[38] are to be found there, specifically between Georgia, Armenia, Azerbaijan and Russia. Prior to the dismemberment of the USSR, in 1988, an armed confrontation between the authorities of Azerbaijan in its territory of Nagorno-Karabakh and the militias of its Armenian population had escalated into a war that lasted until 1994. The Republic of Nagorno-Karabakh (or Artsakh) was proclaimed on 10 December 1991 and subsequently assisted by Russia. It has practically been a part of Armenia since 1992, when Armenian forces took the Lachin district that separates Armenia from Russian territory. The other two conflicts are located in Georgia in areas close to Russia, hence their independence movements enjoy Russian support and actually operate under the strict control of the Russian Government, which helped them militarily in the wars of 1992–1994 and 2008 and continues to provide economic assistance. The Republic of Abkhazia was first proclaimed on 23 August 1990 and again on 23 July 1992, on the latter occasion in response to the suppression of autonomy by the authorities of the then independent Georgia. South Ossetia declared itself independent on 20 September 1990, expressing its desire to join the Russian republic of North Ossetia-Alania.

An internal armed conflict with similar features has been taking place since 2014 in Eastern Ukraine, which contains areas with a majority Russian population. The republics of Donetsk and Luhansk were proclaimed on 7 and 28 April, and subsequently ratified by the voting public in highly questionable referendums on 12 May, which returned favourable results of 89.7 and 96.2%, respectively. The armed struggle against the Ukrainian Government is supported by economic and military aid from Russia, and each republic has its own Constitution, of 15 and 18 May 2014, respectively.

An undoubtedly singular case is that of Somaliland[39], a territory that had been a British colony until 1941 and a protectorate (British Somaliland) until 1960, when it was united with the former Italian colony in the new Republic of Somaliland. During the civil war that began in 1991, it declared itself independent (18 May 1991) and has remained stable since then, barring only a few

38 Belovezha Accords of 8 December 1991 between Russia, Belarus and Ukraine, and Alma-Ata Protocols of 21 December 1991, signed by the same three countries plus Armenia, Azerbaijan, Kazakhstan, Kyrgyzstan, Moldavia, Tajikistan, Turkmenistan and Uzbekistan.

39 See Kibble, Steve. "Somaliland: Surviving Without Recognition". *International Relations*, vol. 15, no. 5, 2001, pp. 5–25 and Ahmed, Dirdeiry M. *Boundaries and Secession in Africa and International Law: Challenging Uti Possidetis*. Cambridge University Press, 2015, pp. 183 et seq.

confrontations with the militias of neighbouring Puntland for the control of the eastern territories of Sanaag and Sool, albeit in a context of permanent internal armed conflict as a consequence of the struggle between Somali clans and the intervention of international terrorist organisations. It has a consolidated political structure, with regular democratic elections, and it maintains incipient low-level diplomatic relations with countries such as Ethiopia, France and the United Kingdom, and even with the African Union and the European Union. The fact that the State of Somaliland created in 1960 had a consensual basis among the previous territories, with certain agreements breached by the southernmost one as a consequence of the dictatorship of Mohamed Siad Barré (1969–1991)[40], makes this case similar to another successful one very nearby, that of Eritrea with respect to Ethiopia in 1993. Moreover, the lack of a forceful and persistent response on the part of the parent State, an unusual circumstance but one that is easily explained given the failed State of Somalia, allows Somaliland to think of itself as an ignored yet tolerated secession.

Completed secessions

In the examples cited, we can see, on the one hand, simple proposals made within the domestic sphere of States, with more or less social impact and violence, and, on the other, secessions that have taken place but which have turned out to be temporary or, having lasted for some time, ultimately unsuccessful, due to lack of acceptance by the parent State or of general recognition by the international community. In the latter category, which we label '*de facto* entities', most cases involve the 'removal' of territories, since they are closely dependent on intervening or controlling States. However, in addition to these examples, there are others involving *completed and accepted secessions*, which have created States that are fully integrated in the international community. This is the case, in the last one hundred years, of Mongolia (1921, from China), Ireland (1922, from the United Kingdom), Bangladesh (1971, from Pakistan), Estonia, Latvia and Lithuania (1991, from the USSR, for the second time), Slovenia, Croatia and Macedonia (1991, from Yugoslavia), Bosnia and Herzegovina (1992, from Yugoslavia), Eritrea (1993, from Ethiopia), East Timor (2002, from Indonesia) and South Sudan (2011, from Sudan); and, in the immediately preceding era, of Romania (1877), Serbia (1882), Bulgaria (1908) and Albania (1912) from the Ottoman Empire, Panama (1903, from Colombia), Finland, Estonia, Latvia and Lithuania (1918, from Russia; first time for the three Baltic republics), Poland (1918, from the neighbouring states), Czechoslovakia (1918, from the Austro-Hungarian Empire) and North Yemen (1918, from the Ottoman Empire).

As a first example of the most recent cases we have Mongolia, which had been an independent State since the third century BC and which succeeded in conquering China and much of Asia in the thirteenth century. The Mongolian

40 See Roethke, Peter, "The Right to Secede Under International Law: The Case of Somaliland". *Journal of Modern African Studies*, 2006, pp. 35–47.

Yuan dynasty was overthrown in 1368 and remained independent from China until its annexation in 1691. With the republican victory in China in 1911, the tribes of Outer Mongolia proclaimed their independence but were defeated by Chinese troops in 1919, and it was not until 1921 that they expelled them with the help of the Russian army, before finally proclaiming the Republic of Mongolia in 1924. In a referendum held on 20 October 1945, voters confirmed their desire to be independent, which persuaded the Republic of China to recognise the Republic of Mongolia in January 1946 despite previously having considered it part of China and objected to both Russian interference since Soviet recognition in 1924 and Japanese annexation in 1941. Although China supported Mongolia's admission to the UN in June 1946, its membership failed to materialise because reports on its actual status allowed the United States to reject it in August 1947, claiming it was a 'satellite state' of the USSR. Eventually, the Republic of China also objected because of an incident on its border[41]; however, the authorities of the People's Republic of China established diplomatic relations with Mongolia in 1951 and it finally joined the UN in 1961. In the context of our study, this case serves both to highlight the determining role of parent State acceptance and to prove that the requirement of genuinely exclusive administration in the cases of current *de facto* entities is actually a test with numerous precedents, as the first thing to be verified in the process of accession to statehood is precisely full compliance with the necessary requirements or elements.

The Lordship of Ireland, ruled by the king of England from 1171, and despite leading various rebellions such as those of 1641 and 1798, finally joined the United Kingdom of Great Britain and Ireland in 1801, pursuant to the Act of Union passed by a Dublin Parliament controlled by the Anglo-Irish minority and the British Government, and despite the formal independence enshrined in the Constitution of 1782[42]. The situation of rebellion generated by the Easter Rising of 1916 and the Anglo-Irish War of 1919–1921 ended with the truce of 11 July 1921, which allowed a bilateral negotiation between the Irish representatives and the Government of David Lloyd George that led to the signing of the Anglo-Irish Treaty in London on 6 December 1921. Both sides thereby accepted the creation of the Irish Free State, which was to become a self-governing dominion of the British Empire, like Canada or Australia. This solution, which also provided for the possibility of withdrawal from the territory of Ulster, was contested by some of Ireland's political parties, causing a civil war. The Statute of Westminster of 1931 put an end to British legislative intervention in the dominions of the Commonwealth, and the Irish Constitution of 1937 erased any vestige of subordination to

41 Regarding the agreements between China and the USSR on the status of Mongolia, as well as its situation after the Second World War, see Rupen, Robert A. "Notes on Outer Mongolia Since 1945". *Pacific Affairs*, vol. 28, no. 1, 1995, pp. 71–79.

42 The Repeal of Act for Securing Dependence of Ireland Act 1782 repealed the Dependency of Ireland on Great Britain Act 1719, which had declared that the Parliament of Ireland depended on the Parliament and Privy Council of Great Britain.

the British Crown[43]. The Irish case is especially relevant because although from the British perspective it has historically been treated as a decolonisation issue (because of its dominion status since 1921), the way it is viewed from the Irish perspective, as a secessionist process, is more appropriate[44], since it is undoubtedly a separation that was initially denied but eventually accepted after successive rebellions and an armed struggle; and also because until 1921 it was a territory that formed part of the United Kingdom, like the rest of its constituent countries, however much of its non-English population was in a situation of inequality (as happens to many national minorities) and its own institutions lacked full powers (which is also typical of centralist States).

A further 50 years would pass before another State was created by secession, namely Bangladesh in 1971, although it should be pointed out that this was preceded by a few thwarted attempts, such as the aforementioned cases of Katanga and Biafra. So exceptional was this form of State creation that contemporary authors writing in the wake of the second partition of the former British colony considered it an exceptional situation in international practice[45]. The Islamic Republic of Pakistan was formed in 1947 with two regions separated by India, the eastern region of which, Bengal, was considered to be discriminated against with respect to the western area both in its culture and in the exercise of political power. In the parliamentary elections of 1970, refusal to recognise the victory of the Awami League (east) on the part of the President, General Yahya Khan (west), to the benefit of the People's Party of Zulfikar Ali Bhutto, caused a Bengali uprising between March and December 1971. West Pakistan's brutally repressive response[46] led to India's military intervention, which soon forced Pakistan's surrender and brought victory to a beleaguered Bangladesh. Independence had been declared in March 1971, at the beginning of the armed conflict, and was prematurely recognised by India on 6 December 1971, one week before the Indian army entered Dhaka. Bangladesh joined the UN in September 1974, having previously been recognised by Pakistan (22 February 1974). The creation of Bangladesh is an interesting example, because it initiates secessionist practice immediately after Resolution 2625 (XXV) of 1970 of the General Assembly, which, as we will discuss in more detail later on, declares the applicability of the right to self-determination of peoples to non-colonial situations where minorities are discriminated against, and because it fulfils – without any doubt whatsoever – all the

43 Regarding the progressive secession of Ireland vis-à-vis the United Kingdom between 1921 and 1949, until all ties were broken, see Mansergh, Nicholas. "Ireland: The Republic Outside the Commonwealth". *International Affairs*, vol. 28, no. 3, 1952, pp. 277–291.

44 In the same vein, see Pavkovic and Radan, op. cit., p. 47.

45 Umozurike, U. Orji. *Self-Determination in International Law*. Hamden: Archdon Books, 1972, p. 199; Buchheit, Lee C. *Secession*. New Haven: Yale University Press, 1978, p. 222; and Nanda, op. cit., p. 272.

46 Operation Searchlight (March–May 1971) caused at least 300,000 civil casualties and gave rise to millions of refugees in India.

conditions for protection under this new normative proposition, in fact being a typical example.

More disconcerting, as regards their basic premises, are the indisputably similar processes whereby the republics of Estonia, Latvia and Lithuania achieved independence during the death throes of the USSR, in September 1991. The fact that they had already seceded from Russia between 1917 and 1920 has meant that certain texts speak of a 'recovery of statehood'[47]. Thus, UNGA Resolution 48/18, of 15 November 1993, literally states that it recalls "with particular satisfaction that *independence was restored* in Estonia, Latvia and Lithuania through peaceful and democratic means", in keeping with the context of the declarations of independence of these three Baltic republics, between March and May 1990[48], given that, as Yakemtchouk[49] states:

> Les Parlements de ces trois républiques ont bien précisé qu'il s'agissait là non pas d'une sécession ou d'une accession au statut d'Etat nouveau, mais du rétablissement d'une indépendance étatique d'avant 1940 qui leur avait été illégalement confisquée par une puissance étrangère: en conséquence, les trois Parlements ont demandé aux autorités de Moscou de déclarer nuls et non avenus les Accords Molotov-Ribbentrop de 1939 et d'abroger les actes législatifs du Soviet suprême qui ont consacré leur annexion en 1940.

As this author explains, the circumstances of the Soviet annexation in 1940 after 20 years of independence, the previous recognition of the Bolshevik State itself in 1920 and its League of Nations membership led some countries (such as the United States) to refuse recognition and even deny the effectiveness of this annexation in keeping with the Stimson Doctrine, and others (such as the United Kingdom) to accept the integration by force but not its legal validity. Therefore, treating their independence in 1990 as a recovery thereof after a situation of illegality stretching across 50 years allowed Washington to maintain this 'legal fiction', which Moscow immediately rejected in order to avoid a domino effect in other peripheral territories. Likewise, Mikhail Gorbachev insisted on applying the 1977 Constitution of the Soviet Union, in which Article 70 proclaimed that "the Union of Soviet Socialist Republics is an integral, federal, multinational state formed on the principle of socialist federalism as a result of the free self-determination of nations and the voluntary association of equal Soviet Socialist Republics", and Article 72 stated that each one had the

47 As well as some authors, such as Pavkovic and Radan, op. cit., p. 161, or Wilson, Gary. "Self-Determination, Recognition and the Problem of Kosovo". *Netherlands International Law Review*, vol. 56, no. 3, 2009, p. 473.

48 Lithuania declared independence on 11 March 1990, Estonia on 8 May 1990 and 20 August 1991, and Latvia on 4 May 1990 and 21 August 1991. Our italics.

49 Yakemtchouk, Romain. "Les républiques baltes en droit international. Echec d'une annexion opérée en violation du droit des gens". *Annuaire Français de Droit International*, vol. 37, 1991, p. 276.

right freely to separate from the USSR[50]. This provision was developed in the Supreme Soviet Law of 7 April 1990 which set out the conditions for this separation of the federated republics. After some incidents of violent repression, which caused the death of 18 people in Vilnius in January 1991 and the intervention of the KGB in Latvia, the Baltic independence leaders exploited the weakening of the USSR caused by the failed coup d'état of August 1991 to redeclare their independence in parliament, restore the validity of their old constitutions (such as the Constitution of the Republic of Latvia of 15 February 1922) and finally obtain recognition from the USSR: Lithuania on 29 July; Estonia and Latvia on 24 August[51]. Although some international recognitions mention "the restoration of the sovereignty and independence of the Baltic States" (EC Declaration of 27 August 1991), this is unquestionably a strictly political assertion.

In the early years of the final decade of the twentieth century, the Socialist Federal Republic of Yugoslavia provides further cases of secession. The SFRY, instead of merely shrinking like the USSR – owing to Baltic secession and the subsequent (voluntary) separation of other federated republics –, actually disappears due to the violent disintegration of the union of States and peoples created after the First World War. In fact, in 1918 the Principality of Montenegro (formally independent since 1878) voluntarily joined the Kingdom of Serbia, and the Kingdom of Serbs, Croats and Slovenes was proclaimed immediately afterwards, incorporating the southernmost territories of the Austro-Hungarian Empire (Slovenia, Croatia, Bosnia and Herzegovina and Vojvodina). In 1929, its name was changed to the Kingdom of Yugoslavia, and after the Second World War – in which pro-German 'satellite States' were created in Croatia, Montenegro and Serbia – it became a republic. Its constitutional system became practically confederal in 1974, given that the highest authorities of the State were to be represented in turn by the six federated republics (Slovenia, Croatia, Serbia, Bosnia and Herzegovina, Montenegro and Macedonia) in the case of the Head of State, and by these six plus the two autonomous provinces (Voivodina and Kosovo, in Serbia) in the case of the Head of Government, with a complex system of territorial balances. Although there had already been incidents in Kosovo in 1981 and 1989, the Yugoslav conflicts began first in Slovenia (declaration of independence on 25 June 1991 and the Customs War in July 1991) and then continued, between July 1991 and November 1995, with the war between Croatia and the Yugoslav Federal Army and, later, with Serbia and the Serbo-Croat militias, after Croatia's declaration of independence on 25 June 1991. Macedonia proclaimed its independence on 8 September 1991, and Bosnia and Herzegovina followed suit on 5 April 1992 (after the referendum held on 1

50 Article 72: "Each Union Republic shall retain the right freely to secede from the USSR".

51 On these events, see Eastwood, Lawrence S. "Secession: State Practice and International Law after the Dissolution of the Soviet Union and Yugoslavia". *Duke Journal Comparative & International Law*, vol. 3, no.2, 1993, pp. 316 et seq.

March 1992, in which 63% of the population voted in favour). In this second scenario, an armed conflict developed between the Bosnian Muslim and Bosnian Croat communities and the Bosnian Serb community. Following the intervention of the UN, the war would eventually end with the signing of the Dayton Accords in 1995. This process of violent disintegration gave rise to six new States corresponding to the formerly federated republics of Yugoslavia.

During the same period, and also in a context of internal armed conflict, albeit of greater duration, the State of Eritrea was created in 1993. As we mentioned when dealing with the case of Somaliland, its most salient characteristic is its voluntary integration into a confederal framework, since, after being an Italian colony under British administration between 1941 and 1952, it was integrated, with the approval of the Eritrean Assembly and the mediation of the UN[52], into the new Federation of Ethiopia and Eritrea (Constitution of 11 September 1952)[53]. However, the agreement was broken by Ethiopia, whose military forces were sent in to occupy the territory in 1962. The Eritrean revolt was severely repressed by the dictatorial regime of Mengistu Haile Mariam (1974–1991), although this did not manage to prevent the Eritrea People's Liberation Front from gradually gaining the upper hand. On 23 April 1993, after decades of international indifference, a referendum took place pursuant to the London Agreements of 1991 and under the auspices of the UN Observer Mission to Verify the Referendum in Eritrea (UNOVER)[54], in which the people voted almost unanimously (99.83%, with a 98.52% turnout) for independence, which was finally proclaimed on 24 May 1993, the country becoming a UN Member State just four days later.

Besides the case of East Timor, described earlier, the last successful secessionist process culminated in 2011 with the creation of South Sudan. Previously having formed part of the Free State of Congo, the British Protectorate of Uganda and Anglo-Egyptian Sudan, this territory, in 1956, instead of being integrated into Uganda or becoming an independent State, was absorbed into the new Republic of Sudan at Britain's behest. From the outset, the fact of having a majority animist and Christian population was a cause of confrontation between the south Sudanese and the Muslim population in the north of the new State, resulting in the First Sudanese Civil War (1955–1972) and, ten years later, a resurgence of the conflict prompted by the establishment of an Islamic regime (Second Civil War, 1983–2005). Thanks to the Naivasha Peace Agreement of 2005, it became an autonomous region and, in accordance with the provisions of the Sudanese Constitution of 5 December 2005, a referendum was held between 9 and 15 January 2011 in

52 UNGA Resolution 390 (V), of 2 November 1950, and 617 (VII), of 17 December 1952.

53 Regarding the integration of Eritrea and Ethiopia and the civil war, see Fox, Gregory. "Eritrea". In *Self-Determination and Secession in International Law*, edited by Christian Walter et al. Oxford University Press, 2014, pp. 275 et seq.

54 Created by UNGA Resolution 47/114 (1992), of 16 December.

which a 99% majority voted for independence. The new State was proclaimed on 9 July 2011 and joined the UN five days later.

Reference to political arguments for secession

Although there are numerous studies on the causes of contemporary secessionism[55], the juridical nature of this work does not allow us to expand on matters that are essentially sociological and political. Nevertheless, it is worth pointing out some of these causes, even though they are merely political claims made by leaders of independence movements that seek to replace the legal arguments laid down in international laws and constitutional provisions.

First, there are those who maintain that the basis is *ethnic identity*, and that therefore the borders of States should coincide with the settled territory of each people. This doctrine is based on purely political criteria, equating ethnic community with State subjectivity. In the nineteenth century and the early twentieth century, it was expressed in the "principle of nationalities", by virtue of which the peoples who were absorbed into or subjugated by the European empires defended their claims to independence. English-speaking authors call it 'ascriptive group theory', as the important thing is objectively belonging to the national community, the latter and its members being differentiated on ethnic grounds, hence it should properly be termed an 'ethno-nationalism'[56]. This kind of argument is usually at the root of most secessionist movements, in which a minority political party, an elite or a social leader promotes it as an untested representative of the whole people, but understanding that said objectively differentiated community must be independent because that is what it is in its very essence. When society mobilises in its defence, this usually ceases to be the initial foundation and becomes just another argument for its territorial claims. Thus, what argument could the Slovenian independence leaders in

55 Among others, we highlight Horowitz, Donald L. *Ethnic Groups in Conflict*. Los Angeles: University of California Press, Updated Edition, 2000; Premdas, Ralphe, W. R. de A. Samarasinghe and Alan Anderson (eds.). *Secessionist Movements in Comparative Perspective*. London: Bloomsbury, 1993; Heraclides, op. cit.; Buchanan, Allen. "Theories of Secession". *Philosophy & Public Affairs*, 1997, pp. 30–61; Wood, John R. "Secession: A Comparative Analytical Framework". *Canadian Journal of Political Science*, vol. 14, 1981, pp. 109–135; and Pavkovic and Radan, op. cit., pp. 173 et seq.

56 In Pavkovic and Radan, op. cit., pp. 199 et seq., that main feature of what the authors call 'justifying or normative theories', together with claims that an independent State would bring prosperity to the people, eliminate the discrimination they suffer or restore their lost dignity, is simply the correlation between the national group and its own State. As an example of this particular argument, Resolution 5/X of the Parliament of Catalonia, of 23 January 2013, adopting the Declaration of sovereignty and right to decide of the people of Catalonia, states that

> the people of Catalonia, throughout its history, has democratically expressed its commitment to self-government, in order to strive for more progress, welfare and equal opportunities for all its citizens, and to reinforce its own culture and its own collective identity.

1991 put forward to obtain the support of the majority of their fellow citizens and even to persuade these citizens to take up arms against the Yugoslav Federal Army? Although there were underlying economic reasons, and certainly the occasional historical claim dating back to the nineteenth century, what proved most popular was to claim an ethnic identity and a settled territory of the 'Slovene nation'. For this purpose, a historical and cultural location was configured in the orbit of the Habsburg Empire (excluding Hungary, to which Croatia was attached, and of course the Ottoman Empire, any Balkan states, such as Serbia, and even the Eastern Roman Empire), a different religion (Catholicism as opposed to the Orthodox Christianity of Serbs and the beliefs of Bosnian Muslims) and a language with some differences in relation to those spoken in other parts of the region. As in other cases, the fact that there is a differentiation in domestic law, with an administrative boundary, a decentralised authority and sometimes even a special set of laws, helps enormously when presenting the public with a supposed equivalence between ethnic identity and territorial heritage, essential for claiming the right to statehood. In the Yugoslav case, the federated republics were considered to be 'constituent nations or peoples' (*narod*), well above the 'ethnic nationalities or minorities' within each one (*narodi*), such as the Romani, the Hungarians or the Ruteni.

A variant of the aforementioned theory is based on the *recovery of statehood*, whereby any people that historically constituted a State are entitled to fight for it. We have seen that this was the argument used by Latvian, Estonian and Lithuanian independence seekers in 1990. The most well-known example is that of the Poles, who for 123 years struggled to rid themselves of Prussian, Austrian and Russian occupation, before eventually achieving statehood in 1918. But it has also been used by many other peoples, such as the Croats (pointing to the Kingdom that existed between the tenth and fourteenth centuries) or the Greeks (recalling the Byzantine Empire that fell in 1453 and even Ancient Greece). As we will see in relation to Catalonia, history can also be manipulated to 'manufacture' a previous state entity that allows this argument to be used.

The third theory we come to posits the possibility of secession based exclusively on the *will of the majority of the population* of a territory. This 'doctrine of the majority' or, in the English-speaking world, 'theory of primary right' or 'associative group theory'[57], goes beyond community identity to defend a kind of democratic principle by virtue of which the internal self-determination of any group equates to its external self-determination. The will of the community as a basis for secession poses a fundamental problem, which is how to determine any potential unit of self-determination, since there is no predetermined criterion for doing so. Thus, to use the example of the Basques, by which we mean a people with a language of its own (given that other cultural characteristics such as religion,

57 Ibid. p. 201, they are called 'the choice theories', considering that the State is a voluntary association that citizens and groups of citizens can enter and leave by their own choice.

history or the economy are shared with the population of the territory to which it belongs or with that of the neighbouring territory), this language (Euskera) accounts for about 50% of the province of Guipúzcoa, 30% of Vizcaya, 20% of Alava and 10% of Navarre, in Spain, and 30% of the Pyrénées-Atlantiques department, in France. With these percentages, some of which clearly indicate a minority, it is very difficult to locate the unit of self-determination in an ethnically identified and delimited territory. Moreover, there is always a tendency to extend it to internal administrative units, not to mention real or mythical historical entities, in this case, for example, the boundaries of the Kingdom of Navarre of Sancho Garcés III in the eleventh century, as if it had been proved that this monarch were the Basque leader of a Basque-speaking people, as opposed to being – as a member of the Jimena dynasty – from a noble Hispano-Roman family that governed a territory whose language closely resembled Castilian. In the end, the problem is a matter of deciding who can self-determine. Should it be whoever identifies voluntarily as a member of the people? Whoever boasts the distinctive ethnic characteristics? Or whoever resides in an internal administrative unit? This is a serious problem that has already been seen, to give just two examples, in the Eritrea and East Timor secessions, and which the UN, as guarantor of the referendums, has always resolved by ignoring the 'people' question and resorting instead to a very broad interpretation of the concept of 'those affected' or 'those concerned' with regard to self-determination, which includes all those residing in that internal administrative unit and at least all those born there who reside elsewhere on the State's territory, and even – on occasion – the refugees outside of it. But obviously, in these cases, the 'people' – neither objectively nor in terms of its mobilisation – do not coincide with the referendum census or with the actual settled territory, when the latter is identifiable, causing subsequent problems such as those detected in Scotland, whose referendum in 2014 foresaw the disaffection of the peripheral areas with a majority against independence.

A fourth theory, which in a certain way has taken its place alongside the other three, and which has enjoyed some degree of political success, is based on *reparations for historical injustices*. It is put forward in those cases where a community has suffered, or believes it has suffered, a serious affront in the past, either because it has lost its status as a State by being forcibly absorbed into another, or because it has been defeated in a domestic armed conflict with important dynamic consequences or significant changes to the internal configuration of the State, or because it has lost settled territories, etc. One example would be the claims of the Kurdish peoples from Turkey to Iraq, where there have been not only historical episodes of harsh repression but also a failure to fulfil international agreements or past promises. Other cases are similarly serious, such as that of Ireland, with a long history of plunder, dependence and discrimination at the hands of English landowners. The major problem with this theory is that history is often manipulated and there is usually very little objectivity in the interpretation of events that actually happened, shaping the feelings of subsequent generations in a self-serving way. Thus, along with facts as verifiable as those mentioned in relation to Kurdistan or Ireland, we usually find others that are either of dubious veracity or impossible to prove. This latter group includes some of the arguments put forward by Catalan pro-independence nationalists, who confuse the War of the Spanish Succession in the early eighteenth century, that is, the armed conflict between European powers, supported by the various factions and territories of Spain, with a supposed war between Castile and Catalonia in which the former sought to take away some freedoms enjoyed by the Catalan people.

Finally, academia has found a place for what is known as *remedial secession theory*, which, because it claims to have a legal basis in UNGA Resolution 2625 (XXV) of 1970, will be analysed in the next chapter. Suffice it to say here that, although similar to the previous theory, it differs inasmuch as the grievance is neither distant nor even remote in time, but instead is currently ongoing in a systematic manner, and that the wrong done to the people necessarily falls within the sphere of the human rights recognised and protected in international law, as opposed to the realm of other circumstances unconnected with such rights, such as failure to comply with founding constitutional agreements (as between the communities of Cyprus or in Ethiopia with respect to Eritrea), or the imbalances in economic contributions to maintain the State or to develop its territories (as between the federated republics of Yugoslavia in 1991).

The possibility of separation under State constitutions

Given that secession has been described in previous sections as a separation of part of the territory and population of a State without that State's consent, separatist processes that are not secessions in the strict sense should be excluded from this diverse phenomenology because they have been provided for in the constitutional rules. Likewise, neither will they be in the future, where applicable, in the few cases in which a national constitution provides for separation – and not, therefore, 'secession', we insist – of a part of the State.

Among the States created by 'separation' we find Montenegro, 55.4% voting for independence[58] in a referendum held on 21 May 2006, a decision that was formally announced on 3 June. This was made possible by Article 60 of the Constitutional Charter of the State Union of Serbia and Montenegro 2003, which states that:

> Upon the expiry of a 3-year period, member states shall have the right to initiate the proceedings for the change in its state status or for breaking away from the state union of Serbia and Montenegro.

58 For the result to be effective, at least half of the electoral census had to vote, and at least 50% had to vote in favour of the referendum proposition. The question was: "Do you want the Republic of Montenegro to be an independent state with full international and legal personality?".

> The decision on breaking away from the state union of Serbia and Montenegro shall be taken following a referendum. The law on referendum shall be passed by a member state bearing in mind the internationally recognized democratic standards. Should Montenegro break away from the state union of Serbia and Montenegro, the international instruments pertaining to the Federal Republic of Yugoslavia, particularly UN SC Resolution 1244, would concern and apply in their entirety to Serbia as the successor.
>
> A member state that implements this right shall not inherit the right to international personality and all disputable issues shall be separately regulated between the successor state and the newly independent state.
>
> Should both member states vote for a change in their respective state status or for independence in a referendum procedure, all disputable issues shall be regulated in a succession procedure just as was the case with the former Socialist Federal Republic of Yugoslavia.

The nearest precedent was the agreement reached on 8 December 1991 in Belovezha for the dissolution of the USSR through the separation of the Soviet Socialist Republics of Russia, Ukraine and Belarus, and, as a consequence, of its remaining constituent republics, with the exception of the Baltic States, which had already seceded. This was made possible by the will of its leaders to reach a consensus on how to dissolve the Soviet Union and avoid a traumatic breakup, as was seen with the Baltic republics, by replacing it with a framework of alliances between the new States (initially the Commonwealth of Independent States created in Alma-Ata on 21 December 1991). But arguably the most important factor was that the decision of the former put the onus of responsibility on all the rest.

To deal with any possible separatist demands, the Soviet Law concerning the Procedure of Secession of a Soviet Republic from the USSR was passed on 3 April 1990, according to which the corresponding referendum could be held at the initiative of the Supreme Soviet of a Republic or 10% of its population, requiring the support of two-thirds of the votes cast to be effective. If the result were in favour of separation, there would be a transitional period for resolving – by agreement with the USSR – any problems posed by the separation in matters of trade, ownership of assets, debt, etc., and especially those relating to military facilities or the rights of individuals, including the right to nationality by choice as a general rule and the right to monetary compensation if they chose to leave their place of residence.

There are currently other constitutions that allow for separation. This is the case of Saint Kitts and Nevis, Uzbekistan and Ethiopia. The Federation of Saint Kitts and Nevis is a State formed by these two islands (the larger one officially called Saint Christopher) which gained independence from the United Kingdom in 1983. The first has around 44,000 inhabitants and the second some 12,000; for this reason and also because the State was created as a combination of decolonised islands (at first with Anguilla, and then without it), its Constitution of 23 June 1983 provides for the possibility of the separation of the smaller island. Article 113, entitled "Separation of Nevis from Saint Christopher", reads as follows:

1 The Nevis Island Legislature may provide that the island of Nevis shall cease to be federated with the island of Saint Christopher and accordingly that this Constitution shall no longer have effect in the island of Nevis.
2 A bill for the purposes of subsection (1) shall not be regarded as being passed by the Assembly unless on its final reading the bill is supported by the votes of not less than two-thirds of all the elected members of the Assembly and such a bill shall not be submitted to the Governor-General for his or her assent unless

   a there has been an interval of not less than ninety days between the introduction of the bill in the Assembly and the beginning of the proceedings in the Assembly on the second reading of the bill;
   b after it has been passed by the Assembly, the bill has been approved on a referendum held in the island of Nevis by not less than two-thirds of all the votes validly cast on that referendum;
   c full and detailed proposals for the future constitution of the island of Nevis (whether as a separate state or as part of or in association with some other country) have been laid before the Assembly for at least six months before the holding of the referendum and those proposals, with adequate explanations of their significance, have been made available to the persons entitled to vote on the referendum at least ninety days before the holding of the referendum.

3 Every person who, at the time when the referendum is held, would be entitled to vote at elections of Representatives held in the island of Nevis shall be entitled to vote on a referendum held for the purposes of this section in accordance with such procedures as may be prescribed by the Nevis Island Legislature for the purposes of the referendum and no other person shall be entitled so to vote (...)

In accordance with these provisions, a referendum on self-determination took place on 10 August 1998. With a favourable result of at least two-thirds being required for effective separation, 61.83% (with a turnout of 58%) was close but insufficient[59].

Article 39 of the Ethiopian Constitution of 8 December 1994, on "Rights of Nations, Nationalities, and Peoples", also provides for – under the misnomer of 'secession' – the right to self-determination of any of its peoples, meaning groups of people who share a common language, customs, culture and psychological make-up, and who inhabit a contiguous territory. The actual text reads as follows:

1 Every Nation, Nationality and People in Ethiopia has an unconditional right to self-determination, including the right to secession.

59 See Mcintosh, Simeon. "The St. Kitts-Nevis question: secession or constitutional reform?". *Caribbean Law Review*, vol. 7, 1997, pp. 419–463.

2 Every Nation, Nationality and People in Ethiopia has the right to speak, to write and to develop its own language; to express, to develop and to promote its culture; and to preserve its history.

3 Every Nation, Nationality and People in Ethiopia has the right to a full measure of self-government which includes the right to establish institutions of government in the territory that it inhabits and to equitable representation in state and Federal governments.

4 The right to self-determination, including secession, of every Nation, Nationality and People shall come into effect: 1. When a demand for secession has been approved by a two-thirds majority of the members of the Legislative Council of the Nation, Nationality or People concerned; 2. When the Federal Government has organized a referendum which must take place within three years from the time it received the concerned council's decision for secession; 3. When the demand for secession is supported by majority vote in the referendum; 4. When the Federal Government will have transferred its powers to the council of the Nation, Nationality or People who has voted to secede; and 5. When the division of assets is effected in a manner prescribed by law.

5 A "Nation, Nationality or People" for the purpose of this Constitution, is a group of people who have or share large measure of a common culture or similar customs, mutual intelligibility of language, belief in a common or related identities, a common psychological make-up, and who inhabit an identifiable, predominantly contiguous territory.

Finally, we have Karakalpakstan, a territory representing one-third of the Republic of Uzbekistan but consisting mainly of desert terrain. It was absorbed into the Soviet Socialist Republic of Uzbekistan in 1932 and became an Autonomous Republic in 1936. In the new State created in 1991 it has maintained this status, as opposed to the rest of the administrative units, which are provinces. The Karakalpaks make up barely 3% of the population of Uzbekistan and do not even constitute the majority in their Autonomous Republic. Nevertheless, the Constitution of 8 December 1992 recognises their singularity and provides for them to have their own Constitution (Article 71), for their territory and borders not to be altered without their consent, and for them to be able to establish their own administrative-territorial structure (Article 73), that the

> mutual relationship between the Republic of Uzbekistan and the Republic of Karakalpakstan, within the framework of the Constitution of the Republic of Uzbekistan, shall be regulated by treaties and agreements negotiated by the Republic of Uzbekistan and the Republic of Karakalpakstan
>
> (Article 75)

and, especially, that "the Republic of Karakalpakstan shall have the right to secede from the Republic of Uzbekistan on the basis of a nation-wide referendum held by the people of Karakalpakstan" (Article 74).

In a different context, as it concerns a different interpretation of constitutional provisions, the sponsors of a referendum held on 25 September 2017 in the autonomous region of Iraqi Kurdistan assumed that it was covered by the Iraqi Constitution of 2005, which not only confirmed the legislation issued by the local authorities of Kurdistan since its *de facto* independence from the Baghdad Government[60], but also stated, in Article 140:

> First: The executive authority shall undertake the necessary steps to complete the implementation of the requirements of all subparagraphs of Article 58 of the Transitional Administrative Law.
>
> Second: The responsibility placed upon the executive branch of the Iraqi Transitional Government stipulated in Article 58 of the Transitional Administrative Law shall extend and continue to the executive authority elected in accordance with this Constitution, provided that it accomplishes completely (normalization and census and concludes with a referendum in Kirkuk and other disputed territories to determine the will of their citizens), by a date not to exceed the 31st of December 2007.

According to this provision, the Iraqi Transitional Government should have acted effectively to take measures that would remedy the injustice caused by the former regime's practices consisting in forcibly altering the demographic composition of Kirkuk and its neighbouring areas. However, regional president Massud Barzani interpreted the legislation in such a way as to satisfy his wish to hold a self-determination referendum, which he did, with a 72.16% turnout and 92.73% of the vote. As a consequence of this, the Iraqi Government stepped in to restore its authority in that city and throughout the regional territory, thus thwarting Kurdish expectations.

In contrast, other recent cases have seen the adoption of clear and explicit fundamental rules that have allowed or envisage the legal possibility of self-determination by holding the appropriate referendum and complying with the terms and conditions set out therein. This has been the case in Scotland and Bougainville and is legally provided for in Canada to deal with the Quebec question.

In the latter case, the Supreme Court of Canada, in its decision of 20 August 1998 on the question of the Quebec independence referendum[61], states that the right to self-determination of peoples established within the scope of the UN is

60 According to Article 141,

> Legislation enacted in the region of Kurdistan since 1992 shall remain in force, and decisions issued by the government of the region of Kurdistan, including court decisions and contracts, shall be considered valid unless they are amended or annulled pursuant to the laws of the region of Kurdistan by the competent entity in the region, provided that they do not contradict with the Constitution.

61 *Renvoi relatif à la sécession du Québec*, published in (1998) 2 RCS, pp. 217–297, www.canlii. org/en/ca/scc/doc/1998/1998canlii793/1998canlii793.pdf.

initially reserved only for those subject to colonial domination (paragraphs 131 and 132) or under any other foreign domination (paragraph 133). Similarly, the Court considers that some authors have interpreted the last section on the self-determination of peoples in Resolution 2625 and other concordant declarative texts as derogating from the protection of the territorial integrity of States when they conduct themselves in a discriminatory manner towards their constituent peoples (paragraph 134). It concludes by adhering – as we will explain in the next chapter – to this 'remedial secession' when stating that:

> … A right to secession only arises under the principle of self-determination of peoples at international law where 'a people' is governed as part of a colonial empire; where 'a people' is subject to alien subjugation, domination or exploitation; and possibly where 'a people' is denied any meaningful exercise of its right to self-determination within the state of which it forms a part. In other circumstances, peoples are expected to achieve self-determination within the framework of their existing state. A state whose government represents the whole of the people or peoples resident within its territory, on a basis of equality and without discrimination, and respects the principles of self-determination in its internal arrangements, is entitled to maintain its territorial integrity under international law and to have that territorial integrity recognized by other states. Quebec does not meet the threshold of a colonial people or an oppressed people, nor can it be suggested that Quebecers have been denied meaningful access to government to pursue their political, economic, cultural and social development. In the circumstances, the National Assembly, the legislature or the government of Quebec do not enjoy a right at international law to effect the secession of Quebec from Canada unilaterally.
>
> (paragraph 154)

After ruling out the colonial nature of the relationship between Canada and its territories and roundly affirming that there is no oppression or discrimination of any kind against the population of Quebec, the Court holds that – at a political-constitutional level – Canada is a voluntary federation of its provinces, as formulated in the 1867 British North America Act[62], and that nobody should remain in it without being willing to do so, as this would be detrimental to the State as a whole. It therefore proposes that Parliament study a legal framework that would enable any people integrated in its territory to secede from it. To this possible end, it believes that a number of conditions must be fulfilled, principally: a clear question[63], a significant majority and a system of protection for the resultant new minorities. This gave rise to the Clarity Act of 29 June

62 Regarding the history of Canada and Quebec secessionism, see Calonge Velázquez, Antonio. "El derecho de secesión en Canadá: una regulación jurídica completa y un problema sin resolver". *Revista de Derecho de la Unión Europea*, 2013, pp. 107–124.

63 Not quite so in the case of the question asked in the referendum of 30 October 1995: "Do you agree that Quebec should become sovereign, after having made a formal offer to Canada for a new Economic and Political Partnership, within the

2000, which regulates referendums on separation, with provisions on the mandatory clarity of the question, the majority required and the effects on issues such as the division of assets and liabilities, borders, indigenous peoples and the rights of minorities. The federal law was developed by the Act respecting the exercise of the fundamental rights and prerogatives of the Quebec people and the Quebec State, of 13 December 2000, which, among other things, sets the majority at half plus one of the voters.

This legal provision coincides, in a certain way, with the UK Parliament's treatment of Scottish separatism. The historical entity of Scotland, united with England by the Acts of Union of 1707, held a referendum on self-determination on 18 September 2014, with a majority voting against independence, after the UK and Scottish Governments had agreed on the referendum conditions in the Edinburgh Agreement of 15 October 2012. To this end, they followed the procedure set out in current legislation (Political Parties, Elections and Referendums Act 2000), although they delegated its implementation to the Scottish regional authorities and demanded compliance with very precise conditions regarding the date, the question, the census and the negotiation procedure that would follow a vote for independence in order to carry it through. There would also be subsequent talks regarding distribution of debt, the future currency and delimitation of the territory of the new State, in this case to exclude from it – in the event of an adverse result – the strip adjacent to England and the islands off its northeast coast.

Finally, with regard to Bougainville, the 2001 peace agreement and the 2005 Constitution of the Autonomous Region of Bougainville (Articles 193 and 194) provided for a future non-binding referendum on self-determination. In the referendum held on 7 December 2019, with 98.31% voting for independence, an 87.59% turnout and a clear question ("Do you agree for Bougainville to have: (1) Greater Autonomy (2) Independence?"), the result was confirmed on 20 January 2020 by the Referendum Commission and is awaiting negotiation at the National Parliament of Papua New Guinea, a process that may take years.

The starting point of the secession phenomenon: peoples and minorities

In the international legal order, we can distinguish three classes of peoples, categorised by having not only a number of typical characteristic elements but also different legal regimes.

First, there are *peoples under colonial domination*, whose characteristic elements are, as set out in UNGA Resolution 1541 (XV), 15 December 1960: a) a territory that is geographically separate from the country administering it, which has traditionally been called the 'saltwater rule'; b) in relation to this metropolitan State, the territory is ethnically or culturally distinct; and c) other elements of an

scope of the Bill respecting the Future of Quebec and of the agreement signed on 12 June 1995?".

administrative, juridical, economic or historical nature that demonstrate that in the relations between the metropolitan state and the territory the latter is arbitrarily placed in a position of subordination. This same Resolution then sets out the ways in which self-government can be attained: independence, free association with an independent State or integration with an independent State (to which Resolution 2625 of 1970 added any other form of relationship with the State, such as a federal or confederal solution). The territories to be decolonised are those included in the list drawn up by the UNGA at the behest of the Special Committee on Decolonization, currently: Western Sahara (Morocco), New Caledonia (France), Tokelau (New Zealand), Gibraltar, Falkland Islands, British Virgin Islands, Montserrat, Anguilla, Bermuda, Cayman, Turks and Caicos, St. Helena and Pitcairn (United Kingdom), Virgin Islands, Samoa and Guam (United States). The legal regime of these peoples currently includes a genuine right to self-determination with the possibility of exercising it through the legal use of force, protection of their territorial integrity and permanent sovereignty over their natural resources. Its recognition began in UNGA Resolution 1514 (XV) of 14 December 1960 and was completed with Resolution 2625 (XXV) of 24 October 1970, both being considered '*jus cogens*' norms in jurisprudence[64]; and with other resolutions that cover important aspects of its regulation, making up a set of international customs on the matter.

Second, there are *national, ethnic, religious or linguistic minorities.* There is no conventional definition, but their characteristics have been listed in different texts. In 1977, the Special Rapporteur of the UN Sub-Commission on Prevention of Discrimination and Protection of Minorities, Francesco Capotorti, ruled that they are:

> a group numerically inferior to the rest of the population of a State, in a non-dominant position, whose members – being nationals of the State – possess ethnic, religious or linguistic characteristics differing from those of the rest of the population and show, if only implicitly, a sense of solidarity, directed towards preserving their culture, traditions, religion or language[65].

Likewise, Recommendation 1201, of 1 February 2003, of the Parliamentary Assembly of the Council of Europe defines a national minority as: residing on the territory of a State and being citizens of that State; maintaining firm and lasting ties with a State; displaying distinctive ethnic, cultural, religious or linguistic characteristics; being sufficiently representative, even if they are a minority in relation to the total population of a State; being motivated by a

64 *Legal Consequences for States of the Continued Presence of South Africa in Namibia (South West Africa) notwithstanding Security Council Resolution 276 (1970)*, Advisory Opinion of 21 June 1970; *Western Sahara*, Advisory Opinion of 16 October 1975; and *East Timor (Portugal v Australia)*, Judgment of 30 June 1995.

65 Study on the rights of persons belonging to ethnic, religious and linguistic minorities, E/CN.4/Sub.2/384, Rev.1, 1979, para. 568.

concern to preserve their common identity, including their culture, traditions, religion or language.

According to the International Meeting of Experts on Further Study of the Concept of the Rights of Peoples, in 1989[66], the definition is as follows:

1 A group of individual human beings who enjoy some or all of the following common features:

    a a common historical tradition;
    b racial or ethnic identity;
    c cultural homogeneity;
    d linguistic unity;
    e religious or ideological affinity;
    f territorial connection.

2 The group must be of a certain number which need not be large (e. g. the people of micro States) but which must be more than a mere association of individuals within a State;
3 The group as a whole must have the will to be identified as a people or the consciousness of being a people - allowing that groups or some members of such groups, though sharing the foregoing characteristics, may not have that will or consciousness.

Recently, however, in the Report of the Special Rapporteur on Minority Issues of 15 July 2019, the following definition is put forward for consideration:

> An ethnic, religious or linguistic minority is any group of persons which constitutes less than half of the population in the entire territory of a State whose members share common characteristics of culture, religion or language, or a combination of any of these. A person can freely belong to an ethnic, religious or linguistic minority without any requirement of citizenship, residence, official recognition or any other status[67].

It differs from the previous definitions in several controversial aspects: first, it removes the temporal connection of residence or nationality, which is a core but problematic issue in Eastern European legislation[68]; and second, it does not include the concern for preserving a common identity or the sense of solidarity, eliminating two elements considered traditional: identification and social mobilisation; since, as Koskenniemi explains, "national identity combines subjective and objective elements (will and culture): a sense of community within

66 Paris Nov. 27–30, 1989, SHS 89/CONF. 602.
67 UN Doc. A /74/160, para. 59.
68 Thus, for example, in Article 1 of Hungary's Law no. LXXVII on the Rights of National and Ethnic Minorities, of 7 July 1993, minorities are defined as "any ethnic group with a history of at least one century residing in the Republic of Hungary".

the relevant population and some linguistic, historical or ethnic criteria to which it refers"[69]. Similarly, until then it had been understood, as stated at the Permanent Court of International Justice in 1928 in Rights of Minorities in Upper Silesia, that claimants could declare that they belonged to the German minority in Poland, as opposed to Poland's position which claimed that this recognition had to be the consequence of an objective fact, such as the language used[70].

The current legal regime pertaining to minorities is situated in the field of human rights and consists mainly of ensuring the exercise of distinctness (language, religion, etc.) and preventing discrimination in the different social spheres of the State on the basis of belonging to a minority. At UN level, it is included, in recommendatory terms, in the Declaration on the Rights of Persons Belonging to National or Ethnic, Religious and Linguistic Minorities, adopted by the UNGA on 18 December 1992 and, by convention, in Article 27 of the Covenant on Civil and Political Rights of 1966; and at a regional level, in documents such as the European Charter for Regional or Minority Languages of 1992 and the Framework Convention for the Protection of National Minorities, of the Council of Europe, which came into effect in 1998.

And third, there are *indigenous populations*. Although there is a conventional definition within the framework of the International Labour Organization (Convention 107 of 1957), the one that appears in Convention 1669 of 1989 (Article 1) is more up to date:

1 This Convention applies to:

a tribal peoples in independent countries whose social, cultural and economic conditions distinguish them from other sections of the national community, and whose status is regulated wholly or partially by their own customs or traditions or by special laws or regulations;
b peoples in independent countries who are regarded as indigenous on account of their descent from the populations which inhabited the country, or a geographical region to which the country belongs, at the time of conquest or colonisation or the establishment of present state boundaries and who, irrespective of their legal status, retain some or all of their own social, economic, cultural and political institutions.

2 Self-identification as indigenous or tribal shall be regarded as a fundamental criterion for determining the groups to which the provisions of this Convention apply.

69 Koskenniemi, Martti. "National Self-Determination Today: Problems of Legal Theory and Practice". *The International and Comparative Law Quarterly*, vol. 43, no. 2, 1994, p. 263.
70 Permanent Court of International Justice, *Rights of Minorities in Upper Silesia (Minority Schools), Germany v Poland*, Judgment of 26 April 1928, A, 15, pp. 46–47.

However, the most widely accepted definition is that provided by Special Rapporteur José R. Martínez Cobo in the Working Group on Indigenous Populations, of the UNGA's Sub-Commission on Prevention of Discrimination and Protection of Minorities:

> Indigenous communities, peoples and nations are those which, having a historical continuity with pre-invasion and pre-colonial societies that developed on their territories, consider themselves distinct from other sectors of the societies now prevailing in those territories, or parts of them. They form at present nondominant sectors of society and are determined to preserve, develop and transmit to future generations their ancestral territories, and their ethnic identity, as the basis of their continued existence as peoples, in accordance with their own cultural patterns, social institutions and legal systems[71].

There is no conventional regime, only the UN Declaration on the Rights of Indigenous Peoples, approved by the General Assembly in 2007, and the American Declaration on the Rights of Indigenous Peoples, approved by the General Assembly of the Organization of American States (OAS) in 2016. The regime is therefore recommendatory, and as such it promotes, in addition to preserving their identity and prohibiting discrimination against them, internal political autonomy, protection of their ancestral territory and ownership of their economic resources.

The secessionist project in Catalonia

Having explained in general terms the international aspect of the secessionist phenomenon, we can now begin to study the particular problems posed in the case of Catalonia. Critical analysis of the secessionist process in Catalonia in recent years requires, in our opinion, an exposition of the most relevant facts and events pertaining thereto, which in this section will be fairly brief, and then – in the following section – an initial explanation of the problems involved in applying the term 'people' – according to the parameters of international law – to the entire population of the Spanish region of Catalonia, or to the part of it that promotes or adheres to the secessionist project. Then we will take a look at the various political arguments used by Catalan secessionism to support its claims to independence, taking into account the theories put forward by international law scholars and other secessionist processes. In the following chapter we will deal with the legal arguments, first by using the precedents of Quebec, Kosovo and Scotland, and then in relation to the remedial secession theory. After dealing with these preliminary matters, we will proceed to study substantive issues such as the problems posed by the lack of effectiveness of the material elements of statehood in the specific case of Catalonia as well as its recognition by States and international organisations.

71 UN Doc. E/CN.4/Sub.2/1986/7, Add. 4, para. 379.

With regard to the account of the most relevant events, it should be noted, first, that when on 27 October 2017 the Catalan nationalist regional MPs approved their Unilateral Declaration of Independence at the seat of their autonomous parliament, in a manner that was as solemn as it was ineffective, this marked the greatest milestone in their recent effort to achieve the secession of Catalonia from the rest of Spain. But this act was not the first, and will surely not be the last, of the steps taken in this direction. The first half of the twentieth century witnessed the pro-independence declarations of the first secessionist politicians, such as Francesc Macià, who in 1919 argued for the participation of an independent Catalonia in the newly created League of Nations[72] and, on 14 April 1931, went so far as to proclaim the Catalan Free State within the Republic recently established in Spain. He himself was President of the Autonomous Government (*President de la Generalitat*) of Catalonia between 1931 and 1933 and sponsor of the Statute of Autonomy of 1932. After his death he was succeeded as president by Lluís Companys, a Member of Parliament in Madrid and formerly Minister of the Navy of the Spanish Government led by President Manuel Azaña. The new Catalan president again proclaimed the constitution of a Catalan State on 6 October 1934, in response to the coalition of conservative parties winning the general election in Spain, but the secessionist leaders were arrested and tried, and autonomy was suspended. Although it was restored in February 1936, the end of the Spanish Civil War also entailed the formal repeal of the Statute of Autonomy (5 April 1939).

The restoration of democracy in Spain in 1977 led to the reinstatement of Catalonia's regional institutions and a new Statute of Autonomy, which was approved by 88.15% of voters in a referendum held on 25 October 1979, with a 59.6% turnout. It is precisely the process of approving the statutory text that replaced it in 2006 that triggered the second stage of Catalan secessionism, in this case well into the first decade of the twenty-first century. The text approved in the Catalan Parliament received the people's blessing in the referendum held on 18 June 2006 (with 73.9% voting in favour in a turnout of only 48.85%), but it was amended in the Spanish Parliament and submitted to proceedings before the Constitutional Court. One of the key amendments made in parliament was the removal of early references to the "right of the citizens of Catalonia to self-determine freely their future as a people", "Catalonia is a nation", "Catalonia considers that Spain is a plurinational State", "Catalan law is preferentially applicable", etc. The main example is the replacement of the initial text "Catalonia exercises its self-government through its own institutions, constituted as an autonomous community in accordance with the Constitution and this Statute" with the definitive "Catalonia, as a nationality, exercises its self-government constituted as an Autonomous Community in accordance

72 The earlier Commonwealth of Catalonia (*Mancomunitat de Catalunya*, 1914–1925) was a unique regional body in Spain in which representatives of the region's four provincial councils could exercise their powers.

with the Constitution and with this Statute, which constitutes its basic institutional regulations", which confirms that its autonomy is the consequence of the current constitutional order and not of alleged earlier rights. Likewise, in its Judgment of 28 June 2010, the Constitutional Court insisted on the constitutional basis of the autonomous institutions, systematically interpreted numerous provisions (on linguistic rights, popular consultations or civil law) and corrected the competencies of some of them (such as the High Court of Justice of Catalonia or the Catalan Ombudsman).

The confirmation that regional MPs could not issue regulations that contradicted the constitutional order, or, in other words, that Catalan autonomy (like that of all the other regions of Spain) was subject to the decisions of the national parliament and the rulings and judgments of the State courts, meant resetting – as in 1934 when the *Generalitat* did not have the support of the central government – the secessionist project that had been suspended in 1936. After some preparatory acts, both in the form of social mobilisations and parliamentary declarations[73], a referendum on self-determination was proposed in 2014. However, the Catalonia's Law on Referendums of 19 September 2014 was provisionally suspended by the Constitutional Court and an alternative 'participative process' was announced for 9 November 2014. Voters would be asked, first, if they wanted Catalonia to be a State and, if so, whether they wanted that State to be independent. The result was 80.76% affirmative on the first and second questions, in a process with a very low turnout of only 37% and no census, no official polling stations and no subsequent supervision and control. The direct sponsors were prosecuted, and Constitutional Court Judgment of 11 June 2015 declared the acts carried out unconstitutional, on the ground that, in short, "it is not for the Autonomous Community to call referendums on matters that affect the established order and the foundation of constitutional order".

Despite the prosecution of those directly responsible and the annulments made by the Constitutional Court, the second – and as of now the latest – chapter of the defiant bid for independence began immediately. Indeed, Resolution 1/XI of 9 November 2015 of the Parliament of Catalonia, on the start of the political process in Catalonia as a consequence of the election results of 27 September 2015, "solemnly declares the start of the process to create an independent Catalan state in the form of a republic" (point 1) and that

> the Parliament of Catalonia, as the repository of sovereignty and the expression of the constituent power, reiterates that this House and the process of democratic disconnection from the Spanish State shall not be subject to the decisions of the institutions of the Spanish State, in particular

73 Among them, Resolution 5/X, of 23 January 2013, of the Parliament of Catalonia, which proclaimed the capacity of Catalan institutions to decide the political future of this region.

> the Constitutional Court, which it considers devoid of legitimacy and jurisdiction following its judgment of June 2010 on the Statute of Autonomy of Catalonia previously voted on by the people in a referendum, among other rulings.
>
> (point 6)

Although it was declared unconstitutional[74], this did not prevent its Parliament from passing Law 19/2017, of 6 September, on the Catalonia Self-Determination Referendum, and Law 20/2017, of 8 September, of Juridical Transition and Foundation of the Republic. And in spite of the warnings, in the form of the Constitutional Court's interim measures[75], a referendum was held on 1 October 2017. Without State authorisation, when asked "Do you want Catalonia to be an independent state in the form of a republic?", an alleged 43% of the census turned out, 90.18% answering in the affirmative. These figures, however, are practically impossible to verify, as there were no mechanisms in place to ensure that the referendum would be carried out correctly, at least not in accordance with the standard parameters of Western democracies. It should be noted that the census was not subject to public scrutiny and voters' objections, the polling stations were staffed by citizens who were sympathetic to the independence option, there was no control over the number of times that votes could be cast, the integrity of the ballot boxes and the votes cast was not guaranteed, and there was no independent mechanism for subsequent verification or appeal to any court or similar body. And most surprising of all, without a doubt, was the use of the 'universal census', an entirely anomalous practice whereby anyone could vote and as many times as they wished.

Finally, in two acts on 10 and 27 October 2017, a Unilateral Declaration of Independence was approved and signed in the Parliament of Catalonia, sponsored and signed by a majority of Catalan MPs (72 of the 135 members of the autonomous parliament). The State took immediate action in response; on the one hand, the proceedings for annulling the laws referred to and Decree 139/2017, of 6 September, on calling the Referendum on Self-Determination in Catalonia, as reflected in the Constitutional Court's Judgments of 17 and 31 October 2017, respectively; and on the other hand, criminal charges were brought against those directly involved, which culminated in Supreme Court

74 Constitutional Court Judgment of 2 December 2015. On the proceedings before this court between 2006 and 2018, see Miguel Bárcena, Josu de. "El proceso soberanista ante el Tribunal Constitucional". *Revista Española de Derecho Constitucional*, vol. 113, 2018, pp. 133–166, and the works of constitutional law scholars cited in this book. Also, among others, Bar Cendón, Antonio. "El proceso independentista de Cataluña y la doctrina jurisprudencial: una visión sistemática". *Teoría y realidad constitucional*, vol. 37, 2016, pp. 187–220; and Álvarez Vélez, M. Isabel. "Cataluña, las consultas populares y el referéndum: comentario a la STC 51/2017, de 10 de mayo 2017". *Teoría y Realidad Constitucional*, vol. 41, 2018, pp. 435–446.

75 Among others, in the decision of 7 September 2017, suspending the Referendum Law and admonishing the participant public authorities.

proceedings leading to conviction, with a Ruling issued on 14 October 2019[76], and prison sentences for most of the defendants. Finally, on 27 October 2017, the Senate agreed to temporarily suspend Catalonia's regional autonomy (until 2 June 2018) by triggering the procedure provided for in Article 155 of the Spanish Constitution.

Consideration of the Catalans as a people and the alleged basis of the secessionist process in political theories concerning recovery of statehood and reparation of historical injustices: a comparative analysis

Analysis of the secessionist phenomenon requires defining the group of people that mobilises itself, or is mobilised, to confront the rest of the population of the State in which it is located in its efforts to promote the independence of the territory on which it is settled. Sometimes this identification is very simple, but on other occasions it is not.

Thus, in the Baltic republics in 1989 we find three administrative units, the Soviet Socialist Republics (SSR) of Lithuania, Estonia and Latvia, each with a defined territory (which is practically the same as when these States were created in 1918, with some differences on the Lithuanian border) and a multi-ethnic population, albeit with varying proportions of minorities. In Estonia, specifically, 62% considered they could identify as Latvian due to their language (Latvian) and 38% as being from other parts of the USSR, especially Russia (30%) and, to a lesser extent, Ukraine and Belarus, as well as from Finland and other territories. Locating the Latvian community was very simple, as only one of the 15 counties (Iva-Virumaa, in the far northeast) had a Russian majority. According to the definitions of minorities provided earlier in this chapter, Latvians in the SSR of Latvia could be described as such in 1990, given that the required objective elements can be ascertained: a considerable number (62% of the population of the SSR, around 960,000 people[77]), a shared historical tradition (although certainly very remote in 1919, since the thirteenth-century Livonian Brothers of the Sword were succeeded by the domination of Danes, Teutons, Swedes, Lithuanians and Russians, sometimes without sharing the same sovereignty and without a significant administrative identity in their States), a language (Estonian, belonging to the Finnic group) and a cultural identity (with oral traditions, literature, medieval music, etc.), a religious affinity (those who claim to be religious – less than

76 Ten senior officials and two leaders of the sponsoring social entities were convicted of sedition, misuse of public funds or disobedience. Nine of the 12 defendants received prison sentences of between nine and 12 years, and the other three were given fines and temporary bans on holding public office. Seven other defendants are in contempt of court, having escaped to various European countries, including the former President of the Autonomous Community, Carles Puigdemont. Other administrative and police charges were brought before the High Court of Catalonia and the National High Court.

77 1989 data according to UN HRI/CORE/EST/2015, 25 November 2016.

half – consider themselves Lutherans) and a territorial connection (majority in 14 of the 15 counties). And as objective elements, a consciousness of being a people that has resulted in national mobilisation, in the nineteenth century at a cultural level and since the early twentieth century in the struggle against Russification imposed from Moscow, the demand for autonomy in 1917 in the final days of the Russian Empire, the declaration of independence of 24 February 1918 and the War of Independence from November 1918 to February 1920, with its recognition as a State until the Soviet annexation in 1940.

The year 1987 saw the beginning of Estonia's 'Singing Revolution', so called because the most popular nationalist events took the form of musical folklore festivals in which hundreds of thousands of Estonians participated. In the years leading up to the dismemberment of the USSR, they managed to front the communist political organisation and subsequently replace its political hegemony with a nationalist party, which won the elections and made Estonian a co-official language. Brought together by their ethnic affinity, they won the majority of seats (73 out of 105) in the first democratic elections held in March 1990, which allowed them to make successive declarations of independence, until the referendum of 3 March 1991 when, with a turnout of 82%, this option was supported by 78%.

In any case, Estonia's independence in 1991 has resulted in an equally multi-ethnic State, as was the former USSR, in which 902,000 ethnic Estonians now live alongside 326,000 of Russian origin and some 60,000 of other origins and languages.

In the case that constitutes the main focal point of this book, which is the secessionist process unfolding in Catalonia since 2014, the difficulties involved in identifying these elements are greater but would lead to a similar situation in the event of a Catalan secession.

Indeed, the main problem in the case of Catalonia is that the four provinces that form this Autonomous Community according to the constitutional regime approved by a majority of the population in 1978[78] have formed part of the Kingdom of Spain, as have nearly all its other territories, since its origins in Hispania or the Visigothic Kingdom in 507. The Arab occupation that began in 711 was followed by a political fragmentation that gave rise to different States – Christian and Muslim – in the north and south of the Iberian Peninsula. In the northeast, by the end of the ninth century, this process had resulted in the Hispanic Marches, under Carolingian (Frankish) rule, from which the Kingdom of Pamplona (later Navarre), the Counties of Aragon, Sobrarbe and Ribagorza (later united in the Kingdom of Aragon, which would absorb Pallars at the end of the twelfth century) and the more eastern counties of Urgel, Cerdanya, Osona, Besalú, Ampurias, Barcelona, etc. would gradually become independent. Until the end of the tenth century, these latter-mentioned counties shifted between independence and dependence on the Frankish kingdom, the Kingdom of Aragon and their

78 Approved in a referendum with 88.54% support in Spain as a whole (with turnout of 67.11%); in the four provinces of Catalonia: 91% in Barcelona (67.6% turnout), 90.4% in Gerona (72.3%), 91.9% in Lérida (66.5%) and 91.7% in Tarragona (67%).

neighbouring counties. Although some retained a certain independence until the fourteenth century, the fact of the matter is that at the end of the ninth century the County of Barcelona took hegemonic control of all of them. This complex of political entities was unified in 1135 with the marriage between Ramón Berenguer IV, Count of Barcelona and holder of other counties, and the heiress to the Kingdom of Aragon, Petronila, thus forming the Crown of Aragon in 1164, their first-born becoming King Alfonso II (of the House of Barcelona). The same would happen in 1469 when his descendant Ferdinand II of Aragon married Isabella I of Castile, which would mark the beginning of the Hispanic Monarchy, their daughter Joanna (of the House of Aragon, formerly Barcelona) inheriting the kingdoms of both. Since then, with different territorial or constitutional systems – more confederal, federal, regional or centralist – the provinces that make up Catalonia and the rest of Spain have shared the same State.

It is not, therefore, as in the case of Estonia, a territory conquered successively by neighbouring countries, but a territory connected to them, first to Aragon and then to Castile, by the will of its monarchs. This dynastic continuity ceased to be led by the Hispanic royal houses when Joanna of Castile married a member of the Austrian House of Habsburg, thus beginning a long historical period which in the early eighteenth century would end with its replacement by the French House of Bourbon, due to the death of the childless Charles II and the ensuing War of the Spanish Succession (1701–1713), which saw the European powers seek to impose a king on the Spanish throne from among his nephews. It was precisely Philip V, the first Bourbon monarch of Spain, on the throne from 1700, who would modify the existing political system with the Nueva Planta decrees for the territories that formed the Crown of Aragon (in 1707 for Aragon and Valencia, in 1715 for Majorca, and in 1716 for Catalonia), abolishing the institutions of the Crown and therefore the complex structure of what is known as the 'Hispanic Monarchy'. This is something that the Count-Duke of Olivares, royal favourite of Philip IV, had already tried to do, and it had resulted in the uprisings of 1640 in Catalonia and Portugal (in the Hispanic Monarchy by hereditary title since 1580 and whose independence was accepted in 1668 after the Portuguese Restoration War).

At this point we can analyse the arguments put forward by some members of the pro-independence movement, who maintain that Catalonia was once a State and therefore has the right to recover its statehood. Thus, the first Article of the Unilateral Declaration of Independence approved by the Parliament of the Autonomous Community of Catalonia on 10 and 27 October 2017 proclaims that:

> Justice and individual and collective human rights, irrevocable foundations which sustain the historical legitimacy and legal and institutional traditions of Catalonia, are the basis of the foundation of the Catalan Republic.
>
> The Catalan nation, its language and culture have a thousand years of history. For centuries, Catalonia has maintained and run its own institutions in complete self-governance, with the Generalitat as the maximum expression of Catalonia's historic rights
>
> (...)

> Today Catalonia restores its complete sovereignty, lost and much sought for, after decades of attempting to maintain institutional coexistence, in an honest and loyal manner, with the other peoples of the Iberian Peninsula.

Likewise, the preamble to Law 19/2017, of 6 September, on the Catalonia Self-Determination Referendum, passed by its Parliament – and declared unconstitutional[79] – claims deprival of "the legal and institutional tradition of the Catalan people – interrupted over the course of centuries only by force of arms– …". This institutional tradition is also mentioned in Resolution 5/X of the Parliament of Catalonia, of 23 January 2013[80], adopting the Declaration of sovereignty and right to decide of the people of Catalonia, which refers to the historical rights of the Catalan people, couched in a subjective account of the political history of Catalonia.

From a reading of these documents, we can deduce that those who support Catalan independence base their self-proclaimed Republic on human rights, on their cultural identity, on the existence of historical self-governing political institutions and on the restoration of Catalan sovereignty, which was lost as a result of the use of armed force. We will discuss these alleged legal grounds in the next chapter when we explain the international laws relating to human rights and the self-determination of peoples. As far as the other arguments are concerned, we should first point out that, *in relation to cultural identity*, the current international legal order no longer accommodates what used to be called, pre-UN, 'the principle of nationalities' and which could be translated today as the capacity of peoples integrated in States to become State subjects by their own will. As we will explain in detail in the next chapter, there is no international law, universal or regional, that enshrines a right with this or similar content that would therefore recognise the external self-determination of what we know as national, ethnic or linguistic minorities.

This voluntarist transformation of ethnic groups into national communities and of these into States has no legal basis and is not supported by any similar widespread international practice; moreover, it creates enormous practical difficulties and, in some cases, serious consequences in terms of regional security. As regards the States that have emerged by secession under the current international system, which is that of the UN, we find identity as a political argument in the Yugoslavian and Baltic processes, although recovery of statehood has also been put forward as a reason; but this is not primarily the case in Bangladesh, East Timor and South Sudan, where the main cause is discrimination on grounds of ethnicity; nor so in the case of Eritrea, where the catalyst was the breach of constitutional agreements on the union of communities.

79 Constitutional Court Judgment of 17 October 2017 (rec. 4334/2017).

80 Regarding this Resolution of 2013 and the Constitutional Court's response thereto, Judgment 42/2014, of 25 March, see Pons Rafols, Xavier. "Sentencia del Tribunal Constitucional (Pleno) 42/2014, de 25 de marzo de 2014", *Revista de Derecho Internacional*, vol. 2, 2014, pp. 201–210, and Pons Rafols, *Cataluña…*, op. cit., pp. 58–73.

As regards the practical difficulties, recent international practice has shown that they stem mainly from two issues: identifying the members of a people and determining its territorial location. Regarding the first issue, in the Estonian example the main identifying element is the use of Estonian, and to a lesser extent – because of the relatively small proportion of churchgoers – (Lutheran) religion, since physical differences are not very marked compared with other populations in the region, and there is no distinctive social structure or economic life. Nor does Estonia have its own political tradition, as it spent eight centuries under the domination of neighbouring countries, except for a brief period of sovereignty from 1919 to 1940. Estonian legislation has used precisely this linguistic element to differentiate its significant minorities to exclusionary ends[81]. In the case of Catalonia, can we say that the Catalan people is that which speaks the Catalan language? Is it that which speaks Catalan and also knows and shares the cultural traditions of the territory? Is it that which speaks this language, has its cultural tradition interiorised and is also mobilised in its defence? Who decides this? As we have already said, there is no law that defines the elements of a minority people. If we follow international practice – not only the reports and non-binding resolutions we have cited, but also cases brought before international courts and human rights supervisory bodies[82] – we should add together certain distinguishing objective elements and certain subjective elements based on defending one's own identity.

With regard to the objective elements, in Catalonia there is a large and proportionally significant number of people who speak Catalan. According to the Statistical Institute of Catalonia (2018 data), 95.12% of its 6,386,000 inhabitants know Catalan, with 55.70% being able to write it, and only 36.10% who "have Catalan as the usual language", according to its own terms[83]. As

81 On this issue, see López Martín, Ana G. and José Antonio Perea Unceta. "Los efectos en los derechos humanos de las secesiones de Estados y entidades no aceptadas por la comunidad internacional". *Foro, Nueva Época*, vol. 21, no. 1, 2018, pp. 57–91.

82 See, among others, Thornberry, Patrick. *International Law and the Rights of Minorities*. Oxford: Clarendon Press, 1991, and Pentassuglia, Gaetano. *Minorities in International Law: An Introductory Study*. Strasbourg: Council of Europe, 2002.

83 According to Oskam, Jeroen. "A New State in Europe? Scenarios for Catalan Self-Determination". *Futures*, 64, 2014, p. 52:

> could language then be considered as an objective indicator of national identity? Hardly, because the choice of a mother language is closely linked to the construction of identity, and can be similarly altered or manipulated (Fishman, 2004). Languages can be suppressed; territories can be 'russified'. In the twentieth century, Yugoslavians spoke a language known as Serbo-Croatian. An emerging language may deliberately diverge—e.g. choose different words or spelling rules—from related languages, such as Norwegian and Danish, or Galician and Portuguese. The Basque common language or Batúa was composed out of seven dialects in the nineteenth century. The differences between Catalan and the Valencian language are distinguished by politicians rather than by linguists…

reflected in its statistical tables, 2,320,000 people have Catalan as their language of identification and 2,978,000 have Spanish, while 2,302,000 opt for Catalan as their usual language and 3,101,000 choose Spanish. Considering these figures and language as the first objective factor of identification of a people, the Catalan people would, according to international law, amount to roughly 2,300,000, 36% of the total population.

Further objective elements may be added, according to international definitions, but we must rule out race and religion, as both are shared with their neighbours. We would be left with a common historical tradition, cultural homogeneity and territorial connection. Leaving this last element until the end, as it entails a specific complexity, the first problem is how to determine whether there is a common historical tradition and, if so, whether there is also a Catalan culture; the second problem is how to measure and locate individually the part of the population resident in or originally from Catalonia that knows both and – focusing now on the subjective element – has interiorised them and defends them. The existence of political, social and cultural institutions specific to Catalonia is indisputable, as is the fact that it shares numerous political, social and cultural institutions with the rest of the population (and peoples) of Spain: in this sense, the residents of Catalonia have a history and a culture in common (over the last 12 centuries as a distinct community), just as they do with the rest of the former Crown of Aragon (at least between the twelfth and the seventeenth centuries politically, and up until the present day culturally) and with the rest of the Kingdom of Spain (since the fifteenth century). The common history of the peoples that have seceded in recent decades is much shorter: South Sudan shared just 55 years with the rest of independent Sudan (1956–2011; previously, only part of it was in Anglo-Egyptian Sudan), East Timor 27 years with Indonesia (1975–2002; previously, Timor had been a Portuguese colony and part of the Dutch East Indies), and Eritrea 41 years with Ethiopia (1952–1993; previously, it had been an Italian colony and before that a part of different empires, Ethiopia meanwhile being an independent State). As for the common history of Estonia – our Baltic example – with Russia, the shared history is longer than in these more recent cases but shorter than that of Catalonia with Spain, totalling 260 years (1710–1919 and 1940–1991), the same as that of Latvia and somewhat longer than that of Lithuania (175 years, the first period having started in 1795). As regards the Yugoslav peoples, despite being a different case due to the dissolution of the existing State, they have a collective common history lasting 73 years (1918–1991), as compared with Croatia and Slovenia's 391 years in the Austro-Hungarian Empire (1527–1918) and Croatia, Slovenia and Bosnia's 40 years in the same empire (1878–1918), and earlier, Bosnia and Macedonia's 415 years in the Ottoman Empire (1463–1878, with the transfer of Bosnia to Austria-Hungary).

As for the subjective elements, it is not surprising that they have been omitted from the most recent UN texts (cited earlier), as they are difficult to ascertain beyond the mechanism of voluntary registration in referendum censuses, and may lead to an absurd conclusion, i.e. that a people can only comprise individuals with common objective characteristics who are effectively mobilised in defence of their identity, whatever that may be, and – certainly in the opinion of nationalist leaders – who effectively support its independence. This would exclude those who are not imbued with its culture, those who do not actively promote its own identity and those who do not mobilise socially and, above all, politically in favour of its national project.

In this context, the greatest difficulty lies in the subjectivation of this historical, political and cultural tradition. The international definitions (with the exception of the last one indicated earlier in this chapter) opted to add some subjective elements comprising defence of common identity and nationalist mobilisation, but given how inadvisable it would be to abide by what each leader, movement or party claims to represent, the criterion chosen in the League of Nations era was self-identification, whereas in the UN era it was much more objective: residence on the territory. In respect of the latter-mentioned criterion, certain exceptions applied where objective identification was possible (for example, on identity documents) and it could encompass – if they chose to register as such on the electoral roll – those residing in the rest of the territory or even in third countries as refugees, as in the case of Eritrea[84]. In general, therefore, the referendums of secessionist processes have tended to equate the unit of self-determination with those residing on the territory concerned. Thus, in the referendums held, for example, in the Baltic republics in 1991, all residents, regardless of national origin, were called upon to vote, with a turnout exceeding 80% in all three cases (82.9% in Estonia, 84.7% in Lithuania and 87.6% in Latvia) and a vote for independence equivalent to the ethnic majority of each if turnout is taken into account (93.2% in Lithuania, 78.4% in Estonia and 74.9% in Latvia).

In the referendum called by the Autonomous Government of Catalonia, officially referred to as a 'consultation' and held in Catalonia on 9 November 2014, Catalans were allowed to participate by registering for the purpose – voluntarily as in South Sudan or Eritrea[85] – it being prescribed that "this registration is voluntary and is intended for those citizens whose political status is Catalan, that is, for Catalans who are Spanish and reside outside Spain, their last legal residence being in Catalonia"[86]. It was specified that anyone over 16 years of age could vote (despite the fact that the legally established rule for all electoral processes sets the minimum voting age at 18 years) and that it was

84 Regarding this type of problem in Eritrea, see Sorenson, John. "Opposition, Exile and Identity: The Eritrean Case". *Journal of Refugee Studies*, vol. 3, no. 4, 1990, pp. 298–319; Hoyle, P.A. "The Eritrean National Identity: A Case Study", *North Carolina Journal of International Law and Commercial Regulation*, vol. 24, 1998, pp. 381–416; and Noronha, Kimberly M. *Refugees and National Identity: National Identity and Eritrean Refugees in the Sudan*. SSR, 2004.

85 More than one million registered, 66,022 being resident in Ethiopia and nearly 280,000 in other States. Badía Martí, Ana. *La participación de la ONU en procesos electorales*, Madrid: McGraw Hill, 1998, pp. 174–175.

86 As published in 2014 on the website of the Department of the Presidency of the Autonomous Government of Catalonia.

necessary either to have an identity document showing a home address in a municipality of Catalonia or to show a document demonstrating Spanish nationality together with proof of registration in the Register of Catalans Abroad or the certificate from the register of Spaniards residing abroad showing territorial attachment to Catalonia. This criterion was broader than that of strict residence used in the Baltic republics in 1991 and of a less restrictive nature than that of birth or kinship used by the UN in East Timor in 1999, but it is strange that the registration of Catalans resident elsewhere on Spanish territory was not provided for. This would have required recourse to another type of identification different from the objective requirement of residence or last residence in Spain, such as birth, kinship, educational background, property assets or economic interests, criteria used in other cases where there was a significant contingent of refugees or exiles, even second-generation ones (as in the Timorese case or, in another context, in New Caledonia, where "material and moral interests" were also referred to[87]).

As can be seen, in some cases it is so difficult to identify the members of the minority people seeking self-determination that a decision is made to widen the net to include at least all the inhabitants of the territory. This is what Castellino calls "geographic factors in determination of identity"[88]. But this is just an illusion, because once this first stage is over, it is common for new governments to enact laws that limit the political participation rights – as well as rights in other areas such as labour or education – of their resulting new minorities, which are considered external to the common national project and affiliated with the old State or neighbouring countries. This is what we were referring to when we mentioned the serious effects of some secessions, and this has been verified before international bodies, such as the UN Human Rights Committee in the case of *Antonina Ignatane v Latvia* (No. 884/1999, 2002), in which it held that Latvia had violated Articles 2 and 25 of the 1966 New York Covenant by preventing a Russian speaker from participating in municipal elections; or in the *Podzolzina v Latvia* case (No. 46726/1999, Judgment of 9 April 2002), before the ECHR, which held that Article 3 of Protocol No. 1 had been violated also in relation to knowledge of Latvian for the purpose of standing for election[89].

Finally, it is also worth emphasising that there may be significant problems involved in locating a people in a given territory, and the more objective the defining elements are, the more these problems are exacerbated. In the case of

87 In the case before the UN Human Rights Committee, *Marie-Hélène Gillot et al. v France*, CCPR/C/75/D/932/2000, para. 2.6 reproduces the legislation passed by France for participation in the referendum of 8 November 1994.

88 Castellino, Joshua. *International Law and Self-Determination*. The Hague: Nijhoff, 2000, p. 73. See also Oeter, Stefan. "The Role of Recognition and Non-Recognition with Regard to Secession". In *Self-Determination and Secession in International Law*, edited by Christian Walter and others. Oxford University Press, 2014, p. 58.

89 For a detailed discussion of this issue in Estonia, Macedonia, Eritrea or Bosnia, see López Martín and Perea Unceta. "Los efectos en los derechos humanos…", op. cit.

Estonia, we have already indicated that one of the country's 15 counties has a majority population of another ethnic group, namely Russian. However, this county has been compulsorily included in the unit of self-determination, showing that in practice territorial identification prevails over personal identification, as it is much more objectifiable and also ensures the preservation of the territorial integrity of the administrative unit or of the historical territory, which is usually an obsession of nationalist movements. Exceptions to this general rule are the referendum held in Scotland in 2014 and Canada's 2000 Clarity Act, which we will discuss in relation to Catalonia in the next chapter.

Both in 2014 and in 2017, with Law 20/2017, of 8 September, of Juridical Transition and Foundation of the Republic, also declared unconstitutional[90], the Catalan Government opted to protect the territorial integrity of the four provinces that make up the Autonomous Community of Catalonia, just as they were designed and with the same historical regional reference as in the Royal Decree of 30 November 1833 that established them. It ignores the fact that the 'linguistic unit' is not fulfilled in the Aranese-speaking rural district of Val d'Aran and that linguistic identification with Catalan varies greatly from one such district to another, according to objective criteria, and that in a referendum with a large turnout (only 33% participated in the 2014 referendum, with 80.76% voting in favour, the corresponding percentages for the 2017 referendum being 43% and 90.18%, respectively) there may be – as was the case in Scotland in 2014 – notable differences between the different parts of the territory of Catalonia. This eventuality could cause problems in those districts with non-nationalist majorities, which in comparative practice have been resolved in very different ways, to a large extent in situations already overcome thanks to international pressure: the de-russification imposed in Estonia and Latvia, the raising of minimum voting percentages throughout the State (as in Lithuania), the manipulation of electoral districts (as in Macedonia), the purging of all former State officials (as in Eritrea and East Timor) or the expulsion of minorities (as in Croatia); or, conversely, without adopting any discriminatory measures at all (as in South Sudan, Serbia and Slovenia).

Second, in relation to the *recovery of statehood* argument, and as stated earlier, there is no international law, either customary or conventional, that recognises this supposed right for a people that has previously been a State, or this obligation for the State in whose territory the people is integrated[91]. It can be argued that the current four Catalan provinces formed a common State at some point in history, although it appears that between the ninth and twelfth centuries there was a certain concentration of the Catalan counties in the hands of the incumbents of the county of Barcelona. The existence of a common

90 Constitutional Court Judgment of 8 November 2017 (rec. 4386/2017).

91 This is the opinion of, among others, Crawford, op. cit., p. 699, and Ahmed, op. cit., p. 184, who refer specifically to the non-existence of an international law that permits reversal in the cases of unions of old States without their consensus, referring, for example, to Eritrea and Ethiopia.

political tradition can also be argued, but the fact is that throughout history there has been a succession of political and social institutions similar in some way to those of today, albeit with very different compositions and powers, such as the Catalan Parliament (*Corts* in Catalan) and Government (*Generalitat*), which existed from the thirteenth century and 1359, respectively, until 1716; between 1931 and 1939; and since 1979 and 1977, respectively. In fact, this is very common in other parts of Spain, with institutions that are not the same as their medieval equivalents but whose similar appearance allows the current manifestations to be considered their successors, such as the *Cortes de León* of 1188 or the *Justicia de Aragón* of 1208 (a form of ombudsman).

Despite the absence of an international law in this respect, there is one minor practice – which as such obviously cannot be considered sufficient to generate an international custom – in the independence of the Baltic republics in 1991 at least in terms of political arguments, given that they received no general recognition.

In this respect, there is no questioning the fact that international law prohibits – since 1945 – the use of force in international relations. It is a structural principle enshrined in Article 2.4 of the UN Charter, developed as a '*jus cogens*' norm in texts such as Resolution 2625 (XXV) of 1970 and recognised as such in the jurisprudence of the ICJ, for example in the Judgment of 27 June 1986 on *Military and paramilitary activities in and against Nicaragua (Nicaragua v United States of America)* [92]. This prohibition imposed in the UN system, and which is one of its characteristic features, given that it also has a counterpart in the Security Council's responsibility for maintaining and restoring peace (Article 24.1 and Chapters VII and VIII of the Charter), has among its effects the unlawfulness of acquiring territory through use of force[93], which already prevailed in the 1930s, albeit with very limited scope (Stimson Doctrine), and, even up to the present day, the prosecution of crimes of aggression before the International Criminal Court (for example, by invasion and occupation, according to UNGA Resolution 3314 of 1974). As a result, in its resolutions following the Iraqi invasion of Kuwait on 2 August 1990, the Security Council warned of the illegality not only of the use of force but also of territorial annexation. Therefore, in Resolution 662 (1990), of 9 August, it "decides that annexation of Kuwait by Iraq under any form and whatever pretext has no legal validity, and is considered null and void".

92 Among others, *Military and Paramilitary Activities in and against Nicaragua (Nicaragua v United States of America)*, Merits, Judgment. ICJ Reports 1986, p. 14, paras 187–190, and *Legal Consequences of the Construction of a Wall in the Occupied Palestinian Territory*, Advisory Opinion, ICJ Reports 2004, p. 136, para. 87.

93 Resolution 2625 specifies that:

> The territory of a State shall not be the object of military occupation resulting from the use of force in contravention of the provisions of the Charter. The territory of a State shall not be the object of acquisition by another State resulting from the threat or use of force. No territorial acquisition resulting from the threat or use of force shall be recognized as legal.

However, the assertion contained in the Law on the Catalonia Self-Determination Referendum, passed by its Parliament in 2017, that "the legal and institutional tradition of the Catalan people – interrupted over the course of centuries only by force of arms – ..." is not only false, as nobody has ever invaded and annexed Catalonia by force, but would also lack any legal effectiveness even if it were true, unless it had occurred after 1945, as until then there was no prohibition on territorial conquests through use of force. If the aim was to prove that its self-government had been suppressed at some point by the armed intervention of another State, then this is not true, either, because its union with the Kingdom of Castile was voluntary and because, once integrated into the Kingdom of Spain, any legislative action was taken within the framework of the powers of the government at any given time, be they legitimate or otherwise, or even within the context of internal armed conflicts, matters which come under the internal and discretionary competence of States according to international law.

The foregoing observations allow us to address, finally, the *reparation for historical injustices* argument, which underlies that assertion and is expressed in the Declaration of Independence when it states that "the Spanish State has answered this loyalty with the refusal to recognise Catalonia as a nation; and allowing a limited and constantly re-centralising autonomy, more administrative than political; with profoundly unjust economic conditions and with cultural and linguistic discrimination".

Obviously, the existence of injustices committed against the people throughout history, at some specific time or in recent times, is a subjective claim made by nationalist movements, but one that can also be verified or refuted after rigorous study. It is not for us to explore this claim in depth, but we do feel bound to point out, first, that the process of centralisation or dismantling of Spain's "composite monarchy" between the fifteenth and seventeenth centuries (like Aragon's between the twelfth and fifteenth centuries), which more closely resembles the complex political structure of the Austro-Hungarian Empire than the simple union established in the United Kingdom in the early eighteenth century, was imposed by the new Bourbon monarchy on all Spanish territories, following the French model and the policy of post-medieval absolutist regimes. In addition, two alleged grievances have emerged in recent years: on the one hand, Catalonia's fiscal deficit; in Oskam's words,

> to avoid misinterpretations, the alleged injustice does not mean that individual residents of Catalonia pay more than tax payers in other regions; but the sum of taxes paid in Catalonia and other affluent regions is higher than that of poorer regions, while the distribution of state investments benefits the latter[94];

94 Oskam, op. cit., p. 52.

and on the other, the amendments made to the Statute of Autonomy by the Congress of Deputies (the lower house of the Spanish Parliament in Madrid[95]), and the annulment of some of its provisions by the Constitutional Court Judgment issued on 28 June 2010, despite it having been approved by the Catalan people in a referendum held on 18 June 2006[96]. This notwithstanding, it is obvious that the State institutions acted pursuant to the powers conferred upon them and in accordance with the ruling constitutional order.

It should also be considered, second, that the decentralised model established in the Spanish constitutional system since 1978 grants broad political autonomy to the Spanish regions and therefore to those that can be considered its peoples, with a legal regime that preserves cultural differences and, in particular, the languages existing in Spain, which are co-official in their respective territories regardless of whether they are used there by a majority or not. There is, therefore, full compliance with international and regional European conventions and recommendations on the protection of national minorities and minority languages, without any legal discrimination on the grounds of belonging to such minorities in social or cultural life, in economic affairs or in the workplace, or in the field of political engagement.

In any case, no international law includes an exceptional derogation from the *jus cogens* norm that prescribes respect for the sovereignty and territorial integrity of States on account of a wrong committed against a people throughout history, just as there is none based either on the recovery of pre-1945 statehood or on the ethnic identity or will of a minority people integrated in a State.

95 The *Cortes Generales* constitute the two-house Spanish Parliament, comprising the Senate and the Congress of Deputies, according to the 1978 Constitution.

96 As pointed out by Guibernau, Montserrat. "Prospects for an Independent Catalonia". *International Journal of Politics, Culture and Society*, vol. 27, 2014, pp. 15 et seq. It should be added that, for other authors, independence is considered an instrumental means of achieving greater social welfare and more democratic government, as argued by Dalle Mulle, Emmanuel and Ivan Serrano. "Between a Principled and a Consequentialist Logic: Theory and Practice of Secession in Catalonia and Scotland". *Nations and Nationalism*, vol. 25, no. 2, 2019, pp. 640 et seq., with references to the messages sent out by the Catalan pro-independence parties and the Parliament of Catalonia.

2 The impossible basis of secession in the right of self-determination of peoples designed by the United Nations

Alleged legal bases of Catalan secessionism

A review of international practice: from the principle of nationalities to the work of the League of Nations

The first regulation of universal scope relating to peoples emerges from the framework of the first general and universal international institution, the League of Nations, created in 1919[1]. The Covenant of the League of Nations, attached to the Peace Treaty of Versailles of 28 June 1919, expressly mentions 'indigenous populations'[2], whose definition and international protection will be undertaken much later by the International Labour Organization[3], created in the same year. Likewise, it outlines a legal regime for some territories that had belonged to the powers defeated in the First World War, of varying scope depending on their degree of political development, some explicitly referred to as 'colonies' and others as 'territories'. We can now identify the latter as 'peoples integrated in States', although they are not just 'national minorities', as we are talking about others, such as Lebanon, Syria and Iraq, with a very heterogeneous ethnic composition.

According to Article 22 of the Covenant, the functions of the new international organisation include supervising the administration of "colonies and territories which as a consequence of the late war have ceased to be under the sovereignty of the States which formerly governed them and which are inhabited by peoples not yet able to stand by themselves". This euphemism actually refers to the victorious powers being handed the territories taken from the vanquished powers, Germany and the Ottoman Empire, who were deprived of – as punishment and to undermine their future economic and military capabilities – their colonial dominions in Africa and Oceania and their extensive empire in the Middle East, which henceforth would be administered by the victors as 'mandates'. Three types of mandate were distinguished, the

1 Regarding precedents in the conventional protection of minorities, see Castellino, op. cit., pp. 49–52, among others.
2 Pursuant to Article 23.b) of the Covenant of the League of Nations, its members undertake the obligation to ensure "just treatment of the native inhabitants of territories under their control".
3 ILO Conventions 107 and 169, of 1957 and 1989, respectively.

DOI: 10.4324/9781003200772-3

first of which, 'Class A mandates', were the territories considered to have a degree of social and political development sufficient to obtain their independence in the short term. As a result of this regime, the mandates exercised in the former Ottoman territories, by the United Kingdom in Mesopotamia and by France in Syria, led to the creation of the new States of Iraq (1932), Syria (1941) and Lebanon (1943). Only the British mandate for Palestine remained pending. Obviously, this is not a process of decolonisation, as these territories neither appeared to be colonies nor were administered as such by the Ottoman Empire, and nor did they meet the requirements for being considered colonies indicated in the previous chapter. In our view, however much accession to independence unfolded with the consent of the administering powers, they are actually and essentially secessions, as these territories were never the sovereign property of the United Kingdom and France, which only exercised a trusteeship, their last possessor being the Ottoman Empire, from which they were forcibly separated in peace treaties (in this case the Treaty of Sèvres of 10 August 1920) which we consider 'unequal' for being imposed on countries defeated in a war. As for the regime established and the practice relating to the 'B and C mandates', in no way do they signify the beginning of a decolonisation process, but rather the transfer of some colonial dominions from their former metropolitan empire (Germany) to new ones[4].

As for national minorities, the Covenant contains no provisions in respect thereof, yet they would be one of the main focal points of the League of Nations up until the outbreak of the Second World War. The great driving force behind the new organisation, US President Thomas Woodrow Wilson, in his speech before Congress on 8 January 1918, known as the "Fourteen Points", had already pointed out that the security of continental Europe required addressing the problems affecting national minorities caused by the readjustments of the Italian borders (point 9), the peoples of Austria-Hungary (10), the Balkan states (11), the non-Turkish nationalities of the Ottoman Empire (12) and the recovery of Poland as an independent State (13). Therefore, when speaking in the same forum on 11 February he stated that "national aspirations must be respected; peoples may now be dominated and governed by their own consent. Self-determination is not a mere phrase, it is an imperative principle of action which statesmen will henceforth ignore at their peril"[5].

4 The Class B mandates were African territories under the colonial administration of the mandatory power with certain limitations set by the Covenant (British mandates of Tanganyika, British Cameroons and British Togoland; French Cameroun and French Togoland; and the Belgian mandate of Ruanda-Urundi), and the Class C mandates were island territories that were directly integrated into those of the victorious powers without any condition (South West Africa in the Union of South Africa, Territory of New Guinea and Nauru in Australia, Western Samoa in New Zealand, and the Japanese Pacific Mandate in Japan).

5 Reproduced by Pierce, Anne Rice. *Woodrow Wilson and Harry Truman: Mission and Power in American Foreign Policy*. Westport: Praeger, 2003, p. 84.

The peace treaties that drew a line under the Great War were the culmination of the nationalist aspirations of many communities that hitherto had formed part of European empires, such as Poland, Estonia, Latvia, Lithuania, Finland, Czechoslovakia, Hungary and Yugoslavia (initially the Kingdom of Serbs, Croats and Slovenes), but they left unresolved ethnic conflicts of an irredentist or border-related nature, such as the Teschen dispute between the new states of Poland and Czechoslovakia (declared a plebiscite territory by the Allied Supreme Council in Versailles and which was the subject of an Advisory Opinion of the Permanent Court of International Justice on 6 December 1923), the Italian claim to Fiume (a free state from 1920 to 1924, annexed by Italy), the war between Poland and Lithuania over Vilnius (1919–1920), the Corfu incident between Greece and Albania (1923), the Incident at Petrich between Greece and Bulgaria (1925) or the dispute over the territory of Memel (administered by the League of Nations until 1923, when it was occupied by Lithuania, and self-governing under international supervision between 1924 and 1939, when it was annexed by Germany). Many populations with ties to neighbouring countries were left out of their national State as a result of the punishment imposed on defeated powers in 1919, especially, therefore, Turks, Hungarians, Germans and Russians. Some disputes were settled by force (such as the Greek-Turkish war over Smyrna) and others through the intervention of the League of Nations, such as the division of Schleswig between Denmark and Germany (plebiscites of 14 February and 14 March 1920), the partition of the Upper Silesia region (which honoured the result of the referendum held on 20 March 1921) or the reintegration of Saarland into Germany (following the referendum of 13 January 1935).

Of these issues dealt with by the League of Nations, the most important in terms of the solution adopted is the dispute between Sweden and Finland over the Åland Islands. In 1917, the inhabitants, of Swedish origin and culture, asked to be separated from the new independent Finnish state and reintegrated into Sweden. Following interventions by Finnish and German armed forces, the League of Nations reached a decision on the matter, proposing that Finland's territorial integrity be maintained and that Swedish be recognised as a language of instruction in schools and as co-official in government, as well as recommending extensive local autonomy, which would eventually be established in 1922. The Committee of Experts of the League of Nations expresses itself in no uncertain terms on a supposed right of self-determination of peoples:

> Although the principle of self-determination of peoples plays an important part in modern political thought, especially since the Great War, it must be pointed out that there is no mention in the Covenant of the League of Nations. The recognition of this principle in a certain number of international treaties cannot be considered as sufficient to put it upon the same footing as a positive rule of the Law of Nations (...). Positive International Law does not recognize the right of national groups, as such, to separate themselves from the State of which they form part by the simple

> expression of a wish (...) The grant or refusal of the right to a portion of its population of determining its own political fate by plebiscite or by some other method is, exclusively, an attribute of the sovereignty of every State[6].

Both in this matter and in that of the minorities of Upper Silesia[7], the League of Nations resolves the problems relating to national minorities located outside their national State in a similar way: by protecting the territorial integrity of the States in which they are integrated after the drawing of borders in 1919, in exchange for granting extensive internal autonomy. In any case, the Committee's opinion on the Åland Islands dispute shows that in the 1920s there was no customary international norm – be it established by convention under the League of Nations system or recognised in jurisprudence – that considered that ethnic groups had the right to secede from the States to which they belonged on grounds of their distinctness, their national aspirations or the simple plebiscitary expression of their will. Thus, the 'principle of nationalities'[8] is shown to be a mere political doctrine; indeed, one that would be especially refuted in the interwar period[9].

Non-colonial peoples in the basic texts of the United Nations

The Charter of the United Nations of 1945 and the Universal Declaration of Human Rights of 1948

At the San Francisco Conference in 1945, the Allied powers of the Second World War, in designing the new universal organisation with general powers that was to replace the League of Nations, focused their priorities concerning the rights of peoples on a proclamation of the principle of self-determination, judiciously placed at the beginning of the 1945 Charter of the United Nations alongside the organisation's other aims and the structural principles that were to inform the general rules and regulations of its incipient legal system. However, the grandiloquent statement in Article 1 (2) of the Charter, according to which it is the purpose of the UN "to develop friendly relations among nations based on respect for the principle of equal rights and self-determination of peoples",

6 Report of the International Committee of Jurists, *Advisory Opinion upon the Legal Aspects of the Åland Islands Question*, League of Nations, O.J. Spec. Supp. 3, 5, 1920.

7 *Case concerning certain rights of minorities in Upper Silesia*, 1928, PCIJ Reports, Series A, No. 15, p. 4.

8 Regarding this principle, see Redslob, Robert. "Le principe des nationalités". *Recueils des Courses de l'Académie de Droit International.* The Hague, vol. 37, no. 3, 1931, pp. 1–82.

9 As is correctly pointed out by Carpentier, Chantal in her analysis of supposed principles with juridical value in this area of secession: "Principe Mythique des Nationalités: Tentative de Dénonciation d'un Prétendu Principe". *Revue Belge de Droit International*, vol. 25, no. 2, 1992, pp. 351–389.

is not fleshed out in any substantive way elsewhere in the text of this treaty[10], and the regime established refers exclusively to colonial peoples and, therefore, makes no reference whatsoever to ethnic minorities or indigenous peoples.

The Conference delegates undertook the Allied powers' prior commitment to restrict the scope of application of this principle of self-determination to only some of the territories under colonial domination, specifically those remaining under the trusteeship regime of Chapter XII of the Charter. These territories, then called 'self-governing', as opposed to the 'non-self-governing' territories regulated in Chapter XI, are limited – pursuant to Article 77 – to the previous mandates (Palestine, pending, and the B and C mandates of the League of Nations), the colonial territories separated from the enemy nations of the Second World War (Italian Somalia and Japan's Pacific dominions) and those voluntarily placed under this regime by the other colonial powers. Although their temporary administration was not expressly imposed until they gained independence, this was the goal promoted in practice by the Trusteeship Council, which remained in operation until 1994 (independence of Palau). Thus, most of the colonial dominions of France, the United Kingdom, Belgium, the Netherlands, Spain, Portugal and the United States remained beyond the scope of the effective application of that principle declared in Article 1(2) of the Charter, since these 'non-self-governing territories' were only subject to very mild obligations relating to information and development.

As for any other classes of people, such as those integrated in the territory of States, there is no reference in the Charter to extending its application and nor was there any intention to do so. On the contrary, all the explicit references are to territories administered by the Members (Art. 73). It was not on the agenda of the major powers at previous conferences, beyond resolving a specific situation that seriously compromised international security (such as the question of Poland's definitive borders), and nor was it among the intentions of any of the other delegations at San Francisco. At the founding conference, for example, the United Kingdom, France and Colombia argued that the self-determination of peoples could not be interpreted as protecting any right to secession within States, the first-mentioned stating that its government did "not believe that the principle of self-determination (is) intended to form a basis upon which provinces or other parts of independent states (can) claim a right to secession"[11]. As the Committee responsible for drafting Chapter I made clear in its preparatory work:

> Concerning the principle of self-determination, it was strongly emphasized on the one side that this principle corresponded closely to the will and

10 See Cassese, Antonio. *Self-Determination of Peoples: A Legal Reappraisal.* New York: Cambridge University Press, 1995, p. 42.

11 Cited by Anderson, Glen. "A Post-Millennial...", op. cit., p. 1207. See Quane, Helen. "The United Nations and the Evolving Right to Self-Determination". *International & Comparative Law* Q., vol. 47, 1998, pp. 539 et seq.

> desires of the peoples everywhere, and should be clearly enunciated in the Chapter; on the other side it was stated that the principle conformed to the purposes of the Charter only insofar as it implied the right of self-government of peoples and not the right of secession[12].

This is confirmed in Principle I of General Assembly Resolution 1541 (XV) of 15 December 1960, when it reveals that "the authors of the Charter of the United Nations had in mind that Chapter XI should be applicable to territories which were then known to be of the colonial type". This was also the case in the discussions for drafting the first human rights texts, such as the Universal Declaration of Human Rights, drawn up by the Human Rights Committee (HRC) and adopted by General Assembly Resolution 217A (III) of 10 December 1948. In the text of this document there is no reference to the self-determination of peoples, thus confirming it was no more, at that point, than a principle of a political nature – and at most a structural principle of as yet unspecified content – and not a genuine right. This was made clear in various debates, both in the HRC and in the Third Committee of the General Assembly, by the delegations of the United Kingdom, France, Australia, the Netherlands and Belgium, among others[13]. Only the USSR argued, from the early 1950s onwards, that it should be included, albeit expressly restricted to colonial peoples[14].

General Assembly Resolution 1514(XV) of 1960 and the International Covenant on Civil and Political Rights of 1966

It was not until General Assembly Resolution 1514 (XV) of 14 December 1960 that the right of self-determination of peoples made its reappearance in UN texts, although, as we will see later on, the work of the Third Committee during the 1950s encompassed a broad debate on the inclusion and scope of this right in its draft general treaties on human rights, which would eventually become what are known as the New York Covenants of 1966. At the same time, the Fourth Committee was preparing a document on decolonisation that was eventually adopted in 1960, entitled "Declaration on the Granting of Independence to Colonial Countries and Peoples", which in keeping with its title refers exclusively to "Trust and Non-Self-Governing Territories or all other territories which have not yet attained independence". Resolution 1541 (XV), adopted the following day, aims to establish the "Principles which should guide Members in determining whether or not an obligation exists to transmit

12 UNCIO, Documents, Volume 6, Document 343, pp. 296–297.

13 Among others, speeches made by the Representative of the United Kingdom on 2 July 1955, of Australia on 20 July 1955 and of the Netherlands on 29 August 1955, UN Doc., A/2910/Add.1, Annexes, 5, 11 and 14.

14 Tunkin, Grigory Ivanovich. *Theory of International Law*. Harvard University Press, 1974, p. 64, and Cassese, op. cit., p. 49.

the information called for under Article 73 of the Charter" and again refers only to colonial situations.

The International Covenant on Civil and Political Rights (ICCPR) and the International Covenant on Economic, Social and Cultural Rights, both of 19 December 1966, have in common an Article 1 that reads as follows:

1 All peoples have the right of self-determination. By virtue of that right they freely determine their political status and freely pursue their economic, social and cultural development.
2 All peoples may, for their own ends, freely dispose of their natural wealth and resources without prejudice to any obligations arising out of international economic co-operation, based upon the principle of mutual benefit, and international law. In no case may a people be deprived of its own means of subsistence.
3 The States Parties to the present Covenant, including those having responsibility for the administration of Non-Self-Governing and Trust Territories, shall promote the realization of the right of self-determination, and shall respect that right, in conformity with the provisions of the Charter of the United Nations.

From a simple reading of this text, it is not possible to tell which types of peoples are being referred to in paragraph 1, but it becomes apparent in the other two. In the second paragraph, since it states that people have the right to dispose of their natural and economic resources, we can only deduce that it is a matter of avoiding all forms of economic neo-colonialism once independence is achieved (for example, the former colonial powers or their companies reserving or controlling mineral resources, hydrocarbons or any other commodity), as established in UNGA Resolution 1803 (XVII) of 14 December 1962. And in the third paragraph it is made explicit by the reference to 'Non-Self-Governing and Trust Territories'.

Various aspects of the problem were discussed during the preparatory phase[15]: first, whether it could be unequivocally stated that there already existed a genuine international right of self-determination of peoples, surpassing its initial status as a political principle, which was finally accepted by all delegations in the terms expressed in Resolution 1514 of 1960, negotiated in parallel; second, whether the self-determination of peoples should be included, given that it is essentially a collective right whereas the instrument being drafted was intended to establish effective mechanisms for claims by individuals – a wasted discussion in that even though the most reticent delegations accepted its inclusion, the final text failed to specify any procedure for claiming this right in

15 Regarding the preparatory work and Article 1 of the ICCPR, see Palmisano, Giuseppe. *Nazioni Unite e autodeterminazione interna*, Giuffrè, Milano, 1997, pp. 107–145; Hannum, Hurst. "Rethinking Self-Determination". *Virginia Journal of International Law*, vol. 34, 1993, pp. 19–25, and Cassese, op. cit., pp. 47–62.

practice, which would have required ascertaining the representativeness of the group of people in question; and third, the scope of this collective human right, that is, whether it should be restricted to peoples under colonial domination, in the strict terms of the 1960 Resolution, or whether it could also be extended to other peoples integrated in States.

This last debate is of most interest in this study, although it should be said that the passage of the original proposals to the ultimately approved text was the result – as is usually the case in these negotiations – of compromises between the different delegations, which in exchange for admitting certain contents added others of political interest to themselves.

When the debate first arose in the early 1950s, the Western bloc understood that it was not necessary to make any reference to this 'principle' set out in Article 1 of the UN Charter, as its mention in the founding treaty was solely for international security purposes. However, the Eastern bloc and the new countries that had emerged from decolonisation insisted that it be addressed in the preparatory work – for the covenants that would be adopted in 1966 and also for the aforementioned Resolution 1514 that would be adopted a few years earlier, in 1960 – because they felt that this political principle had been transformed by international custom into a genuine structural principle of the general international order and that its normative development, its legal regime, should be reflected in a document agreed upon by all concerned. The first stumbling block for the USSR, its European allies and the Afro-Asian countries had been overcome, but now it was time to address the matter of scope: the first discussion centred on the colonial territories, and it was agreed by a slim majority that the colonies in general, that is, the non-self-governing territories, should also be included alongside the territories under trust administration. As the Western countries were defeated in their attempt to exclude their colonial dominions (22 votes against, 28 in favour and five abstentions), which did them serious harm, they – not only the United States and the United Kingdom but also others such as Denmark, New Zealand, Egypt, Afghanistan, India and Lebanon – proposed another area in which they could in turn undermine the internal security of the Eastern bloc, namely by applying this right to oppressed minorities, meaning those who were discriminated against in terms of political participation. It is in this context that we should understand the initial discussion on whether to admit the expression 'peoples and nations', rejected by the delegations led by the USSR, which only argued for the inclusion of colonies ('peoples'), and defended by the United States because it allowed a self-serving interpretation that encouraged the rebellion of the minorities oppressed by its adversaries ('nations'). Although the pairing appears in the text adopted in 1952, it was subsequently withdrawn to leave only the reference to peoples, as numerous delegations considered that it introduced a concept that overstepped the limits of the prevailing international legal system and, in political terms, generated a great deal of insecurity in their respective States. To give just one telling example, the Iraqi delegate believed that "the right of self-determination applied to a people under foreign domination, whether it could be defined as a nation or not, but not to a separatist movement within a sovereign state", while his Iranian counterpart insisted that "the right of self-determination must never be confused with the right of secession"[16]; and the same view was expressed by other delegations such as France, the USSR, Yugoslavia, Greece, Belgium, Saudi Arabia, India, Afghanistan, Ecuador, Venezuela, Syria and New Zealand.

Therefore, although the negotiating game introduced the issue of minorities in the early years of the debate, they were finally left out due to the majority conviction that the right to self-determination of peoples eventually recognised in 1966 referred exclusively to those under colonial domination. Since then, this has been the interpretation of most authors after analysing the debates conducted by this Committee, among them Rigo Sureda, Humphrey, Bossuyt, Higgins, Musgrave and Pentassuglia. Others, in contrast, such as Buchheit, Cassese and Anderson, reach a different conclusion[17]. Thus, paragraph 1 of the common Article 1 is, according to the majority of experts, applicable to all the peoples that make up a State, in the sense of affirming their right to internal self-determination.

This was also the interpretation given by the HRC created by the ICCPR. Thus, in *Diergaardt and Others v Namibia* (1996)[18], representatives of the Rehoboth Baster community, descendants of indigenous Khoi and Afrikaans settlers from the Cape, who had enjoyed self-government between 1872 and 1990, alleged that the new State of Namibia, created in 1990, had violated – among others – the right to internal self-determination enshrined in Article 1 (1) by suppressing their traditional local institutions. The Committee considered that "all peoples have the right of self-determination and the right freely to determine their political status, pursue their economic, social and cultural development and dispose of their natural wealth and resources, as stipulated in article 1 of the Covenant", but – as we have previously noted with regard to its practical effectiveness – that first it is necessary to determine which individuals belong to a people, a matter which does not fall within the remit of this body, and second, that violations of the individual rights of its claimant members must be proved under Articles 25 to 27 of the Covenant, as this is the actual competence of this supervisory body.

16 UN A/C.3/SR.671, 25 November 1955, UN A/C.3/SR.888, 21 November 1958. Cited by Mustafa, Zubeida. "The Principle of Self-Determination in International Law". *The International Lawyer*, vol. 5, no. 3, 1971, p. 484.

17 Rigo Sureda, Andrés. *The Evolution of the Right of Self-Determination*. Leyden: Sijthoff, 1973, pp. 107–110; Humphrey, John P. *Human Rights and the United Nations. A Great Adventure*. New York: Transnational Pub., 1984, p. 129; Bossuyt, Marc J. *Guide to the 'travaux préparatoires' of the International Covenant on Civil and Political Rights*. The Hague: Nijhoff, 1987, pp. 32–37; Higgins, Rosalyn. *Problems and Process: International Law and How We Use It*. Oxford: Clarendon Press, 1994, pp. 111 et seq.; Musgrave, op. cit., pp. 92–93, and Pentassuglia, op. cit., p. 308. For the opposing view, see: Buchheit, op. cit., p. 83; Cassese, op. cit., p. 143, and Anderson, "A Post-Millenial…", op. cit., p. 1213.

18 Doc. CCPR/C/69/D/760/1996, Communication no. 760/1997, 25 July 2000.

The Committee itself expressed this view in its General Comment No. 12 (1984) on Article 1[19]:

> Article 1 enshrines an inalienable right of all peoples as described in its paragraphs 1 and 2. By virtue of that right they freely 'determine their political status and freely pursue their economic, social and cultural development'. The article imposes on all States parties corresponding obligations (…) With regard to paragraph 1 of article 1, States parties should describe the constitutional and political processes which in practice allow the exercise of this right.

Ruling out the practical possibility of admitting communications submitted by alleged representatives of peoples, it is only applicable – on a specific basis – under Article 27 of the ICCPR, which provides that:

> In those States in which ethnic, religious or linguistic minorities exist, persons belonging to such minorities shall not be denied the right, in community with the other members of their group, to enjoy their own culture, to profess and practise their own religion, or to use their own language.

In General Comment No. 23 on this Article, dated 6 April 1994[20], it is clearly stated that Articles 1 and 27 differ in terms of their content and whom they concern, and that the effectiveness of the latter cannot undermine the integrity of the State:

> 1. Article 27 of the Covenant provides that, in those States in which ethnic, religious or linguistic minorities exist, persons belonging to these minorities shall not be denied the right (…) 2. In some communications submitted to the Committee under the Optional Protocol, the right protected under article 27 has been confused with the right of peoples to self-determination proclaimed in article 1 of the Covenant (…) 3.1. The Covenant draws a distinction between the right to self-determination and the rights protected under article 27. The former is expressed to be a right belonging to peoples and is dealt with in a separate part (Part I) of the Covenant. Self-determination is not a right cognizable under the Optional Protocol. Article 27, on the other hand, relates to rights conferred on individuals as such and is included, like the articles relating to other personal rights conferred on individuals, in Part III of the Covenant and is

19 CCPR/C/21/Add. 3 dated 5 Oct. 1984.

20 CCPR/C/21/rev.1/Add.5, para. 5.3. Previously, General Comment no. 12, of 1984, which dealt with the right of self-determination as presented in Article 1, offers few explicit references, although it refers in general to the right of internal self-determination, the economic rights of peoples and the obligations with respect to self-governing and trust territories.

> cognizable under the Optional Protocol. 3.2. The enjoyment of the rights to which article 27 relates does not prejudice the sovereignty and territorial integrity of a State party (...).

The reports and resolutions of other supervisory bodies also follow this same course of action. For example, the Committee against Torture, in its General Recommendation XXI (48) of 8 March 1996, states that:

> The external aspect of self-determination implies that all peoples have the right to determine freely their political status and their place in the international community based upon the principle of equal rights and exemplified by the liberation of peoples from colonialism and by the prohibition to subject peoples to alien subjugation, domination and exploitation (...). The Committee emphasizes that, in accordance with the Declaration on Friendly Relations, none of the Committee's actions shall be construed as authorizing or encouraging any action which would dismember or impair, totally or in part, the territorial integrity or political unity of sovereign and independent States conducting themselves in compliance with the principle of equal rights and self-determination of peoples and possessing a Government representing the whole people belonging to the territory, without distinction as to race, creed or colour. In the view of the Committee, international law has not recognized a general right of peoples unilaterally to declare secession from a State[21].

General Assembly Resolution 2625(XXV) of 1970

The culminating point of the debate on this matter within the bodies of the UN is precisely this text to which the aforementioned resolution refers, the seventh paragraph of the part devoted to the self-determination of peoples contained in UNGA Resolution 2625 (XXV) of 24 October 1970, entitled "Declaration on Principles of International Law concerning Friendly Relations and Cooperation among States in accordance with the Charter of the United Nations". After reaffirming that:

> by virtue of the principle of equal rights and self-determination of peoples enshrined in the Charter of the United Nations, all peoples have the right freely to determine, without external interference, their political status and to pursue their economic, social and cultural development, and every State has the duty to respect this right in accordance with the provisions of the Charter,

and setting out all the general obligations regarding this right, it states that:

21 UN Committee on the Elimination of Racial Discrimination, 'General Recommendation XXI on self-determination' (1996), UN Doc A/51/18, Annex VIII, para. 6.

> Nothing in the foregoing paragraphs shall be construed as authorizing or encouraging any action which would dismember or impair, totally or in part, the territorial integrity or political unity of sovereign and independent States conducting themselves in compliance with the principle of equal rights and self-determination of peoples as described above and thus possessed of a government representing the whole people belonging to the territory without distinction as to race, creed or colour.

This was the umpteenth time that delegations to the UN had discussed the scope of the right of self-determination of peoples, but it was also the first time that they had intended, as is reflected in the preparatory work, to extend this right, in certain cases, to situations outside the colonial context[22]. Although there are no doubts about this intention to include non-colonial peoples, the legal value and practical scope of this provision are far more controversial. We will discuss their inclusion in this section and their practical scope in those that follow.

In fact, the United States and the Western countries rescued the proposal put forward during the discussions leading to the 1966 Covenants, that self-determination should apply not only to the colonies but also to ethnically distinct groups integrated in States, not with the intention of generously recognising a right to secession of the indigenous peoples of the United States or Canada, or of the Corsicans in France, or of the Irish in British Ulster, but of delivering a body blow to the Eastern bloc. The American and British proposal of 1966 maintained that:

> States enjoying full sovereignty and independence, and possessed of a representative government, effectively functioning as such with respect to all distinct peoples within their territory, shall be considered to be conducting themselves in conformity with this principle as regards to those peoples[23].

As we explained in another monograph[24], this proposal – to which the current initial reference to territorial integrity and the final reference to discrimination in government would be added – was wholly in keeping with the strategy employed by these countries in the negotiations of the earlier texts, in which the English-speaking bloc considered the battle over decolonisation to have

22 Regarding the preparatory work, see Emerson, Rupert. "Self-Determination". *American Journal of International Law*, vol. 65, no. 3, 1971, pp. 459–475, and Critescu, Aureliu. "Le droit à la autodétermination: développement historique et actuel sur la base des instruments des Nations Unies". UN Doc E/CN.4/Sub.2/404/Rev.1, N.Y.: UN, 1981.

23 Proposals on self-determination submitted by the United States, UN A/AC.125/L.32 and the United Kingdom UN A/AC.125/L. 1966.

24 López Martín, Ana G. and José Antonio Perea Unceta. *Creación de Estados, secesión y reconocimiento*. Valencia: Tirant lo Blanch, 2018, pp. 162–169.

been lost once and for all, accepting the disappearance of the colonial empires of the Western powers due to the imposition of an inescapable positive law by a majority of States[25] and simply by coming to terms with historical and social events. The intention of the proposal was twofold: 1) to prioritise the principle of respect for the sovereignty and territorial integrity of States over the principle of self-determination of peoples, restricting it to its internal dimension; and 2) failing this, to reformulate it as an emerging democratic principle, so that the principle of respect for territorial integrity would only lose out in its confrontation with that of self-determination in situations in which the populations of States, including minority ones, were not guaranteed internal self-determination equivalent to respect for liberal democracy[26].

The debates on the British-American proposal were conducted on two different levels: on the one hand, in relation to the extension of this right to peoples not subject to colonial domination[27], it being clear from the delegation speeches that the majority did not admit the existence of a right to secession in current international law, as affirmed by India, Nigeria, Algeria, Ecuador and Burma, among others, in whose opinion – as Argentina stated – "le príncipe de l'autodétermination désigne le droit à l'autonomie intrene de toute peuple organicé en Etat indépendant"[28]; and on the other, to establish a 'democratic saving clause', called a 'safeguard clause'. On this second level, the delegations of France, Japan, Canada, Australia, the Netherlands, Argentina and Venezuela supported the British and American proposal for its inclusion, which was opposed by, among others, those of India, Burma, Syria, Bolivia, Ecuador, Guatemala, Kenya, Central African Republic, Ghana, Argelia, Romania and Poland, who considered that the recognition of free internal self-determination was in contradiction with the simultaneous imposition of a specific political system[29], especially if the consequence was a sanction in terms of loss of territorial sovereignty[30]. The USSR tried to skirt round the debate by arguing that the proposed text could be interpreted as meaning that a State should not prevent certain people from participating in political bodies on the grounds that they belong to a minority and not necessarily in terms of the political system implying a liberal democracy, i.e. with plurality of political participation.

To overcome the objections of these States, Italy – supported by Czechoslovakia – suggested adding the original paragraph that was eventually approved

25 As acknowledged by Michel Virally, French delegate at the debates of the Sixth Committee. UN Doc. A/AC.125/Sr.69, pp. 13–15.
26 Positions of the United States and the United Kingdom, in UN Doc. A/AC.125/Sr.92, pp. 21 and 141–143. See the comments of Tancredi, Antonello. *La secessione nel diritto internazionale*, Padova: Cedam, 2006, p. 254.
27 Interventions, among others, of United Kingdom, Japan, Australia, the Netherlands and France, as reported by Palmisano, op. cit., pp. 224–225.
28 According to Argentina UN Doc. A/AC.125/sr.70, p. 16. "[T]he principle of self-determination implies the right to internal self-government of any people organised into an independent State" (author's translation).
29 Cassese, op. cit., pp. 115 et seq.
30 As expressed by the Kenya delegation. UN Doc./A/AC.125/Sr.69, p. 21.

("nothing in the foregoing paragraphs shall be construed as authorizing or encouraging any action which would dismember or impair, totally or in part, the territorial integrity or political unity of...") and Lebanon successfully proposed in an amendment the final paragraph with the discriminatory condition. The reasons for this Lebanese amendment are unknown, but it was certainly made with the intention of reducing the scope of the proposals put forward, given that the aim was to satisfy the Eastern bloc countries and developing nations with a participation clause in which the important thing was not their access through democratic channels but the absence of discriminatory, racial or religious motives[31]. This interpretation is borne out by the rejection it provoked in South Africa, with its segregationist regime that flagrantly breached the safeguard clause[32]. Therefore, we can state that Resolution 2625 declares the extension of the right of self-determination to all peoples, including national minorities, but limits its exercise to those situations in which the States where they reside do not permit the political participation of persons belonging to one of these peoples on racial or religious grounds. A different matter is the legal scope of this declaration, as this text would be reproduced verbatim in other international documents, but all of them of a non-conventional nature, such as the Declaration of the World Conference on Human Rights, held in Vienna on 25 June 1993.

The Declarations on Minorities (1992) and Indigenous Peoples (2007)

When referring specifically to the human rights of peoples integrated in States, whether they be ethnic minorities or indigenous peoples, the approach of the UN basically involves proclaiming, in international declarations (i.e. non-binding instruments), certain ambitious goals and, in conventions for the formulation of individual rights, recognition of the exercise of distinctness and the prohibition of discrimination, although it is true that there are certain differences between the regime of minorities and that of indigenous peoples.

By Resolution 47/135 of 18 December 1992, the General Assembly adopted the Declaration on the Rights of Persons Belonging to National or Ethnic, Religious and Linguistic Minorities, inspired by Article 27 of the 1966 New York Covenant. In general, it recommends that States recognise the right of minorities situated within their territory to use their language, enjoy their culture and practise their religion, but makes no reference to a supposed right to internal political autonomy, let alone to external self-determination.

However, the treatment given to indigenous peoples in the UN Declaration on the Rights of Indigenous Peoples, adopted by the General Assembly on 13 September 2007 (UNGA 61/295), differs on some matters, as it recommends recognition of certain rights that are essentially collective, not only of an economic nature but also concerning political autonomy. In relation to self-

31 Cassese, op. cit., pp. 117–118.
32 GAOR, 25th Session, Sixth Committee, 1148th Mtg., para. 15.

determination, although the Annex states that "indigenous peoples are equal to all other peoples" (first paragraph), that

> the Charter of the United Nations, the International Covenant on Economic, Social and Cultural Rights and the International Covenant on Civil and Political Rights, as well as the Vienna Declaration and Programme of Action, affirm the fundamental importance of the right to self-determination of all peoples, by virtue of which they freely determine their political status and freely pursue their economic, social and cultural development,
>
> (fifteenth paragraph)

and that "nothing in this Declaration may be used to deny any peoples their right to self-determination, exercised in conformity with international law" (sixteenth paragraph), the text nevertheless interprets this self-determination exclusively in its internal aspect, confirming international practice in relation to any people integrated in a State.

In fact, during the debate on this declaration, some delegations – Sweden, Norway, New Zealand and Switzerland, among others – submitted an amendment whose wording was based on the safeguard clause in Resolution 2625, but they did not receive the support of the representatives of indigenous peoples, who felt that it detracted from the inherent right of peoples to full self-determination, even externally, assuming they were democratic States. The eventual solution was to add an Article 4 in which it is stated that "indigenous peoples, in exercising their right to self-determination, have the right to autonomy or self-government in matters relating to their internal and local affairs, as well as ways and means for financing their autonomous functions"[33]. This internal autonomy is completed with Article 5, which provides that:

> indigenous peoples have the right to maintain and strengthen their distinct political, legal, economic, social and cultural institutions, while retaining their right to participate fully, if they so choose, in the political, economic, social and cultural life of the State;

Article 19, according to which:

> States shall consult and cooperate in good faith with the indigenous peoples concerned through their own representative institutions in order to obtain their free, prior and informed consent before adopting and implementing legislative or administrative measures that may affect them;

33 At the General Assembly it received 141 votes in favour and four against (Australia, New Zealand, Canada and the United States), with 11 abstentions, mainly from African countries.

and other provisions regulating the right to self-identification (Article 33(1)) and the right to their ancestral lands (Articles 25, 26 and 27)[34].

Limited scope of the collective rights of non-colonial peoples as recognised in regional international law

In addition to the international instruments of the UN – binding or non-binding – outlined in the previous section, which in different areas and in different forms are aimed at peoples, be it those integrated in States or mainly those subject to colonial domination, there are others drawn up within the framework of regional organisations that also include references to all peoples and colonies, or to ethnic minorities or indigenous peoples.

In the OAS there is no reference to national minorities, but there *is* to indigenous peoples. Likewise, although there is no specific provision for minority and indigenous peoples in the American Convention on Human Rights adopted in 1969 in San José, Costa Rica, the Rapporteurship on the Rights of Indigenous Peoples, created in 1990, promoted the development of the American Declaration on the Rights of Indigenous Peoples, which was adopted by the OAS General Assembly on 14 June 2016. Once again, it is reproduced in a declaration, and therefore, formally, is only of a recommendatory nature, but the Inter-American Commission on Human Rights has recognised that:

> the Commission will, to the extent appropriate, interpret and apply the pertinent provisions of the American Declaration in light of current developments in the field of international human rights law, as evidenced by treaties, custom and other relevant sources of international law[35].

In content it is very similar to the UNGA Declaration, as it recognises their right to internal self-determination (Article III) and political autonomy (Article XXI), with the same proviso that:

> nothing in this Declaration may be interpreted as implying for any State, people, group or person any right to engage in any activity or to perform any act contrary to the Charter of the Organization of American States or the Charter of the United Nations or construed as authorizing or encouraging any action which would dismember or impair, totally or in part, the territorial integrity or political unity of sovereign and independent states.
>
> (Article IV)

34 Regarding this Declaration, see, among others, Xanthaki, Alexandra. *Indigenous Rights and United Nations Standards. Self-Determination, Culture and Land*. New York: Cambridge University Press, 2007, and Stavenhagen, Rodolfo. *Los pueblos indígenas y sus derechos*, México: UNESCO, 2007.

35 Report N° 40/04, Case 12.053, Merits, Maya Indigenous Communities of the Toledo District, Belize, October 12, 2004, para. 88.

In the European regional setting, in contrast, references are explicit and limited to ethnic minorities. In the Final Act of the Conference on Security and Cooperation in Europe (Helsinki, 1 August 1975), which in 1994 became the Organization for Security and Co-operation in Europe (OSCE), a distinction is made between national minorities (Principle VII) and other peoples (Principle VIII). According to the former,

> the participating States on whose territory national minorities exist will respect the right of persons belonging to such minorities to equality before the law, will afford them the full opportunity for the actual enjoyment of human rights and fundamental freedoms and will, in this manner, protect their legitimate interests in this sphere.

According to the latter:

> The participating States will respect the equal rights of peoples and their right to self-determination, acting at all times in conformity with the purposes and principles of the Charter of the United Nations and with the relevant norms of international law, including those relating to territorial integrity of States.
>
> By virtue of the principle of equal rights and self-determination of peoples, all peoples always have the right, in full freedom, to determine, when and as they wish, their internal and external political status, without external interference, and to pursue as they wish their political, economic, social and cultural development.

Despite only five years having passed since Resolution 2625, there is neither express reference to the self-determination of minorities nor a similar safeguard clause, initiating the characteristic regulation of minorities – as already mentioned in relation to the 1992 UN Declaration – based on the right to differentiation and the prohibition of discrimination, without any mention of external self-determination. These are the terms of the Charter of Paris for a New Europe of 21 November 1990, which states that:

> the ethnic, cultural, linguistic and religious identity of national minorities will be protected and that persons belonging to national minorities have the right freely to express, preserve and develop that identity without any discrimination and in full equality before the law.

The Lund Recommendations of 1 September 1999, drawn up by the OSCE Office for Democratic Institutions and Human Rights and the High Commissioner on National Minorities, and which deal with the participation in public life of persons belonging to national minorities, seek to promote – unlike other texts on minorities – "non-territorial or territorial arrangements of self-governance or a combination thereof" and because "appropriate local, regional, or autonomous administrations that correspond to the specific historical and territorial circumstances of national minorities may undertake a number of functions in order to respond more effectively to the concerns of these minorities" (para. 20)[36].

As for the Council of Europe, although here too we find no recognition of external self-determination, there are, on the other hand, many exhortations to respect the territorial integrity of States. This can be seen in the European Charter for Regional or Minority Languages of 5 November 1992, in Recommendation 1201 of the Council of Europe Parliamentary Assembly, adopted on 1 February 1993, on the Additional protocol on the rights of minorities to the European Convention for the Protection of Human Rights and Fundamental Freedoms relating to National Minorities, and in the Framework Convention for the Protection of National Minorities of 1 February 1995, whose Article 21 states that:

> nothing in the present framework Convention shall be interpreted as implying any right to engage in any activity or perform any act contrary to the fundamental principles of international law and in particular of the sovereign equality, territorial integrity and political independence of States.

Other documents, such as Recommendations 928 (1981), 1134 (1990) and 1177 (1992), and the reports of the Committee of Experts on Issues relating to the Protection of National Minorities, include a comprehensive list of rights and a complaints procedure, but nothing about external self-determination or any possible right to internal self-governance[37].

Finally, the treatment given to this question in Africa differs in form but not in content. Logically, its international treaties condemn all forms of colonialism and repeatedly promote the right to self-determination of peoples, without making any specific reference to minorities[38] or indigenous peoples. The

36 Along the same lines, the Bolzano/Bozen Recommendations on National Minorities in Inter-State Relations of the High Commissioner on National Minorities (20 June 2008). Regarding the protection of minority rights and the OSCE, see Helgesen, Jan E. "Protecting Minorities in the Conference on Security and Co-operation in Europe (CSCE) Process". *International Journal on Group Rights*, vol. 2, no. 1, 1994, pp. 7–34, and Wright, Jane. "The OSCE and the Protection of Minority Rights". *Human Rights Quarterly*, vol. 18, no. 1, 1996, pp. 190–205.

37 Regarding the protection of minority rights and the Council of Europe, see Gilbert, Geoff, "The Legal Protection Accorded to Minority Groups in Europe". *Netherlands Yearbook of International Law*, vol. 23, 1992, pp. 67–104; Díaz Barrado, Castor. "La protección de las minorías en el seno del Consejo de Europa". *Anuario de la Facultad de Derecho, Universidad de Extremadura*, vol. 17, 1999, pp. 125–170; and Weller, Marc. *The Rights of Minorities in Europe*. Oxford University Press, 2005.

38 As criticised by most of the authors who have studied the regional system, such as, among others, Howard, Rhoda E. *Human Rights in Commonwealth Africa*. N.J.: Rowman and Littlefield, 1986, p. 95. Other authors point out, in contrast, that this silence has not prevented their protection by the AU, for example, Dersso,

founding Charter of the Organisation of African Unity (replaced in 2002 by the African Union), signed in Addis Ababa on 25 May 1963, states, in Article 2.1.d, that one of the organisation's aims is to eradicate all forms of colonialism, and in the preamble to the African Charter on Human and Peoples' Rights, of 27 July 1981, the signatories recognise their duty to:

> achieve the total liberation of Africa, the peoples of which are still struggling for their dignity and genuine independence, and undertaking to eliminate colonialism, neo-colonialism, apartheid, zionism and to dismantle aggressive foreign military bases and all forms of discrimination, language, religion or political opinions,

while Article 21 goes into more detail and reads as follows:

1 All peoples shall freely dispose of their wealth and natural resources. This right shall be exercised in the exclusive interest of the people. In no case shall a people be deprived of it.
2 In case of spoliation, the dispossessed people shall have the right to the lawful recovery of its property as well as to an adequate compensation.
3 The free disposal of wealth and natural resources shall be exercised without prejudice to the obligation of promoting international economic cooperation based on mutual respect, equitable exchange and the principles of international law.
4 State Parties to the present Charter shall individually and collectively exercise the right to free disposal of their wealth and natural resources with a view to strengthening African Unity and solidarity.
5 State Parties to the present Charter shall undertake to eliminate all forms of foreign exploitation particularly that practised by international monopolies so as to enable their peoples to fully benefit from the advantages derived from their national resources.

In spite of this silence on minorities, in the cases heard by the African Commission on Human and Peoples' Rights, this body has consistently maintained that Article 20 can also be applied to post-colonial situations, but only in the case of peoples subjected to serious violations of their human rights, discrimination and oppression by the government of the State in which the minority groups are located. This was the view taken in Cases 75/92 (*Congrès du peuple katangais/DRC*), 266/03 (*Kevin Mgwanga et al/Cameroon*) and 328/06 (*Front for the Liberation of the State of Cabinda v Republic of Angola*). As it explains in these cases, "the Commission is aware that post-colonial Africa has witnessed numerous cases of domination of one group of people over others, either on

Solomon. "The African Human Rights System and the Issue of Minorities in Africa". *African Journal of International and Comparative Law*, vol. 20, no. 1, 2012, pp. 42–69.

the basis of race, religion, or ethnicity, without such domination constituting colonialism in the classical sense" (Communication no. 266/03, para. 181); therefore, "the right to self-determination cannot be exercised, in the absence of proof of massive violation of human rights under the Charter" (266/03, para. 199); so that:

> in the absence of concrete evidence of violations of human rights to the point that the territorial integrity of Zaire should be called to question and in the absence of evidence that the people of Katanga are denied the right to participate in government as guaranteed by Article 13 of the African Charter, the Commission holds the view that Katanga is obliged to exercise a variant of self-determination that is compatible with the sovereignty and territorial integrity of Zaire,
>
> (75/92, para. 6)

concluding that "the Commission states that the various forms of governance or self-determination such as federalism, local government, unitarism, confederacy, and self-government can be exercised only subject to conformity with state sovereignty and territorial integrity of a State party" (266/03, para. 199). Africa's institutional response is, consequently, one of 'jurisprudential' recognition of remedial secession but with its effects limited to internal self-determination.

Although, as we have pointed out, there are no specific laws on minorities in the African system, those of a general nature prohibiting discrimination (Article 2)[39] are applicable, as is – most especially, because of the problems it could generate in relation to the 'democratic clause' of Resolution 2625 – Article 13:

1 Every citizen shall have the right to participate freely in the government of his country, either directly or through freely chosen representatives in accordance with the provisions of the law.
2 Every citizen shall have the right of equal access to the public service of his country.
3 Every individual shall have the right of access to public property and services in strict equality of all persons before the law.

Formulation of a possible customary right based on remedial secession

A review of the international texts on the rights of peoples, whether they concern accession to statehood or regulate the human rights of their constituent

39 The accumulated Communication nos 27/89, 46/91, 49/91 and 99/93, *Organisation Mondiale Contre la Torture and Association Internationale des Juristes Démocrates, Commission Internationale des Juristes and Union Interafricaine des Droits de l'Homme v Rwanda*, condemn Ruanda's actions against the Tutsi community pursuant to, in the first instance, Article 2, which prohibits discrimination on the grounds of "race, ethnic group, national or social origin".

individuals, shows that no international treaty recognises a right of self-determination until 1966. Although the San Francisco Charter of 1945 proclaims a principle of a political nature, there is no real normative development of this principle in its articles. Moreover, these articles only refer to, and indeed were only intended for (as evidenced by the preparatory work), a first type of peoples, those under colonial domination. Such a political nature and limited scope is demonstrated, as we have seen, by its absence from the text of the Universal Declaration of Human Rights of 1948.

It is in the resolutions drafted by the committees set up by the General Assembly that this principle proclaimed in the Charter is transformed into a genuine structural principle of the international legal order and where its content and normative scope are developed. Resolution 1514 (XV) of 1960 and Resolution 2625 (XXV) of 1970, among others, reflect – in most cases with declaratory effect, although in some with crystallising effect[40] – an international custom that had been developing since the late 1940s with the independence of Libya, India, Pakistan, Burma, Ceylon, Indonesia, Laos, Vietnam, Tunisia, Ghana, etc. This is, in any case, a custom whose object is peoples under colonial domination rather than other cases – which are also the subject of debate – such as ethnic, national, religious or linguistic minorities. The legal significance of these resolutions, as regards the right of self-determination of colonial peoples, did not, however, remain a matter of customary corroboration, as the will of the international community to develop a structural principle and its approval by consensus classify its content as a *jus cogens* norm, as has been recognised in various cases – cited earlier – by the ICJ's jurisprudence and as is unanimously accepted by legal scholarship[41].

The problem arises in extending colonial peoples to cover other classes of peoples, those integrated in States, what we call ethnic minorities or indigenous peoples. In this respect, in some cases the wording and in all cases the debates in the committees responsible for drafting the UNGA resolutions on the self-determination of peoples and the general international conventions on human rights show that, although some delegations were in favour of their assimilation into the decolonisation regime, this would not be possible until 1970 due to the opposition of the majority of States. This is the case in UNGA Resolution 1514 (XV) of 1960 and in shared Article 1 of the 1966 Covenants on Civil and Political Rights and on Economic, Social and Cultural Rights.

40 Some aspects of the decolonisation regime are included in the resolutions without it yet having been generated as a complete custom or having reached any milestones in practice, as is the case of States having the duty to help peoples immersed in their armed struggle to obtain independence.

41 Among others, in those years, Abi-Saab, Georges and Michell Virally. *Les Résolutions dans la formation du droit international du développement*. Genève: Librairie Droz, 1971, and Arangio-Ruiz, Caetano. "The Normative Role of the General Assembly of the United Nations and the Declaration of Principles of Friendly Relations". *Recueil de Cours*, vol. 137, no. 3, 1972, pp. 418 et seq.

Similarly, international texts that make recommendations or positively regulate the human rights of the constituent members of 'internal peoples', be they minorities or indigenous peoples, at both universal and regional level, do not recognise any right to external self-determination of these peoples. As far as minorities are concerned, the specific UN text – the 1992 UN Declaration on the Rights of Persons Belonging to National or Ethnic, Religious and Linguistic Minorities – is a mere declaration of the General Assembly and therefore promotes a number of rights of persons belonging to minorities, but it is undoubtedly a faithful reflection and a development of the normative provision of Article 27 of the 1966 ICCPR, as are these documents of other international treaties of a regional scope, such as the Conventions on Minority Languages (1992) and on National Minorities (1995) of the Council of Europe, and other regional texts, binding or recommendatory, such as the Helsinki Act of 1975 or the Charter of Paris of 1990, within the sphere of the OSCE. The normative texts and the practice of the supervisory bodies for the protection of human rights of the UN, OAS, OSCE, Council of Europe and AU show that where minorities are concerned, differentiation of their constituent members is protected and discrimination against them is prohibited, but without recognition of collective rights, including internal autonomy.

With regard to indigenous peoples, both the UN Declaration on the Rights of Indigenous Peoples of 2007 and the OAS Declaration of 2016 contain, in addition to these obligations to admit distinctness and prohibit discrimination (applied by the supervisory bodies of both organisations as if dealing with ethnic minorities), some proposals – as yet without conventional or customary force – for the recognition of collective rights, in the form of internal autonomy and rights pertaining to economic resources and territorial administration. But in neither case is any right of external self-determination ever proposed, despite the demands of the representatives of indigenous peoples.

As we have seen, the first international text in which the international community as a whole intends to propose new rules for extending the right of self-determination, already enshrined for the colonies, to all other classes of peoples is the seventh paragraph of the section on this right in Resolution 2625 of 1970. We say 'new rules' because in the quarter of a century between 1945 and 1970, no people without colonial status gained independence by secession; the first case was Bangladesh in 1971. After the independence of Mongolia and Ireland in 1921 and 1922, respectively, 50 years passed without any cases of accession to statehood by secession, which is why, unlike in the case of decolonisation, it is not possible to speak of the existence of a perfectly formed custom or the crystallisation of a custom in the making.

Having ruled out the existence of a custom in 1970[42], and in view of the fact that there is no international treaty that recognises the right of self-determination outside the context of colonial domination and no ICJ jurisprudence that declares the existence of a *jus cogens* norm in respect thereof, it is a matter of

42 For Arangio-Ruiz, op. cit., p. 571, it is a proposal *de lege* ferenda.

ascertaining whether a customary norm concerning the right to self-determination of non-colonial peoples has been generated since that date and that resolution.

In the 1970s and 1980s, some authors formulated a theory – which today we know as 'remedial secession' or the last resort for ending repression – according to which the aforementioned paragraph of Resolution 2625 of 1970 recognises the right of non-colonial peoples to exert their self-determination if they are subject to discrimination in the States in which they are integrated. This was the initial understanding of Rosenstock[43], for whom:

> Although paragraph 7 is drafted in a somewhat remote manner in the form of a saving clause, a close examination of its text will reward the reader with an affirmation of the applicability of the principle to peoples within existing states and the necessity for governments to represent the governed. The fact that these aspects of the principle must be extracted by an a contrario reading of the paragraph should not be misunderstood to limit the sweep and liberality of the paragraph. Moreover, paragraph 7 must be read in light of the state's duty to promote respect for an observance of human rights and fundamental freedoms in accordance with paragraph 3.

This author points out the difficulty of applying this 'saving clause' in practice, referring to the contemporaneous case of Pakistan and Bangladesh. Other authors would also consider the statement contained in Resolution 2625 sufficient and that there would have to be a discriminatory violation of the minority's human rights, referring to this case or others. In this regard, Kamenu considers its possible application to the events that were taking place in the early 1970s in South Sudan and Eritrea, and with the Somalis in Kenya, and analyses the frustrated experience of Biafra (1967–1970), arguing that it is not enough for a people to be different but that it is essential, in order for an exception to be made to the principle of respect for the territorial integrity of States, that peaceful coexistence within the State be impossible due to the oppression to which the minority population is subjected and that there be no other solution to prevent it. This, therefore, would be a remedial secession to prevent oppression but also the last resort, considering that this is what happened in Biafra, despite the lack of international community consensus[44]. Precisely, in relation to the attempted secession of Biafra, Nayar argued – after acknowledging the mass and flagrant violation of the fundamental rights of the Ibos by the Nigerian Government – that the right to remedial secession as a last resort existed and that the problem lies in its practical application, because:

43 Rosenstock, Robert. "The Declaration of Principles of International Law Concerning Friendly Relations: A Survey". *American Journal of International Law*, vol. 65, no. 5, 1971, p. 735.

44 Kamenu, Onyeonoro S. "Secession and the Right of Self-Determination: An OAU Dilemma". *Journal of Modern African Studies*, vol. 12, 1974, p. 361.

self-determination was denied to the Ibos, because they lacked the power to sustain Biafra's independence. The Bengalis of Bangladesh have been able to assert their right of self-determination, because they won their war. Significantly, the preamble to the Universal Declaration of Human Rights contains the statement that "it is essential, if man is not to be compelled to have recourse, as a last resort, to rebellion against tyranny and oppression, that human rights should be protected by the rule of law." This seems to concede a right to rebel, if it becomes unavoidable, for the sake of self-determination, which, it has been recognized, "is a prerequisite to the full enjoyment of all fundamental human rights"[45].

The retrospective application of the provision of Resolution 2625 to the case of Biafra moves Suzuki to claim, along the same lines, that:

> the Ibos became the principal target of a systematic and deliberate massacre by the Northerners and began fleeing into their Eastern homeland. Confronted with the genocide of their people and the earlier denial of equal participation in the election process, the Ibos inevitably considered secession.

He also points out that the case of Bangladesh in 1971 is very similar, but, as Kamenu indicates, with a notable difference: its eventual success. Suzuki[46] highlights the different treatment given by the UN to these two situations: the Nigeria/Biafra case is deemed a domestic problem when Secretary General U Thant declares that "the United Nations has never accepted and does not accept and I do not believe will ever accept the principle of secession of a part of its Member State"[47], whereas in relation to Pakistan/Bangladesh, the same Secretary General states:

> A problem which often confronts us, and to which as yet no acceptable answer has been found in the provisions of the Charter, is the conflict between the principles of the integrity of sovereign States and the assertion of the right to self-determination, and even secession, by a large group within a sovereign State. Here again, as in the case of human rights, a

45 Nayar, M.G. Kaladharan. "Self-Determination Beyond the Colonial Context: Biafra in Retrospect". *Texas International Law Journal*, vol. 10, 1975, p. 343. Of the same opinion, in much later studies, but also after analysing the case of Biafra, see Okoronkwo, op. cit., pp. 85 et seq., and, in relation to the Ogoni people, Ezetah, Chinedu Reginald. "International Law of Self-Determination and the Ogoni Question: Mirroring Africa's Post-Colonial Dilemma". *Loyola of Los Angeles International and Comparative Law Journal*, vol. 19, August 1997, pp. 811–856, especially pp. 834 and 843.

46 Suzuki, Eisuke. "Self-Determination and World Public Order: Community Response to Territorial Separation". *Virginia Journal of International Law*, vol. 16, 1976, pp. 799 and 805 et seq.

47 7 UN Monthly Chronicle 36 (Feb. 1970).

> dangerous deadlock can paralyse the ability of the United Nations to help those involved[48].

For Don Johnson, the Bangladesh conflict would have been the perfect opportunity to apply what is provided for in Resolution 2625, which, although considered essentially a political commitment, embodied by consensus an emerging legal obligation, since:

> Admittedly, the significance of the principle of self-determination continues to evoke question and sustain discord. The principle is seen by some as 'the hope for the future of mankind', while skeptics of the principle dispute its viability, and label its proponents as 'politically naive'. And though recent international declarations and covenants speak authoritatively of a 'right of self-determination', in the Indo-Pakistani conflict where application of such a right would have seemed most appropriate, it was neither respected nor even formally asserted. Every effort to utilize the principle of self-determination as a vehicle for preserving world order and basic human rights of all people is apparently overwhelmed by forces that see it as promoting anarchic nationalism and infringing upon the sovereign integrity of states[49].

The proliferation of secessionist movements in the 1970s and 1980s led some authors towards a kind of wishful thinking that brushed over the shortcomings of what Ofutaey-Kodojoe described at the time as "the most confused expressions in the lexicon of international relations"[50]. This is the case of Nanda, who, after relating the numerous cases of what he regards as secessionist claims in the early 1980s (Basque Country, Taiwan, South Sudan, Eritrea, Tibet, Northern Ireland, Quebec, etc.) and despite recognising that it is an imprecise concept lacking in objective regulatory norms and "viable machinery to apply" it, considers that it would be useful and desirable to regulate the circumstances in which the secession of a people could occur when it is the "only viable remedy for the manifest abuse of its human rights within the body politic". To this end, from a reading of Resolution 2625 he deduces that:

> Consequently, a state has to meet the requirement of possessing a "government representing the whole people, before it is entitled to protection from any action which would dismember or impair… [its] territorial integrity or political unity …" Thus, under special circumstances, the

48 26 UN GAOR, Supp. (No. IA) 1, at 18, UN Doc. A/8401/Add.1 (1971).

49 Johnson, C. Don. "Toward Self-Determination – A Reappraisal as Reflected in the Declaration on Friendly Relations". *Georgia Journal of International and Comparative Law*, vol. 3, no. 1, 1973, pp. 145 and 149.

50 Ofuatey-Kodjoe, W. *The Principle of Self-Determination in International Law*. New York: Nellen, 1977, p. VII.

> principle of self-determination is to be accorded priority over the opposing principle of territorial integrity.

Although he considers the examples of Katanga, Biafra and Bangladesh to be inconclusive, criteria of political expediency having prevailed instead of legal reasons[51], he maintains the need to establish certain conditions for exercising the right enshrined in Resolution 2625:

> To establish the minimum standards of legitimacy, it is necessary to identify: 1) the group that is claiming the right of self-determination; 2) the nature and scope of their claim; 3) the underlying reasons for the claim; and 4) the degree of the deprivation of basic human rights[52].

Sornarajah introduces his concept of 'internal colonialism' into the debate: "Internal colonialism results where an ethnic group in control of a government systematically exploits resources of the regions occupied by minority ethnic groups". He goes on to make the following qualification:

> However, preservation of peace may require that claims to secession be dealt with by the international community. Hitherto, the technique for dealing with such situations, as evidenced during the Biafran and Bangladesh crises, has been to recognize overtly the sovereignty of the dominant state, to condone the atrocities committed, and passively to accept covert intervention in the dispute by interested states. It may be preferable to recognize a right to secession in certain well-defined circumstances. Thereafter, intervention by an outside state in an ethnic conflict within a state would be illegal, at least until the objective criteria giving rise to a right to secession in the minority are satisfied...[53]

This author thereby adheres to the thesis that in 1970 a limit to the principle of the territorial integrity of States really has been acknowledged, namely, the fulfilment of the human rights of all the peoples therein, and provided that secession is the last possible remedy, as would other international law scholars from the same period, such as Saxena, Umozurike, Buchheit and Pomerance[54]. Much more moderate is Critescu, who, in his Special Rapporteur's report of 1981, merely affirms:

51 As argued by Smouts, Marie-Claude. "Décolonisation et sécession: double morale à l'ONU?". *Revue Française de Science Politique*, vol. 22, no. 4, 1972. pp. 832–846.

52 Nanda, op. cit., pp. 265, 270 and 275.

53 Sornarajah, M. "Internal Colonialism and Humanitarian Intervention". *Georgia Journal of International and Comparative Law*, vol. 11, 1981, pp. 46 and 49.

54 Saxena, J.N. *Self-Determination: From Biafra to Bangla Desh*, University of Delhi, 1978; Umozurike, op. cit.; Buchheit, op. cit., p. 94; and Pomerance, Michla. *Self-Determination in Law and Practice: The New Doctrine of the United Nations*, The Hague: Nijhoff, 1982.

> ... that the right of peoples to self-determination has been written into international instruments, not in order to encourage secessionist or irredentist movements. By virtue of this principle it is necessary to avoid any act likely to prejudice the national unity and territorial integrity of a State — particularly a State which respects the principle of equal rights and self-determination of peoples and has a Government representative of the population as a whole.
>
> (para. 228)[55]

With the cases of the 1990s, in the USSR, Yugoslavia, Eritrea, Kurdistan, Bougainville, Quebec, Somaliland, Sri Lanka, etc., other authors gradually come to favour a remedial secession[56], in line with those that preceded them, based mainly on the 1970 starting point, on 1990s State practice and on a broad interpretation of the validity of human rights, in such a way that would allow the structural principle of protecting human rights to take precedence over – in certain very serious circumstances and after ruling out all other possible solutions – the equally structural principle of territorial integrity of States. In spite of rather inconsistent State and international practice, McCorquodale, a defender of this thesis, considers that[57]:

> The equivocal support -balanced as it is against the significant State practice- does not prevent a customary international law rule operating, particularly in the field of human rights where obligations of States are not solely reciprocal and where broader values than sovereignty are taken into account. The acceptance of these values is seen in the international

55 Critescu, Aureliu. "Le droit à la autodétermination: développement historique et actuel sur la base des instruments des Nations Unies". UN Doc E/CN.4/Sub.2/404/Rev.1, N.Y.: UN, 1981.

56 Among others, Buchanan, Allen. *Secession: The Morality of Political Divorce from Fort Sumpter to Lithuania and Quebec.* Boulder: Westview Press, 1991; Gjidara, Marc. "Cadres juridiques été règles applicables aux problèmes européens de minorités". *Annuaire Français de Droit International*, vol. 37, no. 1, 1991, pp. 365 et seq.; Islam, op. cit., pp. 456–460; Murswiek, Dietrich. "The Issue of a Right of Secession Reconsidered". In *Modern Law of Self-Determination*, edited by Christian Tomuschat. Dordrecht: Nijhoff, 1993, pp. 26–27; Tomuschat, Christian, "Self-Determination in a Post-Colonial World". In *Modern Law of Self-Determination.* Dordrecht: Nijhoff, 1993, p. 7; Dinstein, Yoram. "Is There a Right to Secede". *American Society of International Law Proceedings*, vol. 90, 1996, p. 299–302; Kooijmans, P.H. "Tolerance, Sovereignty and Self-Determination". *Netherlands International Law Review*, vol. 43, 1996, pp. 212 et seq.; and Christakis, Theodore. *Le droit à l'autodétermination en dehors des situations de décolonisation.* Paris: La Documentation Française, 1999, p. 192. In Spain, Mariño Menéndez, Fernando. "Naciones Unidas y el derecho de autodeterminación". *Balance y perspectivas de las Naciones Unidas en el cincuentenario de su creación.* Madrid: Universidad Carlos III, 1996, pp. 89–90; and Díaz Barrado, op. cit., pp. 139–140.

57 McCorquodale, Robert. "Self-Determination: A Human Rights Approach". *International and Comparative Law Quarterly*, vol. 43, no. 4, 1994, pp. 862–863.

> community's vigorous attempts to eradicate oppression of people and its aim to protect human rights in all circumstances. Thus there is sufficient evidence to conclude that today the right of self-determination applies to all peoples subject to oppression by subjugation, domination and exploitation by others.

In favour of basing remedial secession on Resolution 2625, Cassese argues that:

> Although secession is implicitly authorized by the Declaration, it must however be strictly construed, as with all exceptions. It can therefore be suggested that the following conditions might warrant secession: when the central authorities of a sovereign State persistently refuse to grant participatory rights to a religious or racial group, grossly and systematically trample upon their fundamental rights, and deny the possibility of reaching a peaceful settlement within the framework of the State structure. Thus, denial of the basic right of representation does not give rise per se to the right of secession. In addition, there must be gross breaches of fundamental human rights, and, what is more, the exclusion of any likelihood for a peaceful resolution within the existing State structure[58].

Prudence prevails, however, in some specialists, such as Eastwood, for whom:

> The adoption of a United Nations declaration or an international convention on secession would clarify the limits of a secession right, thus providing some useful direction both to potential secessionists and to states dealing with secessions. Although such an instrument would not create a secession right, it would provide evidence of the international community's collective opinion on secession, which could speed the process of establishing secession as a recognized norm of customary international law. However, such a development appears unlikely due to states' concerns that secession will threaten their sovereignty and international stability. It is more probable that states will continue to deal with secession responsively, on a case-by-case basis, such as occurred with the secessions of the Baltic states and Yugoslavia. In time, this state practice could establish a secession right under customary international law. This development is likely to be slow, however, and could produce an amorphous, loosely defined right, less useful as a guide than if states had adopted a declaration or other international agreement concerning secession and its limits. Until either a coordinated approach to secession is developed by the international community or a coherent secession right is recognized under customary international law, states will be free to respond to individual secession movements in accordance with their own political interests. This prospect appears more uncertain and destabilizing than the likely effects of

58 Cassese, op. cit., pp. 119–120.

recognizing a carefully limited secession right derived from the framework outlined here[59].

In the twenty-first century, certain domestic events, such as those in Quebec, Scotland and Catalonia, and the ICJ's opinion on Kosovo, have reopened the academic debate about the possible right of secession of non-colonial peoples[60], in most cases assuming the existence of an international custom in respect thereof in the practice of States and international organisations alike, a conceptual extension of the right of self-determination to all kinds of peoples based on a transposition of its internal and external dimensions, and a certain interventionist doctrine whereby protection of human rights takes precedence over any other principles, rights and values promoted by current international law[61]. This doctrine is forcefully and cogently defended by Ryngaert and Griffioen, for whom:

> That self-determination is a universal human right which is applicable outside the colonial context, and should be defined as broadly as possible, including both internal and external aspects. For reasons of international peace and security, the right of self-determination needs to be balanced

59 Eastwood, op. cit., p. 349.

60 Authors who have expressed themselves in favour of remedial secession include, among others, Radan, Peter. "Post-Secession International Borders: A Critical Analysis of the Opinions of the Badinter Arbitration Commission". *Melbourne University Law Review*, vol. 24, no. 1, 2000, p. 52; Tancredi, Antonello. *La secessione nel diritto internazionale*. Padova: Cedam, 2006, p. 689; Kohen, Marcelo G. "La création d'états en droit international contemporain". *Cursos Euromediterráneos Bancaja de Derecho Internacional*, vol. 6, 2002, p. 594; Dugard J. and David Raic. "The Role of Recognition in the Law and Practice of Secession". In *Secession. International Law Perspectives*, edited by Marcelo Kohen. Cambridge University Press, 2006, pp. 94–137; Pavkovic and Radan, op. cit., pp. 232–239; Xanthaki, op. cit.; Brewer, Evan M. "To Break Free from Tyranny and Oppression: Proposing a Model for a Remedial Right to Secession in the Wake of the Kosovo Advisory Opinion". *Vanderbilt Journal of Transnational Law*, vol. 45, no. 1, January 2012, pp. 245–292; Vidmar, Jure. "The Annexation of Crimea and the Boundaries of the Will of the People". *German Law Journal*, vol. 16, 2015, p. 370; and Fisher, Steven R. "Towards Never Again: Searching for a Right to Remedial Secession under Extant International Law". *Buffalo Human Rights Law Review*, vol. 22, 2015–2016, pp. 261–296. In Spain, Soroeta Liceras, Juan. "La opinión consultiva de la Corte Internacional de Justicia sobre Kosovo de 22 de julio de 2010". *Revista Electrónica de Estudios Internacionales*, vol. 25, 2013; Martínez Jiménez, op. cit.; and Pons Rafols, Xavier. Cataluña: Derecho a decidir y Derecho internacional. Madrid: Reus, 2015, pp. 149, 215 and 308.

61 As expressed in other words by Roch, François. "Réflexions sur l'évolution de la positivité du droit des peuples à disposer d'eux-mêmes en dehors des situations de décolonisation". *Revue québécoise de droit international*, vol. 15, no. 1, 2002, pp. 76 et seq., for whom, however, in spite of numerous attempts by legal scholars to legitimise a secession right based on the exercise of the right of peoples to self-determination, international law is still fundamentally resistant to this idea (p. 73).

> with other principles of international law, in particular the sovereignty and territorial integrity of States. That is why, outside the colonial context, the emphasis must be on the internal aspect of self-determination (…). There are four cumulative conditions that must be fulfilled before the right of external self-determination may be invoked. First of all, the group invoking the right is a 'people'. The 'people' has a distinct identity, and represents a clear majority within a given territory. A minority is not necessarily a 'people'. Second, massive violations of basic human rights and systematic discrimination at the hands of a repressive regime have taken place. Third, violations cannot be prevented and remedied because the 'people' is excluded from political participation, and is not given internal self-determination (e.g., through devolution or federalism). Finally, negotiations between the 'repressive' regime and the 'people' lead nowhere[62].

These authors, and others like them, take international practice as proof of the existence of an international custom that vouches for remedial secession. They consider decisive the League of Nations' opinion on the Åland Islands, Resolution 2625, *Katangese Peoples' Congress v Zaire of the African Commission on Human and Peoples' Rights*, the Supreme Court of Canada's decision on Quebec and the ICJ's opinion on Kosovo, as well as practice relating to Bangladesh, the former Yugoslavia, the *de facto* Caucasus entities and Chechnya[63].

Other international law scholars, such as Anderson, rely on a broad interpretation of the text and on the consensus for the adoption of Resolution 2625, to assert that:

> There are also implied requirements, however, which have to be satisfied before a right to UNC secession will arise. First, the discrimination must be of a deliberate, sustained, and systematic nature, with "the exclusion of any likelihood for a possible peaceful solution within the existing state structure". This means that a government must knowingly and intentionally inflict discrimination against a people. Mere de minimis or unknowing instances of discrimination will not do. Something more is required, namely, governmental behavior which evidences dolus, or intentional malice, towards a people. Additionally, there must be a fundamental loss of rapport between the parties to the dispute, precluding the likelihood of a harmonious resolution. These requirements function as a threshold test for the operation of paragraph 7 rights, ensuring that UNC secession is only available under especially egregious conditions[64].

62 Ryngaert, Cedrick and Griffioen, Christine W. "The relevance of the right to self-determination in the Kosovo matter: in partial response to the Agora papers". *Chinese Journal of International Law*, vol. 8, no. 3, 2009, pp. 575–576.

63 Ibid., pp. 579 et seq.

64 Anderson. "A Post-Millennial Inquiry…", op. cit., p. 1218.

The validity of this remedial secession has also been admitted in jurisprudence, be it in national or international courts. Thus, the 1999 Canadian Supreme Court decision on Quebec states that:

> in summary, the international law right to self-determination only generates, at best, a right to external self-determination in situations of former colonies; where a people is oppressed, as for example under foreign military occupation; or where a definable group is denied meaningful access to government to pursue their political, economic, social and cultural development[65].

Although the Supreme Court of Canada does not explain from which treaties or international jurisprudence it derives this statement, various politicians and judges have also reproduced this paragraph without confirming its veracity. Thus, the Spanish Constitutional Court, in its Judgment of 17 October 2017, after correctly explaining the importance of the principle of territorial integrity, the scope of Article 1 of the 1966 New York Covenant and the natural scope of self-determination in the colonial context, states that "the defended right of separation is only possible in cases of colonial domination, peoples annexed by conquest, foreign domination or occupation, and peoples oppressed by massive and flagrant violation of their rights"[66]. A few years earlier, in the case of *Chiragov and Others v Armenia*, with Judgment issued on 16 June 2015, Armenia's *ad hoc* judge Alvina Gyulumyan, in her dissenting opinion regarding the majority decision, in relation to the secessionism of Nagorno-Karabakh with respect to Azerbaijan, states that recent developments in matters relating to the self-determination of peoples increasingly confirm the existence of a right to remedial secession (para. 17) consisting of a community seceding from a State when it is subjected to gross human rights violations and repression, the supporting arguments here being the same as those used by Ryngaert and Griffioen, in addition to the works of other authors cited earlier. In another ECHR case, *Loizidou v Turkey*, with Judgment dated 18 December 1996, the opinion of judges Wildhaber and Ryssdal who took the same position[67] was not accepted by the majority.

65 Renvoi relatif à la sécession du Québec, *Jugements de la Cour Suprême de Canada*, 2, 1998, pp. 217–297.

66 Constitutional Court Judgment 114/2017, of 17 October 2017, appeal on grounds of unconstitutionality 4334–2017, against Catalan Parliament Law 19/2017, of 6 September, on the self-determination referendum.

67 In recent years a consensus has seemed to emerge that peoples may also exercise a right to self-determination if their human rights are consistently and flagrantly violated or if they are without representation at all or are massively under-represented in an undemocratic and discriminatory way. If this description is correct, then the right to self-determination is a tool which may be used to re-establish international standards of human rights and democracy.

(Report of Judgements and Decisions of the ECHR, 1996, VI, p. 2216)

Refutation of remedial secession

As we have seen, our analysis of UN texts and those of the regional organisations shows that there is no conventional norm that recognises and regulates a right of secession in favour of peoples integrated in States. The international norms – conventional and *jus cogens* contained in General Assembly resolutions and recognised as such by the ICJ – whose object is the international institution of the right to self-determination of peoples refer to those under colonial domination. The preparatory work confirms that this was the will of the negotiating States. And the conventional norms and non-binding texts whose object is the rights of minority or indigenous peoples integrated in States do not recognise any right to external self-determination. For this reason, and in the absence of an explicit positive law, it is necessary to analyse international practice in order to ascertain whether an international custom exists, as is claimed by some of the authors we have cited.

For there to be an international customary norm there needs to be uniform practice and a conviction that such practice is legally binding. In our opinion, shared by some legal scholars, these elements of international custom are nowhere to be found in the actual creation of States or in the rejection thereof, a practice that we will analyse first. And nor are they to be found in any other practice arising from the actions of national and international courts, so we will go on to analyse the Canadian Supreme Court's Opinion on Quebec and, finally, the ICJ's Advisory Opinion on Kosovo, as these are recurrent milestones in the debate around this problem.

Practice in the creation of States and in the rejection of secessionist entities

As we have pointed out, there is no practice prior to Resolution 2625 of 1970[68], as 50 years separate the successful secessions preceding the UN Charter (Mongolia, Finland and Ireland in the 1920s) and the independence of Bangladesh in 1971. Therefore, it cannot be said that the General Assembly resolution reflects previous practice. On the contrary, the most recent cases of secessionism are negative, since both in Katanga (1960–1963) and in Biafra (1967–1970), the UN, the OAU and the international community in general (except for Tanzania, Ivory Coast, Zambia and Haiti) did not consider the humanitarian situation of the Ibo and Katanga peoples in Nigeria and the Democratic Republic of the Congo; on the contrary, they helped prevail respect for the territorial integrity of these States and non-intervention in their

68 In the same vein, James Crawford in "State Practice and International Law in Relating to Unilateral Secession", Report for the Attorney General of Canada, 19 February 1997. Consulted in Bayefsky, Anne. *Self-Determination in International Law: Quebec and Lessons Learned*. The Hague: Kluwer, 2000, pp. 31–61, in particular when she states that "this had, and has, nothing to do with any pre-existing right in international law on the part of any group or territory to secede. In international law before 1945, there was no such right" (para. 9).

internal affairs[69], despite the evidently grave, large-scale and systematic violation of the fundamental rights of the Ibo people that was taking place in the Nigerian case.

As regards practice since 1970, successful secessionist processes have taken place in Bangladesh (1971), Lithuania, Estonia and Latvia (1990), Croatia, Slovenia and Macedonia (1991), Bosnia and Herzegovina (1992), Eritrea (1993), East Timor (2002) and South Sudan (2011). These cases have different causes and factors in the process of secession from their respective States, but they all share effective accession to independence, subsequent consent of the parent State and acceptance on the part of the international community. These features distinguish them from others in which even an incipient independence failed to materialise (Gorkhaland, Mindanao, Ulster, Corsica, Catalonia, Basque Country, Flanders, Kurdistan, Tibet, Kashmir, etc.) or where it was obtained but lasted only until the parent State regained its territorial integrity (Aceh 1976–2003, Bougainville 1990–2001, Tamil Ealam 1990–2009, Krajina 1991–1995, Chechnya 1991–2009, Sprska Republic of Bosnia 1992–1995, Anjouan 1997–2008, ISIS 2006–2017 and Azawad 2012–2013), or where they remain *de facto* entities separated from their parent State but without any recognition or acceptance by the international community, in most cases surviving thanks to military intervention and aid of all kinds provided by like-minded third States (TRNC since 1983, Transnistria since 1990, Nagorno-Karabakh since 1991, Abkhazia and South Ossetia since 1992 and, with different characteristics, Somaliland since 1991).

The examples of completed practice are the 11 listed earlier on p. 28. It is debatable whether any of them is actually a completed secession, but there are no more cases that could be included, given that the States created since 1970 stem from other circumstances. Indeed, full sovereignty has been acquired in situations in which previous States had been subject to 'protection' by a power, under what might be called 'covert colonialist imperialism' (this being the case of Bahrain, Qatar, Oman and the United Arab Emirates in 1971 and, in another non-colonial context, Andorra in 1993); also a union of States (Yemen); various separations, consented to or agreed upon (Serbia and Montenegro, Ukraine, Belarus, Moldova, Georgia, Armenia, Azerbaijan, Uzbekistan, Kazakhstan, Turkmenistan, Tajikistan, Kyrgyzstan, Czech Republic, Slovakia and Montenegro); but above all, numerous cases of decolonisation (Fiji, Namibia, Brunei, Saint Kitts and Nevis, Antigua and Barbuda, Belize, Vanuatu, Saint Lucia, Saint Vincent and the Grenadines, Dominica, Djibouti, Seychelles, Angola, Cape Verde, Comoros, Mozambique, Papua New Guinea, Sao Tome and Principe, Solomon Islands, Suriname, Grenada, Guinea-Bissau, Bahamas, Marshall Islands, Micronesia, Tuvalu, Kiribati, Nauru, Tonga and

69 As Suzuki points out, op. cit., p. 802, the Assembly of Heads of State and Government of the OAU, condemning "secession in any Member States", termed the Biafran situation "an internal affair, the solution of which is primarily the responsibility of Nigerians themselves".

Palau). The new States created by secession account for 11 of the 62 cases of accession to statehood since 1970. Depending on the author, all or some of these 11 States appear in their lists of successful secessions, but the fact of the matter is that all these cases of practice have been considered by one international law scholar or another as examples of secession. Doubts generally arise when verifying the defining requirement of the concept of secession consisting of the absence of parent State consent. In our view, what matters is that there be no such consent during the initial stages and principal development of the secessionist process, as in all cases there has been consent at some point, either just after independence was declared with more or less public unrest and government repression (Lithuania, for example), or after an armed conflict (Eritrea)[70], or after a diplomatic or international security intervention (East Timor). In all these cases the peoples in question have achieved independence through their struggle over a long period of time (South Sudan) or through rebellion while taking advantage of certain internal circumstances (Croatia), and in none because it was provided for in their constitutional order, agreed in their parliament or a result of a national agreement; the consent of the parent State was always forced by circumstances, and not derived from its will and generosity.

Before analysing the unsuccessful cases and their impact on all secession processes, essential for determining whether there is a general and uniform practice, we must ask ourselves: do these successful processes meet the discriminatory conditions contained in the safeguard clause of Resolution 2625? Was independence accepted by the parent State and the international community because they considered it legally binding?

The answer to the first question varies. In our opinion, there are very obvious cases of discrimination against the ethnic minority and even gross violations of fundamental rights (South Sudan), as well as cases where there is not even the slightest hint (Slovenia).

In the first case, Bangladesh, there is a very peculiar situation, in that although the East Pakistanis shared many cultural characteristics with their western counterparts, until 1970 they had been discriminated against in their political engagement, a situation that was resolved for the first time in the elections at the end of that year. However, the non-recognition of the election results and the repression following the Bengali uprising place this process in

70 Hence it is considered secession, as argued by Borgen, Christopher J. "The Language of Law and the Practice of Politics: Great Powers and the Rhetoric of Self-Determination in the Cases of Kosovo and South Ossetia". *Chicago Journal of International Law*, vol. 10, no. 1, Summer 2009, p. 10, note 28, which refutes the claims of other authors:

> Crawford disqualifies Eritrea because the Transitional Government of Ethiopia supported Eritrean independence after a plebiscite; I view this as a successful secession because the overthrow of the previous Ethiopian government and the installation of the Transitional Government can be viewed as part of the overall conflict.

the context of the provisions of Resolution 2625[71]. Although the remedialist literature cites as an argument the fact that the International Commission of Jurists, in its 1972 report, accepts the safeguard clause when stating that:

> it is submitted, however, that this principle is subject to the requirement that the government does comply with the principle of equal rights and does represent the whole people without distinction. If one of the constituent peoples of a state is denied equal rights and is discriminated against, it is submitted that their full right of self-determination will revive[72],

the rest of the report denies not only that the provisions of Resolution 2625 are applicable to this case, but even that this is a conflict of international jurisdiction. The Commission is forthright in its opinion that the Bengalis have no international right to secede[73] and that the military imposition of a regime other than the one voted for by a majority at the polls is a matter of domestic order[74]. Castellino, although in favour of the doctrine of remedial secession, considers that the situation of East Pakistan was very unusual, due to the territorial separation and an economic neo-colonialism on the part of West Pakistan, incidentally the less populated of the two[75], which distances it considerably from the standard definition of a minority.

Moving ahead to 1990, the Baltic independence processes took place in a very particular context, as their sponsors' claims were rooted in the sovereignty lost in 1940 owing to military occupation and annexation by the USSR. In essence, they represent – certainly in 1919, to a lesser extent in 1991 – an application of the classic principle of nationalities, which permitted the creation of new States on the basis of their ethnic identity (Estonia and Latvia) or the recovery of national identity (Lithuania). Undoubtedly, Estonians, Latvians and Lithuanians were part of a population in which there was no respect for human rights, but this situation was not in itself discriminatory, given that all the inhabitants of the USSR suffered it. In fact, the legislation in force as from 1990 provided for separation by means of referendum, but with majorities

71 In the same vein, among others, Musgrave, op. cit., p. 189; Crawford, James. *The Creation of States in International Law.* Oxford: Oxford University Press, 2nd ed., 2006, p. 393; and Anderson. "Unilateral Non-Colonial Secession…", op. cit., p. 216.

72 Secretariat of the International Commission of Jurists, *The Events in East Pakistan 1971*, Genève, 1972, p. 69.

73 "The Awami League leaders were not entitled in international law to proclaim the independence of Bangladesh in March 1971 under the principle of the right of self-determination of peoples" (p. 73).

74 They were, however, justified under domestic law in using force to resist the attempt by the self-appointed and illegal military regime to impose a different form of constitution upon the country to that approved by the majority of the people in a fair and free election.

(pp. 97–98)

75 Castellino, op. cit., p. 171.

(two-thirds) and deadlines (five years) that were dangerous for the Latvian and Estonian independence leaders, with sizeable Russian minorities on their territories, and onerous for the Lithuanians, who without delay wanted to take advantage of the particular difficulties the Russian Government was experiencing.

The Yugoslav case, with the secessions of Croatia, Slovenia, Macedonia, and Bosnia and Herzegovina between 1991 and 1992, merits similar attention. Although the SFRY had a non-democratic regime in 1990, it cannot be argued that there was any discrimination against the Croatian, Slovenian, Bosnian or Macedonian populations as regards their participation in politics and public life. In a country with no ethnic majority of any of its peoples (with 36.2% Serbs, 19.7% Croats, 9.8% Bosnian Muslims, 9.2% Albanians, 5.8% Macedonians, 2.3% Montenegrins and 13% other minorities), not even the most populous group, the Serbs, had a monopoly on political and social power[76]. As we have already explained, the quasi-confederal design of the State established collective heads of state and heads of government among the federated republics (plus two autonomous provinces in the head of government) and not only was there no discrimination among the different Yugoslav nations and nationalities, but each exercised autonomous powers in its territories in coexistence with other minorities. As for the dissolution of Yugoslavia, one of its worst contributions – in legal terms but also in terms of international security – is the Badinter Commission's application of the principle of *uti possidetis iuris*, in its Opinion No. 2 of 1 January 1992[77], transposing it from the borders between decolonised States to this entirely different context. In its application, it was prescribed that the Yugoslav republics' accession to independence could not entail changes to the previous internal administrative borders, the authority to secede being reserved for the larger federated entities and denied to the smaller ones, such as Kosovo (Autonomous Province in the Federal Republic of Serbia) or the Bosnian Serb communes or municipalities in the Federal Republic of Bosnia and Herzegovina. The latter was afforded – without any conventional or customary foundation – the right of self-determination of the constituent Yugoslav nations – interpreted in a constitutional rather than historical sense – while the other ethnic, religious or linguistic minorities had to settle for the right to their identity, enjoyment of their distinctiveness, and non-discrimination. In this respect, as Buchanan points out:

> some who cite the Yugoslav case as a precedent for the application of uti possidetis to Quebec secession may have a different argument in mind. On their interpretation, international acquiescence to the dissolution of

76 See Perea Unceta, José Antonio. *La actuación de …*, op. cit., p. 45.

77 Criticised in numerous works, including that of Radan. "Post-Secession…", op. cit., pp. 52 et seq., with a comprehensive analysis. For an opposing view, see Peters, Anne. "The Principle of Uti Possidetis Iuris: How Relevant is it for Issues of Secession?". In *Self-Determination and Secession in International Law*, edited by Christian Walter and others. Oxford University Press, 2014, pp. 95–137.

> Yugoslavia along republic boundaries implies acknowledgment of a presumptive right to independence to federal units as such. This argument, however, is not cogent. There is nothing in international legal doctrine or practice, and certainly nothing in the concept of a federation, that imputes a presumptive right to Independence to federal units[78].

The next success story, Eritrea in 1993, unquestionably contains evidence of discrimination in connection with the political participation of the different Eritrean ethnic groups in Ethiopia[79], including serious human rights violations, especially during Mengistu Haile Mariam's dictatorship between 1974 and 1991. The novel aspect of the Eritrean case is that it also involves a breach of the State's founding agreement[80], in the precise terms used by the International Commission of Jurists for East Pakistan in 1972, mentioned earlier, in that by the end of 1962 the Ethiopian side had unilaterally abolished the federal scheme proposed by the UN ten years earlier.

The secessionist process in East Timor – as explained in the previous chapter – is to some extent confused with a decolonisation phenomenon, in that Portugal's exit from the territory in 1975 did not bring about its independence, as in so many other cases, but its annexation by Indonesia. However, as has also been pointed out, what takes place in 2002 is not a decolonisation process, as it is not an Indonesian colony, but rather a secession from the State it had been forced to join. As in the previous case, the Portuguese and Tetum-speaking Timorese, with a Catholic majority, unlike their Indonesian neighbours, were brutally repressed during 27 years of occupation until they achieved independence thanks to international intervention.

Finally, South Sudan is the case whose circumstances most closely fit the discrimination criterion[81]. This is because the southern Christian and animist

78 Buchanan, Allen. "The Quebec Secession Issue: Democracy, Minority Rights, and the Rule of Law". *Nomos*, vol. 45, 2003, p. 252.

79 In this case there is no objective ethnic difference that distinguishes a single people, but instead a shared aversion to integration in Ethiopia among the nine peoples inhabiting the territory; as pointed out by Erlich, Haggai. *The Struggle over Eritrea, 1962–1978: War and Revolution in the Horn of Africa*. Stanford: Hoover Institution Press of Stanford University, 1983, pp. 18–19: "Eritreanism (...) was essentially the negation of Ethiopianism rather than a historically rooted supratribal, supralinguistic, and suprareligious sense of Eritrean affiliation".

80 See Fox, op. cit., pp. 281 et seq., who considers that in addition to this Eritrean claim there was a breach of the international agreement to replace decolonisation within ten years (like Italian Somaliland) with the federal solution, as well as an internal discrimination, due to the exclusion of Tigrinya and Arabic as official languages to the exclusive benefit of Ethiopian Amharic, repeal of the constitution and Eritrean laws, etc., and then in the civil war, severe repression by the Ethiopian Government. As this author points out, another peculiar feature of this case is that "as a former colony territory Eritrea would always be entitled to self-determination" (p. 291).

81 Day, Joel. "The Remedial Right of Secession in International Law". *Potentia*, vol. 4, 2012, p. 31.

population have been socially and politically marginalised by the northern Muslims, in a situation of constant internal armed confrontation between the two communities since Sudanese independence in 1952. On occasions this discrimination has turned into repression, especially following Yaffar al-Numeiry's military takeover in 1962 and the imposition of *sharia* throughout the territory in 1983.

Within the category of discrimination as provided for in Resolution 2625, we can only include, therefore, four of the 11 successful secessionist processes. First, Bangladesh, not because there is any proof that Pakistan, the UN or States such as neighbouring India accept and support the secession under those provisions, but rather because it has been accepted as a *fait accompli* – due to the effectiveness of independence – and because of India's indispensable military intervention. Eritrea, too, although in this case it was Ethiopia's failure to comply with the federal agreement sponsored by the UN in 1950 that carried most weight. Likewise, in East Timor the international community intervened for humanitarian and security reasons, mainly due to the mass exodus of Timorese to neighbouring Australia. And finally, South Sudan, although the security situation and the desire to put an end to internal armed conflicts outweigh other presumed legal obligations. No UN or AU document makes any reference to a broad right of self-determination that protects their independences, or to a secession right based on serious violations of the human rights of these peoples at least on the ground of discrimination in respect of participation in the political bodies of the State.

In addition to successful practice, it is also necessary to analyse the thwarted processes and those that endure but without international acceptance. With regard to the former, an example of the absence of discrimination is the Sprska Republic, a Bosnian Serb entity that rose up at the start of the Bosnian Civil War (1992–1995) in opposition to the attempted independence of the new State and with the aim of joining the largest and most homogeneous territory possible in the new Yugoslavia, the one formed by Serbia and Montenegro. Indeed, many of the crimes committed systematically for ethnic cleansing purposes were executed precisely, albeit not exclusively, by Bosnian Serb and Serbian militias, as was reflected in the report of Special Rapporteur Tadeusz Mazowiecki[82]. Another example, both geographically proximate yet utterly different, is that of Krajina, whose Serbo-Croat population was clearly discriminated against by the Zagreb Government, as the Security Council confirmed in several resolutions[83], demanding that "the Government of the Republic of Croatia respect fully the rights of the Serb population including their freedom of movement" (Res. 994 de 1995), bearing in mind:

82 Report dated 18 December 1995, UN Doc. A/50/441-S/1995/801.

83 Resolutions 994 (1995), 1019 (1995), 1023 (1995), 1025 (1995), 1120 (1997) and 1145 (1997).

> reports, including by UNCRO and United Nations humanitarian agencies, of serious violations of international humanitarian law and of human rights in the former sectors West, North, and South, in the Republic of Croatia, including burning of houses, looting of property, and killings of civilians.
>
> (Res. 1019 of 1995)

However, as regards the independence aspirations of both Serbian entities, the UN response was the same: denial of any possibility of secession. Thus, Resolution 787, adopted on 16 November 1992, demands that the Security Council "respect strictly the territorial integrity of the Republic of Bosnia and Herzegovina", stating that "any entities unilaterally declared or arrangements imposed in contravention thereof will not be accepted".

The enormous UN contradiction in these cases is that in the same scenario one or two years earlier it had admitted the secessions of the larger entities from Yugoslavia, i.e. Croatia and Bosnia and Herzegovina, but not those of its Serbian entities (or, subsequently, that of Kosovo in Serbia). This rejection is undoubtedly due to the doctrine established by the Badinter Commission, according to which only the constituent nations could create new States, even though Opinion No. 2 – on the right of self-determination of these Serbian entities – offered no international legal basis for this, or for denying this right to the smaller communities belonging to the former federal republics, except for the strange and untimely application – in Opinion No. 3 when asked about the borders of the new States – of the principle of *uti possidetis iuris*, reserved in international jurisprudence for territorial disputes between States created through decolonisation[84]. It begins in Opinion No. 2 by saying, in relation to the principle of self-determination of peoples, that "in its present state of development, international law does not make clear all the consequences which flow from this principle". It also states that ethnic minorities must be respected in their fundamental rights, that they have the power to identify themselves, and that they cannot be discriminated against in any way, not admitting, however, any external self-determination due to application of the aforementioned principle and because the existing borders could not be changed, since Article 5 of the Yugoslav Constitution did not allow the territory of the federated republics to be altered without the consent of their governments. What Pellet politely calls choosing a middle way between strict application of the existing rule and "the application of adventurous visions"[85] can be deemed rigorous as regards the denial of self-determination of minorities, but not as

84 ICJ Judgment of 22 December 1986, *Frontier Dispute (Burkina Faso v Republic of Mali)*, indicates that it is a principle that transforms the old administrative boundaries established during the colonial era into international borders, and therefore concludes that it is a general principle necessarily linked to decolonisation.

85 Pellet, Alain. "The Opinions of the Badinter Arbitration Committee. A Second Breath for the Self-Determination of Peoples". *European Journal of International Law*, vol. 3, January 1992, p. 181.

regards its legal justification. The latter does not lie in maintaining the internal administrative divisions of the State undergoing dissolution but in respecting the territorial integrity of States, a general obligation that does not apply in the context of the right of self-determination of peoples exclusively for colonies and precisely without entailing any contradiction with it, given that they do not form part of the State territory. As Pomerance points out:

> Upon closer examination, however, the Commission appears to have misused more than used the International Court's jurisprudence. Far from serving as the lodestar for the Commission, that jurisprudence instead provided a reservoir of formulas (themselves not free of ambiguity) which were unquestioningly repeated and, in some cases, questionably extended by the Commission in inappropriate contexts. The long-range results of the Commission's application of ICJ law could more plausibly harm than facilitate the goal of having self-determination questions adjudicated in judicial and quasi-judicial fora[86].

The questions the Badinter Commission does not answer are the ones this professor asks:

> Whose territorial integrity was deserving of preservation, and why? If the secession of the republics from the SFRY was permissible because the Federation was disintegrating, on what legal grounds could further secession from those republics be legitimately opposed? Why was one unit's self-determination more sacrosanct than that of another? Why was the territorial integrity of the whole federation less holy than that of the sub-units? And what of the territorial integrity of the sub-sub-units, like Drajina and Petrinja within Croatia? (Or, for that matter, of Kosovo and Vojvodina within Serbia?) By saying that uti possidetis applies to internal administrative divisions, the Commission was establishing them as the new 'selves' entitled to self-determination and territorial integrity. But denying self-determination to sub-units was not really sustainable on legal grounds[87].

In any event, in these examples and others such as Aceh, Bougainville, Tamil Ealam, Chechnya, Anjouan, ISIS or Azawad, the reasons given by the international community for rejecting their secession were not the absence of discrimination-driven human rights violations – which could certainly have been claimed in the case of the Tamils after the government established Sinhalese as

86 Pomerance, Michla. "The Badinter Commission: The Use and Misuse of the International Court of Justice's Jurisprudence". *Michigan Journal of International Law*, vol. 20, no. 1, 1998, p. 31.

87 Ibid., p. 56. For a critical analysis of these Badinter Commission opinions, see Radan, "Post-Secession…", op. cit., and Hannum, Hurst. "The Specter of Secession: Responding to Claims for Ethnic Self-Determination". *Foreign Affairs*, vol. 77, no. 2, 1998, pp. 13–18.

the sole language, Buddhism as the official religion and other measures restricting the rights of that minority[88] – but respect for the sovereignty and territorial integrity of Indonesia, Sri Lanka or the Comoros. In the latter case, at the Tenth Ordinary Session of the AU Assembly in 2008, the Comoros Government requested international assistance to restore the territorial integrity of its country, receiving military support from several countries, in line with previous AU resolutions in which it:

> requests all Member States capable of doing so to provide the necessary support to the Comorian Government in its efforts to restore, as quickly as possible, the authority of the Union in Anjouan and to put an end to the crisis born out of the persistent refusal by the illegal authorities of Anjouan to comply with the relevant texts governing the functioning of the Union of the Comoros[89]

and repeatedly urges them to help "facilitate the restoration of the Union's authority on Anjouan"[90].

As for the *de facto* entities, Transnistria, Nagorno-Karabakh, Abkhazia and South Ossetia, they have characteristics in common because they were created during the break-up of the USSR and as a result of the existence of significant minorities similar to their neighbouring populations. Thus, the Armenian population of Nagorno-Karabakh is fully integrated in Armenia and at odds with Azerbaijan, from whose territory it has been forcibly separated; the same applies to the Abkhazians and Ossetians, who since 1992 have been supported by Russia in their confrontation with the authorities of their State, Georgia. These three conflicts are of an inter-ethnic and strategic nature, but their cause is to be found not in blatant discrimination[91] but in the acts of ethnic cleansing committed by both parties during the armed conflicts[92]. In the eastern territory of Moldova known as Transnistria, Russians, Ukrainians and Moldovans

88 Weiss, Gordon. *The Cage: The Fight for Sri Lanka and the Last Days of the Tamil Tigers*. New York: Bellevue Literary Press, 2012. Regarding the Tamil secession process, see Welhengama, Gnanapala and Nirmala Pillay. *The Rise of Tamil Separatism in Sri Lanka: From Communalism to Secession*. New York: Routledge, 2014.

89 Assembly/AU/Dec.186 (X).

90 Peace and Security Council. 'Communique', PSC/PR/Comm (XCV), 10 October 2007, 46 Peace and Security Council. Also in 'Report of the Chairperson of the Commission on the situation in the Comoros since the 10th Ordinary Session of the Assembly of the African Union Held in Addis Ababa from 31 January to 2 February 2008'. PSC/PR/2 (CXXIV), 30 April 2008.

91 For Burri and Oeter, these cases cannot be used as examples of remedial secession. Burri, Thomas. "Secession in the CIS: Causes, Consequences and Emerging Principles". In *Self-Determination and Secession in International Law*, edited by Christian Walter and others. Oxford University Press, 2014, pp. 138–154; and Oeter, "The Role of Recognition…", op. cit., pp. 54–60.

92 Such as those indicated in UN Security Council Resolution 1716, adopted on 13 October 2006, regarding refugees and internally displaced persons in the Abkhazia conflict.

coexist, and its confrontation with Moldova is due to the national government's campaign of gradual Romanization since 1989, particularly in terms of language and education[93], given the imposition of the Latin alphabet and the withdrawal of Russian as a co-official language. In the case of Transnistria there is linguistic discrimination, which would surely have triggered the gradual expulsion of Russians and Ukrainians from public life, as occurred in Estonia, Latvia and Lithuania[94], but by no means was their political non-participation comprehensive.

All these secessionist processes got under way and have been maintained with the indispensable assistance of Russia and, in the case of Nagorno-Karabakh, of Armenia. This situation of dependence is such that the ECHR, in various cases it has heard, has been consistent in attributing international responsibility for human rights violations to both countries (as it also does with Turkey in relation to the Turkish Republic of Northern Cyprus)[95]. What little recognition these entities have received has come from Russia and, in the case of South Ossetia, also from Venezuela, Nicaragua, Syria, Nauru and Tuvalu[96], and in the case of Abkhazia, these as well as Vanuatu. The UN position is firm and unequivocal in its respect for the territorial integrity of the States concerned. This view is reiterated in the numerous resolutions adopted by the Security Council since 1993 in relation to Abkhazia, in which it doggedly maintains that it:

> reaffirms the commitment of all Member States to the sovereignty, independence and territorial integrity of Georgia within its internationally recognized borders, and the necessity to define the status of Abkhazia within the State of Georgia in strict accordance with these principles.
>
> (Res. 1462 of 30 January 2003)[97]

93 There was also a plan in 1991 to join Romania.
94 López Martín and Perea Unceta. "Los efectos…", op. cit., pp. 57–91.
95 *Loizidou v Turkey* (1995), *Cyprus v Turkey* (2001), *Ilascu and Others. v Moldova and Russia* (2004), *Catan and Others v Moldova and Russia* (2012) and *Chiragov and Others v Armenia* (2015), mainly, analysed in Perea Unceta, "Los derechos de las minorías nacionales…", op. cit.
96 Tuvalu revoked its recognition of both entities in March 2014 following events in Crimea.
97 The Independent International Fact-Finding Mission on the Conflict in Georgia, II, September 2009, pp. 135, 138 and 141, known as the Tagliavini Report, states that:

> as evidenced by state practice and United Nations resolutions, the right to secede unilaterally is uncontested for colonial peoples, and peoples subject to foreign occupation. This situation is not present in South Ossetia and Abkhazia;
>
> with a view to that state practice, the prevailing scholarly opinion shares the view that – as a matter of international law as it stands – the savings clause does not imply that whenever the principles of non-discrimination and adequate representation are violated a 'people' can lawfully claim a right to secession;

It therefore describes the parliamentary elections in this Georgian territory as illegal acts (Res. 1096 of 30 January 1997); also, in the few resolutions on the conflict in Azerbaijan, in which its view is also based on the "inviolability of international borders and the inadmissibility of the use of force for the acquisition of territory" (Res. 822 of 30 April 1993), without explicitly mentioning Nagorno-Karabakh.

In relation to Transnistria, Russia has made sure that this conflict has not been addressed by the Security Council[98]. Nevertheless, the European Parliament, in spite of expressing its support for "a peaceful reunification of the state, with minority language rights and local autonomy being safeguarded", has taken a clear position, stating that it:

3 Fully rejects the organisation and outcome of the 'referendum' on independence for the Transnistrian region of Moldova and its possible accession to the Russian Federation, as this is in sharp contradiction with the internationally recognised sovereignty and territorial integrity of the Republic of Moldova and as the repressive regime in Transnistria does not allow for the free expression of the popular will;
4 Stresses that the resolution of the Transnistrian issue constitutes a crucial element for promoting political stability and economic prosperity in the Republic of Moldova and in the whole region; stresses the need for a peaceful solution to the conflict, in line with the UN Charter and Conventions and OSCE declarations and with full respect for the sovereignty and territorial integrity of the Republic of Moldova within its internationally recognised borders[99].

The case of the TRNC is somewhat special in that the Turkish military invasion of 1974 – which preceded the proclamation of that entity in 1983 – was the consequence of the Cypriot Government's failure to comply with the international and constitutional agreements of 1960, reached between the Turkish and Greek communities under the aegis of the United Kingdom amid the threat of union with Greece (*enosis*)[100]. It shares some of the causes of the

to sum up, outside the colonial context, self-determination is basically limited to internal self-determination. A right to external self-determination in form of a secession is not accepted in state practice. A limited, conditional extraordinary allowance to secede as a last resort in extreme cases is debated in international legal scholarship. However, most authors opine that such a remedial 'right' or allowance does not form part of international law as it stands. The case of Kosovo has not changed the rules.

98 Richter, Dagmar. "Illegal States?". In *Unrecognised Subjects in International Law*, edited by Władysław Czapliński and Agata Kleczkowska. Warsaw: Scholar Publishing House Ltd., 2019, p. 40.
99 European Parliament Resolution on Moldova (Transnistria) 2006/2645(RSP), Official Journal 313 E, 20/12/2006, pp. 427–429.
100 See Rodríguez Villena, op. cit., pp. 59–72.

Eritrean secessionist conflict, but in this case the international position is markedly different, given that the UN Security Council condemned the Turkish intervention (Res. 353 of 20 July 1974) and also the declaration of independence of the Turkish Cypriots, as stated in Resolution 541 of 18 November 1983, in which it deplores the secession of part of the Republic of Cyprus and declares it "legally invalid", urging all States not to recognise any Cypriot state other than the Republic of Cyprus. The ECHR, in its Judgment of 18 December 1996 on the *Loizidou v Turkey* case, puts it as follows:

> It is evident from international practice and the various, strongly worded resolutions referred to above (see paragraph 42) that the international community does not regard the 'TRNC' as a State under international law and that the Republic of Cyprus has remained the sole legitimate Government of Cyprus[101].

What is most relevant for the purposes of this study is that neither of the two third States involved in the creation and survival of these *de facto* entities has claimed a right of remedial secession. Russia has long insisted that the assistance provided to these entities has always been driven by the right to self-defence and an obligation to defend the like-minded population abroad, as confirmed by Sergei Lavrov, Ministry of Foreign Affairs of the Russian Federation:

> By its answer to the Georgian aggression Russia has established a standard for responding which is fully in line with current international law, including the right to self-defense under Article 51 of the Charter of the United Nations and our concrete obligations regarding the settlement of this conflict, and with the principles of moderateness and proportionality. Russia's actions pursued no aims other than those dictated by the necessity of providing effective guarantees of non-resumption of aggression against the Republic of South Ossetia and the Republic of Abkhazia (…) We can't understand why those who are talking about the responsibility to protect and about security of the person at every turn, forgot it when it came to the part of the former Soviet space where the authorities began to kill innocent people, appealing to sovereignty and territorial integrity. For us, the issue in South Ossetia was to protect our citizens directly on the borders of Russia, not in the Falkland Islands[102].

101 Section 44. See sections 19, 21 and 42 which cite the Resolution of the Committee of Ministers of the Council of Europe, of 24 November 1983, and the statement issued by the European Communities on 16 November 1983.

102 Cited by Borgen, "The Language…", op. cit., p. 18, note 48, who considers that "thus, Russia has taken neither the moral high ground nor the jurisprudential high ground, but it has used international law in an attempt to seize the narrative high ground" (p. 25).

In fact, Russia accepts that the right of South Ossetians and Abkhazians to secede cannot be fully justified, no matter that when the conflicts began it recognised them as States on the ground that this was the will of their respective populations. No doubt Russia considers that maintaining the *de facto* secession situation, indefinite until there is such an agreement between the parties and guaranteed by its military and economic assistance for the separatists, is an acceptable solution, as evidenced by its already having lasted three decades.

In conclusion, after analysing this international practice it can be stated that there is no international custom that justifies extending the right of self-determination of peoples and/or establishes a right to secede as a last resort due to the serious and discriminatory violation of a minority population within a State. Its existence has not been claimed by the majority of States or international organisations, neither in most of the successful cases nor in rejecting those that have been thwarted or that survive without general recognition. Nor is there a majority – whether or not claims have been made for the existence of such a custom – of successful cases that could possibly fit into the "discrimination" category; in our view, there are only four of the 11: Bangladesh, Eritrea, East Timor and South Sudan. And there are secessions that have been rejected which, had remedial secession been in force, would have constituted a notorious and scandalous contravention, namely, in our opinion, Krajina and Tamil Ealam. This same view has been taken by some international law scholars[103], for as Oeter asserts:

103 Among other authors who deny its validity, Rousseau, Charles. *Droit international public*. Paris: Dalloz, 1974, p. 32; Guilhaudis, Jean François. *Le droit des peuples à disposer d'eux-mêmes*. Grenoble: Presses Universitaires, 1976; Gros Espiell, Héctor. "En torno al derecho a la libre determinación de los pueblos". *Anuario de Derecho Internacional*, vol. 3, 1976, pp. 56–57; Thornberry, op. cit., p. 14; Seara Vázquez, Modesto. *Derecho internacional público*. México, 1991, p. 90; Ruiz Fabri, Hélène. "Genèse et disparition de l'État à l'époque contemporaine". *Annuaire Français de Droit International*, vol. 38, 1992, pp. 153–178; Clark, Donald and Robert Williamson. *Self Determination. International Perspectives*. Basingstoke: Macmillan Press, 1996, p. 30; Quane, op. cit., p. 571; Onguergouz, Fatsah. *The African Charter on Human and Peoples' Rights: A Comprehensive Agenda for Human Rights and Sustainable Democracy in Africa*. The Hague: Kluwer Law International, 2003, p. 251; Kohen. "Introduction", op. cit., p. 9; Eudes, Marie. "Retour sur une réussite passée inaperçue: L'Accord de Belfast et la nouvelle lecture du droit à l'autodétermination". *Revue générale de droit international public*, vol. 110, no. 3, 2006, pp. 631–646; Crawford, *The Creation…* 2nd ed., op. cit., pp. 127–128; Combacau, Jean and Serge Sur. *Droit international public*. Paris: Montchrestien, 8th ed., 2008, p. 273; Van Den Driest, Simone F. *Remedial Secession: A Right to External Self-Determination as a Remedy to Serious Injustices*. Antwerp: Intersentia, 2013, p. 331; Ahmed, op. cit.; and Summers, James. "Kosovo". In *Self-Determination and Secession in International Law*, edited by Christian Walter et al. Oxford University Press, 2014, pp. 235 et seq. In Spain, Andrés Sáenz de Santamaría, Paz "La libre determinación de los pueblos en la nueva sociedad internacional". *Cursos Euromediterráneos Bancaja de Derecho Internacional*, vol. 1, 1997, pp. 160 et seq.; Acosta Sánchez, Miguel A. "Kosovo: ¿una (nueva) piedra en el zapato de la política exterior de la UE?".

State practice has never shown any tendency to embrace seriously such a justification of secession – too many states in our globe (in particular large parts of the Third World) feel threatened by secessionist movements and perceive it as dangerous to open the Pandora's box of decomposition of statehood by justifying secession, be it even under very limited circumstances (as in the doctrine of 'remedial secession')[104].

The Canadian Supreme Court Decision on Quebec, 20 August 1998

Along with the creation of States or the rejection of entities emerging from secessionist processes, the Decision issued by the Supreme Court of Canada on 20 August 1998[105] frequently crops up in the debate about the international legality of secession. In *Reference re Secession of Quebec*, on 20 September 1996, the House of Commons, the Minister of Justice and Attorney General of Canada, through the Governor in Council, asked the Supreme Court three questions:

1 Under the Constitution of Canada, can the National Assembly, legislature or government of Quebec effect the secession of Quebec from Canada unilaterally?
2 Does international law give the National Assembly, legislature or government of Quebec the right to effect the secession of Quebec from Canada unilaterally? In this regard, is there a right to self-determination under international law that would give the National Assembly, legislature or government of Quebec the right to effect the secession of Quebec from Canada unilaterally?
3 In the event of a conflict between domestic and international law on the right of the National Assembly, legislature or government of Quebec to effect the secession of Quebec from Canada unilaterally, which would take precedence in Canada?

Revista de Derecho Comunitario Europeo, vol. 31, 2008, pp. 777 and 786; Carrillo Salcedo, Juan Antonio. "Sobre el pretendido derecho a decidir en Derecho internacional contemporáneo". *El Cronista del Estado Social y Democrático de Derecho*, vol. 33, 2012, pp. 20–22; Gutiérrez Espada, Cesáreo and Romualdo Bermejo García. "El derecho de libre determinación de los pueblos no coloniales a la luz del Derecho internacional", in *La autodeterminación a debate*, edited by J.J. Solozábal. Madrid: Edit. P. Iglesias, 2014, pp. 93–108; and Fernández de Casadevante, Carlos. "El derecho de autodeterminación: una lectura desde España". *Revista Electrónica Cordobesa de Derecho Internacional Público*, vol. 1, 2018.

104 Oeter, Stefan. "Secession, Territorial Integrity and the Role of the Security Council". In *Kosovo and International Law: The ICJ Advisory Opinion of 22 July 2010*, edited by Peter Hilpold. Leiden: Nijhoff, 2012, pp. 109–138. In the words of Walter, Christian. *Self-Determination and Secession in International Law*, edited by Walter, Ch., Anetje Von Ungern-Sternberg and Kavus Abushov. Oxford University Press, 2014, p. 305, "a general right of secession as part of the right to self-determination overwhelmingly rejected. It also finds no support in international practice".

105 Renvoi relatif à la sécession du Québec, published in (1998) 2 RCS, pp. 217–297.

The debate before the Canadian Supreme Court raised matters of a domestic order, relating to the country's constitutional system and the court's jurisdictional competence to hear this question[106], but also others of great interest for international law – although not all of the general scope claimed by some secessionist politicians – such as those relating to the 'people' concept and the regulation of secession in this legal system. First of all, it is worth highlighting the discussion between the jurists proposed by the Public Prosecutor's Office and those of the amicus curiae on the Quebec side.

In James Crawford's report of 19 February 1997 on "State Practice and International Law in Relation to Unilateral Secession", with comments by Luzius Wildhaber, they argue that there is no international right of secession. In Crawford's opinion,

> if international law does not confer any right to unilateral secession outside the colonial context - and in my opinion it does not - then the only way in which an entity can unilaterally secede is by the traditional means of winning a war of independence – as Bangladesh did in 1970 – with India's help and as Chechnya is trying to do now.
>
> (para. 10)

With regard to this international practice, he maintains that:

> By comparison with the acceptance of self-determination leading to the independence of colonial territories covered by Chapters XI and XII of the Charter (so-called 'external self-determination'), the practice regarding unilateral secession of non-colonial territories is clear and distinct. Since 1945 the international community has been extremely reluctant to accept unilateral secession of parts of independent states, in situations where the secession is opposed by the government of that state. In such cases the principle of territorial integrity has been a significant limitation. There is only one clear example of successful unilateral secession during this period, viz. Bangladesh. Since 1945 no state which has been created by unilateral secession has been admitted to the United Nations against the declared wishes of the government of the predecessor state.25 By contrast there are many examples of failed attempts at unilateral secession, including cases where the seceding entity maintained de facto independence for some time.
>
> (para. 26)

106 Regarding these constitutional matters and others relating to Canadian domestic law, see the detailed explanation of Bienvenu, Pierre. "Secession by Constitutional Means: The Decision of the Supreme Court of Canada in the Quebec Secession Reference". *Hamline Journal of Public Law & Policy*, vol. 23, no. 1, Fall 2001, pp. 185–254.

And so "to summarize, outside the colonial context, the principle of self-determination is not recognised in practice as giving rise to unilateral rights of secession by parts of independent states" (para. 60). In spite of proposals such as that contained in Resolution 2625, which he does not consider a reflection of international practice, he understands that "these developments are still tentative (*de lege* ferenda), and they do not affect the established rules and practices with respect to self-determination and the territorial integrity of state" (para. 62). In his opinion, therefore:

> there is a distinct issue of internal self-determination, in the sense of the recognition of cultural identity and internal self-government for different groups or peoples within the state. But these developments do not affect the established rules and practices with respect to self-determination and the territorial integrity of states. They lend no support to the view that peoples within independent states have a unilateral right to secede.
>
> (para. 67.e)

In contrast, Alain Pellet, Thomas Franck, Malcolm Shaw and George Abi-Saab issued their reports for the *amicus curiae*, with opinions that differed from those set out on p. 109. Pellet, in his report on "Legal Opinion on Certain Questions of. International Law Raised by the Reference", considers that "obviously, secession ('unilateral', but all secession is unilateral…) is 'possible' in international law" (para. 8). For Franck, "international law does not prohibit secession (although it may prohibit unlawful means for attaining it)" (para. 3); "there is no right to secession, nevertheless secession is in no sense unlawful per se" (para. 181)[107].

The Supreme Court, in its consideration of the three questions asked, makes some points that are certainly interesting for the purposes of this study. The first concerns the constitutional principles to be taken into account in this matter, mainly the principle of democracy (invoked by the Quebec side), that of legality (invoked by the Canadian Government) and those of constitutionalism[108], federalism, respect for minorities and effectivity (highlighted by the Court). Indeed, the Court considers that "it would be a grave mistake to equate legitimacy with the 'sovereign will' or majority rule alone" (para. 67), since the will of the people must be expressed within the framework of the procedures

107 All these reports can be consulted in Bayefsky, op. cit., especially those cited on pp. 177–212.

108 Constitutionalism facilitates—indeed makes possible—a democratic political system by creating an orderly framework within which people may make political decisions. Viewed correctly, constitutionalism and the rule of law are not in conflict with democracy; rather they are essential to it. Without that relationship, the political will upon which democratic decisions are taken would itself be undermined.

(para. 78)

legally established by the representatives of the entire population of the federal State. It maintains that the latter is the sum of all its citizens and all its peoples, in their respective territories, voluntarily and successively throughout the country's history. It understands, moreover, that the Canadian Constitution protects minorities from any possible measures of assimilation on the part of the majority, as it would violate their right to exist and be different, and that federalism requires that actions affecting these minorities be negotiated among others and not imposed by the majority (para. 91 et seq.).

Second, although it asserts that "International law contains neither a right of unilateral secession nor the explicit denial of such a right", it adds that "although such a denial is, to some extent, implicit in the exceptional circumstances required for secession to be permitted under the right of a people to self-determination" (para. 112). In an attitude that will subsequently be adopted by other courts (the ICJ on Kosovo, or the Spanish Constitutional Court with regard to Catalonia), it also affirms the general rule of prevalence of the territorial integrity of States and the exception on grounds of gross human rights violations without any other possible remedy (not applicable to the case in question, of course[109]), as well as international law's silence on the creation of States by secession and its referral of such cases to the sphere of domestic law (para. 143). In our opinion these statements are completely unwarranted, as nothing is said about their foundations in law. The following chapters will also refute this alleged silence, mistakenly deemed so by the Canadian court, as the principle of respect for the sovereignty and territorial integrity of States is absolutely valid in the international legal order[110] and therefore enforceable in respect of the response of third States to an act of secession within another State. The Court is right, however, in its assessment of the principle of effectivity:

> Although there is no right, under the Constitution or at international law, to unilateral secession, that is secession without negotiation on the basis just discussed, this does not rule out the possibility of an unconstitutional declaration of secession leading to a de facto secession. The ultimate

109 The following are legally possible pursuant to international law, according to the Supreme Court:

> situations of former colonies; where a people is oppressed, as for example under foreign military occupation; or where a definable group is denied meaningful access to government to pursue their political, economic, social and cultural development. In all three situations, the people in question are entitled to a right to external self-determination because they have been denied the ability to exert internally their right to self-determination. Such exceptional circumstances are manifestly inapplicable to Quebec under existing conditions. (para. 138)

110 In the same vein, see Buchanan, "The Quebec Secession…", op. cit., pp. 257–259.

> success of such a secession would be dependent on recognition by the international community, which is likely to consider the legality and legitimacy of secession.
>
> (para. 155)

And third, it asks whether we are actually dealing with a people in this case, since this is the presupposition necessary for proposing any kind of self-determination. It recognises the specificity of indigenous peoples[111], but only for the purposes of protecting their human rights as minorities, and it has doubts on this (para. 112). Therefore, it states that: "much of the Quebec population certainly shares many of the characteristics (such as a common language and culture) that would be considered in determining whether a specific group is a 'people', as do other groups within Quebec and/or Canada" (para. 125).

In our opinion, the Supreme Court of Canada's decision cannot be used as an infallible benchmark to defend the validity of a remedial secession, because it neither conducts nor refers to a rigorous study of international law and practice. Its assertions about its existence are not only arbitrary – in the sense of not being substantiated – but are also contradicted in other passages (the previously cited para. 155, "although there is no right…") and are unsystematic, as they do not take into account all the structural principles and concepts of international law (territorial integrity, recognition, etc.).

The ICJ's Advisory Opinion on Kosovo, 22 July 2010

In 2008, Professor Malcolm Shaw, one of the informants of the *amicus curiae* in the Quebec case, stated that "self-determination as a concept is capable of developing further so as to include the right to secession from existing states, but that has not as yet convincingly happened"[112]. The scholarly debate, with its lack of proof of a uniform practice, acquired a new element of confusion when the ICJ issued its Advisory Opinion on Accordance with International Law of the Unilateral Declaration of Independence in Respect of Kosovo, on 22 July 2010[113]. Because in answer to the question, "Is the unilateral declaration of independence by the Provisional Institutions of Self-Government of Kosovo in accordance with international law?", the Court sidestepped the underlying question, that is, whether there exists an international norm that protects and regulates the secession of non-colonial territories.

On 17 February 2008, 109 of the 120 members of the Autonomous Parliament of Kosovo voted to adopt a statement, to which the President of Kosovo adhered, declaring its independence in the following terms:

111 During the proceedings, the Grand Council of the Crees requested recognition of their right to secede from Quebec to join the rest of Canada. See Bienvenu, op. cit., p. 227.

112 Shaw, Malcolm. *International Law*. Cambridge University Press, 8th ed., 2017, p. 203. This observation had already appeared in the sixth edition, published in 2008.

113 ICJ Rep. 403.

> 1. We, the democratically-elected leaders of our people, hereby declare Kosovo to be an independent and sovereign state. This declaration reflects the will of our people and it is in full accordance with the recommendations of UN Special Envoy Martti Ahtisaari and his Comprehensive Proposal for the Kosovo Status Settlement.

These autonomous institutions had been established by the international authority that has been administering the territory since 1999, following the military operation carried out by the North Atlantic Treaty Organization (NATO) to prevent the ethnic cleansing actions initiated by the Serbian Government against the Kosovar Albanian population in 1998, which led to the Serbian authority being expelled from Kosovo and replaced, as provided for in Resolution 1244 (1999) of 10 June, by the UN Secretary-General's Special Envoy and UNMIK, with the military assistance of NATO (Kosovo Force, KFOR). Annex 1 to this Resolution sets out the general principles for this international administration and for the resolution of this conflict:

1. end of hostilities;
2. withdrawal of Serbian armed forces;
3. deployment of international civil and security presences;
4. establishment of an international interim administration;
5. return of all refugees and displaced persons;
6. establishment of a framework agreement providing for self-government;
7. respect for the sovereignty and territorial integrity of the Federal Republic of Serbia;
8. demobilisation of the Kosovar Albanian militias;
9. adoption of measures for economic development and stabilisation; and
10. interim authority of the UN.

The functions of the civil presence are, as indicated in Annex 2, to promote self-government, create provisional democratic institutions, perform basic administrative functions for as long as necessary, protect the human rights of the population, support economic and institutional rebuilding, distribute humanitarian aid, facilitate the return of refugees and displaced persons and propose a political process aimed at determining the future status of Kosovo, taking into account the Rambouillet Agreement. The Rambouillet conference was an attempted negotiation between the NATO countries and the Government of the Federal Republic of Yugoslavia, with the participation of Kosovar Albanian representatives, prior to the military intervention.

The Court holds that analysis of international practice in non-colonial situations does not reveal the appearance in international law of a new rule prohibiting the adoption of a declaration of independence by one part of a State. Furthermore, whenever the Security Council has condemned such declarations of independence it has done so owing to the specific circumstances, especially when one State had used force against the independence and territorial integrity of another. And it considers that it should not take a position on the question of whether, outside the context of colonial territories and those subjugated by force, international law confers on a part of the population of a State a right to secede from it or whether there is a right of remedial secession, as these questions are deemed to be beyond the scope of the question posed by the General Assembly.

This ICJ opinion is undoubtedly frustrating – for not taking the opportunity to resolve the scholarly dispute[114] – and extremely cowardly, as its purely advisory nature means that it could have been extended to other matters deemed to be connected to the literal question, as the validity and conditions of a possible international law of secession clearly are.

In any case, at least it allows us to look back at the first decade of this century and check the *opinio iuris* of States in relation to this issue, thanks to the written statements they made during the proceedings. Thus, for the United Kingdom, Russia, Germany, Japan, Ireland, Slovenia, the Netherlands, Switzerland, Albania, Estonia, Latvia, Finland, Slovenia, the Czech Republic, Poland and Jordan – 16 of the 43 States that submitted written statements – the international order allows for an exceptional secession for which there needs to be a serious violation of human rights and which must be the only remaining solution possible[115]. Of these States, Poland, the Netherlands and Australia considered that remedial secession is supported by Resolution 2625, as a sanction against the State responsible for gross human rights violations[116]; and Russia, while recognising the existence of remedial secession, nevertheless considers that it is not applicable to the case of Kosovo[117].

114 As stated by judges Yusuf, Simma and Sepúlveda-Amor in their separate opinions. Criticisms of this inaction are numerous; for instance, Vashakmadze, Mindia and Matthias Lippold. "Nothing but a Road towards Secession – The International Court of Justice's Advisory Opinion on Accordance with International Law of the Unilateral Declaration of Independence in Respect of Kosovo". *Goettingen Journal of International Law*, vol. 2, no. 2, 2010, pp. 646–647; Roben, Volker. "The ICJ Advisory Opinion on the Unilateral Declaration of Independence in Respect of Kosovo: Rules or Principles". *Goettingen Journal of International Law*, vol. 2, no. 3, 2010, p. 1071; and Burri, Thomas. "The Kosovo opinion and secession: the sounds of silence and missing links". *German Law Journal*, vol. 11, 2010, pp. 881 et seq.

115 Thus, for Poland, "remedial right to secession is based on a premise that a state gravely violates international human rights and humanitarian law against peoples inhabiting its territory". Written statement of Poland dated 14 April 2009, para. 6.5.

116 As stated in Poland's written statement dated 14 April 2009, para. 6.5: "remedial right to secession is based on a premise that a state gravely violates international human rights and humanitarian law against peoples inhabiting its territory".

117 Written statement of Russia dated 16 April 2009, para. 88:

> in this regard, the Russian Federation is of the view that the primary purpose of the 'safeguard clause' is to serve as a guarantee of territorial integrity of States. It is also true that the clause may be construed as authorizing secession under certain conditions. However, those conditions should be limited to truly

Against these arguments in favour of the existence of a remedial right to secession, other States maintained that the right to self-determination was formulated exclusively for peoples under colonial domination or ruled by force. This is the opinion of Brazil, Argentina, Iran, Serbia, China and Chile, whose delegation declared:

> While the claim that there is a 'right of secession of last resort' has been supported by some writers and by a contrario reasoning [...], it is without support in State practice. It has not emerged as a rule of customary law. It is not found in any treaty. And it has no support from the practice of the UN[118].

The fact that the remaining States did not declare themselves in favour of accepting remedial secession shows how legally unconvincing this supposed legal concept is[119], but even more so does the fact that even the majority of those who accepted it ruled out its application in the case in question, as Russia did. In our opinion, there is no doubt that if the question had been raised in early 1999, before NATO's armed intervention, the existence of a grave situation of systematic violation of the human rights of the Kosovar Albanian population would have been established[120], with the clearly discriminatory intention of provoking this population's exit from Serbian territory. This was the aim of the measures taken between 1989 and 1999, which abolished the province's self-governing bodies, suspended its participation in the federal government, prohibited teaching in its language, forced the property of displaced persons and refugees to be sold to Serbs and expelled this majority ethnic group in Kosovo from public office as well as from Albanian state

> extreme circumstances, such as an outright attack by the parent State, threatening the very existence of the people in question.

118 Written statement of the Republic of Cyprus dated 3 April 2009, para. 143.
119 We agree with Arp in that:

> the ICJ did all it could to circumvent the question of the legal qualification of remedial secession. The Court briefly addressed this argument by stating that remedial secession was a subject on which radically different views were expressed by those taking part in the proceedings and expressing a position on the question. From this it can be inferred that the Court may consider that there is no consolidated legal opinion (opinio iuris) in international law on this topic.
>
> (Arp, Björn. "The ICJ Advisory Opinion on the Accordance with International Law of the Unilateral Declaration of Independence in Respect of Kosovo and the International Protection of Minorities". *German Law Journal*, vol. 11, 2010, p. 853)

120 Report of the Special Envoy of the Secretary-General on Kosovo's future status (S/2007/168, 26 March 2007), para. 6.

enterprises and from universities[121], which resulted in more than 400,000 refugees and displaced persons[122]. However, this humanitarian situation was resolved in 2008 when independence was declared and in 2010 when the ICJ heard the case, and therefore it is not relevant[123].

Aside from this contribution towards proving the existence of an international custom, clearly unfavourable as it requires generality, this case is neither particularly relevant from the perspective of legal analysis nor useful for secessionist arguments, as the vagueness surrounding the existence or non-existence of a secession right deprives us of jurisprudence. Of interest in this respect is Bolton and Visoka's analysis, according to which only five of the first 75 countries to recognise Kosovo as a State (one of the five being Slovenia) based their decision on the right to self-determination claimed by the Yugoslav republics during the process of dissolution, ignoring the Badinter Commission's reasoning against the minor entities and minorities; another five (including Ireland) on the majority will of the population, in accordance with identity-based political theories and those based on an isolated or unsystematic democratic principle; 73 on other grounds, such as effectivity, acceptance of international supervision, the impossibility of negotiating another solution or regional security; and only five on the violation of human rights (Canada, Costa Rica, Samoa and Australia, and Ireland again)[124].

The ICJ's other opinions – this is an advisory opinion – are at the very least open to criticism. First, in relation to the international legality of a unilateral declaration of independence, the Court concludes that no international law prohibits such declarations, which occur in the domestic sphere of States. As Gutiérrez Espada and Bermejo García point out[125]:

121 Kumbaro, Dajena. *The Kosovo Crisis in an International Law Perspective: Self-Determination. Territorial Integrity and the NATO Intervention*. NATO Report, 2001, pp. 42 et seq.

122 European Action Council for Peace in the Balkans and Public International Law and Policy Group of the Carnegie Endowment for International Peace, Kosovo – From crisis to permanent solution, Report of 1 November 1997, p. 6.

123 For the opposing view, see Musgrave, op. cit., pp. xv et seq.

124 Bolton, Grace and Gezim Visoka. "Recognizing Kosovo's Independence: Remedial Secession or Earned Sovereignty?". *South East European Studies at Oxford Occasional Paper*, vol. 11/10, October 2010, p. 19.

125 Gutiérrez Espada, Cesáreo and Romualdo Bermejo García. "De la opinión consultiva de las Corte Internacional de Justicia, de 22 de julio de 2010, sobre Kosovo". Real Instituto Elcano, Working Document no. 35, 2010, p. 26. See also their criticisms on pp. 45 et seq. In the words of Christie, Emily. "Accordance with International Law of the Unilateral Declaration of Independence in Respect of Kosovo, ICJ Advisory Opinion 22 July 2010, General List No. [4]". *Australian International Law Journal*, vol. 17, no. 1, 2010, p. 212,

> the opinion of the ICJ that there is no prohibition in international law on declarations of independence per se, without providing any commentary on possible entitlements to such a declaration, unfortunately does very little to

> Obviously, these statements of the Court are worrying, since according to its theses any infra-state entity could declare its independence, generating not only insecurity but, what is more serious, possible conflicts within States and even between States. It is therefore understandable that several States participating in the proceedings before the Court have affirmed that this prohibition is implicitly deduced from the principle of territorial integrity[126].

And second, on the accordance of the unilateral declaration of independence with the legal regime established in Resolution 1244 (1999) of the Security Council, suffice it to say that the latter constitutes the specific legal framework of this conflict and on several occasions it stresses the prevalence of the principle of territorial integrity:

> Reaffirming the commitment of all Member States to the sovereignty and territorial integrity of the Federal Republic of Yugoslavia and the other States of the region, as set out in the Helsinki Final Act and annex 2 (…)
>
> 1 Decides that a political solution to the Kosovo crisis shall be based on the general principles in annex 1 and as further elaborated in the principles and other required elements in annex 2 (…)
> 11e Facilitating a political process designed to determine Kosovo's future status, taking into account the Rambouillet accords (S/1999/648) (…)
>
> A political process towards the establishment of an interim political framework agreement providing for a substantial self-government for Kosovo, taking full account of the Rambouillet accords and the principles of sovereignty and territorial integrity of the Federal Republic of Yugoslavia and the other countries of the region, and the demilitarization of the KLA (…)[127]

> 5 Establishment of an interim administration for Kosovo as a part of the international civil presence under which the people of Kosovo can enjoy substantial autonomy within the Federal Republic of Yugoslavia, to be decided by the Security Council of the United Nations. The interim administration to provide transitional administration while establishing and overseeing the development of provisional democratic self-governing institutions to ensure conditions for a peaceful and normal life for all inhabitants in Kosovo[128].

further the jurisprudence on sovereignty and statehood, arguably creating more questions than it answers.

126 Author's translation.
127 Annex 1.
128 Annex 2.

The Rambouillet Agreement, signed by the Kosovar representatives, and which serves as the basis for Resolution 1244, states that "acts outside those powers and responsibilities shall be null and void" (para. 6). According to this provision, the unilateral declaration of independence would be null and void, as they undertake to join Yugoslavia as a self-governing territory and respect its territorial integrity (article 1.2 of the Agreement). The opinion of the majority of the ICJ judges that this declaration does not actually breach the legal framework of Resolution 1244 because it falls outside of the powers that had been conferred upon the self-governing institutions is surprising in general terms, as it clearly circumvents the sovereignty of the Yugoslav people and seeks to destroy the territorial integrity of Yugoslavia (now Serbia). Yet it is also possible to detect a questionable interpretive technique as provided for in Articles 31 and 32 of the 1969 Vienna Convention – which are applicable to international treaties but also by analogy to other written rules – given that it is necessary to analyse the context and purpose of the norm and the preparatory work. In this respect, both the preamble and the annexes to Resolution 1244 clearly protect Serbian integrity and the Rambouillet agreements are an unequivocal foundation, and they should operate as complementary means of interpretation. Judge Bennouna was far more moderate in his dissenting opinion when stating that what the Court is being asked to do is to rule on the accordance with international law not of any declaration of independence, but of the one adopted on 17 February 2008 by the Provisional Institutions of Self-Government of Kosovo, institutions established by the United Nations with specific powers (para. 30).

These objections are particularly relevant in the context of remedial secession, since it is conceived of as a last resort to resolve the discriminatory situation. Indeed, the autonomy imposed by the Security Council allows the political participation of the Kosovar Albanians, and it is therefore an effective alternative that would preclude independence. In the words of Wilson:

> It is difficult to base Kosovo's secession upon the terms of resolution 2625 for several reasons. Firstly, the exact legal status of its 'saving' clause is not clear, especially in light of the general reluctance of states to sanction a right of secession within international law. Secondly, even if a right of secession can be established it is difficult to sustain the argument that the population of Kosovo currently endures oppressive discriminate treatment carried out by the federal authorities, and that no alternatives exist for affording Kosovo with Powers of self-government without recourse to secession. Thirdly, no universal agreement exists upon the meaning of 'peoples' capable of benefiting from any right of secession which resolution 2625 might confer[129].

Consequently, we agree with Walter that "the judicial minimalism of the Court" has helped Kosovo remain independent from Serbia but has not

129 Wilson, op. cit., p. 472

contributed to the development of international law[130], and also with the cited Tagliavini Report on Georgia and the secessionism it suffers, when it states that:

> since the unilateral declaration of independence of Kosovo in 2008, the discussion has gained momentum. However, most commentators remain sceptical. Only a few international legal scholars have diagnosed a change of international law[131]. In any case, it is more than doubtful that a new rule of customary international law has been created on the basis of the Kosovo case[132].

The secessionist process in Catalonia and the precedents of Quebec, Kosovo and Scotland

In addition to the political arguments referred to in the previous chapter, Catalan independence advocates, at a legal level, have also resorted to using the most immediate precedents, i.e. the Canadian Supreme Court's 1998 decision on the self-determination referendum in Quebec and the subsequent 2000 Clarity Act, the 2008 ICJ Advisory Opinion on the legality of Kosovo's declaration of independence, and the Scottish independence referendum approved by the UK Parliament in 2014.

In our opinion, both the Canadian Supreme Court's *dictum* and the legal reform carried out for its application in Canada do not favour the Catalan pro-independence theses. In relation to the 1998 decision, it is important to bear in mind, first, that the constitutional circumstances of Spain and Canada are very different, especially because the latter is a federal State created on a consensual basis in the nineteenth century. Spain does not have a federal constitutional system and currently is not set up on a consensual basis. To claim that Spain today is the voluntary sum of the countries that have been part of it throughout its long history (Asturias, Galicia, Leon, Castile, Navarre, Aragon, the Catalan and the Aragonese counties), Valencia, Majorca, the Caliphate of Cordoba, the Kingdom of Granada and all the Muslim *taifas*, or at least the union of the Crown of Aragon (not Catalonia) and the Kingdom of Castile, has no legal or constitutional basis and therefore is hardly likely to be recognised as such by the Spanish Constitutional Court in a consultation similar to that carried out by the Canadian Government in 1997.

In relation to the Canadian Supreme Court's considerations regarding the separation of Quebec, we could transfer to the Catalan case its doubts concerning the existence in Quebec of a 'people' eligible for self-determination, as we pointed out in the first chapter. Likewise, the debate about constitutional

130 Walter, op. cit., p. 5.
131 Specifically, Weller, Marc. *Escaping the Self-Determination Trap*. Leiden: Nijhoff, 2008.
132 Op. cit., p. 147.

principles is extremely interesting, especially the balance between democracy or the will of the people and legality or compliance with the procedures provided for.

In this respect, the Judgment issued by the Spanish Constitutional Court on 17 October 2017, which declares the unconstitutionality of the Referendum Law passed by the Catalan Parliament, states that:

> by renouncing -as we observe in Legal Basis 2 of this Judgment- any presumption of constitutionality, the autonomous legislature has not been able to legitimately claim obedience for this Law. A power that expressly denies the law denies itself as an authority worthy of compliance. Such a serious attack on the rule of law violates, with equal intensity, the democratic principle, the Parliament having ignored that the submission of all to the Constitution is another form of submission to the popular will, expressed this time as a constituent power held by the Spanish people, not by any fraction of it. In the constitutional state, the democratic principle cannot be separated from the unconditional primacy of the Constitution...

Like this Spanish court, the Canadian Supreme Court opts to consider that citizens adopt decisions by means of certain procedures, within the framework of certain established rules and jurisdictions that cannot be altered by the simple will of the people, let alone by a part of the people in their local institutions, as this would clash head-on with the principles of legality, constitutionalism and federalism. The end result of this combination of principles is also unfavourable for the Catalan secessionists, as it advocates that the will of the people in one part of the territory cannot be imposed on the constitutional and legal system democratically established by the whole population of the State. For this reason, the Court holds that it must be all the representatives of the entire State, in its federal parliament, who decide to authorise the separation – consented to and therefore not secession – of a part of the State, under such conditions or requirements as may be established.

In this respect, Spain's Constitutional Court is categorical in its Judgment, of 8 November 2017, on the Juridical Transition Law, just three weeks after the Judgment on 17 October:

> The people of Catalonia, as we have already said, and the same applies to the people of Aran, 'is not the holder of a sovereign power, exclusive to the [Spanish] Nation constituted as a State' (STC 42/2014, FJ 3), nor is it 'a legal subject that enters into competition with the holder of national sovereignty' (STC 259/2015, FJ 3), nor, lastly, can the citizens of Catalonia can be confused with the sovereign people conceived of as 'the ideal unit of imputation of the constituent power and, as such, source of the Constitution and the legal system' [SSTC 12/2008, FJ 10; 259/2015, FJ 3; 90/2017, FJ 6 a); 114/2017, FJ 5 B)] .

The 2000 Clarity Act (or Bill C-20), passed in the House of Commons on 20 March 2000 and in the Senate on 29 June 2000, authorises the separation and establishes some requirements for this that are very unfavourable for secessionist claims in Catalonia. First, and intrinsically, it implies that Canada does not permit 'secession', only 'separation', and not as an immanent right of its peoples but as a right granted by its federal parliament and under the conditions established by it[133]. Second, the conditions themselves are not very favourable. In general terms and for the purposes of this study, we should highlight four:

1 The competence of the House of Commons to determine whether a question proposed by the legislative assembly of a province is clear, especially if "the question would result in a clear expression of the will of the population of a province on whether the province should cease to be part of Canada and become an independent state".

2 To determine whether there is a sufficient majority:

> consider and, by resolution, set out its determination on whether, in the circumstances, there has been a clear expression of a will by a clear majority of the population of that province that the province cease to be part of Canada[134], without pre-establishing it, as the following will be taken into account: "(a) the size of the majority of valid votes cast in favour of the secessionist option; (b) the percentage of eligible voters voting in the referendum; and (c) any other matters or circumstances it considers to be relevant".

3 It is necessary to proceed, after the referendum, to amend the Constitution:

> It is recognized that there is no right under the Constitution of Canada to effect the secession of a province from Canada unilaterally and that, therefore, an amendment to the Constitution of Canada would be required for any province to secede from Canada, which in turn would require negotiations involving at least the governments of all of the provinces and the Government of Canada.

133 The Act Respecting the Exercise of the Fundamental Rights and Prerogatives of the Québec People and the Québec State, passed on 7 December 2000 in the National Assembly of Quebec, contradicts some essential aspects of the decision and Canadian federal law; for example, on this question, as in Article 1 it states that "the right of the Québec people to self-determination is founded in fact and in law. The Québec people is the holder of rights that are universally recognized under the principle of equal rights and self-determination of peoples", and in Article 2 that "the Québec people has the inalienable right to freely decide the political regime and legal status of Québec".

134 In the Act Respecting the Exercise of the Fundamental Rights and Prerogatives of the Québec People and the Québec State, it is set at 50%, which does not correlate with what is provided for in the Clarity Act.

4 To determine the clarity of the question, the opinion of all the parties and indigenous peoples will be taken into account, and when establishing the conditions of separation, all the relevant circumstances will be determined, among them "the division of assets and liabilities, any changes to the borders of the province, the rights, interests and territorial claims of the Aboriginal peoples of Canada, and the protection of minority rights".

Of course, clarity is lacking in the question asked in the Quebec referendum in 1995 ("Do you agree that Quebec should become sovereign after having made a formal offer to Canada for a new economic and political partnership within the scope of the bill respecting the future of Quebec and of the agreement signed on June 12, 1995?") as well as in the one posed by the Catalan Government in 2014 ("Do you want Catalonia to be a State? If so, do you want this State to be independent?"). Even the one in 2017 would be questionable, not for the clarity in opting for independence (which is not apparent in the first question asked in 2014), but for being coupled with a single constitutional form ("Do you want Catalonia to be an independent state in the form of a Republic?"). Excellence in clarity is a quality of other referendums, such as that of Eritrea ("Do you approve Eritrea to become an independent, sovereign state?") or that of Scotland ("Should Scotland be an independent country?"). On the contrary, other questions contain unnecessary words or are incomplete or confusing: "Do you want the Republic of Montenegro to be an independent state with full international and legal personality?", "Do you accept the proposed special autonomy for East Timor within the Unitary State of the Republic of Indonesia?". And some are tendentious: "Do you want the restoration of the national independence and sovereignty of the Republic of Estonia?"

As for the significant majority, the most important thing is that it is determined by the federal parliament, which it can do afterwards – as can be gathered from reading its articles – by taking into account the percentage of votes cast and the percentage of votes in favour. And even the net percentage of support for separation in each of the different areas of the territory concerned can be taken into account, as the final condition mentions consideration of the territory's borders. Undoubtedly, those in favour of Catalan independence are not in favour of a separation of any part of Catalonia depending on the referendum result in each part. For this reason, its territorial integrity is proclaimed in Article 6 of the (unconstitutional) Law 20/2017, of 8 September, on the Juridical Transition and Foundational of the Republic.

Furthermore, the prior participation of all political parties and subsequent negotiation with all the territorial governments that make up the State is necessary, which in the case of Catalonia is the polar opposite of both the pro-independence parties' monopoly of representation of the Catalan people and the unilateral nature of their alleged right to self-determination, expressed in, among others, Article 2 of the (unconstitutional) Law on the

Self-Determination Referendum in Catalonia[135]. Among the issues that have to be negotiated are borders, as mentioned earlier, as well as matters relating to property, assets and economic affairs (provided for in the final paragraphs of the Declaration of Independence of Catalonia), and the rights of minorities. The latter issue is an extraordinarily sensitive one for Catalan secessionists, who are currently disinclined to use the Spanish language under the self-governing regime. Although Article 24 of the Transition Law covers the linguistic rights of speakers of Catalan, Spanish and Aranese, and Articles 10(2) and 15 declare the provisional continuity of the international treaties concluded by Spain, when Article 22 says it guarantees respect for the rights recognised in the Universal Declaration of Human Rights, the ICCPR, the International Covenant on Economic, Social and Cultural Rights, the European Convention on Human Rights and its additional protocols, and the Charter of Fundamental Rights of the European Union, it fails to mention the other regional treaties, namely the Framework Convention for the Protection of National Minorities of 1995 and the European Charter for Minority Languages of 1992.

As for the ICJ's Advisory Opinion on Kosovo of 2010, the Court's vagueness is, initially, favourable to secessionist interests, given that it states that international law does not prohibit declarations of independence; however, it is detrimental to them in that the legality of these declarations of independence is determined by domestic law, and in the Spanish legal system they are flagrantly unconstitutional, as the Constitutional Court declared in its Judgment of 8 November 2017:

> In fact, the Resolutions adopted by the Parliament of Catalonia on 27 October 2017, entitled 'Declaration of the Representatives of Catalonia' and 'Constituent Process', reflect the stubborn will of this House to evade the procedures of constitutional reform in order to carry out its political project of separating from the Spanish State, and the Parliament of Catalonia disregards the repeated pronouncements and warnings of this Court and once again seeks to cancel de facto, in the territory of Catalonia and for the entire Catalan people, the validity of the Constitution, the Statute of Autonomy and any rules of law that may not conform to the dictates of its will....

Therefore, the Spanish Government's pronouncements in the written statement submitted to the ICJ were clearly opposed to the legality of a declaration of independence of a non-State actor and to the existence of remedial

135 "The people of Catalonia are a sovereign political subject and as such exercise their right to decide freely and democratically, their political status" (in Catalan "el poble de Catalunya és un subjecte polític sobirà i com a tal exerceix el dret a decidir lliure i democràticament, la seva condició política").

secession: "as a form of sanction or remedy (...) has no proper place in contemporary international law"[136].

The example of Scotland is also difficult to extrapolate to Catalonia, given that Spain's current constitutional system has nothing similar to the Act of Union of 1707 whereby the Scottish and English parliaments agreed to create the new State of Great Britain (Article 1), with a united parliament (Article 3) and separate judiciaries (Article 19). Therefore, there is no precedent like the one that led the UK Parliament to approve the Edinburgh Agreement of 15 October 2012 authorising a referendum on self-determination for Scotland. This agreement permitted the Scottish Parliament to amend the Scotland Act 1998, allowing it to call a referendum through the Scottish Independence Referendum Act 2013 of 17 December, which eventually took place on 18 September 2014. This agreement also established, as in the Quebec case, the need for a clear question[137], and other conditions are set out in the agreements entered into by both governments. None of these conditions respond to Scottish nationalist claims, especially those that refer, again as in the Quebec case, to subsequently determining the effects of the separation by mutual agreement and the possibility of some areas of Scotland remaining part of British territory. With regard to the latter, it should be borne in mind that the northern isles (Hebrides, Orkney and Shetland) had expressed their will to not join an independent Scotland in the Joint Position Statement of 2013[138]. In fact, in the referendum, with a 84.9% turnout and only 44.7% voting in favour of independence (which only four of the 32 local government areas voted for), there was far less support in areas such as the Scottish Borders and the aforementioned isles (just 32.8% in Orkney, 36.3% in Shetlands, 34.3% in Dumfries and Galloway, and 33.4% in the Scottish Borders).

In any case, the arguments of the pro-independence SNP (Scottish National Party) are much more rigorous than those of the Catalan nationalist parties, since, as Dalle Mulle and Serrano indicate, "in essence, the SNP's argument for Independence is based on the idea of recovering Scotland's sovereignty, since

136 Written Statement of Kingdom of Spain on Accordance with International Law of the Unilateral Declaration of Independence in Respect of Kosovo (April 2009), p. 5. Regarding Spain's position, see Borgen, Christopher J. "From Kosovo to Catalonia: Separatism and Integration in Europe". *Goettingen Journal of International Law*, vol. 2, no. 3, 2010, pp. 1018 et seq., and Escobar Hernández, Concepción. "La posición del Reino de España en el procedimiento consultivo: una aproximación general". *Revista Española de Derecho Internacional*, vol. 63, no. 1, 2011, pp. 11–27.

137 Art. 5: "Both governments agree that the referendum question must be fair, easy to understand and capable of producing a result that is accepted and commands confidence".

138 López Basaguren, Alberto. "Escocia: el referéndum sobre la independencia y la propuesta de reforma de la Devolution". *Revista Española de Derecho Constitucional*, vol. 104, 2015, p. 142.

the union with the rest of the United Kingdom does not serve Scottish interests anymore"[139]. As the Scottish Government declared in January 2012:

> Scotland is not oppressed and we have no need to be liberated. Independence matters because we do not have the powers to reach our potential. We are limited in what we can do to create jobs, grow the economy and help the vulnerable. We shouldn't have a constitution which constrains us, but one which frees us to build a better society. Our politics should be judged on the health of our people, the welfare of young and old and the strength of our economy.

The impossible application of remedial secession in the case of Catalonia

In addition to these precedents, the Catalan secessionist process has drawn on – again, at a legal level – the doctrine of remedial secession, comparing itself with successful secessions such as those of the Baltic states.

Before analysing it, we should briefly refer to the claim contained in some statements and documents that this secessionist process is protected under the regime of self-determination of peoples. Among others, Catalan Parliament Resolutions 98/III, of 12 December 1989, 679/V, of 1 October 1998, 631/VIII, of 3 March 2010, and 6/IX, of 10 March 2011, reiterated, as in the latter, that:

> the Parliament of Catalonia considers the right to self-determination of peoples as an inalienable right of the people of Catalonia. This has been made explicit in repeated votes by the Parliament, as the seat of the sovereignty of the people of Catalonia.

The Declaration of Independence of 2017 proclaims that "the Government of Catalonia has called a referendum to exercise the right to self-determination as recognised in international law", while the preamble to the annulled Referendum Law of the Catalan Parliament states that:

> the Covenants on Civil and Political Rights and on Economic, Social and Cultural Rights, approved by the United Nations General Assembly on December 19, 1966, ratified and in force in the Kingdom of Spain since their publication in the BOE[140], 30 April 1977, recognize the right of peoples to self-determination as the first of human rights.

These affirmations contradict, as explained in this chapter, current international law, since it is not proven, nor has it been recognised by international courts,

139 Dalle Mulle and Serrano, op. cit., p. 635.
140 BOE is the official journal of Kingdom of Spain.

that a right to self-determination exists outside the international context, and those who maintain that the 1966 New York Covenants extend its external aspect to national minorities are few and far between, as is revealed by studying the preparatory work[141]. Of course, as has also been stated, there are authors, and even governments, who have spoken of the emergence of an international right to remedial secession, yet not in the strict context of the general regime of the right to self-determination, but rather as an autonomous institution of the latter, more in the context of the protection of human rights and even of the doctrine – not consolidated as an international norm – of the responsibility to protect.

Given that Catalonia is obviously not a territory under colonial domination, for many reasons, one of them being that it does not satisfy the 'saltwater rule', the only possible interpretation of these declarations is that they refer precisely to this remedial secession, and not to the general right of self-determination, as other texts seem to confirm. In this respect, the Declaration of Independence of 2017 contains such notorious falsehoods as that in Spain, with respect to Catalonia, there is "a linguistic and cultural discrimination", or that:

> the brutal military-style police intervention orchestrated by the Spanish State against Catalan citizens repeatedly violated their civil and political liberties and the principles of human rights, and contravened international accords signed and ratified by the Spanish State itself. Thousands of people, among them hundreds of elected and government officials and professionals in the communications and media sector, the administration and in civil society, have been investigated, detained, charged, interrogated and threatened with lengthy prison sentences.

The seriousness of these accusations is made more evident by the fact that the human rights supervisory bodies to whose jurisdiction, in the broadest sense, Spain is subject, both in the UN and in the Council of Europe, have not found that, during recent decades or specifically in 2017, there has been a situation of linguistic and cultural discrimination, a general violation of human rights, or military-style police repression of the Catalan people. On the contrary, leaving aside the warnings or convictions for particular acts that also occur in other European countries, the situation regarding observance of human rights in Spain is very healthy; and specifically in relation to language, the complaints come, conversely, from those who speak Spanish in Catalonia, especially in the field of education, because they feel discriminated against and ignored by the State institutions. On this issue, we agree with Professor Alonso de Antonio that the Spanish Constitutional Court itself has done very little to protect

141 On the contrary, other authors, such as Ridao, Joan. *El dret a decidir. La consulta sobre el futur politic de Catalunya*. Barcelona: Institut d'Estudis Autonòmics, 2014, especially pp. 57–90, consider that international law endorses a right to self-determination of the Catalan people.

Spanish as an official language of the State, particularly in education, but also in other areas of everyday life[142].

The claims of Catalan independence supporters are similar, in this context, to those made in other secessionist processes, be they successful (Bangladesh, Eritrea, East Timor and South Sudan), fruitless (Biafra, Krajina, Tamil Ealam, etc.) or in gestation (Kosovo or Transnistria), in some especially due to linguistic discrimination (Eritrea and Transnistria). The difference is that the violation of human rights in these territories was real.

In any case, the factual and legal shortcomings of these texts drawn up by the Catalan nationalists are less surprising than the imprecisions of the Spanish Constitutional Court in its Judgment of 17 October 2017 annulling Law 19/2017, of 6 September, on the Catalan Self-determination Referendum. Therein, following a correct exposition of the international legal regime in relation to self-determination of peoples and secession of territories, in which it states that:

> International Law has evolved, configuring the principle of self-determination within a framework of respect for the territorial integrity of existing States and does not grant the constituent parts territorial-based political subdivisions of a democratic State the right to unilaterally separate from the State,

it finally asserts that "The defended right of separation is only possible in cases of colonial domination, peoples annexed by conquest, foreign domination or occupation, and peoples oppressed by massive and flagrant violation of their rights". The final part of this sentence is included without any reasoned justification.

The arguments put forward by the Catalan secessionists are thus completed. In the first chapter we set out and refuted their alleged basis in ethnic identity, historical grievances, recovery of statehood and the will of the inhabitants. In

142 Alonso de Antonio, Ángel L. "La cuestión lingüística en la Sentencia del Tribunal Constitucional sobre el Estatuto de Autonomía de Cataluña". *Teoría y Realidad Constitucional UNED*, vol. 27, 2011, p. 460. Regarding the use of Spanish in Catalonia's educational linguistic model, see Álvarez Ortega, Miguel. "El castellano en las aulas catalanas: claves de una incómoda recurrencia". *Revista de Estudios Políticos*, vol. 169, 2015, pp. 267–298:

> it can be said that the decisions of the Constitutional Court in the field of language have shown little respect for Spanish as the sole official language of the State, that there has been no desire to thoroughly resolve the practical questions, such as education, which arise on a daily basis, and that the sometimes naïve interpretation of the articles under appeal opens the door to political decisions that could jeopardise the equal rights of the citizens of Catalonia depending on which shared language they use.
>
> (Author's translation)

this chapter we have done likewise with other supposed bases such as the precedents of Quebec, Kosovo and Scotland and the concept of remedial secession. Although the secessionists usually insist on these arguments, in recent years they have resorted to a new term, the 'right to decide', which seeks to sum up all these arguments and make their aspirations revolve around the will of the Catalan people.

This right to decide, which was first mentioned in a text issued by Catalonia's principal self-governing institution in 2012[143], appears to restrict self-determination to the simple will of the population, as maintained by the theories of primary rights discussed in our first chapter. However, in Catalan secessionism there is no detachment from the other arguments put forward. On the contrary, the self-determination of the Catalan people is exercised according to its own will and its own will alone, that is, without taking into account constitutional procedures or the opinion of the rest of the Spanish population. And the purpose of this voluntarist reductionism is precisely to recover the statehood lost during the course of history and the continuity of the legal and political institutions wrested away by Spain, to defend Catalan culture, traditions and language, to ensure a more effective government that is fair in its taxation of Catalan citizens and businesses and promotes their economic and social development, and to defend itself against repression and serious human rights violations on the part of the Spanish authorities. Yet, as we have explained, not only are these accusations unfounded, but neither these claims nor any of the other arguments put forward are recognised in current international law as a basis for a right of secession.

143 Pons Rafols. Cataluña…, op. cit., p. 47. Resolution 742/IX, of 27 September 2012, of the Parliament of Catalonia:

> …Catalonia must start a new stage based in the right to decide. 3. The Parliament of Catalonia expresses the need for Catalonia to make its own path and that the Catalan people can decide freely and democratically their collective future, to guarantee social progress, economic development, democratic strengthening and the promotion of its own culture and language.

3 State creation and accession to statehood in international law

First lesson to bear in mind in secessionist attempts such as Catalonia's

The obvious goal of any secessionist entity, as is the case of Catalonia, is to become a State. In this respect, it is very important to bear in mind that determining accession to statehood, that is, the possibility of becoming a State, is a matter regulated exclusively by international law. For this reason, it is essential to carry out a detailed analysis of the relevant international rules and regulations – be they customary, conventional and/or institutional – and how they apply to secessionist attempts such as Catalonia's.

The aim of this chapter is to clearly explain the international laws governing the creation of new States, which constitute a handbook to be studied carefully by any secessionist entity that aspires to statehood; in our particular case study, by Catalonia. Yet it should also be consulted by all the States and international organisations that make up the international community when deciding how to react to the unilateral declarations of independence made by these secessionist entities.

The notion of State and statehood in the international sphere

The State constitutes the principal and undisputed subject of international law. It is both the origin and the core of this legal order, despite the many changes it has undergone throughout the history of international relations, particularly since the mid-twentieth century.

Therefore, the State and the notion of 'statehood' occupy a fundamental place in the structure of international law and are key to understanding this system, which is predominantly decentralised inasmuch as the international community is based on, among others, two basic principles that make States its subjects: the principle of sovereign equality and that of non-interference in internal affairs.

As a starting point, we believe it is necessary to address the concept or definition of 'State' and, therefore, of 'statehood', insofar as this will give us our first point of reference for determining the requirements or conditions that an entity aspiring to statehood must meet in order to actually become a State, particular attention being paid to the case of secession. And we will do so both from an academic point of view and from the perspective of the international legal order itself.

DOI: 10.4324/9781003200772-4

Academic approach to the notion of statehood

The indisputable prominence of the State has made the question of statehood in international law a favourite among jurists since time immemorial. Thus, we find that countless international law scholars have offered an explanation of what should be understood by 'State', contributing their own particular view of what it means. This has given rise to numerous and varied academic definitions of statehood. We will refer to just a few of them and do so from a historical perspective in order to trace the evolution of this concept, which is directly connected to that of the international legal order itself.

Hugo Grotius defined the State as a complete association of free men, joined together for the enjoyment of their rights and for their common interest[1]. In contrast, and only half a century later, Vitoria provided a much more juridical definition, albeit one still based on scholastic arguments, when he described a State as being:

> one which is complete in itself; that is, one which is not part of another community, but has its own laws and its own counsel and its own magistrates, such as the Kingdom of Castile and Aragon and the Republic of Venice, and which, as such a State, has the authority to declare war, itself alone and no one else[2].

It is important to note how this definition shows, even at this early stage, the emergence of government and independence as key components of statehood.

At the beginning of the positivist period, Vattel defined nations or States as bodies politic, societies of men united together for the purpose of promoting their mutual safety and advantage by their combined strength[3]. Following in the wake of Vitoria, Vattel indicates that one of the basic criteria of statehood is the fact that such nations are independent of others, thereby adding a further element: equality among nations. He understands equality in terms of each State being the sole arbiter of its rights and obligations under the law of nations. This also introduces a terminological component that had not emerged until then: this definition refers to the 'sovereign' State.

In the early twentieth century, Franz von Liszt wrote that independence (*Selbständigkeit*) and supremacy over territory (*Landeshoheit*) were indispensable attributes of the State[4]. A decade or so later, Fiore emphasised the need to combine both political power and law to give rise to the existence of a State:

1 Grotius, Hugo. *De Iure Belli ac Pacis*. 1646, p. xiv. Thomas Hobbes and Samuel von Pufendorf expressed similar views. All of them believed that natural law and the law of nations were the same.
2 Vitoria, Francisco. *De Indis ac de Iure Belli Relectiones*. Ed. Simon. 1696, pp. 425–426.
3 Vattel, Emer de. *Le Droit des Gens*. 1758, p. 15.
4 Liszt, Franz von. *Das Völkerrecht: Systematisch Dargestellt*. 1904, pp. 65–66.

> The State is an association of a considerable number of men living within a definite territory, constituted in fact as a political society and subject to the supreme authority of a sovereign, who has the power, ability and means to maintain the political organization of the association, with the assistance of the law, and to regulate and protect the rights of the members, to conduct relations with other states and to assume responsibility for its acts[5].

Baty, on referring to the State in 1930, put the emphasis on sovereignty, meaning the existence of an organised political power over a territory and a population. He also proposed as a criterion for statehood a characteristic resembling what we now understand as independence: "the existence among the people, or the bulk of the people, of a certain mutual reliance, not participated in by the outside world"[6].

Scelle, meanwhile, described the State as "une collectivité –fixée sur un territoire délimité–, juridiquement organisée"[7].

In the direction marked by Fiore, it was Kelsen who strove hardest to define statehood in terms of law, pointing to a new academic line that would eventually establish itself following the advent of the age of contemporary international law. Kelsen stated that:

> The state is not its individuals; it is the specific union of individuals, and this union is the function of the order which regulates their mutual behavior... One of the distinctive results of the pure theory of law is its recognition that the coercive order which constitutes the political community we call a state, is a legal order. What is usually called the legal order of the state, or the legal order set up by the state, is the state itself[8].

As we can see, the essence of the State for Kelsen is the existence of a legal system that exercises control over a territory and over the people living on that territory who are the population in the sense of positive international law. However, Kelsen's formulation does not emphasise the independence factor, as the previous definitions did. Nor does it emphasise territoriality, since he believed that territorial supremacy is less a criterion in itself than a reflection of its defining characteristics.

This promising Kelsenian definition of the State as a legal system fell out of favour after the Second World War, although the need to understand statehood in terms of law did come back into focus. Since then, few authors have played down the role of territory and population in accession to statehood as

5 Fiore, Pasquale. *International Law Codified and Its Legal Sanction or the Legal Organization of the Society State*. 1918, p. 106.
6 Baty, Thomas. *The Canons of International Law*. 1930, pp. 9–10.
7 Scelle, George. *Précis de Droit des Gens: Principes et Systématique*. Paris: Dalloz, 1932, p. 74.
8 Kelsen, Hans. "The Pure Theory of Law and Analytical Jurisprudence". *Harvard Law Review*, vol. 55, 1941–1942, pp. 64–65.

Kelsen did. In stark contrast, contemporary international law scholars are unanimous in demanding both elements among the criteria for statehood, together with the existence of a governmental organisation.

Among others, Lauterpacht[9] and Cavaré[10] put the emphasis on these factors. It is worth noting that although these authors do not expressly mention the need for international legality as a prerequisite for statehood, they do insinuate it. In subsequent editions of their handbooks, in the wake of the Rhodesian crisis of the 1960s, both assert that statehood, in addition to entailing effective control, requires compliance with certain international legal standards. Thus, we see how a new requirement for accession to statehood, as indicated previously by Kelsen, begins to emerge: respect for international legality. This condition has been accepted by contemporary scholars and now prevails in current international law.

Continuing with the introduction of new criteria for accession to statehood, from the 1970s onwards we find that various authors, especially from the English-speaking world, include the need for independence in their definitions of what constitutes a State, in addition to the three already widely accepted requirements of population, territory and governmental organisation. This is the case of Dahm, Delbrück and Wolfrum in Germany; Carter and Trimble in the United States; Higgins, Starke and Shearer in the United Kingdom; and Crawford in Australia; as well as Dinh, Dailier and Pellet in France[11]. In the opposing camp, many others believe that independence does not constitute a standalone criterion but instead is inseparable from the element of governmental power.

As regards Spanish academic opinion, it has also striven to provide a clear concept of statehood. In fact, we find that a significant number of legal scholars take the aforementioned three classic elements and add the note of sovereignty which appears linked to that of independence. This is the case, among others, of Sánchez Rodríguez, who states that:

> The conception of the State as a legal phenomenon presupposes the existence of a human community, politically organised on a territory; this necessary condition is not, however, sufficient. What characterises the State as a singular entity is that it is not subject to any foreign power or authority; it is the note of *sovereignty*... Sovereignty is an attribute that the international order recognises solely in States, and for sovereignty to exist, it is necessary that they be independent[12].

9 Lauterpacht, Hersch. *Oppenheim, International Law: A Treatise*. London, 8th ed., 1955, pp. 118–123.

10 Cavaré, Louis. *Le Droit International Public Positif*. 1962, pp. 253–303.

11 See the reference in Grant, Thomas. "Defining Statehood: The Montevideo Convention and its Discontents". *Columbia Journal of Transnational Law*, vol. 37, 1998–1999, pp. 412–413.

12 González Campos, Julio D., Luis Ignacio Sánchez Rodríguez and Paz Andrés Sáenz de Santa María. *Curso de Derecho Internacional Público*. Madrid: Civitas, 2008,

A similar assessment can be gleaned from a reading of Latin American legal scholarship. Both Barboza and Pagliari, among others, take the traditionally accepted triumvirate and add a fourth element: sovereignty. The latter-mentioned author also introduces respect for international legality as a condition for accession to statehood[13].

At this point it is clear that, in terms of attempting to provide a definition of 'State', the contribution of legal scholarship is of great value. Having analysed it we can conclude that, beyond the logical historical evolution, there is currently absolute academic unanimity regarding the necessary concurrence of three constituent elements: population, territory and governmental organisation. At the same time, we see, on the one hand, a lack of consistency in relation to other possible criteria and, on the other, the emergence of a fourth condition: legality in the formation process.

The existence of the State in the international legal framework. The Montevideo criteria

States are both political and legal entities. When an entity accedes to statehood, it acquires full international legal personality with all the rights and duties this entails. It follows, therefore, that the creation of the State constitutes a fact, but an international legal fact with its corresponding legal effects. This being so, it is only logical that its formation be regulated by international law. And international law does not disregard accession to statehood.

Therefore, for the purpose of determining when a new State comes into being, what really matters are the relevant provisions of international law, and not so much academic opinion, although its constant effort to take account of or reflect the law means that it should not be dismissed. In this respect, we should highlight the evident paucity of written international law sources that offer a clear and practical definition of what a State is. In fact, there is no treaty or resolution of universal scope on the subject. There is, however, a text that is commonly accepted and cited, both by legal scholars and by States themselves, as a textual basis for determining accession to statehood: the Convention on the Rights and Duties of States, adopted in Montevideo on 26 December 1933[14], and, in particular, Article 1, which reads as follows:

p. 426. In the same vein, see Díez de Velasco, Manuel, *Instituciones de Derecho internacional Público*. Madrid: Tecnos, 2009, or Remiro Brotons, Antonio et al. *Derecho internacional*. Madrid: MacGraw Hill, 1997.

13 Barboza, Julio. *Derecho internacional público*. Buenos Aires: Zavalía, 2001, p. 201; Pagliari, Arturo S. *Curso de Derecho internacional público*. Córdoba: Advocatus, 2nd ed., 2013, p. 254.

14 League of Nations Treaty Series, vol. 165, p. 19. The States that signed this Convention were: Honduras, United States, El Salvador, Dominican Republic, Haiti, Argentina, Venezuela, Uruguay, Mexico, Panama, Bolivia, Guatemala, Brazil, Ecuador, Nicaragua, Colombia, Chile, Peru and Cuba.

The State as a person of international law should possess the following qualifications:

I. a permanent population;
II. a defined territory;
III. government; and
IV. capacity to enter into relations with the other states.

There is no doubt that, since being adopted at the Seventh International Conference of American States, this provision has been and continues to be the reference point for defining statehood and determining the requirements a State must meet in order to be considered as such. Following its signing in 1933, it was cited repeatedly over the next two decades[15]. Even today, the elements of statehood offered by the Montevideo Convention are still the benchmark in matters of statehood. In this respect, Crawford states that this article is "the best known formulation of the basic criteria for statehood"[16].

However, there are those who question the universal validity of the Montevideo criteria because the Convention is a regional agreement signed by only 16 States. In this regard, we should emphasise that international practice on this issue leads us to conclude that this provision reflects general customary law. This is considered to be the case by legal scholars and States alike. Along these lines, some States have included its content in their own domestic legislation, one example being the United States, whose Restatement (third) defines the State according to international law, in Article 201, as follows:

> Under International Law, a state is an entity that has a defined territory and a permanent population, under the control of its own government and the engages in, or has the capacity to engage in, formal relations with other such entities[17].

Similarly, if we analyse international practice in relation to recognition of new States, we find that a large majority of the recognitions given by States expressly mention fulfilment of the qualifications set out in Article 1 of the Montevideo Convention on the part of the entity to be recognised[18]. Jurisprudence had occasion to rule likewise some years before the Convention was

15 Grant. "Defining Statehood…", op. cit. pp. 413–414.
16 Crawford, James. *The Creation of States in International Law.* Oxford: Oxford University Press, 1st ed., 1979, p. 36.
17 Restatement (Third) of the Foreign Relations Law of the United States, vol.1, 1987, p. 72. As also stated in Restatement (Second) of 1965.
18 This can be seen in the First Report of the International Law Association's Committee on Recognition and Non-recognition, presented at the Sofia Conference in 2012 (International Law Association, Report of the Seventy-Fifth Conference, Sofia, 2012, pp. 164–198).

adopted. The Judgment delivered on 1 August 1929 by the German-Polish Mixed Arbitral Tribunal declares that:

> a State exists only on the condition that it possesses a territory, a human community that inhabits said territory, a public power that is exerted over that community and that territory. These conditions are recognised as indispensable and a State cannot be conceived of without them[19].

To underline this customary quality, we can also mention that Fitzmaurice, the Special Rapporteur of the International Law Commission (ILC) in charge of codifying Treaty Law, included the following definition in his proposed Article 3:

> For the purposes of the present Code… the term 'State'
>
> i means an entity consisting of a people inhabiting a defined territory, under an organized system of government, and having the capacity to enter into international relations […]
>
> ii includes the government of the State[20].

We believe it is important to emphasise that, while there is no doubt about the existence of a customary norm, such a statement clearly encompasses only the first three criteria mentioned – population, territory and government – in respect of which there is consensus and widespread acceptance. It is far more difficult to reach the same conclusion about the fourth criterion, given that international practice is not consistent enough for it to be considered a qualification for achieving statehood. Some States have questioned whether it is really an autonomous element in itself, maintaining that capacity to enter into relations with others is a consequence of acquiring statehood. This is why it is commonly regarded as the 'most questionable' of the four elements of the Montevideo formula.

Forms of State creation established by contemporary international law

From a historical point of view, States have emerged in a wide variety of ways: through a foundational process of political integration that overcame feudal polycentrism; by emancipation; by war; by treaties; by decisions of other States[21].

At present, according to the provisions of positive law, new States can appear in the international sphere as a result of one of the modes of what is known as 'succession of States'. This phenomenon, according to the definition given by the Vienna Conventions on Succession of States – in Article 2 of each Convention – refers to "the replacement of one State by another in the responsibility for the international relations of territory": the (new) successor State

19 Case no. 1877, 2 (1/2) *ZaöRV*, 1930, part 2, p. 22.
20 ILC Yearbook, 1956-II, p. 107.
21 Pagliari, op. cit., pp. 299–300.

replaces the (previous) predecessor State in the exercise of sovereignty over the territory in question; that is, there is a change in territorial sovereignty.

In this respect, following the typology established by the ILC in its effort to codify the various problems generated by succession of States, and set out in the two resultant Vienna Conventions to which we have just referred – in respect of treaties (1978) and in respect of property, archives and debts (1983) –, we can identify four forms of succession that result in the emergence of a new State in the international arena. The first of these concerns the phenomenon of decolonisation; the other three are forms of creation based on the territory of a pre-existing State.

Newly independent States

Despite the confusing terminology that might lead one to think that this category would include any entity that declares itself independent for the first time (secessionist entities, for instance), it is important to clarify that it refers only to non-self-governing territories – colonies – that accede to independence, thereby becoming new States; and that they do so by exercising their right of self-determination of peoples – in its external application – recognised for the first time in Resolution 1514 (XV) of the UNGA. There are copious examples of this practice, the latest being that of the Democratic Republic of Timor-Leste, a territory that gained independence in 2002 following the self-determination referendum held in 1999. It is clear, therefore, that secession does not fit into this category and that decolonisation is not an example of secession. As soon as non-self-governing territories cease to be subject to the sovereignty of the colonial power and have a separate and distinct existence from the State that administers them, it is no longer possible to speak of secession when they declare themselves independent States.

Unification and absorption

Unification occurs when two or more States voluntarily decide to merge, thereby forming a new successor State, which coincides with the disappearance of all the predecessor States. This is the case of North Yemen (Mutawakkilite Kingdom of Yemen, 1918) and South Yemen (People's Democratic Republic of Yemen, 1967) which merged in 1990 to form the new Republic of Yemen. By contrast, in the case of absorption, although the result is also the voluntary union of two or more States, the process differs in that it is one of the States that absorbs the other (s), keeping its international legal personality intact; whereas the absorbed State or States disappear(s) to become part of the former, which becomes responsible for the international relations of the territory of the predecessor States[22]. This is what

22 The possibility of *annexation*, that is, adding one State to another through the use of armed force – very frequent in the history of international relations before 1945 (as suffered by, among others, Austria, Czechoslovakia, Ethiopia and Poland) – is totally excluded and prohibited under contemporary international law for being a violation of a *jus cogens* norm; as expressly stated in Resolution 2625 (XXV).

happened with the German Democratic Republic, voluntarily absorbed by the Federal Republic of Germany in 1990.

Separation

Separation is when one or more part(s) of the territory of a (predecessor) State separate(s) from it and form(s) a new (successor) State with the consent or assent of the former, which continue(s) to exist. A recent example is Montenegro, which separated from Serbia in 2006. In the event of a separation without consent or agreement, it cannot be considered a *strictu sensu* separation, which we refer to in this section and which is provided for by international law. This is because the two Vienna Conventions of 1978 and 1983, which regulate this matter, as we have mentioned, and are therefore the reference texts in this respect, expressly state – in Articles 6 and 3, respectively and identically – that they apply "only to the effects of a succession of States occurring in conformity with international law and, in particular, the principles of international law embodied in the Charter of the United Nations"; it follows that when we speak of secession we are referring to a disintegration of a part of the territory of a State that has not been consented to or agreed upon by the latter, i.e. that is in violation of the principle of territorial integrity of the predecessor State – a principle of international law embodied in the Charter of the United Nations – and therefore outside the scope of the international law referred to.

Dissolution

Dissolution occurs when a (predecessor) State dissolves and ceases to exist, with two or more successor States forming the parts of its territory. The best-known recent examples are the dismemberment of the USSR (Agreement of 8 December 1991 and Alma-Ata Protocol of 21 December 1991) and the latest break-up of Czechoslovakia (Agreement of 31 December 1992), which gave rise to the new States of Slovakia and the Czech Republic.

The constituent material elements of a State

Taking as reference points the provisions of the Montevideo Convention, as well as international practice and the different academic opinions on the matter, we will now present and analyse the traditional material elements that must necessarily coincide for a given entity to achieve statehood, with a view to possible problems that secession might pose in this regard.

Permanent population. Some problems this concept poses in the case of secession

The State is a human community that does not exist without a population. This is obvious, since the exercise of government authority requires the existence of a group of people over whom it can be deployed. However, the population need not be composed of nationals. This criterion refers to the human element of the State, i.e. the set of people – both nationals and aliens – who inhabit permanently the territory of the State, and among whom multiple relations coexist. In terms of number and density, the population of a State varies considerably from one to another. In this respect, international law does not prescribe a minimum population size. This is proved by the fact that there are States with extremely small populations, as is the case of what are known as 'micro-states': Liechtenstein, Micronesia, Marshall Islands, San Marino, Andorra, Palau and Tuvalu, contrasting with the world's most populous states, such as China, India, the United States, Indonesia, Brazil and Russia. Some States are very densely populated, such as Monaco, while others are very sparsely populated, such as Australia. What international law does require is that the population residing on a territory be of a stable and permanent nature. In this respect, Brownlie points out that this "criterion is intended to be used in association with that of territory, and connotes a stable community"[23].

As for determining who the nationals of a State are, it is clear that granting and regulating *nationality* is an attribute of the State and depends on its domestic laws. As the Permanent Court of International Justice stated in its advisory opinion on the *nationality decrees issued in Tunisia and Morocco*, "in the present state of international law, questions of nationality are … in principle within this reserved domain"[24]. In other words, nationality depends on the existence of the State and not vice versa. The creation of the nationality link is, therefore, the corollary of the existence of the State. Once it has acceded to statehood, each State determines freely the conditions that must be met for the acquisition and loss of nationality of natural persons, legal persons and the objects subject to its authority.

Such a legal situation sometimes poses major *problems* when a new State emerges on the territory of another State that continues to exist – particularly in cases of separation and secession –, in relation to the nationals of the predecessor State who habitually reside in that territory. Take, for example, the events that followed Eritrea's separation from Ethiopia, and the problems of loss and/or suspension of nationality suffered by many Ethiopian nationals residing in the new Eritrean territory, which eventually had to be settled by the Eritrea-Ethiopia Claims Commission, the principle of nationality by estoppel playing a fundamental role in its decision[25]. Several questions arise in this context: Do they keep their nationality? Do they lose their previous nationality and automatically acquire that of the new State? Do they become stateless? This is an issue that should be resolved by agreement between the two States, which is feasible in the case of an agreed separation, but extremely difficult to achieve in a case of secession from a territory without the consent of the parent

23 Brownlie, Ian. *Principles of Public International Law*. Oxford: Clarendon Press, 7th ed., 1998, p. 71.

24 PCIJ, Series B, no. 4, p. 24.

25 Award of 17 December 2004 (ILM, vol. 44, pp. 601–610).

State. This can lead to a clash of contradictory domestic laws, triggering problems of statelessness or multiple nationalities.

In order to ensure greater legal certainty and reach a solution that does not violate the rights of the individuals concerned – in particular their right to nationality as recognised in Article 15 of the 1948 Universal Declaration of Human Rights –, it is important to bear in mind the United Nations General Assembly Resolution adopting the Sixth Committee's report on "Nationality of natural persons in relation to the succession of States"[26], which was based on the ILC's 1999 draft on the subject and whose chief goal is to avoid situations of statelessness[27]. This instrument stems from the recognition of the right to nationality (Article 1) and recommends that the States concerned take into account the will of the persons concerned – nationals of the predecessor State – whose usual place of abode is in the territory of the new State, and grant them the right to choose between maintaining the nationality of the former or acquiring that of the new State, provided that they meet the conditions required for this purpose (Articles 11 and 24). This solution is based on the customary norm, recalled by the ICJ in the *Nottebohm* case, according to which nationality requires the existence of a genuine link between the person and the State. In the Court's opinion, nationality constitutes expression of the fact that the individual on whom it has been conferred is in fact more closely connected with the population of that State than with that of any other[28]. As regards its composition, the population might be homogeneous or heterogeneous; in practice it could encompass a diversity of races, religions, economic levels, etc., notwithstanding the predominance of a homogeneous majority that serves as a basis for the national consciousness[29]. In the context of this heterogeneity, a nomadic people can be considered a permanent population, as the ICJ stated in its Advisory Opinion on Western Sahara[30].

Sometimes, population composition poses the problem of *minorities*, i.e. groups that, because of their race, religion, nationality, culture, etc., differ from the majority population group and are sometimes subjected to legislative

26 Resolution A/55/153, of 30 January 2001, adopted on the basis of the Sixth Committee's report (A/55/610).

27 The ILC's work on succession of States and its impact on the nationality of individuals was included in its agenda in 1993. Initially, the aim was to address the nationality of individuals as well as groups, but in 1996 the General Assembly recommended that its work should focus solely on natural persons and not on legal persons.

When the Draft Articles were adopted in 1999, the ILC recommended that they be approved in the form of a General Assembly declaration instead of a Convention, as is customary in the codification process. This proposal undoubtedly stems from the fact that although nationality problems resulting from succession of States concern the international community, regulation of the acquisition of nationality is an exclusive competence of each State.

28 ICJ Reports 1955, pp. 20–26.

29 Pagliari. op. cit., p. 254.

30 ICJ Reports 1975, p. 40.

discrimination on such grounds. This situation is particularly significant in cases of *secession*, especially in relation to the population that maintains the nationality of the predecessor State.

It is important to emphasise that minorities must be respected, both as a group and in relation to their constituent individual members; their identity must be recognised and their rights respected, as provided for in international law. In this regard, general consideration should be given to the provisions of the Declaration on the Rights of Persons Belonging to National or Ethnic, Religious and Linguistic Minorities, adopted by the General Assembly on 18 December 1992[31], and derived from Article 27 of the ICCPR of 1966; and, in the European setting, to the Framework Convention for the Protection of National Minorities (No. 157 of the Council of Europe), adopted at Strasbourg on 1 February 1995, to which Spain is a party. In this respect, it is important to stress that there is a customary norm of general international law which establishes that, in the event of succession of States – except in the case of newly independent States – the *principle of continuity of the treaties* to which the predecessor State was a party applies. Consequently, new successor States remain bound by the international treaties to which they were bound previously. This means that if a territorial entity separates, for example, from a State that is party to the 1995 Convention – as is the case of Spain – and accedes to statehood, it must comply with the provisions of that Convention in respect of the resulting minorities in that new State; in addition to all the human rights treaties that also address the issue.

Defined territory

Territory is an essential condition *sine qua non* for the birth, existence and persistence of a State, which cannot be conceived of without a territorial foundation. States are territorial entities and therefore require a physical, spatial and geographical basis in order to exist as such. As Philip C. Jessup stated, the need for this essential attribute is explained by the fact that a State cannot be represented in the form of a sort of disembodied spirit[32].

The concept of territory has evolved hand in hand with international society. At present we can define it as the spatial area over which the State exercises its powers fully, autonomously and exclusively; it is the physical basis of territorial sovereignty. This means that it is the area or space where the State exercises both its authority over the territory itself and its control over the persons located and the situations arising thereon. As Judge Huber stated in *the Island of Palmas case*, "territorial sovereignty… involves the exclusive right to display the activities of a State"[33]. With this definition in mind, from a spatial perspective it

31 Resolution 47/135.

32 A statement he made as US representative during the Security Council's deliberations on the admission of Israel as a member of the UN (Doc. N.U. S/FV 383rd session, 2 December 1948, p. 11).

33 Award of 4 April 1928 (RIAA Vol. II, p. 838).

can be said that the State's territory includes a necessarily terrestrial, possibly maritime, and complementary aerial dimension.

The Montevideo Convention refers to the existence of a defined territory. In this respect, as with population, international law does not establish a minimum size, as proved by the existence of States with a very small territory, such as the Vatican, Monaco, Liechtenstein and San Marino, contrasting with the vast territorial extent of Russia, China, Australia, Brazil, the United States and Canada, which account for 90% of the planet's land surface. What is essential is that there be a defined and basically stable territory, no matter how small. Whether or not this territory should have clearly defined borders is a different matter. In this connection, the Mixed Arbitral Tribunal that settled the *Deutsche Continental Gas-Gesellschaft v Polish State* case (1929) held that "In order to say that a State exists and can be recognised as such ... it is enough that ... [its] territory has a sufficient consistency, even though its boundaries have not yet been accurately delimited"[34].

Four decades later, the ICJ confirmed in the *North Sea Continental Shelf* case that international law does not require the boundaries of a State to be fully delimited and defined[35].

It is clear, therefore, that although the existence of a territory is necessary, it is not essential that all the borders be precisely defined. Proof of this is that no one doubts the existence of China as a State, even though long stretches of its border with its neighbours remain undefined – a situation it has in common with many other States. Indeed, numerous States have come into being and been admitted as members of the United Nations without having clearly defined borders; such is the case of Israel, Mauritania and Kuwait. Similarly, the existence of territorial or border disputes in relation to a new State is not an obstacle to its being considered as such, unless such a dispute affects the whole of the territory claimed by the State, in which case this territorial element would not be fulfilled. Having a defined territory does not necessarily mean that it is recognised, delimited and, even less, demarcated[36]. The indispensable requirement is that the State should have a certain defined territory governed effectively.

Government

The third of the elements required for the existence of a State lies in government, according to the Montevideo terminology. However, it would be more accurate and closer to reality to refer to it as a political, institutional and effective organisation through which the functions of public authority can be carried out on its territory and over the national population.

34 Annual Digest of Public International Law, no. 5, pp. 14–15.
35 ICJ Reports 1969, para. 3 and para. 32.
36 Remiro Brotons. op. cit., p. 45.

It is very important to bear in mind that the organisation of political power does not boil down to what is known as executive power but to the plurality of bodies, authorities and powers that express sovereign power in the political and legal order. In other words, in order to accede to statehood, it is imperative that the aspiring entity be equipped with all the organs of the various spheres – executive, judicial, legislative, administrative, police, military, etc. – through which it can exercise public power, which is a quality inherent in the nature of the State, and which manifests itself internally as supreme power, and externally as independence. In this regard, as Pagliari indicates[37], the 'government' element implies having sufficient institutional apparatus capable of imposing actions backed by legal sanction and, where appropriate, the use of force. It has the nature of a legal power, and the institutionalisation of power allows the decisions taken by those in power to be legally attributed to the State. This legal power is autonomous, centralised and territorially defined. The *legality* of power materialises as soon as it is exercised through the imperatives of the law and of legal coercion. It is *autonomous* because it does not recognise in law the existence of a higher power, defining itself as independent outwardly and supreme inwardly. It is *centralised* because it emanates from a single clearly defined core, from which stems the hierarchy of the other powers of a society. All of its constituent institutions have a common focal point that representatively personifies the unity of the State. The *territorial determination* of State power is a consequence of coexistence with the other States that make up the international community.

For international law, the form of government or its particular organisation, even decentralisation, is irrelevant; this is a domestic matter. In this respect, Resolution 2625 (XXV) states that "every State has the inalienable right to choose its political system". In a similar vein, the ICJ stated in its *Advisory Opinion on Western Sahara* that no rule of international law requires the State to have a particular structure. What matters is the effective exercise of power, with full jurisdiction and exclusive authority over the population and the territory[38]. What is required, therefore, is that this institutional apparatus, whatever its form, perform all the activities proper to the State, including that of participating in international society. For this supreme decision-making power, which is the element of government, is not limited to exercising its authority in the territorial sphere but, from the point of view of international law, must also have the capacity to interact with other State entities in creating and applying the law. This requires appropriate institutional bodies. The same occurs when there is a serious breakdown in international relations, because in order to preserve territorial integrity against the use of force by other States, internal political power must translate into security and defence services that guarantee a minimum of permanence in the face of foreign aggression.

37 Pagliari. op. cit., p. 256.
38 ICJ Reports 1975, p. 43.

Capacity to enter into relations with other States

A State's capacity to engage in international relations with other States basically means it can not only obtain advantages from other States but also grant them. In other words, it must be able to grant rights to other States and to exercise the obligations inherent in statehood. This obviously requires reciprocity, and so to some extent, achieving this objective may depend on obtaining recognition from other States. It is important to bear in mind that there is no obligation for any State to establish relations with other States, therefore the existence or absence of such relations depends on the will of already existing States.

According to Crawford, this is not so much a preliminary element as a consequence of statehood. He maintains that the capacity to enter into relations with other States is a prerogative of the State[39]. This assertion may be questionable in the current context of international law, insofar as there are certain 'non-State' subjects that also have the capacity to enter into relations with States; this is the case of insurgents and national liberation movements. Irrespective of the opportuneness of Crawford's affirmation, we understand that this element actually refers to having the necessary government apparatus to be able to establish inter-state relations and not so much to the fact of maintaining such relations, for which purpose it is necessary to have an effective and independent government. If we go by the description we have developed in relation to government, we see how part of it is political power needing sufficient apparatus to allow it to participate in international society, having the capacity to interact with other State entities, and being capable of ensuring the stability of international relations vis-à-vis other States. This encompasses the fourth Montevideo criterion.

Some jurists who deny the autonomous nature of this element consider that it is contained within a broader notion of something else the State must have: *independence*. We understand that independence, which is fundamental for accession to statehood, is not an element added to the three traditional ones, but that it is inherent in the element relating to the existence of government. For, as we have ascertained, the latter must consist of a definitive and foundational power in the sense that its authority neither derives from nor depends on any other State group, i.e. that it is independent.

Other possible elements indicated by legal scholarship, with special reference to the necessary independence of secessionist entities in accession to statehood

For some jurists, the existence of a State requires an additional criterion: *sovereignty*. By this we mean having full powers, which implies a supreme power (*suprema potestas*) in the sense of the State not being subject to an internal or external authority or power that could be considered superior.

39 Crawford. *The Creation of States…* 2nd ed., p. 61.

In our opinion, sovereignty should not be considered as a fourth element added to the three traditional ones. Instead, and very much on the contrary, it is inherent in and a consequence of their existence and, therefore, of the State. It is a fundamental principle of the international legal order from which arise most of the other structural principles set out in Article 2 of the UN Charter and Resolution 2625 (XXV). It is the most characteristic feature of the international community. Its essence is the right to exercise the functions of the State on a plane of independence and equality with respect to other States. As Salmon rightly points out, sovereignty is a concept that applies equally to all States from the moment they accede to statehood, whatever the size of their territory and population, whatever the form and nature of their government[40].

Other authors insist on the need to add the element of independence, that is, non-dependence on any other external authority, or with respect to any other State or States. We had occasion to confirm this in the first part of the section devoted to the academic approach to the notion of statehood (see p. 130). Currently, it is Crawford who most insists on the need for this element. For this author, independence is the central criterion for statehood[41]. Following Huber, he takes it to mean the right to exercise State functions within the territory, to the exclusion of any other State. Thus considered, it is evident that autonomous deployment of all governmental power over the territory and the population is key to acceding to statehood. If an entity is not independent, that is, if there exists another State that is actually operating on the territory on which the new State intends to establish itself, that controls the deployment of the aforementioned governmental power, then accession to statehood is impossible. The 'separate existence' of the entity aspiring to statehood is necessary in order for it to become a State.

Independence, moreover, must be *formal* and *functional*. Formal independence exists when the powers that govern a territory are held by authorities separate from the State. Functional independence exists when a certain minimum level of real power is exercised by the State's authorities. Formal independence without functional independence is not sufficient to be able to conclude that the entity is independent in its actions. The 1928 report of the Committee of Jurists on the case of the Åland Islands is highly instructive in this regard. After highlighting the conditions of revolution and internal disorder that had prevailed in Finland up until that time, it states:

> It is therefore difficult to say at what exact date the Finnish Republic in the legal sense of the term actually became a definitely **constituted sovereign state. This certainly did not take place until a stable political organization had been created, and until the public authorities had become strong enough to assert themselves**

40 Salmon, Jean. "L'État dans le droit international d'aujourd'hui". *Recueil des Cours*, vol. 347, 2010, p. 57.

41 Crawford. *The Creation*... 2nd ed., op. cit., p. 62.

> **throughout the territories of the state without the assistance of foreign troops**[42].

Regarding this important aspect, the key is knowing how to assess whether independence has been obtained. George Canning formulates the test in the following manner:

> … that such State shall have shown itself substantially capable of maintaining an independent existence, of carrying on a Government of its own, of controlling its own military and naval forces, and of being responsible to other nations for the observance of international laws and the discharge of international duties.
>
> These are questions of fact. By acknowledgement we can only acknowledge what is. We have never recognized in Spanish America any State in whose territory the dominion of the mother-country has not been practically extinguished, and which has not established some form of government with which we could treat[43].

Determining whether the necessary independence exists is particularly significant in the case of *secession*. A new State can only be constituted as such and considered definitively created if it demonstrates total independence (not only formal but real) in respect of the State it previously formed part of. If the parent State still exercises some kind of power over that territory, it is clear that its sovereignty over the territory in question has yet to be extinguished and that, therefore, the secessionist entity has not achieved real independence; therefore, the aspiring State cannot accede to statehood.

Likewise, if the secessionist entity has a 'sponsor' State which has supported it in its attempt to secede, and which actually controls the seceded territory in such a way that the entity depends on that State to be able to exercise governmental power, that entity has not achieved the independence necessary to obtain statehood in the international arena. This would be the case of the Turkish Republic of Northern Cyprus (TRNC) in relation to Turkey, which is its 'sponsor' State; or of Abkhazia and South Ossetia in relation to Russia.

In relation to independence, we should point out that some descriptions of it veer closer to sovereignty than to independence. Judge Anzilotti, in his individual opinion in the advisory opinion on the *Austro-German customs regime*, linked independence to existence "comme État séparé et non soumis à l'autorité d'aucun autre État ou groupe d'États"[44]. Along these lines, Rousseau noted that independence implies exclusiveness, autonomy and full power[45]. In

42 League of Nations Off. J., Spec. Supp. No. 3, at 3 (1920). Bold is ours.
43 British and Foreign State Papers, vol. 49, p. 1216.
44 Advisory Opinion of 5 September 1931. PCIJ, Series A/B, no. 41, p. 57.
45 Rousseau. op. cit., p. 72. "Independence is both the condition and the criterion of sovereignty; once this is recognised by a community that also has the attributes of a State entity … sovereignty will in turn act as the guarantor of independence. The

this regard, we observe a certain confusion and conflation between sovereignty and independence in some academic quarters. Following Salmon, we can affirm that sovereignty is a legal concept distinct from independence or political power. And it is necessary to draw a distinction between the two. We are dealing with two State characteristics that, although very closely linked, correspond to two substantially different moments in the process of acceding to statehood. On the one hand, if we recall what the third Montevideo qualification consists of, we can clearly see how independence forms part of it, as we have already pointed out. More precisely, we can affirm that the State is not definitively constituted until, on a given territory, a government apparatus is established that is capable of effectively controlling the population that occupies it, without any kind of external control, i.e. an independent government apparatus. It is in this sense that independence is a requirement of statehood. Once this is achieved, the State becomes a sovereign entity which, in turn, is also independent.

We could say that if independence is the criterion for sovereignty, then sovereignty is the guarantee of independence. Which demonstrates the close connection between the two. They are different concepts but inextricably linked. P.M. Dupuy explains this situation very well:

> L'indépendance est à la fois la condition et le critère de la souveraineté; une fois celle-ci reconnue à une collectivité possédant par ailleurs les attributs de l'entité étatique… le souveraineté jouera à son tour comme le garant de l'indépendance. Celle dernière constitue une situation de pur fait, mais la souveraineté en constitue la formalisation juridique[46].

In other words, we must distinguish the dual role that independence plays in the State process. On the one hand, it is a fundamental qualification for becoming a State, linked to the element of government. On the other hand, once statehood has been achieved, independence is a right of the State which, along with sovereignty and equality, also forms part of its legal status.

Finally, we can draw attention to the fact that other authors refer to the need for other requirements to converge in order to be able to speak of the existence of a State, such as the socio-ethical purpose it should pursue as an organised political community, a certain degree of civilisation, or the protection of human rights; specifically, it would be a matter of an entity that is unwilling to respect human rights or incapable of doing so not being able to accede to statehood. We believe that there is no international practice that vouches for such criteria being constitutive elements of statehood. Where we do find reference to some of these criteria is in the context of recognition of States, in the sense

latter constitutes a situation of pure fact, but sovereignty constitutes its legal formalisation" (author's translation).

46 Dupuy, Pierre-Marie. "L'unité de l'ordre juridique international: Cours général de droit international public". *Recueil des Cours*, vol. 297, 2002, p. 95.

that some States, availing themselves of what is known as 'conditional recognition', make their recognition of new States conditional on the latter fulfilling certain conditions such as guaranteeing human rights or having a democratic political regime[47].

The decisive role of the principle of effectiveness in accession to statehood and its particular expression in the case of secession

In view of our analysis of the 'Montevideo criteria' and of other possible elements, it is easy to reach a number of important *conclusions*. On the one hand, all the material elements of the State are closely interlinked, since each one complements the others in the process of acceding to statehood: a group of people without a territory cannot become a State and vice versa; and a government cannot exist without a territory and a population, because the political and legal authority has to exercise its obligations over a certain group of people and a defined territory. On the other hand, notwithstanding the previous elements, it seems evident that to some extent they all revolve around the element of government authority – assuming the necessary independence of public power is inherent therein – and are even subsumed in it. This might lead to the third criterion of 'government' itself being considered the central material element of statehood.

Likewise, we have seen how the ascertainment of each and every one of the material elements of the State requires them to possess an essential condition: *effectiveness*. As Cançado Trindade indicates[48], such factual preconditions of statehood arise from and are essentially based in the principle of effectiveness. This being so, effectiveness plays a crucial role in the concept of statehood and in accession thereto. Therefore, we believe it is necessary to address this aspect in detail, with particular reference to its significance in the case of secessionist entities aspiring to statehood.

The function of the principle of effectiveness in State creation

The principle of effectiveness can be defined as that which allows international law to establish certain circumstances in 'facts and/or conditions' and thereby attribute legal consequences to certain real situations. Thus understood, it is clear that the principle of effectiveness plays an important role in many areas of

47 This happened after the break-up of the USSR when the then 12 Member States of the European Community, through a joint declaration in 1991, made recognition of the new States, among other aspects, conditional on their respect for human rights (Declaration on the "Guidelines on the Recognition of New States in Eastern Europe and in the Soviet Union," 16 December 1991, *ILM*, vol. 1486, no. 31, 1992).

48 Cançado Trindade, Augusto Antonio. "International Law for Humankind: Towards a New *Ius gentium*. General Course on Public International Law". *Recueil des Cours*, vol. 316, 2005, p. 205.

the international legal order, such as: creation of laws (effective practice is necessary for custom to arise), acquisition of territorial sovereignty (effective possession), occupation, blockade, diplomatic protection (effective exhaustion of domestic remedies and genuine link of nationality in order to exercise it), international responsibility (link between effective control and the attribution of the act) or in the field of human rights.

And as is only to be expected, it is decisive in the accession to statehood of an aspiring entity, which imperatively needs to have an effective government. We focus on the element of *effective government* because, as we have already noted, this is the defining element of statehood par excellence, around which the others revolve.

This requirement of effective government produces, as Sánchez Rodríguez points out[49], the following legal effects. From a negative point of view, the lack of an organised form of government in a given territory makes it unlikely for that territory to belong to a State, to be its physical foundation. In this respect, tribes or nomadic groups that are not politically organised have a certain legal personality but cannot really be classified as having effective governments, as described earlier, and therefore they are not States in the strict sense of the term[50]. From a positive point of view, the existence of effective government over a territory and its continuity over time constitute a presumption of the existence of a State in that territory and is an indispensable requirement for engaging in international relations. Likewise, it may so happen that internal upheavals in the territory of a State prevent the effective exercise of government power thereon, as a result of internal clashes between belligerent groups that seek either to overthrow the established government or simply destabilise the peace that has existed hitherto (Afghanistan with groups confronting the Taliban Government, Somalia, etc.). In some of these cases, the situation of government ineffectiveness reaches such an extreme point that we can describe these States as 'failed'. Finally, in cases where different groups control part or parts of the territory of a State and become, for some States, the actual government (Taiwan for example, which is considered by some States, such as Honduras, as the true government representative of China); or where a part of the territory of a State seeks to secede in order to become an independent State by obtaining recognition as such from certain States (the case of Kosovo). In such cases there is also an alteration of the effectiveness of State power that will significantly affect its foreign relations, depending on the recognition received from other States in each case.

Therefore, given the importance of effective government, the first question to ask relates to the meaning of effectiveness. In this regard, we can point out that the concept of effectiveness refers to what is real and true, as opposed to

49 In González Campos, Julio D., Luis Ignacio Sánchez Rodríguez and Paz Andrés Sáenz de Santa María. Curso de Derecho Internacional Público. Madrid: Civitas, 2008, p. 430.

50 Advisory Opinion on Western Sahara, ICJ Reports, 1975, p. 39.

what is fanciful or dubious; its meaning is closely linked to realities, certainties, guarantees, actions, power, as opposed to what is apparent, illusory or ineffective.

And what does this mean when applied to the emergence of new States? This question is the key to determining as from which specific moment we are in the presence of a new State. Here we should point out that in spite of the importance of effectiveness in this sphere, there is very little literature on the subject. No doubt this is because it is a difficult concept to pin down and define objectively, together with the fact that, as Couveinhes-Matsumoto points out, the principle of effectiveness is a malleable argument, whose invocation is accounted for by political and unpredictable considerations[51]. The most objective reference we find is that made by the Permanent Mandates Commission of the League of Nations, in its document entitled "Conditions générales à prévoir avant qu'il puisse être mis fin au régime du mandat dans un pays placé sous ce régime". According to the Commission, the conditions whereby a territory under mandate becomes a State are as follows:

a Être doté d'un gouvernement constitué et d'une administration propre à assurer le fonctionnement régulier des services essentiels de l'État;
b Être capable de maintenir son intégrité territoriale et son indépendance politique;
c Être en mesure d'assurer la tranquillité publique dans toute l'étendue du territoire;
d Être assuré de disposer de ressources financières telles qu'elles puissent régulièrement pourvoir aux besoins normaux de l'État;
e Posséder une législation et une organisation judiciaire qui assurent une justice régulière à tous les justiciables[52].

As we have just said, the question to be answered is: *When can we say that effective government exists*? As a first answer we could say that there must be a government with sufficient legal authority and effectiveness to undertake the external and internal functions of the State, that is, to ensure both material and legal order. And when can we say that there exists a government with sufficient

51 Couveinhes-Matsumoto, Florian. *L'effectivité en droit international.* Bruxelles: Bruylant, 2014, p. 271.
52 Société des Nations, *Journal Officiel*, November 1931, p. 2057.

a) Have a constituted government and an administration capable of ensuring the regular functioning of essential State services;
b) To be able to maintain its territorial integrity and political independence;
c) To be able to ensure public tranquillity throughout the territory;
d) To be assured of having financial resources such that they can regularly meet the normal needs of the State;
e) To have legislation and a judicial organisation which ensure regular justice to all litigants.

(Author's translation.)

authority to assume said functions over the population and territory in respect of which it intends to exercise them? This is a crucial question, but one that is also permeated by uncertainty and subjectivity, insofar as international law lacks a body with the power to decide objectively on such a fundamental issue as the emergence of a new international subject.

So, what happens? In the context of an eminently decentralised order such as international law, it is the other States, through their recognition, who will make the decision in this respect, i.e. who will confirm that "a politically organised society exists on a given territory, independent of any other existing State, which is capable of observing the requirements of international law"[53]. And this insofar as recognition is but "l'instrument polyvalent de la constatation des faits juridiques dans l'ordre international"[54]. However, it is very important to bear in mind that this is unquestionably a subjective issue with a considerable margin of discretion and even partiality, not to mention its undeniable political component, as we will discuss in the next chapter. Hence it is not surprising to see that when faced with the same situation, some States deny recognition while others grant it – even prematurely, as occurred when France recognised the United States; when the latter recognised Panama; or as happened more recently with Kosovo.

In any case, in our opinion, and in answer to the question posed, we can state unequivocally that a mere declaration of independence is not enough to become a State, that such a declaration does not in itself produce any legal effect. It is evident that the irruption of the principle of effectiveness, which, as we have indicated, refers to something real, means that there is nothing automatic about the objective creation of a State, i.e. even though it may be a fact, it is not an automatic fact. On the contrary, it is a process. The "instantaneous" creation of a State is not conceivable; it is not possible. Necessary effectiveness – imperative for a State to be created under international law – demands that this declaration be bolstered and consolidated by the government exercising general and exclusive control – without taking any orders from others – over the population and territory, so that it is capable of not only establishing but above all maintaining internal order, and of engaging independently in international relations; requirements that are imposed by international law, as stated in the previous section.

Thus, a mere act of effectiveness is not sufficient. It needs to have continuity, with guarantees that it will endure in the future – what we might call 'lasting effectiveness'. First of all, what is required is a genuine deployment of all State functions, similar to that which international law requires for being able to acquire sovereignty over a given territory through effective possession

53 Definition of recognition proposed by the *Institut de Droit International*, at its Brussels session in 1936, www.idi-iil.org, last consulted 27 August 2017.

54 Virally, Michael. "Panorama du droit international contemporain. Cours général de droit international public". *Recueil des Cours*. vol. 183, no. 5, 1983, p. 52.

thereof[55]. This means that the government element must comprise all the bodies necessary to perform the functions of a State: executive, judicial, legislative, administrative and, of course, military. Furthermore, these functions must be performed continually and over a long period of time. And in order to maintain this extensive government apparatus and, consequently, ensure that it functions effectively, it is obvious that the necessary economic backing is required. In other words, it is necessary to have sufficient *liquidity* and an effective system of financing in order to be able to continue functioning in the future; otherwise, survival will be impossible. And, of course, it must be an authority that acts with total independence, be it in decision making, in the existence of the bodies necessary for the State to perform its functions, or in the aforementioned liquidity. This means that it must be able to function as a State in its various aspects and without being subject to any other State or international organisation. Because if its officials are appointed by an international organisation, as in Kosovo; if its army is that of the sponsor State, as in Transnistria; or if its liquidity is provided by an international organisation, as in Kosovo, or by the sponsor State, as in the TRNC, it is patently clear that the element of effective government does not exist, and therefore there is no State.

If we apply these parameters to the different existing secessionist entities, the result is, as we have pointed out, that they lack the necessary effectiveness in the material elements to be considered States under international law. Kosovo lacks an effective and independent government[56], as well as liquidity and a financing system, given that this is provided by the EU and the UN. Likewise, South Ossetia, Abkhazia, Transnistria, Nagorno-Karabakh and the TRNC do not really meet the effectiveness requirement in that they do not enjoy full independence, as they are entirely dependent on their sponsor State, which also directly performs certain State functions. Russia does so in the first three cases, while also exercising complete military control over these territories, which is a key aspect of the "instrumentalization"[57] of these entities. They are also subject to a policy of 'passportisation', because not belonging to the International Organization for Standardization (ISO) means they do not have the codes they would need to be able to issue their own passports, and so each population makes do with Russian passports. All this, as well as being an instrument for increasing Russian influence in these regions, constitutes a serious violation of the territorial sovereignty of Georgia, in the case of South Ossetia and Abkhazia, and of Moldavia, in the case of Transnistria. The level of control and

55 See, in this respect, López Martín, Ana Gemma. *El territorio estatal en discusión: la prueba del título*. Madrid: McGraw Hill, 1999.

56 The international Administration itself declared in late October 2019 that it did not have the capacity to issue legislation in matters of nationality, which constitutes the most basic of State functions. This reliably proves that Kosovo is not a State.

57 Souleimanov, Emil Aslan, Abrahamyan, Eduard and Aliyev, Huseyn. "Unrecognized States as a Means of Coercive Diplomacy? Assessing the Role of Abkhazia and South Ossetia in Russia's Foreign Policy in the South Caucasus". *Southeast European and Black Sea Studies*, 2018, vol. 18, no.1, p. 80.

influence is similar to that exerted by Armenia in Nagorno-Karabakh and by Turkey in the TRNC. In other words, in none of these cases is the principle of effectiveness upheld. The reality is that these secessionist entities are mere puppets of their respective sponsor States.

We could sum up the foregoing in the words of Roth: "the Montevideo criteria only confer sovereign rights, obligations, powers, immunity – that is, legal personality – on a territorially coherent political community when it is under the *effective long-term control of an independent government*"[58].

In this framework, recognition by third States, as we have already pointed out, plays an important role in crystallizing the necessary effectiveness, and for some it is even "the key to statehood"[59]. Nevertheless, we should make it clear that recognition does not always, by any means, hold the key to statehood; which is entirely logical given its merely declarative nature[60], a matter we will analyse in more detail in the next chapter. This is demonstrated by the 112 recognitions accumulated by Kosovo, which still does not meet the requirements for effectiveness; or the six recognitions of South Ossetia, Abkhazia, Transnistria or Nagorno-Karabakh[61]. None of them can be considered a State according to the principle of effectiveness. Indeed, recognising them as such without applying the effectiveness test also entails the risk of creating States with an inherent weakness or lack of capacity (ideal candidates for becoming 'failed' States or 'puppet' States). In contrast, on the other side of the coin, we find States lacking recognition, such as Somaliland, which fulfil the three constituent criteria with full effectiveness.

All these examples simply confirm two things: first, that recognition is ultimately a political decision; and second, the important role played by the superpowers in this field. It is quite obvious that if Kosovo has received so

58 Roth, Brad. "Secession, Coups and the International Rule of Law: Assessing the Decline of the Effective Control Doctrine". *Melbourne Journal of International Law*, vol. 11, 2010, p. 7 (italics are ours).

59 Kreijen states that:

> An entity may be formally independent, but without being recognised as such it cannot possibly materialise its capacity to enter into relations and, consequently, lacks real independence. Thus, in the sense that the capacity to enter into relations expresses both the ability to enter into the whole scale of international relations and its actual realisation –thereby giving evidence of a State's full independence– it may be regarded as a useful criterion for statehood.
>
> The same author makes a curious comparison between recognition and 'peer review', currently so widespread in the field of scientific publications (Kreijen, Gerard. *State Failure, Sovereignty and Effectiveness*. Leiden: Martinus Nijhoff, 2004, pp. 13 and 22, respectively).

60 In this respect, Article 3 of the Montevideo Convention of 1933 begins by stating: "The political existence of the state is independent of recognition by the other states…".

61 Those of Russia, Nicaragua, Venezuela, Vanuatu, Nauru and Tuvalu. Leaving aside the recognition that these four secessionist entities have given each other, which is of no value in this context.

many recognitions, it is because it is a personal 'wager' by the United States, which in itself also demonstrates that the United States wields greater influence than Russia, whose personal 'ventures' have only mustered five more recognitions in addition to its own. Moreover, this shows that recognition is the tool that the most powerful governments use to decide whether or not a State exists, which might lead us to describe recognition as a tool of diplomatic coercion.

Lack of effectiveness in the material elements of statehood in the case of Catalonia

The foregoing inevitably raises the question of whether, based on current data, Catalonia would effectively possess the material elements required for statehood under international law.

In this respect, it is clear that it could be endowed with the element of *population*. The number of people residing in the Autonomous Community of Catalonia is over 7,600,000[62], in respect of whom the regional government exercises numerous powers assumed under Article 148 of the Spanish Constitution. It exercises these powers throughout the *territory* that makes up Catalonia, which covers an area of 32,123 km2[63]. It is true that these powers must be exercised in accordance with Spanish law, because otherwise the central government of Spain could temporarily suspend the exercise of such powers and assume control of the entire territory of this Autonomous Community by triggering Article 155 of the Constitution[64], as occurred after Catalonia's

62 According to the National Statistics Institute of Spain (INE), as of 1 January 2020 the population of Catalonia was 7,675,217 (www.ine.es/jaxiT3/Datos.htm?t=2915#!tabs-tabla).

63 www.ine.es/inebaseweb/pdfDispacher.do?td=154090&L=0

64 Article 155 of the Constitution complements the provision of ways or means of (ordinary) control of the activity of Autonomous Communities contained in Article 153 by providing for a subsidiary control mechanism, of an exceptional or extreme nature (and in scope even coercive) for equally exceptional or extreme situations, consisting in their failure to comply with obligations imposed by the Constitution or other laws or in actions deemed detrimental to the general interests of Spain. This provision derives from the "federal coercion" (*Bundeszwang*) provided for in Article 37 of the Basic Law of the Federal Republic of Germany, and it reads as follows:

> If an Autonomous Community does not fulfil the obligations imposed on it by the Constitution or other laws, or acts in a way that is seriously prejudicial to the general interests of Spain, the Government, after having lodged a complaint with the President of the Autonomous Community and failed to receive satisfaction therefore, may, following approval granted by an absolute majority of the Senate, take any measures necessary to compel the Autonomous Community forcibly to meet said obligations, or to protect the abovementioned general interests. With a view to implementing the measures provided for in the foregoing paragraph, the Government may issue instructions to all the authorities of the Autonomous Communities.

unilateral declaration of independence in 2017 (as indicated in the first chapter). The activation of Article 155 following the Catalan secession attempt led to the dismissal of the entire regional government, to limits being placed on the Catalan Parliament's functions, and to the complete takeover of control of the Autonomous Community. This shows that when dealing with an illegal unilateral declaration of independence of Catalonia, the Spanish Government has the legal and material instruments necessary to take full and effective control of Catalan territory, and to take legal action against those responsible for the declaration. It is therefore questionable whether the element of territory could be said to exist effectively in the case of a hypothetical Catalan republic.

Finally, we must consider the possible effectiveness of the third criterion relating to the existence of a *political, institutional and effective organisation* through which the functions of public authority can be performed on its territory and over the existing population. It would appear that Catalonia has many of the bodies and elements needed to become a State. It has a parliament, a court of justice, an executive and an autonomous police force. It also has its own telecommunications regulatory body, and even representative offices abroad that promote trade and investment in Catalonia worldwide. In addition, it manages important public services such as education and healthcare, and it even possesses emblems such as a flag and its own language.

However, this is not enough to have the element of government and be able to act as a sovereign State. It would need much more, including border management, customs control, an air traffic control authority, its own currency (as it would be outside the eurozone), a central bank, a tax collection agency and, of course, everything related to national defence – an army, for example, which it does not have. It would also be necessary to establish appropriate international relations, including trade agreements, for which international recognition would be required, which, as we have pointed out and will see in detail in the next chapter, would not occur until Spain had recognised its independence. Likewise, in order to function fully, it would need to be a member of different international organisations so that it could have such basic things as the internet, telephony, a postal service, passports, air and sea corridors, etc. Access to membership which, as we will also point out later, would be impossible without the Spanish State's acceptance of secession.

In order to maintain the elements that it possesses and create all the new ones it needs to be able to function as a State, it must have liquidity and viable sources of financing. The transition to an independent State is costly and, at present, Catalonia does not have the necessary economic solvency[65], as it depends on the Spanish Government's funding streams. Of the Catalan tax system, 90% corresponds to the Spanish State and, although Catalonia has a tax agency, the taxes it collects amount to very little.

65 A detailed study of all these economic problems can be found in García Pedraz, Fernando. *Consecuencias económicas de una eventual secesión de Cataluña sobre Cataluña.* Madrid: Facultad de Ciencias Económicas y Empresariales. ICADE, 2015.

As an immediate economic consequence of its independence and, as a direct result, its non-membership of the EU, Catalonia would suffer the effect on the various components of its current account balance[66]. Independence would have effects on goods trading that in turn would affect its exports, as the Common External Tariff would be applied to it as a non-EU member and the tariff reductions of the preferential agreements signed by the EU would be eliminated, with the consequent loss of competitiveness of Catalan firms. The effect on Catalonia's trade balance could be even worse on leaving the Economic and Monetary Union, not to mention that its foreign balance reflects a deficit of 21% of its GDP. To the fall in exports, we should add the relocation of companies – something we have already seen since the bid for independence began, with more than eight thousand companies having relocated in the past ten years – with the resultant reduction in exports and revenue. Independence would also have negative effects on investment flows, as Catalonia's legal, political, administrative and fiscal framework would have to be redefined. However, besides financing difficulties, Catalonia has another serious economic problem: its debt. According to the latest available figures, the Catalan Government owes some 2.65 billion euros, or 125% of its GDP. The balance sheet could hardly be more catastrophic: Catalonia cannot afford to maintain the institutional apparatus necessary to function as a State. A hypothetical Catalan republic would be born with 'lead in its wings' that would prevent it from 'taking off'.

If we compare this situation in Catalonia with that of the other secessionist entities that have unilaterally declared themselves States – Abkhazia, South Ossetia, Nagorno-Karabakh, Transnistria and TRNC – and that continue to defy the parent State, the reality we find is certainly different insofar as they function as States, not because they actually have the governmental and institutional apparatus necessary to do so, but because the material and economic means they need to operate effectively are 'loaned' to them by the sponsor State that supports their secession – Russia, Armenia or Turkey, as the case may be. In other words, it is the latter that actually controls the territory, which means that these secessionist entities lack the necessary independence which, as we have pointed out, is equally necessary for acceding to statehood under international law.

The theory of eventual success as a corollary of effectiveness in cases of secession. An insurmountable obstacle for Catalonia

In light of the foregoing, it is easy to conclude that, in the case of secession, it is not the 'initial success' of the secession arising from the mere declaration of

66 Report of the Ministry of Foreign Affairs and Spanish Cooperation, available at www.exteriores.gob.es/Portal/es/SalaDePrensa/ElMinisterioInforma/Documents/Consecuencias%20econ%C3%B3micas%20de%20una%20hipot%C3%A9tica%20independencia%20de%20Catalu%C3%B1a.pdf

independence that is taken into account by the law. In other words, a unilateral declaration of independence is not enough to be able to corroborate that the necessary effectiveness required by international law has been achieved; therefore, such a declaration simply does not grant statehood, and nor does it imply that there is now a new State in the international arena. What is actually taken into account in terms of necessary effectiveness is the '*ultimate or eventual success*' of said declaration; that is, the secessionist entity's capacity to impose itself on the parent State and create a seemingly irreversible situation.

This being the case, we find that there is a fairly well-established theory that 'eventual success' cannot be achieved through State effectiveness alone. A secession should be considered successful only if the former sovereign State takes no further steps to contest the validity of the secession, i.e. that it does not continue to try by all means to regain full control of the territory. Or, at least, that it is clearly established that the parent State is not going to succeed in restoring its authority. Or that it tacitly accepts the factual situation created: acquiescence.

Lauterpacht referred to this in 1947 when he stated that effectiveness must be established "beyond all reasonable doubt" and that, in cases of secession, recognition can only be given when "the parent State must in fact have ceased to make efforts (giving de facto its acquiescence), promising success, to reassert its authority"[67]. Thus, if we already have this 'tacit' consent, there is no violation of territorial integrity. In the same vein, Crawford maintains that the secessionist entity must firmly establish its control beyond any hope of return in relation to the predecessor State. In such a case, the latter's mandatory consent would no longer be required[68].

In other words, as Christakis points out, even if international law does not prohibit secession, it is clearly hostile to it and puts major obstacles in its way. The first one derives from effectiveness itself and consists of a presumption against the effectiveness of secession and in favour of the territorial integrity of the parent State, insofar as secession requires the latter's acquiescence or resignation, which occurs when it ceases to attempt to regain control over the seceded territory[69].

This same idea of 'ultimate success' finds support in the internal practice of some States. Thus, in the case of *Madzimbamuto v Lardner-Burke & Phillip George* (1969), the British Privy Council refused to recognise any legal value in the decisions adopted by the Government of Southern Rhodesia, considering that it was not an independent State and that the "eventual success" of secession had not been achieved, bearing in mind that the British Government still had

67 Lauterpacht, Hersch. *Recognition in International Law*. Cambridge: Cambridge University Press, 1947, p. 8.

68 Crawford, James. "La pratique des États et le droit international relativement à la sécession unilatérale". *Cour Suprême du Canada*, no. 25508, 1997, para. 28.

69 Christakis, Theodore. "The State as a 'Primary Fact': Some Thoughts on the Principle of Effectiveness". In *Secession. International Law Perspectives*, edited by Marcelo G. Kohen. Cambridge: Cambridge University Press, 2006, pp. 147–149.

control[70]. Likewise, international practice concerning recognition of secessionist entities seems to confirm this theory of 'eventual success' based on the irreversibility of the situation, either due to the parent State's express acceptance or its tacit agreement to abandon its attempts to regain control. For example, no secessionist entity has ever been admitted as a member of the United Nations until the parent State has consented to the situation.

Furthermore, State practice in this area demonstrates the existence of a clear position of recognising the secessionist entity as a new State only when the parent State consents to the *de facto* situation generated[71]. To corroborate this assertion, we can take the case of Bangladesh as a reference point. On the one hand, it was not admitted as a member of the UN until Pakistan – the parent State – expressly recognised its independence in 1974, i.e. until it declared its consent. Moreover, Bangladesh was not recognised by any State until secession became an apparently irreversible *fait accompli*, with the exception of India, which was ultimately the State that 'sponsored' its independence. In this respect, Summers points out that Bangladesh became a State not because it exercised any right of secession but because its independence became "un fait accompli apparemment irréversible"[72]. This *fait accompli* was the result of the establishment of an effective government, with considerable popular support. This took place when Pakistan lost the war caused by India's armed intervention, after which came Pakistan's tacit acceptance, which in turn corroborated that this was now an irreversible fact.

Moreover, proof of the application of this theory of eventual success is the fact that no State has recognised as a State those secessionist entities that fulfilled the three constituent criteria, and effectively over time, but in respect of which the parent State maintained intact its claims to recovery, which it finally achieved. Such has been the case of Chechnya (Russia), between 1991 and 1994; Katanga (Congo); Biafra (Nigeria); and the Sprska Republic (Bosnia and Herzegovina). The case of the TRNC (Cyprus) can also be regarded as an

70 The Privy Council expresses its view in the following terms:

> That the conceptions of international law as to de facto or de jure status were inappropriate where a court sitting in a particular territory had to decide upon the validity or otherwise of a new regime which had gained control of the territory; and that, accordingly, the usurping government in control in Southern Rhodesia could not, for any purpose, be regarded as a lawful government, since the United Kingdom Government, acting upon behalf of the lawful Sovereign, was still taking steps to regain control.
>
> (www.uniset.ca/other/cs2/19691AC645.html, para. 649)

71 In the same vein, albeit in the context of colonial peoples, when Great Britain recognised the independence of Spain's former colonies in America from 1823 onwards, Spain protested; but Great Britain argued that it had done so once it had seen that there was no possibility of the independent territories being recovered, and that the struggle had already ceased.

72 Summers, James. *People and International Law – How Nationalism and Self-Determination Shape a Contemporary Law of Nations.* Leiden: Martinus Nijhoff, 2007, p. 335.

example of the validity of this theory put into practice, since apart from its sponsor state (Turkey), no other State has recognised it as such, because, among other reasons, Cyprus still seeks to re-establish full sovereignty over the seceded territory. Similarly, the UN has been extremely reluctant to award member status to secessionist entities against the will – express or tacit – of the government of the State in which the secession has taken place. There has been no case since 1945 where this has happened.

If we look closely, this theory of 'eventual success' bears an undeniable resemblance to the controversial figure of acquisitive *prescription*, which is usually included – although it has quite a few detractors – among the modes of acquiring the title of territorial sovereignty arising from a *de facto* situation. This resemblance is not without its logic, as secession and prescription function in very similar ways: in both cases it is a matter of 'adverse contrary possession' against the sovereign State of the territory. In both cases we assume that a State has sovereign control over a given territory, in respect of which there is a transfer/change of sovereignty without its (initial) consent: to another existing State in the case of prescription; to a new State created thereon in the case of secession. This being so, if international law requires the acquiescence of the sovereign State in order for prescription to be perfected and to produce legal effects, the State's acceptance is also necessary in cases of secession. In this regard, it is worth bearing in mind the novel formula used by the ICJ in 2008 to grant Indonesia title of sovereignty over Pedra Branca: *effective possession +acquiescence* [73]. In fact, the Court decided to grant Indonesia sovereignty over the small island on the basis of not only its actual possession thereof but, above all, the acquiescence of Malaysia (Sultanate of Johor), the original sovereign State, vis-à-vis such possession. However, it declined to reach the same conclusion with respect to Middle Rocks and South Ledge because, despite Indonesian possession, there has been no acquiescence on the part of Malaysia, which therefore maintains its sovereignty over these islands.

As a matter of pure logic, it can be concluded that not only material effectiveness in controlling the territory but also the acquiescence of the parent State is required in order for secession to produce legal effects under international law.

In the previous section we indicated that, in response to Catalonia's *unilateral declaration of independence* in 2017, the Spanish State reacted forcefully by activating Article 155 of the Constitution. The plenary session of the Senate on 27 October 2017 approved the measures requested by the Spanish Government, under Article 155, "necessary to guarantee the fulfilment of constitutional obligations and to protect the general interest on the part of the Autonomous

73 In fact, in its Judgment of 23 May 2008 in the case concerning *Sovereignty over Pedra Branca/Pulau Batu Puteh, Middle Rocks and South Ledge*, the ICJ 'created' this new formula of acquisition of title of territorial sovereignty: effective possession +acquiescence; which, admittedly, is merely a periphrasis of acquisitive prescription (ICJ Reports, 2008, para. 273–275).

Government of Catalonia"; and the subsequent Resolution of 27 October 2017 of the Presidency of the Senate made this agreement public[74]. Following this agreement, the then Prime Minister of the Spanish Government, Mariano Rajoy, dismissed the President of the Autonomous Community of Catalonia, Carles Puigdemont, Vice President Oriol Junqueras, the entire Catalan Government and various other public officials. In total, 254 people were removed from office. Prime Minister Rajoy also limited the functions of the Catalan Parliament[75] and took control of the entire Catalan administration, including economic intervention. Forty bodies were dissolved or taken over, including the Advisory Council for National Transition, the *Patronato Cataluña Mundo-Consejo de Diplomacia Pública de Cataluña* (DIPLOCAT, a public–private entity engaged in public diplomacy), and the Catalan Government's offices in various countries. This suspension of autonomy was maintained until 2 June 2018, following regional elections called by the Spanish Prime Minister as a further measure in the application of Article 155. These events show that, in view of the illegal unilateral declaration of independence by Catalonia, the Spanish Government has the legal and material instruments necessary to take full and effective control of Catalan territory, as well as legal action against those responsible for such a declaration.

Indeed, as a consequence of the unilateral declaration of independence, on 14 September 2019 the Spanish Supreme Court sentenced ten members of the Catalan executive and two other people to prison terms for committing various crimes such as sedition, embezzlement of public funds (aggravated by the amount involved), rebellion or disobedience, depending on the individual case. Meanwhile, seven Catalan leaders are currently outside Spain, on the run from justice so as to avoid imprisonment. This course of action taken by the Spanish courts against the forces of Catalan pro-independence has continued as further events have unfolded. Thus, the Spanish Supreme Court, in its Ruling of 28 September 2020, confirmed the disqualification which the High Court of Justice of Catalonia had imposed on the President of the Autonomous Community, Quim Torra, for refusing to remove a banner in support of those he considered 'political prisoners', despite having been ordered by the Central

74 *BOE* (Official Gazette of the Spanish State) no. 260, of 27 October 2017. The Senate's Plenary Resolution of 27 October 2017, approving the measures required by the Government under Article 155 of the Constitution, as well as the provisions issued to develop, complement or add to these measures, was the object of an appeal on grounds of unconstitutionality (no. 143–2018), filed by the Parliament of Catalonia. The Spanish Constitutional Court, in Judgment 90/2019, of 2 July 2019, declared the resolution and the measures adopted thereunder to be constitutional (*BOE* no. 192, of 12 August 2019).

75 Which put paid to 108 policy initiatives (bills presented by the Government, bills presented by the lower house of parliament, citizens' initiatives, legislative initiatives, regulatory initiatives).

Electoral Board to guarantee the neutrality of public buildings during the April 2019 campaign[76].

In view of the precedents of practice, it could be concluded that the immediate implementation of Article 155 of the Constitution and all the measures this entails, with the suspension of autonomy and the Spanish Government's takeover without any noteworthy resistance (beyond street disturbances) on the Catalan side, demonstrate that Spain is not going to cease in its efforts to maintain or, if necessary, regain control of the territory in the face of secessionist attempts. Experience has also shown that Spain has the means to do so and that its power to control is greater than Catalonia's. Therefore, it is very difficult to imagine that the declaration of independence could result in eventual success, both because the material elements would not achieve total effectiveness, given that the parent State – Spain – would not cease in its attempts to regain control (having the legal means and material resources to do so), and because of the lack of acquiescence to this declaration. All of this represents an insurmountable obstacle to the success of Catalan secession and, therefore, accession to statehood in accordance with the requirements established by international law.

Following this reflection on Catalonia, it might be worth asking why the reaction of the parent States has not had the same result in the other cases of recent secessionist attempts, such as those of Abkhazia, South Ossetia, Transnistria, Nagorno-Karabakh and the TRNC. The reason is blatantly obvious: because from the outset they have had a sponsor State that has supported and encouraged secession and continues to do so. A sponsor State that, moreover, carries greater specific weight in the international arena than the parent State. In the case of Somaliland, the situation is different because there has been no reaction from the parent State (Somalia), which is a failed state with no capacity to act in response to secession.

This is not the situation in Catalonia. No State supports this secessionist entity, and so while Spain continues to reject the secession it will not succeed; that is, the attempted creation of the Catalan republic will not be consummated.

Respect for international legality as a necessary condition for achieving statehood

The exposition and analysis carried out so far would correspond to what we might call the 'classical academic position' in relation to State formation and accession to statehood. According to this 'classical' position, supported in the early twentieth century by Jellinek and since followed by many others, the existence of a State is a matter of fact, a political matter, outside the 'realm of

76 In Ruling on Supreme Court appeal no. 203/2020, he is declared to have "stubbornly and obstinately" disobeyed the constitutional body that safeguards the integrity of electoral processes.

law'[77]. This is a generalised statement that we find not only in all the authoritative handbooks but also among some contemporary authors. The Arbitration Commission of the International Conference on the Former Yugoslavia (Badinter Commission) made the same point in its Opinion No. 1 of 29 November:

> a) that the answer to the question should be based on the principles of public international law which serve to define the conditions on which an entity constitutes a state; that in this respect, the existence or disappearance of the state is a question of fact [...];
> b) that the state is commonly defined as a community which consists of a territory and a population subject to an organized political authority; that such a state is characterized by sovereignty[78].

In the context of this traditional position, the birth of a State is compared to the birth of a natural person, in the sense that the law may or may not stimulate the birth rate, but it cannot cause the birth of a human being; it takes note of its existence once it has been born[79]: if an entity has all three of the elements described on p. 137, it is automatically a State. This approach would lead us to the conclusion, for example, that Taiwan must be a State because it clearly meets the requirements for being one, which is truly paradoxical if we take into account that Taiwan, for the time being, does not claim statehood for itself. This is certainly an interesting point to remember when questioning the efficacy of the approach based purely on effectiveness.

Within this same approach, the problem of *secession* cannot be considered in terms of 'authorisation' or 'prohibition' by law, but instead in terms of 'success' or 'failure'. Therefore, according to this classical view, any infra-state entity can try to secede if it wants to, without any legal condition or limit. If it does not succeed, then so be it. But if, on the contrary, it manages to establish the constituent elements with effectiveness – as analysed on p. 147 – then the result would be the birth of a new State. For as Anzilotti pointed out, "the legitimacy of the state resides in its existence"[80]. In other words, the Latin maxim *ex factis jus oritur* would serve as the premise.

In opposition to this classical position, according to which the existence or non-existence of a State was purely a matter of fact dependent solely on its effectiveness, a new trend has gradually taken hold in contemporary international law, according to which the requirement of effectiveness is not sufficient for attaining statehood. The introduction of certain fundamental principles of the international legal order into contemporary law has added the requirement

77 Jellinek, Georg. *Allgemeine Staatslehr*. Berlin: Verlag von O. Haring, 1905, p. 329.
78 ILR, vol. 92, p. 162.
79 Abi-Saab, George. "Cours général de droit international public". *Recueil des Cours*, vol. 207, 1987, p. 68.
80 Anzilotti, Dionisio. *Corso di Diritto Internazionale* (vol. I). Roma: Athenaeum, 1928, pp. 154–155.

of legality in accession to statehood, whereby only those who have obeyed these structural principles during the creation process can be considered States. Conversely, this means that if an entity does not obey such principles, it does not become a State under international law, and nor should it be treated as such. The logic of this new legal approach is very convincingly explained by Couveinhes-Matsumoto in the following terms:

> Le droit international ne prescrit cependant jamais, au titre de l'effectivité, une approche uniquement fondée sur l'admission du fait, et sur l'exclusion de tout critère ou toute finalité dans l'appréciation de sa signification et de sa valeur en droit. Il est impensable que des éléments d'ordre juridique ne guident pas sourdement l'application d'un critère ou d'une exigence de l'effectivité, et qu'il soit possible de faire entièrement fi des autres règles juridiques dans cette opération[81].

It follows that the previously analysed constituent material elements of the State are no longer sufficient. A fourth criterion must be added, which will be decisive for being able to affirm that we are in the presence of a sovereign State. This decisive element is respect for international law, which we will now proceed to discuss.

Analysis of the contemporary approach to the requirement of the criterion relating to respect for legality

In the early days of contemporary international law, Verdross stated that "the principle of effectiveness is not without international legal limits: it only functions within the framework established by international law. If it were to apply without restrictions, the whole of international law would dissolve"[82]. In the same vein, Professor Carrillo Salcedo maintained that "the autonomy of the will of subjects is not unlimited in any legal system, as this would be tantamount to negation of the legal system in question"[83]. And in relation to the aforementioned *ex factis jus oritur* premise, which is part of classical legal scholarship, Jennings warned that it expresses a reality entailing dangers that no system can afford to ignore[84].

81 Couveinhes-Matsumoto. op. cit., p. 47. "However, international law never prescribes, in terms of effectiveness, an approach based solely on the admission of the fact, and on the exclusion of any criterion or any purpose in the assessment of its meaning and value in law. It is unthinkable that legal elements do not guide the application of a criterion or a requirement of effectiveness, and that it is possible to completely ignore other legal rules in this operation" (author's translation).

82 Verdross, Alfred. *Derecho internacional público* (translated by Antonio Truyol Serra). Madrid: Aguilar, 1957, p. 116.

83 Carrillo Salcedo, Juan Antonio. *Soberanía del Estado y Derecho Internacional*. Madrid: Tecnos, 1976, pp. 257–258.

84 Jennings, Robert Yewdall. "Nullity and Effectiveness". In *Cambridge Essays in International Law Essays in Honour of Lord McNair*. London: Stevens & Sons, 1965, p. 74.

In view of both the legal limits pointed out by Verdross and Carrillo Salcedo and the 'dangers' that, according to Jennings, lurk within the *ex factis jus oritur* maxim, applied to cases of secession – where the creation of a State is proposed in a non-peaceful manner, without the consent of the parent State and even through the use of force, which could mean giving way to another Latin maxim: *ex iniuria oritur ius* –, we find an increasingly consolidated academic trend that, without denying the factual grounds and effectiveness necessary for the creation of a new State, affirms the need to also take into account respect for legality in the process of accession to statehood.

In other words, effectiveness is and should be necessary as a criterion for statehood, but it is not sufficient; it must be accompanied by legality, i.e. by respect for current international law.

In this respect, it seems that a matter of pure logic also prevails. According to classical academic opinion based solely on effectiveness, it would appear that Manchukuo, Southern Rhodesia, the Homelands or Bantustans of South Africa (Transkei, Bophuthatswana, Venda and Ciskei), the TRNC or the Republic of Sprska are or have been States at some time. It is certainly difficult to accept and more than dubious that positive international law can prohibit armed attacks, interference in internal affairs and serious violations of human rights or the right to self-determination, and at the same time have no qualms about allowing a State to emerge while manifestly flouting these prohibitions. It is a matter of being consistent.

Furthermore, such a possibility would lead to a situation as inconsistent as this: it is patently obvious that within the framework of contemporary international law, a State cannot use force to acquire the sovereignty of a territory belonging to another State, so that if it invades it would clearly be an act of aggression, an extremely serious illegal act, which furthermore would be devoid of any international validity. However, following the factual approach, it could succeed in taking over the territory indirectly. How? By supporting a group, a national minority that declares itself independent within that State, which achieves effectiveness in its elements, i.e. effective government. According to the doctrine of effectiveness, it would automatically become a State, and would be protected by all the principles of international law that statehood entails, including that of territorial sovereignty. This would lead to the paradoxical consequence of the parent State being prevented from making any attempt at recovery, because it would be an attack on its sovereignty and territorial integrity. Later on, the new State may decide to join the State that supported it.

The situation described here is no mere laboratory hypothesis. Quite the opposite, in fact, as this is basically what has happened in Crimea with its declaration of independence and subsequent incorporation into Russia, the State that promoted the whole secessionist process. Is this not a blatantly clear violation of international law? Should it be admitted simply on the basis of facts, i.e. the effectiveness of the situation generated, given that according to classical academic opinion there are no legal requirements?

As early as 1947, many decades before the arrival of this secessionist maelstrom that we see today, Lauterpacht referred to the existence of entities that are not legally States[85]. However, it is undoubtedly Crawford who has most forcefully demanded the establishment of a legality criterion in accession to statehood. In this regard, and a relatively long time ago – 1977 – he maintained that there had been a change in what were traditionally considered the necessary conditions for State formation, and that, as a result, objective rules of legality should also be observed[86]. It is an argument he has continued to reaffirm in his subsequent works – most recently in 2006 –, drawing on international practice for support.

In this regard, since the early days of contemporary international law, with the irruption of a new institutional structure in the international community (represented mainly by the UN) and especially, since the 1970s, coinciding with the consolidation of the legal category of *jus cogens* (fundamentally with the adoption of the 1969 Vienna Convention on the Law of Treaties and Resolution 2625 (XXV)), we have seen how a growing number of authors insist on the existence of what some call a *fourth element* necessary for the existence of a new State[87]: the 'legality' of the creation process. It follows that if the process of State creation is the product of a violation of international law, then the *de facto* entity would not achieve statehood. In other words, an illegal State formation process entails denial of statehood.

Even authors clearly in favour of the purely factual approach, such as Degan, have come to acknowledge that although the creation of a State is a matter of fact that escapes the grasp of the ordinary rules of law, it "could be legally limited"[88].

Thus, the introduction of the legality criterion – which is an objective criterion – represents an important factor of legal security, to the extent that it serves to counteract subjectivity, which, as we have seen, permeates the mere consideration of effectiveness. With this approach, effectiveness and legality

85 Lauterpacht. *Recognition*..., op. cit., p. 9.

86 Crawford, James. "The Criteria for Statehood in International Law". *BYIL*, 1977, pp. 94 and 144.

87 Tancredi, Antonello. "A Normative 'Due Process' in the Creation of States Through Secession". In *Secession. International Law Perspectives*, edited by Marcelo G. Kohen. Cambridge: Cambridge University Press, 2006, pp. 182–183. Many authors affirm that effectiveness is necessary but not sufficient to create a State; by way of example, in addition to those referred to in this section and those cited by Tancredi (notes 30–31 of his work), they include, among others, Chemillier-Gendreau, Monique. "A propos de l'effectivité en Droit International". *Revue Belge du Droit International*, vol. 11, 1975, p. 41; or Taki, H. "Effectiveness". In *Max Planck Encyclopedia of Public International Law*, vol. III. Oxford Public International Law, 2010, para. 10.

88 Degan, Vladimir Djuro. "Création et disparition de l'État (à la lumière du démembrement de trois fédérations multiethiques en Europe)". *Recueil des Cours*. vol. 279, 2007, pp. 227 and 249.

would not be at odds, but instead complementary, rather like communicating vessels[89].

This contemporary approach limits the validity of the maxim *ex factis jus oritur* and its possible drift towards *ex iniuria oritur ius*, countering it with another Latin maxim, *ex iniuria ius non oritur*, which is a rule of law that responds to an evident imperative of legal security; a kind of 'cornerstone' of any legal system, as Corten indicates[90], which, moreover, has been recognised by the ILC as a general principle of international law.

In this regard, it cannot be admitted that by virtue of recognition or tolerance an illegal act can have legal effects, especially when such illegality arises from a conflict with *jus cogens*, as is the case with a secession that has not been agreed upon or consented to. In Orakhelashvili's view, this approach "is inherent in the idea of public order that it must apply to any conflicting act"[91].

Miaja de la Muela had already warned about the risks of overestimating the consequences of effectiveness in legal life, as this could lead us from *ex factis jus oritur* – recognising the configuration of law by its socio-political structure – to maintaining that *ex iniuria oritur ius*, i.e. that the antilegal act can give birth to law as a rule of conduct and to a subjective right for the perpetrator of the illegal act[92]. According to the same author, it is not the case that *ex iniuria oritur ius* is a governing principle in international law. The opposite is true[93]. In the same vein, Touscoz states that no legal system can accept this maxim, since it is a contradiction and an anomaly. In fact, the principle of effectiveness cannot have the effect of allowing a right to emerge from illegality; this only happens in a primitive system and highlights, purely and simply, the failure of the law in the face of the fact[94].

Therefore, in view of the *ex iniuria ius non oritur* principle, the antilegal act cannot by itself create any legal situation, i.e. an illegal act should not create a subjective right in favour of its perpetrator. For, as Verdross pointed out, he who infringes the right cannot acquire the right to which he aspires[95]. If that

89 Peters, Anne. "Statehood after 1989: 'Effectivités' between Legality and Virtuality". *Proceedings of the European Society of International Law*, vol. 3, 2010, p. 13.

90 Corten, Olivier. "Commentaire de l'article 52". In *Les Conventions de Vienne sur le droit des traités. Commentaire article per article*, edited by Olivier Corten and Pierre Klein. Bruxelles: Bruylant, 2006, pp. 1867–1900. In the same vein, see Lagerwall, Anne. *Le principe ex injuria jus non oritur en droit international*. Bruxelles: Bruylant, 2016.

91 Orakhelashvili, Alexander. Peremptory Norms in International Law. Oxford: Oxford University Press, 2006, p. 213.

92 Miaja de la Muela, Adolfo. "Nuevas realidades y teorías sobre la efectividad en Derecho internacional". *ADI*, vol. 3, 1976, p. 45.

93 Miaja de la Muela, Adolfo. "El principio de efectividad en Derecho internacional". In *Cursos de Derecho internacional de Vitoria 1957*. Universidad de Valladolid, 1958, p. 50.

94 Touscoz, Jean. *Le principe d'effectivité dans l'ordre international*. Paris: Librairie générale de droit et de jurisprudence, 1964, p. 256.

95 Verdross. op. cit., p. 83.

were to happen, it would be tantamount to introducing a contradiction into the legal system, which could only be resolved by denying its legal character[96]. Wallace-Bruce has formulated this theory as follows:

> [A]n entity, in satisfying the traditional criteria must do so in accordance with international law … when an entity claims to be a state; it has to satisfy the international community that it is not the product of international illegality. Put another way, the process by which the entity emerges should not have breached any international rule… If an entity emerges into the international scene through acts which are illegal under international law, no matter how effective it might be, its claim to statehood could not be maintained. It is an illegitimate child which cannot be clothed with legitimacy by the international community. The effect is that the claimant fails this new test of international legality and so its claim should be denied[97].

Thus, if no rule has been violated in the process of accession to statehood, once the necessary effectiveness has been obtained, a State emerges and the *ex factis jus oritur* maxim is fully valid; see, for example, the separation of Montenegro. On the other hand, if the process has taken place in violation of the law, the governing maxim is *ex iniuria ius non oritur* and, even though there may a certain degree of effectiveness, the State does not emerge: Republic of Sprska, Bantustans, Rhodesia, Biafra, Katanga; and, of course, Transnistria, TRNC, etc.

However, this is not a mere isolated opinion of international law scholars. When the ILC's Working Group on the Long-term Programme of Work proposed "Statehood" as a possible topic, in its report of 26 June 1996, it proposed to tackle the issue of *which factors should be taken into account when an entity claims to be a State in order to determine whether it should be treated as such.* In this regard, the Group noted that statehood should be considered in light of the principles of modern international law, including respect for the principles of the Charter and, in particular, the principles of self-determination of peoples and territorial integrity of States, prohibition of use of force in international relations, non-intervention in internal affairs – including domestic armed conflicts –, and respect for the fundamental principles of human rights and humanitarian law by all entities involved, including their interaction[98]. In other words, the ILC itself – the UN subsidiary body responsible for codifying international law – affirms that the creation of a State is subject to respect for the fundamental principles of the international legal order. Which means nothing other than introducing the criterion of legality as a necessary requirement for accession to statehood.

96 Lauterpacht. *Recognition…*, op. cit., p. 421.
97 Wallace-Bruce, Nii Lante. *Claims to Statehood in International Law.* New York: Carlton Press, 1994, p. 66.
98 See the text in Crawford. *The Creation…*2nd ed., op. cit., pp. 757–759.

In the context of this consolidation of the requirement of the legality criterion to form a new State, we should refer to the recent milestone that is the Resolution adopted by the *Instituto Hispano Luso Americano de Derecho Internacional* (IHLADI), at its session held in Lima (Peru) in December 2016, within the framework of its Third Committee "The Creation of States in Contemporary International Law in Cases of Secession: Effectiveness/Legality". It includes the following conclusions, thereby referring to the topic under analysis:

1 International Law only recognizes the right to independence to peoples subjected to colonial domination and to peoples subjected to subjugation, domination or foreign exploitation.
2 International Law does not recognize a right to secession. Peoples within a sovereign State have only the right to internal self-determination, that is, the right to decide their own political organization and without discrimination on the basis of race, creed or color. Likewise, the territorial integrity of the State in which they are located must be respected.
3 In contemporary International Law the creation of a new State must comply with the requirements of effectiveness and legality.
4 Effectiveness implies the general and exclusive control by the government of the state functions, on a continuous and prolonged basis, and independent of another State or International Organization.
5 The requirement of legality implies that the creation of the State must be carried out in accordance with the fundamental principles of International Law, especially the prohibition of the use of force and that of sovereignty and territorial integrity of States. Consequently, any unilateral declaration of Independence in violation of any of these Principles lacks validity and legal effects in application of the maxim *ex injuria non oritur ius*[99].

International practice supporting the requirement of the legality criterion in accession to statehood

Beyond the obvious scholarly debate generated by the introduction of the legality criterion, we understand that, in view of the absence of a conventional regulatory text on the subject, what really matters is State practice and whether a customary norm could be derived from it. In our opinion, there are sufficient elements in international practice to be able to support the establishment of, or at least the process of establishing, this condition of legality in the framework of State creation in contemporary international law.

The first aspect of State practice that we should take into consideration relates to the fact that, as we have already indicated, with the exception of Bangladesh and outside the context of decolonisation, no State has emerged without the consent of the parent State under contemporary international law; that is, there is no practice in favour of secession, and even in this exceptional

99 See the full text at http://ihladi.net/, as well as in *AHLADI*, vol. 23, 2015–2016.

case, Pakistan finally acquiesced to the secession. This is all the more significant if we bear in mind that the list of failed secessionist attempts is very long. To mention just a few well-known cases: Biafra (Nigeria), Katanga (Congo), Bougainville (Papua New Guinea), Aceh (Indonesia), Anjouan and Mayotte (Comoros), Jura in the canton of Berne (Switzerland), the Tamils in Sri Lanka, as well as the South African Bantustans. None of these attempts has been successful or supported by any other State or by any international organisation; on the contrary, they have expressed their opposition. Even in the case of Bangladesh, with the exception of India, the 'sponsor' State, no other State recognised it as such until the 'eventual success' of the secession, that is, until the situation was consummated, with the parent State renouncing recovery; it was at that moment, for example, when it was admitted to the Commonwealth. Similarly, States have not recognised any secession attempt until the consent of the parent State has been given. This happened in the cases of South Sudan (Sudan), Singapore (Malaysia) and Eritrea (Ethiopia).

In response to this claim, one might argue that Kosovo has accumulated 112 recognitions of independence, even without Serbia's consent. This is worth reflecting on. Certainly, as we will see later on, Kosovo is a peculiar and multifaceted case. In this respect, we have already noted that this entity does not yet meet the material requirements to be considered a State in the international sphere and that these recognitions are therefore premature and invalid. But there is also another very important fact to consider: according to Serbian Government sources, 18 States have withdrawn or revoked this recognition. The latest to have done so are Nauru (November 2019) and Sierra Leone (March 2020), which, in the notes sent by their respective foreign ministries, argue that the reason for withdrawal is that the decision to recognise Kosovo's independence was premature and contrary to Security Council Resolution 1244[100]. Others have claimed that recognition is on hold until there is an agreement between Kosovo and Serbia[101]. This confirms that States still acknowledge the need to respect international legality, as well as the need for the parent State's consent in order for a secession to be deemed successful.

Conversely, we find that, for example, no State has yet recognised Somaliland as a State despite it having operated effectively as such for over 20 years, no doubt because Somalia has not consented to its separation. It should be emphasised, however, that this is a special case for two reasons: first, because Somalia is a failed State, which prevents this consent from being given; and second, because Somaliland, a British protectorate, proclaimed its independence on 26 June 1960, deciding to join Italian Somaliland to form Somalia on 1 July; which means we could be dealing with a case of 'recovered identity'.

100 https://es.news-front.info/2019/11/23/la-independencia-de-kosovo-continua-disminuyendo-otro-pais-retiro-el-reconocimiento-del-cuasi-estado/.

101 www.prensa-latina.cu/index.php?o=rn&id=346747&SEO=anuncia-serbia-retirada-de-sierra-leona-del-reconocimiento-a-kosovo.

It is also worth referring to the repeated refusal of the vast majority of States – all but six – to recognise South Ossetia, Abkhazia, Transnistria, Nagorno-Karabakh or the TRNC. Similarly, no secessionist entity has been admitted as a member of the UN until the parent State has consented to the separation (Bangladesh[102]). Kosovo has been admitted to various international forums, such as the IMF, but has not been admitted as a member of any international organisation, not even by UNESCO or the Council of Europe, where some States that have supposedly recognised its statehood voted against its applications in 2017.

We even find that many States have clearly stated that they did not recognise attempts to secede because secession is contrary to international law, to the territorial integrity of the State, or because they considered that it was a matter of domestic law in which they should not interfere – the case of Chechnya. Just a few of many such examples will suffice.

Thus, with regard to Abkhazia, Italy has expressly stated that it does not recognise it as a State; that such recognition by third States has no basis in international law and is in opposition to the territorial integrity of Georgia. It stressed these arguments in the debate before the UN Secretary General on 28 August 2008, where it referred to Russia's recognition of Abkhazia having no basis in international law, while Georgia's territorial integrity is an indisputable principle thereof[103]. Similarly, Japan has not recognised South Ossetia or Abkhazia because it argues that the territorial integrity of Georgia should be respected and that both are still provinces of Georgia[104]. Likewise, Australia maintains that South Ossetia and Abkhazia are part of Georgia, subject to its sovereignty, and rejects Russia's recognition. The UK has also declared that it does not recognise South Ossetia and Abkhazia as States and that they should not be recognised as such; at the same time, it accuses Russia of violating Georgia's sovereignty and territorial integrity by supporting these secessionist entities. The USA's declarations echo this view. Brazil's position is even more categorical, as it does not recognise any secessionist entity, not even Kosovo; with regard to its declaration of independence, Brazil argues that it violates the integrity of Serbia and Security Council Resolution 1244[105].

In the same context, the interventions of the States that participated in the proceedings leading to the ICJ's Advisory Opinion on Kosovo speak volumes[106]. We see how those who opposed the legality of the unilateral declaration expressly stated that they did not recognise Kosovo as a State because the unilateral declaration of independence is contrary to international law – territorial integrity of Serbia and/or Security Council Resolution 1244

102 Resolution 3203 (XXIX) of the General Assembly.
103 UN Doc, S/PV.5969.
104 www.mofa.go.jp/announce/announce/2008/8/1182958_1040.html.
105 The texts of these declarations can be consulted at www.ssrn.com.
106 Of the States that participated at some stage during the proceedings, 25 declared they were in favour of the conformity of the declaration of independence, and 18 against.

(Argentina, Brazil, Spain, Russia, among others). Only the States clearly in favour of the conformity of the declaration of independence with international law stated that the applicable law was limited to the principle of effectiveness, which is contradictory to say the least, given that such effectiveness neither existed nor exists. That said, it should also be stressed that the Kosovo situation was an exception, a unique or *sui generis* case, justified, in general terms, by the serious human rights violations suffered by the Kosovar population at the hands of the Yugoslav Republic. From which it may be inferred, *a contrario sensu*, that in other cases of secessionism they would not have proceeded with recognition, as they did with Kosovo. Indeed, the same States have not recognised the independence of other secessionist entities, and they have even opposed such recognition as being contrary to international law (this is the case, among others, of Australia, Italy, Japan and the UK). Moreover, these States which claimed that the Kosovo declaration did not violate international law went so far as to state that although international law does not regulate this question, and therefore cannot be violated, secession attempts are subject to the peremptory norms of general international law[107].

Very eloquent in this regard is Judge Stotnikov in his dissenting opinion, in which he reflects on the Court's assertion that general international law does not prohibit declarations of independence (para. 84):

> This is a misleading statement which, unfortunately, may have an inflammatory effect. General international law simply does not address the issuance of declarations of independence, because declarations of independence do not 'create' or constitute States under international law. It is not the issuance of such declarations that satisfies the factual requirements, under international law, for statehood or recognition. Under international law, such declarations do not constitute the legal basis for statehood or recognition[108].

As regards internal practice, and in addition to the earlier references to the theory of 'eventual success', which are equally relevant, the Supreme Court of Canada's decision of 20 August 1998 with respect to Quebec cannot be overlooked. The Court's decision affirms, contrary to the claim of the National Assembly, the legislature or the Government of Quebec that they could be independent through *faits accomplis*, that the principle of effectiveness has no constitutional or legal status in the sense that it provides no explanation or justification prior to the act. Acceptance of this principle would mean that the Quebec authorities could act without regard for the law, for the simple reason that they claim they can. If this proposition is presented as a statement of law,

107 See, in this respect, the written statements of Denmark (pp. 2–4) or Switzerland (pp. 26–29).

108 Therein, Judge Stotnikov echoes the statement of the Norwegian Government (www.icj-cij.org/docket/files/141/16002.pdf, para.17).

the implication is that the law can be violated if the violation is successful, and "une telle affirmation est contraire à la primauté du droit et doit donc être rejetée"[109].

Equally relevant is *the practice of international organisations*, which follows in the wake of the State practice referred to earlier, in that they do not accept and do condemn declarations of independence that are contrary to international law. The League of Nations did so in relation to Manchukuo in 1932. UN practice is very explicit in this respect, in relation to various attempts at secession. Over a period of 15 years, the Security Council repeatedly condemned Rhodesia (for violating the right of self-determination of peoples), insisting that it did not consider it a State and that the declaration of independence was not legally valid. It maintained exactly the same position in relation to the South African Bantustans, because of apartheid. Equally forceful was the Council's reaction to the declaration of the TRNC – owing to the use of armed force – where it repeatedly affirmed its invalidity, describing it as 'legally void', and that all its actions were null and void, illegal and invalid[110].

Resoundingly clear and forceful is Resolution 787 (1992) adopted in relation to the Republic of Sprska, where the Security Council "calls on all parties and others concerned to respect strictly the territorial integrity of the Republic of Bosnia and Herzegovina, and affirms that any entities unilaterally declared or arrangements imposed in contravention thereof will not be accepted". Likewise, Resolution 874 (1998) affirms the territorial integrity of Azerbaijan with respect to Nagorno-Karabakh, while Resolutions 1393 (2002) and 1808 (2008) defend Georgia's territorial integrity against Abkhazia's attempt to secede from it. And, of course, Resolution 1244 (1999) in favour of the territorial integrity of Serbia, which, until the Council issues another resolution to the contrary, remains fully in force.

We should even bear in mind an important fact regarding Bangladesh. Unquestionably, the success of the secession was due to the assistance provided by India, which, claiming self-defence (not armed support for the liberation of Bangladesh), invaded Pakistan, causing a war between the two countries which was lost by the latter and led to secession. Well, a Security Council resolution condemning India's intervention and defending Pakistan's territorial integrity was proposed but did not see the light of day due to the USSR's veto.

The UN General Assembly has also had occasion to determine the invalidity of these declarations of independence. The first was in relation to Katanga, in respect of which it declared in Resolution 1474 (XVI) that all secessionist activities were contrary to fundamental principles. Subsequently, it expressed its

109 http://scc-csc.lexum.com/scc-csc/scc-csc/fr/1643/1/document.do, p. 275.

110 Among many other resolutions, see, respectively, for each one of the three cases: 216 and 217 (1965); 402 and 407 (1976); 541 (1983) and 550 (1984). Previously, it had argued against the secession of Katanga (Resolution 169 of 1961).

position regarding Biafra and Mayotte. In all cases it denied their recognition, even arguing against the obligation to respect territorial integrity[111].

Of great significance in this respect was the declaration made on 4 June 1970 by the UN Secretary General U. Thant, at a press conference in Dakar following the Biafra crisis, according to which the UN, as an international organisation, has never accepted, nor will ever accept, the secession of a part of one of its Member States[112].

Along the same lines, we should look at the practice of some regional organisations. At a European level, the position of the Council of Europe, the European Union and the OSCE is very clear. All these organisations have condemned the secessions of South Ossetia and Abkhazia as an attack against the territorial integrity of Georgia, or because of the use of force, or for contravening both principles[113]. Likewise, the OSCE reaffirmed the territorial integrity of Moldova, in relation to Transnistria, and condemned the secessionist attempt by Chechnya for violating Russia's territorial integrity.

In the African arena, the OAU has rejected the secession attempts of Biafra, Katanga and the island of Anjouan, invoking the principle of territorial integrity and the national unity of Nigeria, Congo and Comoros, respectively. It should be recalled that the 1963 OAU Charter recognises the territorial integrity of its Member States as a fundamental principle (Article III)[114]. In the same African context, it is necessary to refer to the jurisprudence of the African Commission on Human Rights. In its 1994 decision on the *Katangese People's Congress v Zaire* case, when questioned about Katanga's right to secede in the context of the right to self-determination, the Commission argued that no such right existed and that Katanga could only exercise the internal dimension of self-determination, stating, moreover, that "the Commission is obligated to uphold the sovereignty and territorial integrity of Zaire, a member of the OAU and a party to the African Charter on Human and Peoples Rights"[115]. The Commission took the same position in its decision on the *Kevin Mgwanga Gunme et al/Cameroon* case, adopted in 2009[116].

As we can see from an examination of practice, the response of States and international organisations is very clear and unequivocal, as well as widespread, consistent and uniform (requirements that give rise to a customary norm in the international legal order): they do not accept the accession to statehood of secessionist entities that unilaterally declare their independence, because this constitutes a violation of the territorial integrity of the parent State and, as the

111 Resolutions 1746 (XVI), 1752 (XVII), 2230 (XXI), 2355 (XXII), 3385(XXX), 31/4, 1976 and 34/91, 1979.

112 United Nations Monthly Chronicle, no. 7, 1970, p. 3.

113 A detailed list of all the decisions adopted by these three European organisations can be found in Peters. "Statehood after 1989...", op. cit., pp. 8–9.

114 A fundamental principle that is also laid down in the Helsinki Final Act of 1 August 1975 (IV).

115 Communication 75/92, para. 27–28.

116 Communication 266/03, para. 194–195.

case may be, prohibition of use of force, self-determination or protection of human rights. In other words, they are not States because of this violation.

Legal limits on accession to statehood. The fundamental principles of international law that intervene in cases of secession and apply to the case of Catalonia

Without a doubt, the fundamental issue that remains to be clarified involves determining exactly what these legal limits are. In other words, what are the rules that, if not obeyed, would prevent an aspiring entity from becoming a State?

In this respect, Salvioli maintained that if a State had emerged in ignorance of the fundamental principles of international law, its effectiveness would not compel other States to recognise it, and nor would it give that State any international legal status[117]. For his part, Grant states that: "Statehood has come to be defined as more than effectiveness. New criteria of statehood such as compliance with ius cogens norms, guarantee of minority rights, and democracy, reflect new claims to international competence over internal governance"[118].

It is worth remembering what the ILC's Working Group on the Long-term Programme of Work said about the factors to be taken into account when an entity claims to be a State in order to determine whether it should be treated as such. According to the Group, the matter should be considered in the light of the principles of modern international law, including respect for the principles of the Charter and, in particular, the principles of self-determination of people and territorial integrity of States, prohibition of the use of force in international relations, non-intervention in internal affairs – including armed conflicts –, respect for the fundamental principles of human rights and of humanitarian law by all entities involved, including their interaction.

Of the utmost importance in this context – as they are the only international rules of positive law we have in this respect – are Articles 6 and 3 of the Vienna Conventions on Succession of States in respect of Treaties, of 23 August 1978, and on Succession of States in respect of Property, Archives and Debts, of 8 April 1983, respectively. The identical content of these articles is as follows: "The present Convention applies only to the effects of a succession of States occurring in conformity with international law and, in particular, the principle of international law embodied in the Charter of the United Nations".

These clauses are clearly derived from the *ex iniuria ius non oritur* principle, on stipulating that an unlawful succession – because it violates the fundamental

117 He also added that legitimising *de facto* situations because they have been realised effectively is tantamount to an inversion between law and fact, and to the elimination of any assessment of what is lawful and unlawful (Salvioli, Grabiele. "L'effettività in Diritto internazionale". *Rivista trimestrale di Diritto Pubblico*, 1953, p. 279).

118 Grant. "Defining Statehood…", op. cit., p. 213.

principles of international law – does not produce legal effects in favour of the acting entity, whatever its effectiveness. In this legal framework, secession is traditionally included within the succession of States, and is termed 'separation' in both Conventions. This being the case, and with a *sensu contrario* interpretation of the aforementioned articles, we find that they clearly recognise the possibility of successions that do not occur in conformity with international law; such are those that do not respect the fundamental principles embodied in the UN Charter, which is precisely where secession is situated. The consequence is that no legal effects arise in such cases[119]. Indeed, Bedjaoui, ILC member and participant in the process of drawing up these provisions, states in relation to this clause: "The successor who has violated the law is simply a 'non-successor', and the rights of the successor should not be established, simply because he has none, because he cannot have any"[120].

Thus, both provisions confirm two fundamental aspects relating to secession: first, that contemporary international law does regulate, to some extent, accession to statehood for secessionist entities and, therefore, the non-existence of a right of secession; and second, that the international legal order establishes legal limits for statehood and that these are the fundamental principles of international law.

The raison d'être of this legal limit formed by these principles lies in their very nature, for they are principles that embody the fundamental values that affect the entire international community as a whole. They are the materialisation of the universal consensus on the essential legal values that inform all international law, that make up its general frame of reference. Consequently, these principles will form a kind of boundary for this whole system, in that they constitute the fundamental core of *jus cogens* norms[121]. And this includes, obviously, the most important aspect of the international legal order, which is none other than the formation of its central subject, the State, in such a way that obstacles must be overcome in order for new State entities to be created. This being their nature, it goes without saying that the fundamental principles must be respected not only by States but by all the constituent parts of the international community whose fundamental values they protect.

In light of all this, especially with regard to international practice and international laws and norms, the conclusion seems very clear: the legal limit on accession to statehood for aspiring entities consists of the *fundamental principles of international law*. This is an evolving legal category, and therefore such principles have emerged as the international community and the international order itself have evolved. Some date back to the very origin of international law, such as the principle of sovereign equality; others appeared and developed during the

119 The same wording appears in Article 3 of the ILC's draft articles on nationality in cases of succession (1999), included in United Nations General Assembly Resolution A/55/153, of 30 January 2001.

120 ILC Yearbook 1974, I., p. 81.

121 López Martín, Ana G. *Derecho internacional público*. Madrid: Dilex, 5th ed., 2019, p. 35.

nineteenth century, such as the principle of peaceful cooperation or that of non-interference. Yet most of them have taken shape since the advent of contemporary international law, such as prohibition of use of force, self-determination of peoples, protection of human rights, etc. These principles are set out in Article 2 of the UN Charter and in General Assembly Resolution 2625 (XXV). Some others, not referred to in these legal texts, have arisen from State practice and have been recognised as such by the ICJ – protection of human rights and the environment, principles of international humanitarian law. This general rule, which makes accession to statehood conditional on respect for the fundamental principles of international law, is applicable irrespective of the form of State creation, but is undoubtedly more far-reaching and significant in the case of attempted secession.

In this respect, we ask ourselves what are the fundamental principles of international law that more specifically must be respected by secessionist entities in the process of accession to statehood. Aside from the fact that they are all effective, we believe that the principles that play a predominant role in this process of creating a new State are the following[122]: non-interference in internal affairs; prohibition of the threat or use of force; self-determination of peoples; respect for fundamental human rights; and territorial integrity of the State.

Principle of non-interference in internal affairs

The principle of non-interference in the internal affairs of a State is the corollary of the principle of sovereign equality of States and is also based on the principle of freedom of States to choose their political, economic, social and cultural system. It is closely linked to both the principle of territorial integrity and the principle of prohibition of the threat or use of armed force.

In relation to this principle, Resolution 2625 (XXV) specifies that no State may intervene either directly or indirectly, for any reason whatsoever, in the internal or external affairs of another State, which includes not only armed intervention but any other form of interference or "attempted threats" against the personality of the State or its political, cultural or economic elements, which "are in violation of international law". Neither may States use economic, political or any other form of coercion against another State in order to subordinate the exercise of that State's sovereign rights. Likewise, no State shall "organize, assist, foment, finance, incite or tolerate subversive, terrorist or armed activities directed towards the violent overthrow of the régime of another State, and interfere in civil strife in another State". Under this principle, in the event of an attempt to constitute a new State from a pre-existing one, third States must disregard this attempt and not interfere. States must also refrain from giving any form of assistance to any secessionist forces or groups that may arise within another State.

122 Such principles are also referred to by Kohen as those directly involved in the process of creating new States: Kohen. "La création …", op. cit., p. 576.

Obviously, given that secession is radically different from decolonisation, supporting the struggle of peoples in the context of decolonisation is not affected by this principle.

Furthermore, we should also bear in mind that, as Kohen indicates[123], failure to respect the principle of non-interference may take more serious forms, constituting a violation of the obligation to respect the territorial integrity of States and of the prohibition of use of armed force. The assistance provided by the Milosevic regime to the Serbian secessionist entity in Bosnia and Herzegovina is an example of contravention of the three aforementioned principles. As is Turkey's involvement in the secessionist declaration of the TRNC.

Principle of prohibition of the threat or use of armed force

According to this principle, States shall refrain from threatening or using force in their international relations, against the territorial integrity or the political independence of any State, or in any other manner incompatible with the purposes of the UN. In terms of the limits that this principle imposes on the process of creating a new State, we should first stress the fact that no State may assist a secessionist movement by using armed force. Doing so quite clearly contravenes this principle, as well as the principle of non-interference in internal affairs, as we have just indicated. The case of the TRNC, which declared itself an independent State in 1983 after the Turkish army had invaded Cypriot territory, is paradigmatic in this respect. This proclamation resulting from the use of armed force was declared null and void by the Security Council.

There is another question concerning the applicability of this principle in the process of State creation, which is that Article 2.4 of the United Nations Charter only prohibits the use of force in *international relations*. In this regard, unlike what happens in the context of decolonisation or foreign occupation, the relationship between a State and a secessionist movement that emerges within its territory is substantially an internal matter, governed, therefore, by the domestic laws of the State concerned. This being so, the customary rule of the prohibition of use of force enshrined in Article 2.4 does not apply to their mutual relations.

This means, in concrete terms, that the authorities of the State affected by the attempted secession may resort to the legitimate use of armed force to quell it, whereas use of force by separatist movements has no legal foundation. However, international law is not completely removed from an armed conflict of this nature, as the rules of humanitarian law governing internal armed conflicts will apply. An example of this is Chechnya's attempt to secede from Russia (1991–1994).

Principle of self-determination of peoples

First, we must differentiate the principle of self-determination of peoples from the principle of nationalities. The former is a legal principle, whereas the latter,

123 Ibid., pp. 581–582.

despite playing an important role in the development of national movements in the nineteenth and twentieth centuries, has only reached the level of a political principle on an international scale. The first mention of the principle of self-determination in a legal context can be found in the Charter of the United Nations, although the references are rather general, vague and even contradictory (Articles 1.2 and 55), and at no point is it explicitly recognised as a principle. It has been the subsequent practice of the UN itself that has led to the establishment of the self-determination of peoples as a structural principle. Here we are bound to mention General Assembly Resolutions 1514 (XV), 1541 (XV) and 2625 (XXV). The last of these represents a key milestone in the evolution of this principle, insofar as it recognises it for all peoples – not only colonial peoples – and configures it not only as a right of peoples but also as a duty of States. According to its wording, all peoples have the right freely to determine, without external interference, their political status and to pursue their economic, social and cultural development, and every State has the duty to respect this right in conformity with the provisions of the Charter.

To give an idea of the limits that it imposes on the process of accession to statehood, it would suffice to refer to the fact that within the framework of this principle, the right to independence – external self-determination – is recognised only for peoples under colonial domination and peoples subjected to foreign subjugation, domination and exploitation[124]. Other 'peoples' – those that exist within the territory of a sovereign State – are entitled only to 'internal' self-determination, that is, the right to decide their own political organisation and without discrimination on the basis of race, creed or colour; but they lack 'external' self-determination, so they do not have the right to separate themselves from the State they form part of in order to set up a State of their own, as they are limited by the obligation to respect the principle of territorial integrity of the State they form part of. This being the case, peoples existing within a State only have the right to separate in two cases: with the express consent of the predecessor State (e.g. Singapore); and if so permitted by domestic law (e.g. Article 39 of the 1994 Constitution of Ethiopia; 1983 Constitution of the Federation of Saint Kitts and Nevis).

Furthermore, the principle of self-determination also implies that an entity which declares itself independent does not attain statehood if, in the process, it does not respect the right of self-determination of the peoples integrated in the territory on which it declares its independence. In this regard, we could mention Rhodesia's declaration of independence in 1965, made by the white minority in violation of the rights of the black population, which was

124 As expressly stated in Resolution 1514 (XV) of the General Assembly, and as endorsed by ICJ jurisprudence (paragraph 79 of the Advisory Opinion on Kosovo of 2010). As regards the case of subjugation and foreign exploitation, it refers to territories that have been illegally annexed; once the use of force is prohibited by contemporary international law, foreign domination is equated with colonial domination in the context of self-determination; this could be the case of the 'recovery of identity' of the Baltic republics.

condemned by both the Security Council (Resolution 217) and the General Assembly (Resolution 2151). Katanga's declaration of independence from the Congo in 1960, which was also condemned and declared illegal by the Security Council (Resolution 169), would also fall into this category.

Principle of respect for fundamental human rights

Mentioned tangentially both in the Charter (Preamble and Articles 1, 55 and 56) and in Resolution 2625 (XXV), there is no doubting today that it is a structural principle. In this respect, the basic frame of reference would be Resolution 217 A (III) of 10 December 1948, i.e. the Universal Declaration of Human Rights, although its ultimate recognition occurred on the occasion of the Declaration marking the 50th anniversary of the UN (General Assembly Resolution 50/6 of 24 October 1995), in which the universality of human rights and the protection thereof is enshrined as a fundamental principle. The relationship between this principle and the creation of new States constitutes a complex problem, which raises a number of questions[125], because it could be argued that new States would only be obliged to respect standards relating to human rights that they themselves bind themselves to from the moment of accession to statehood. If this were the case, then how can their respect be a condition for the creation of a new State? Is respect for human rights a condition to be met for accession to statehood or not? If what occurs is a massive violation of human rights when proclaiming independence, is the emergence of a new State prevented? Is there a right to create a new State that arises from the massive violation of the rights of the individuals that exist in the territory in question?

As we have already stated and been able to verify, the fundamental principles impose obligations on all members of the international community, who not only benefit from them but are also bound by them. The principle of universal respect for fundamental human rights is no exception in this regard. Even more so, in this particular case, given that the direct beneficiaries of this principle are natural persons, it is clear that they not only obtain the right to respect their fundamental rights, but also the obligation to do so; proof of this is international law's recognition of their criminal liability in the event of serious violations of those rights. The members of a secessionist group are but natural persons.

In this respect, international practice shows that when entities claiming to be States declare their independence, and when this has been done in serious violation of fundamental human rights, the existence of such a State is excluded by international law. This was the case in Rhodesia[126], as we have already

125 Kohen. "La création…", op. cit., p. 588.

126 We should also not forget that self-determination is a fundamental right, as recognised in Article 2 of the International Covenant on Civil and Political Rights of 1966.

pointed out, and, above all, of the Bantustans in South Africa (Transkei, Ciskei, Bophuthatswana and Venda), whose proclamation of independence took place in a context of systematic racial discrimination – apartheid – and denial of human rights, which led to condemnation by the United Nations General Assembly and refusal to consider them States (Resolution 1474).

Political rights are of prime importance when demanding that a new State meet its obligation to respect fundamental human rights. Especially significant are the right to equality before the law and without discrimination, the right of citizens to engage in public affairs, the right to universal suffrage, the right of access to public office, etc.[127] And let us not forget the importance, as previously mentioned, of respecting the rights of any national, religious and ethnic minorities that may arise within the context of the secession process.

Principle of territorial integrity and its obligatory nature in relation to secessionist movements

The principle of territorial integrity is the one most closely linked, almost inextricably so, to the principle of sovereign equality of States, which is, as we have indicated, the founding structural principle of today's international community and, perhaps, the most fundamental of those that form the core of international law. Indeed, it could be described as the fundamental rule of the international legal order[128]. In this respect, Resolution 2625 (XXV), in describing the content and scope of the principle of sovereign equality enshrined in Article 2(1) of the UN Charter, expressly declares that:

> In particular, sovereign equality includes the following elements:
>
> [...]
>
> e) The territorial integrity and political independence of the State are inviolable.

One of the most important consequences of the principle of territorial integrity is that it stands as a guarantee against any dismemberment of the territory of a State without its consent. This derives specifically from the term "integrity". It is essential to understand that it is a matter of respecting territorial integrity as well as sovereignty. Without a shadow of a doubt, the most obvious hypothesis of failure to respect the principle of territorial integrity, in the context of the creation of new States, is the case of one part of the territory of a State seceding in an attempt to become a State artificially, against the will and/or domestic

127 Kohen. "La création...", op. cit., p. 588.

128 In the same vein, Tomuschat, Christian. "International Law: Ensuring the Survival of Mankind on the Eve of a New Century. General Course on Public International Law". *Recueil des Cours*, vol. 281, 2001, p. 13.

law of that State. The cases of Manchukuo, the TRNC and Kosovo are just some of the examples that could be mentioned in this context.

The obligation to respect the territorial integrity of a State clearly extends to all States. International treaties and international jurisprudence are very explicit in this regard: any action taken by one State against the territorial integrity of another State constitutes a violation of international law. Article 10 of the Covenant of the League of Nations had already compelled all States to protect the integrity of all Member States against external aggression. We have seen how Article 2(4) of the Charter prohibits the threat or use of force against the territorial integrity of States. Bearing in mind that both direct and indirect use are prohibited, any support for a rebel group – including a secessionist movement – provided by a State violates international law. The Helsinki Act also compels States to respect territorial integrity. As for jurisprudence, the ICJ has repeatedly maintained that States have a duty to respect the territorial integrity of other States[129].

The crucial question in this respect is whether this obligation also extends to non-State international actors and subjects. Specifically, is a people, a group or an entity within a State bound to respect territorial integrity within that State?

In relation to this question, the ICJ concluded in its *Advisory Opinion on Kosovo* that "the scope of the principle of territorial integrity is confined to the sphere of relations between States"[130], and therefore private individuals cannot violate such integrity. We believe it is important to put this statement in its proper context and thereby determine its real meaning and true scope. To this end, the first thing we should bear in mind is that the Court's decision on this point is adopted on the basis of Article 2(4) of the Charter, which, as we have seen, limits the prohibition of use of force – against the territorial integrity of States – to the sphere of relations between States; as well as the Helsinki Act, which states the same. However, it ignored all the other legal instruments that were absolutely relevant to the case and which would lead to a manifestly different conclusion, particularly the Security Council resolutions on the matter.

Therefore, what we should bear in mind above all is that the assertion made by the Court forms part of the whole architecture it has constructed since it 'amended' the question put to it by the General Assembly, to make the action relating to the unilateral declaration of independence rest not with a people, an authority representative of a people, or a minority, but with some private individuals who, as we all know, lack subjectivity in this sphere; and thus arrive at the predetermined response of its Opinion. This being the case, if we ignore this ICJ 'manoeuvre' and situate ourselves, as we should, in the scenario of a

129 We could mention, among others, the Corfu Chanel case (1949), or the case concerning *Military and Paramilitary Activities in and against Nicaragua* (1986).

130 ICJ Reports, 2010, p. 403. An opinion which, however, contrasts with that of several States that participated in the process, who argued that the principle of respect for territorial integrity extends not only to States, but also to international organisations and non-State actors, such as secessionist groups within a State (Argentina, Serbia, Spain, Iran, Cyprus, among others).

secessionist entity that intends to exercise its 'self-determination', as they all so insistently claim, it is clear that we are not dealing with mere individuals, but with a 'people' that enjoys subjectivity precisely in this area, and that *is* bound to respect territorial integrity insofar as international law so requires. General Assembly Resolutions 1514 (XV) and 2625 (XXV), among others, are very clear in establishing the 'safeguard clause' that the principle of self-determination shall not impair the territorial integrity or political unity of sovereign and independent States. In addition, these resolutions also advise States that they should refrain from any action directed towards the partial or total violation of the national unity and territorial integrity of any other State.

The legal basis of this obligatory nature in relation to non-State actors lies in the fact that entities which are recognised as having a certain international legal subjectivity – peoples, minorities, individuals, etc. – are bound to respect the fundamental principles of international law and to behave in accordance with its provisions, particularly those that specifically address them.

There is also a chronological factor we should not overlook, which is that although the references to the obligation to respect territorial integrity were originally addressed to States, at the time of adoption of the different texts that include these references, States were the only entities that could endanger the territorial integrity of their peers. Today, however, individuals and, fundamentally, groups – with varying intensity in terms of international subjectivity – have the capacity to jeopardize the territorial integrity of States. This is borne out by the fact that the 2007 UN Declaration on the Rights of Indigenous Peoples specifically extends the obligation to respect the territorial integrity of States to peoples, groups and individuals. It expressly states in Article 46 that:

> Nothing in this Declaration may be interpreted as implying for any State, *people, group or person* any right to engage in any activity or to perform any act contrary to the Charter of the United Nations or construed as *authorizing or encouraging any action which would dismember or impair, totally or in part, the territorial integrity or political unity of sovereign and independent States* [131].

Furthermore, the practice of UN bodies – subsequent to the legal texts that bind this principle to relations between States – in relation to secessionist attempts endorses the obligatory nature of respect for territorial integrity on the part of secessionist groups. In all cases in which secessionist movements have proclaimed their independence by means that contravene domestic law and have no basis in international law, these bodies have invoked the territorial integrity of the sovereign State from which the movement has sought to secede in order to condemn or challenge the validity of such proclamations of independence, maintaining that the obligation to respect that integrity is binding on secessionist movements. This has been the case with regard to Bosnia and

131 The Declaration was adopted on 13 September 2007, by a majority of 144 votes in favour, four against and 11 abstentions (italics are ours).

Herzegovina (Republic of Sprska), Georgia (South Ossetia and Abkhazia), Comoros, Somalia (Somaliland and Puntland), and even Kosovo.

The resolutions adopted by the Security Council concerning the unilateral proclamation of independence of the Republic of Sprska, in Bosnia and Herzegovina, are extremely explicit in this respect. Resolution 787 (1992) states that "any entities unilaterally declared" – without mentioning the name of the republic – cannot be accepted, and it calls on "all parties" to respect strictly the territorial integrity of Bosnia and Herzegovina, a term that clearly encompasses the secessionist entity. In several subsequent resolutions, the Security Council condemned the "Bosnian Serbs" of that State for not respecting the territorial integrity of Bosnia and Herzegovina[132]. The Serbs in Croatia – in the enclave of Krajina – were also condemned for refusing to respect the territorial integrity of Krajina[133]. In Somalia, the Security Council dismissed the secessionist aspirations of Somaliland and Puntland by reaffirming the importance of the territorial integrity and political unity of the State[134]. Likewise, the Security Council has strongly insisted that it would not accept the secession of any of the peoples of Darfur, reaffirming the need to respect the territorial integrity of Sudan[135].

Therefore, contrary to the Court's opinion – based on a treaty clause of 1945 relating only to a tangential aspect of the problem –, international practice clearly shows that the obligation to respect territorial integrity is not confined to relations between States and that it affects all subjects interacting in the international community, as we have been able to ascertain.

Legal consequence of failing to fulfil the criterion of legality in aspiring to statehood: invalidity of the unilateral declaration of independence

Having reached this point, there is one last important question to answer in the context of this contemporary approach to the criterion of legality. What is/are the legal *consequence(s)* of an aspiring State's failure to respect the fundamental principles of international law in the process of attempting to become independent?

In this respect, as our analysis has shown, the language used both by legal scholarship and by States and international organisations is far from uniform, to the extent that they even refer to cumulative consequences.

Thus, some argue that what occurs in these cases is the *invalidity* of the act of declaration of independence[136]. As Miaja de la Muela rightly pointed out:

> An act that contravenes the rules of international law is, as in any legal order, invalid [...]

132 Resolutions 859 (1993) and 942 (1994).
133 Resolution 981 (1995).
134 Resolutions 1766 (2007) and 1772 (2007).
135 Resolutions 1566 (2004) and 1769 (2007).
136 Among others, Tancredi. "A Normative 'Due Process'...", op. cit., p. 200.

> According to the jurisprudence of the international courts (*Nottebohm, Fisheries, Greenland*, etc.) and State practice, effectiveness alone does not create legal effects if it is not accompanied by the conformity of the factual situation with international law or, if it contravenes the latter, by the recognition of the State vis-à-vis whom the effects of that situation are intended to be made enforceable. The fundamental criterion of enforceability is not effectiveness but legality. Factual situations in conformity with international law take effect vis-à-vis third parties without need for recognition. Not vice versa. If the effective situation contravenes international law, it lacks enforceability until it is recognised
>
> [...]
>
> Without recognition, the effectiveness of a situation can only take effect if it has been created in accordance with international law. It is necessary to remember this in order to reduce the principle of effectiveness in international law to its proper limits and to prevent an alleged realism from leading us to negate international law through an unconditional and absolute admission of the principle of effectiveness[137].

Others also refer to the *nullity* of the unilateral declaration of independence, when this act of proclamation takes place in contravention of the peremptory norms of general international law[138]. It is important to recall, in this respect, that a significant proportion of the fundamental principles of international law have given rise to peremptory norms of general international law, as they are defined in Article 53 of the Vienna Convention on the Law of Treaties of 1969,

> a norm accepted and recognized by the international community of States as a whole as a norm from which no derogation is permitted and which can be modified only by a subsequent norm of general international law having the same character[139].

Identifying which rules have a peremptory character is certainly one of the greatest challenges facing our legal order, given the special legal consequences that they entail. In this regard, while it may be noted that recognition of the

137 Miaja de la Muela. "El principio de efectividad...", op. cit., pp. 60, 64 and 99, respectively.

138 For example, Peters. "Statehood after 1989...", op. cit., p. 6. Exactly the same view is taken by many States, such as South Africa or Israel.

139 Article 53 in full:

> A treaty is void if, at the time of its conclusion, it conflicts with a peremptory norm of general international law. For the purposes of the present Convention, a peremptory norm of general international law is a norm accepted and recognized by the international community of States as a whole as a norm from which derogation is permitted and which can be modified only by a subsequent norm of general international law having the same character.

existence of peremptory norms as part of the modern structure of international law is not currently a source of controversy, and that there is even consensus on the very notion of *jus cogens*, the consensus disappears when it comes to their content and individualisation. This situation is aggravated by the lack of authorised norms for determining their exact legal content or the process by which international norms can attain peremptory status[140]. We will return to this essential and complex task of identifying the peremptory norms of international law when discussing the obligation of non-recognition in the next chapter. However, by way of briefly approaching the question of the nullity of unilateral declarations, we can affirm that there is a certain degree of unanimity in relation to some of them. This is the case of the prohibition of use of force, as well as respect for the 'hard core' of fundamental rights – prohibition of genocide, apartheid, slavery, torture and forced disappearance of persons[141]. We also observe a significant degree of consensus regarding the sovereign equality of States, non-interference in internal affairs and the self-determination of (colonial) peoples. Thus, when a declaration of independence has been made in contravention of any or some of these fundamental principles – legal limit on accession to statehood – it has also been in contravention of the norm or norms of *jus cogens* that have stemmed therefrom.

Given this state of affairs, we could place the declaration of independence within the framework of the international legal regulation of unilateral legal acts. In this legal setting, the "Guiding Principles applicable to unilateral declarations of States capable of creating legal obligations" (2006) maintain that: "8. A unilateral declaration which is in conflict with a peremptory norm of general international law is void".

This assertion is also supported by the ICJ in its 2002 Judgment on *Armed Activities on the Territory of the Congo*, when it states that a unilateral declaration that contravenes a norm of *jus cogens* would be invalid[142]. In this regard, the ILC adds in the commentary to guiding principle no. 8 that "the invalidity of a unilateral act which is contrary to a peremptory norm of international law derives from the analogous rule contained in article 53 of the 1969 Vienna Convention on the Law of Treaties". The majority of the members of the Commission considered that there was nothing to prevent this rule from being transposed to the case of unilateral declarations[143].

140 Such is the importance of this question that the ILC proposed it in 2015 as one of the possible topics to be addressed by the Sixth Committee of the General Assembly of the United Nations; although finally it was not included (A/CN.4/678).

141 See the interesting study carried out by Orakhelashvili. *Peremptory Norms…*, op. cit., pp. 36–66.

142 ICJ Reports 2002, para. 69.

143 Official Records of the General Assembly, Fifty-fourth Session, Supplement No. 10 (A/54/10), p. 292, para. 557; ibid., Fifty-fifth Session, Supplement No. 10 (A/55/10), p. 178, para. 597.

In light of this more than obvious analogy, we should also take into account the legal consequences that the 1969 Vienna Convention indicates for the case of a treaty being null and void because it conflicts with a peremptory norm. Namely, the parties shall:

> eliminate as far as possible the consequences of any act performed in reliance on any provision which conflicts with the peremptory norm of general international law, and bring their relations into conformity with the peremptory norm of general international law.
>
> (Article 71)

To elaborate on the nullity of unilateral declarations of independence in cases of secession, it is important to recall the content of the ninth report submitted by the ILC's Special Rapporteur in charge of codifying unilateral declarations, specifically the first part thereof concerning grounds for nullity. The report includes contravention of a peremptory norm as a ground for nullity, and the Special Rapporteur also considered that a unilateral act is null and void if *it conflicts with a norm of fundamental importance to the domestic law of the State* that formulates it, provided that the conflict is manifest (Principle 6)[144]. In the context of this possibility pointed out by Víctor Rodríguez Cedeño, the ILC's Special Rapporteur, it is obvious that a declaration of independence by a secessionist movement would be null and void on both grounds: on the one hand, for being contrary to a peremptory norm of general international law (sovereignty/territorial integrity; self-determination of peoples); and on the other hand, bearing in mind that, except in the aforementioned cases, no State allows the possibility of secession, especially if its constitution safeguards national sovereignty against separatist movements – as is the case with the 1978 Spanish Constitution –, such a declaration would also be null and void for contravening the fundamental law of the State where it occurs.

This important legal consequence is rooted in the primacy of the peremptory norms of general international law, which in turn lies in the fact that they protect collective interests shared by all States. This is why they generate obligations and rights *erga omnes*, which the latter assume or may enforce, as the case may be, not simply vis-à-vis another State in particular, but in respect of all others. In other words, it has its basis in the quality of the protected legal right. Such primacy entails the nullity of any other norm or act which is contrary thereto. As Crawford points out: "By virtue of their primacy, then, peremptory norms may invalidate not just treaties but other inconsistent legal acts, as well as affecting the legal consequences which would otherwise flow from factual situations inconsistent with them"[145].

144 A/CN.4/569 and Add. 1 (our italics).
145 Crawford. *The Creation*...2nd ed., op. cit., p. 102.

This being the legal regulation, it is clear that declarations of independence formulated contrary to a peremptory norm of general international law are null and lack validity.

Many disagree with this position of nullity, arguing that it is not possible to declare the act of unilateral declaration of independence null and void given that the international legal order lacks a process for such purpose[146]. Without discussing the matter in great detail, this latter argument could be countered with the *theory of the nullity of the juridical act*, which is fully applicable in this context, specifically the part relating to tacit nullity:

> Tacit or virtual nullity is that which, without being declared directly by the hypothetical premise of a legal rule or regulation, is tacitly contained and becomes evident when a particular legal act has an unlawful content, not only because it contravenes peremptory norms, but also because it contravenes public policy or an accepted principle of morality.
>
> These nullities are inferred from an inclusive interpretation of the legal system as a whole. In other words, determining them requires an interpretation not only of the legal norm but also of the bases or foundations of the legal system, which is made up of peremptory norms, public order and good customs. Nullity is deduced or inferred indirectly from the legal system, the requirement of a textual or direct prohibition being unnecessary.[147].

As for the various UN Security Council resolutions adopted in relation to secessionist declarations, they have referred to them using the terms 'illegality', 'invalidity' and 'nullity' interchangeably.

Faced with this dichotomy, Czaplinski rightly states that when reference is made to the nullity of any international legal instrument because it is contrary to a *jus cogens* norm, the term is used in the sense of 'invalidity', this being its legal consequence[148]. Thus, nullity and invalidity are inseparable terms. The same conclusion can be drawn from an analysis of the ILC's work on matters relating to the invalidity of treaties on the ground that they conflict with a peremptory norm of general international law.

146 This is the case of Tancredi. "A Normative 'Due Process'…", op. cit., p. 197, who maintains invalidity but not the nullity of the declaration. Verhoeven, Joe. "La reconnaissance internationale: Déclin ou renouveau?" *AFDI*, vol. 29, no. 9, 1993, p. 21; or Talmon, Stefan. *La non-reconnaissance collective des États illégaux*. Cours et travaux no 9. Paris: Université Pantheon-Assas, 2007, p. 25.

147 Caballero Huayllani, Julio César (www.monografias.com/trabajos88/nulidad-del-acto-jurdico/nulidad-del-acto-jurdico.shtml#efectosdea#ixzz4OwkuRQCL).

148 Czaplinski, Wladyslaw. "Ius Cogens and the Law of Treaties". In *The Fundamental Rules of the International Legal Order. Ius Cogens and Obligations Erga Omnes*, edited by Charles Tomuschat and Jean-Marc Thouvenin. Leiden/Boston: Martinus Nijhoff Publishers, 2006, pp. 87–91.

It follows that whether we speak of invalidity or of nullity or of both at once, the legal consequence is substantially the same: *lack of validity of the declaration of independence and, therefore, lack of legal effects*. This means that the secessionist entity *does not attain statehood*, i.e. it is not a State. And this is because for international law there are only States, which means that you either are a State or you are not. As Anzilotti said, there are no legitimate or illegitimate States[149].

Therefore, if it could be argued that a secessionist entity that declares itself a State should be considered a State because it possesses the material elements, but having acceded to statehood in violation of fundamental principles should be deemed an illegitimate State, such a position is clearly wrong and has no place in international law. The same conclusion must be reached if a distinction is made between *de jure* States, which would be those created not only with effectiveness but also in compliance with the law, and *de facto* States, which are those that meet the material requirements and fulfil the criterion of effectiveness, but not that of legality.

In any event, as Costelloe points out[150], when a unilateral declaration of an act of secession occurs, there is no need to resort to peremptory norms to explain why it has no legal effect. In international law, a declaration of secessionist independence does not have the effect of conferring international legal personality on that entity.

A secessionist entity that has violated the fundamental principles of international law does not become a State, since it does not meet the fourth criterion of legality. It therefore lacks the legal status that comes with statehood and the rights attached thereto. This being so, such an entity cannot be treated as a State in the field of international relations. This question is directly linked to the obligation not to recognise secessionist entities as States, which is incumbent on all States in the international community, as well as on international organisations, and which we will discuss in detail in the following chapter.

149 Anzilotti. *Corso di Diritto...*, op. cit., p. 154.
150 Costelloe, Daniel. *Legal Consequences of Peremptory Norms in International Law*. Cambridge: Cambridge Studies in International and Comparative Law, 2017, p. 168.

4 The role of recognition in accession to statehood and the obligation not to recognise a secessionist entity as a State

Second lesson for Catalonia and other secessionist entities

The concept of recognition in international law and its role in accession to statehood, particularly in cases of secession such as Catalonia

In the international order, many situations require the reaction of one or more States, the nature of the reaction being subject to legal assessment and producing legal consequences[1]. In this regard, as Grant holds, recognition "is a procedure whereby the governments of existing states respond to certain changes in the world community"[2]. Thus, when an alteration in the international order affects a State that has not participated in the change, it cannot be opposed until the State recognises it as such[3].

This being so, recognition can be defined as the unilateral act whereby a State establishes the existence of certain facts that may have legal consequences for its rights, obligations or political interests, and declares that these facts are the elements on which future legal relations will be based.

In an international society based on the juxtaposition of state sovereignties and devoid of higher authorities, recognition is a fundamental concept for clarifying the effects of inter-State relations. We are referring to an act of State that evaluates State conduct in respect of a certain event with legal consequences on the international plane. However, there is no general theory of recognition, no uniform practice and no formal set of rules governing it, and so it has become more of a political than a legal issue that protects the interests of the State carrying out the recognition. The area in which the concept of recognition has traditionally been most widely used is that of statehood. The creation of new States and their subsequent recognition by other States plays a

1 Quel López, F. Javier. "La práctica reciente en materia de reconocimiento de Estados: Problemas en presencia". *Cursos de Derecho Internacional de Vitoria-Gasteiz*. Madrid: Tecnos, 1994, p. 43.

2 Grant, Thomas D. *The Recognition of States: Law and Practice in Debate and Evolution*. Westport: Praeger, 1999, p. xix.

3 Charpentier, Jean. *La reconnaissance internationale et l'évolution du Droit des gens*. Paris: Pedone, 1956, p. 10.

DOI: 10.4324/9781003200772-5

huge role in world politics[4]. This is not the only area in which it operates, however. Other objects of recognition might be mentioned, such as certain subjects that are not fully legal entities in the international order (belligerents, insurgents, national liberation movements), changes that have occurred in governments, or specific legal situations (neutrality, protectorate, etc.). In other words, the objects of recognition may be numerous, but they have in common the active subject of recognition, which can only be the State.

Focusing on *recognition of States*, Brownlie[5] points out that it has a twofold basic legal function: on the one hand, that of determining statehood as a strictly legal matter with the jurisdictional consequences that such status may entail; and on the other, that of being a precondition for establishing bilateral relations between the new State and the recognising State, such as diplomatic relations or the conclusion of treaties. It is clear that, aside from the political issues that accompany it, recognition of States is of great importance within the framework of accession to statehood, especially in the context of new secessionist challenges such as those posed by Catalonia.

We need to be realistic. Even if, as we have seen, there is no right to unilateral secession under international law and it is not recognised in the constitution of the parent State, this does not rule out the possibility of a unilateral declaration – unlawful and unconstitutional – of independence, leading to a *de facto* secession.

It should be borne in mind that a right is one thing and freedom is another, and although secessionist peoples, groups or entities do not have that right, they do have the freedom to declare themselves independent. They are free to do so. And if the factual situation occurs, the question then is, *and what now?*

In the previous chapter we saw that such a declaration *would be devoid of legal effects at the international level* because it is *illegal* – for violating one or more of the fundamental principles of international law – and, consequently, *invalid*. The question is, *who declares the nullity and/or the lack of legal effects of the declaration of independence of a secessionist entity* such as the one made by Catalonia in 2017?

Well, the truth is that, in a decentralised society such as the international one, verification of such illegality is in the hands of the other States, through the act of recognition or, rather, of non-recognition. Because recognition is approval and non-recognition is censure. Therefore, it is not surprising – quite the opposite – that in the Declaration signed on 10 October 2017 and reiterated on 27 October, whereby the Catalan republic is proclaimed, the representatives of Catalonia: "CALL on states and international organisations to recognise the Catalan Republic as an independent and sovereign state"[6].

Obviously, it is States that have the power of self-appraisal, that can determine whether or not the act of declaration of independence of a secessionist

4 Visoka, Gëzim, John Doyle and Edward Newman. *Routledge Handbook of State Recognition*. Routledge, 2019, p. 16.

5 Brownlie. *Principles of…*, op. cit., p. 89.

6 www.dipublico.org/107654/cataluna-texto-de-la-declaracion-de-independencia/ (original in Spanish).

entity is null and void, and that can oppose it simply by not recognising the aspiring entity as a State; or, better still, by explicitly stating that it will not give such recognition to the entity that declares itself independent because it has violated international law. Such a statement was made on 29 September 2017 by US Secretary of State Rex Tillerson following the illegal independence referendum held on 25 September by the Kurdish authorities, in which Tillerson said that "the vote and the results lack legitimacy, and we continue to support a united, federal, democratic and prosperous Iraq"[7].

The international response to the various declarations made by the Parliament of Catalonia has been far more forceful. Following the illegal referendum of 1 October 2017, the French Government, to give but one example, stated on 9 October that "la Catalogne ne reconnaîtra pas si le gouvernement régional avance avec une déclaration unilatérale d'indépendance"[8]. After the unilateral declaration of independence on 27 October, France, Germany and the United Kingdom immediately rejected it and did not recognise it[9]. The President of the European Parliament, Antonio Tajani, even warned that "no one in the European Union is going to recognize" a declaration "contrary to the rule of law", to the Spanish Constitution and to the Catalan Statute of Autonomy, "which are part of the EU legal order"[10]. The reaction was identical in many other countries, such as Morocco, Turkey, Colombia, Argentina, Mexico, Canada, the United States and Serbia.

But the act of recognition is political (with legal effects), free and discretionary. Leaving it to such a concept to 'sanction' the invalidity of the unilateral declarations of independence of secessionist entities entails numerous risks, especially of partiality and arbitrariness. That said, we must bear in mind that recognising secessionist entities that do not comply with the law in the sense we have seen in the previous chapters constitutes a violation of the principle that prohibits abuse of the law.

Therefore, it is of great importance to analyse the role and legal consequences of recognition in the process of State creation in international law, focusing specifically on the case of State proclamation by secessionist movements such as in Catalonia.

Legal nature of recognition of States

Recognition of States was very precisely defined by the *Institut de Droit International* (IDI), in its Brussels resolution of 1936, as:

7 www.reuters.com/article/us-mideast-crisis-kurds-usa/u-s-does-not-recognize-kurdish-independence-vote-in-iraq-tillerson-idUSKCN1C42TS.

8 www.clarin.com/mundo/francia-dice-independencia-cataluna_0_r1uJxdKh-.html.

9 www.leparisien.fr/international/la-france-et-l-ue-ne-reconnaissent-pas-l-independance-de-la-catalogne-27-10-2017-7358976.php.

10 www.europapress.es/nacional/noticia-mapa-recoge-reacciones-lideres-internacionales-declaracion-independencia-cataluna-20171027210525.html.

> the free act by which one or more states ascertain the existence on a given territory of a politically organized human society, independent of any other existing state, capable of complying with the requirements of international law, and consequently express their willingness to consider it as a member of the International Community[11].

The free and discretionary nature that seems to characterise the unilateral act of recognition has given rise to different academic positions regarding its legal nature. In this respect, two models represent opposite poles in the classical debate about recognising new legal personalities under international law: the declarative model and the constitutive model. The divide between the two theories reflects the different conceptions of State formation.

The question is: can a given political entity be considered a State under international law even if it has not been recognised as such by existing States? The constitutive theory answers in the negative; the declarative theory seems to conclude that it can.

The constitutive theory is so called because it posits that recognition constitutes an essential part of a State's international legal personality. According to the constitutive model, the State only obtains its genesis through recognition. Thus, recognition in itself becomes a requirement of statehood, that is, it forms or constitutes the State. Oppenheim, one of the staunchest defenders of this academic position, expresses it in the following terms:

> Through recognition only and exclusively a State becomes an International Person and a subject of International Law (...)
>
> As soon as recognition is given, the new State's territory is recognized as the territory of a subject of International Law, and it matters not how this territory is acquired before the recognition[12].

Constitutive theory is the expression of a positivist understanding of international law as an order of a purely contractual and consensual nature, in which legal relations can only be established with the consent of the parties concerned. The fundamental consequence of this theory is that whether an entity becomes a State or not depends on the action of pre-existing States, since the theory maintains that the legal existence of new States derives from the will of those that already exist. Although the attributes of population, territory and organised government are elements of statehood, for the constitutive theory these are but nothing in the absence of recognition. Recognition perfects statehood. The proposition that follows the constitutive premise is that recognition resides in the absolute discretion of existing States. The decision to recognise is subject exclusively to their sovereign will and is made unilaterally, without reference to

11 IDI, *Annuaire*, 1936, p. 300.

12 Oppenheim, Lassa. *International Law: A Treatise. Vol. I. - Peace.* New Jersey: The Lawbook Exchange. Clark, 3rd ed., 1920, pp. 175 and 373.

the action of other members of the international community. This liberation from the law becomes a tool of the art of governance.

The main reproach that can be brought against the constitutive theory is that it leads to a relativity of the State as a subject of international law. What constitutes a State for one may not do so for another. In this respect, the decision of one State regarding the international legal personality of another may contradict the principle of sovereign equality[13]. This is why the creation of a State cannot fail simply because it is not recognised. On the other hand, this theory does not accommodate the international accountability of non-recognised States, since by denying their legal capacity, they are deprived not only of their rights but also of their obligations under the international legal order.

In contrast, under *declarative theory*, the State is constituted independently of its recognition. The latter simply declares that a community has managed to obtain all the requirements of statehood. Thus, the declarative conception of State recognition denies that the act of recognition alone grants legal personality. It presupposes the existence of the State but does not create it. According to this model, recognition is the evidence that a State already exists, but it is not an instrument for its creation; it is simply the declaration that statehood has been achieved. From this declarative standpoint, it is clear that the moment at which recognition should be given is when there is real and objective evidence that the constituent elements of the State are actually in place. Therefore, an entity cannot be recognised as a State prior to the existence of such elements. If it were, we would be dealing with what is called 'premature recognition', which has no legal validity or effect, as we will see later on. It is not possible to record the existence of what does not yet exist, so a premature recognition – beyond any possible violation, as the case may be, of non-intervention in matters which are essentially within the domestic jurisdiction of a State – constitutes an act devoid of the legal effects that accompany recognition; the main one being proof of the existence of a new State. *Tertium non datur.*

Recognition of States was initially based on the constitutive theory of statehood. It was devised at the Vienna Peace Congress in 1815, whose Final Act recognised only 39 sovereign States in Europe, while also establishing that any future State could only be accepted as such through recognition given by previously existing States. The reason for such a distinction between established States and any future claim to statehood was based on the 'historical longevity' of the former[14]. In contrast to this conception, declarative theory gradually imposed itself in the early twentieth century, and so we find that it now seems to have the support of most legal scholars and the majority of States. It is the one we have seen was adopted by the International Institute for Learning, Inc. (IIL) in its resolution of 1936. It is expressly included in some treaties, such as

13 Talmon. *La non-reconnaissance...*, op. cit., pp. 6–7.

14 Holsti, Kalavi J. *Taming the Sovereigns: Institutional Change in International Politics.* Cambridge: Cambridge University Press, 2004, p. 129.

in Article 3 of the 1933 Montevideo Convention or in Article 13 of the 1948 OAS Charter, as amended by the Buenos Aires Protocol[15]. Similarly, jurisprudence has also supported the declarative theory of recognition. Thus, in the *Tinoco* case, the Court suggests that recognition is simply evidence that the requirements of international law have already been met[16]. Judge Kreça, in his dissenting opinion in the case concerning the Application of the Convention on the Prevention and Punishment of the Crime of Genocide[17], took the same view.

Contemporary State practice also seems to support the declaratory model, as demonstrated by numerous examples[18]. In the same regard, the first opinion of the Arbitration Commission of the International Conference on the Former Yugoslavia asserted that recognition of States by other States had only "declaratory effects"[19]. Subsequently, it noted that recognition:

> tout comme la qualité de membre d'organisations internationales, témoignent de la conviction de ces États que l'entité politique ainsi reconnue constitue une réalité et lui confèrent certains droits et certaines obligations –non autrement précisés- au regard du droit international[20].

15 Article 13 provides that:

> The political existence of the State is independent of recognition by other States. Even before being recognized, the State has the right to defend its integrity and independence, to provide for its preservation and prosperity, and consequently to organize itself as it sees fit, to legislate concerning its interests, to administer its services, and to determine the jurisdiction and competence of its courts. The exercise of these rights is limited only by the exercise of the rights of other States in accordance with international law.

And article 14 adds that: "Recognition implies that the State granting it accepts the personality of the new State, with all the rights and duties that international law prescribes for the two States."

16 Award of 18 October 1923, UN *RSA*, vol. I, p. 369. Subsequently, in the same vein, *Deutsche Continental Gas Gesellschaft v Poland*, 1929.

17 ICJ Reports, 1996, pp. 595 and 686.

18 This is the case, for example, with the letter of the German Federal Foreign Minister of 10 February 1994 (*ZaöRV* 56, 1996, pp. 1007–1008); Australia's statement to the ICJ in the *East Timor* case (CR 95/10, 9 February 1995, p. 52); as well as the positions taken by Guyana, Ecuador, Mexico and Algeria in the Special Committee on the Question of the Definition of Aggression (UN Doc. A/AC.134/SR.52–66, p. 66; A/AC.134/SR.79–91, pp. 21 and 56).

19 Opinion of 29 November 1991 (*RGDIP*, 1992, p. 264). The same view was expressed in its opinion no. 10 (*RGDIP*, 1993, p. 595).

20 Opinion no. 8, of 4 July 1992 (*RGDIP*, 1993, p. 589). "[J]ust like the membership of international organisations, testify to the conviction of these States that the political entity thus recognised constitutes a reality and confers on it certain rights and certain obligations – not otherwise specified – under international law" (author's translation).

In the absence of a general procedure for recognition of new States by a higher authority, or at least a duty to recognise arising once the requirements for the existence of a State under international law are fulfilled, it is impossible to consider the political act of recognition as having a constitutive effect. The existence of a State cannot be subject to the whim or arbitrariness of pre-existing States, especially since its status as such has been acquired through the fulfilment of a set of predetermined requirements or elements. If in reality this entity meets the criteria established by international law, it exists as such and its existence cannot be denied.

Furthermore, in line with this theory, it should also be borne in mind that there exists no right by virtue of which the entity that meets the criteria of statehood can be recognised as a State, but instead simply the possibility of being recognised once those requirements are met.

The eclectic model operating in practice

The existence of a State is, in principle, a matter of fact which implies that a particular government apparatus exercises its power effectively and independently over a given territory and human society. From this perspective, it should be said that it is not necessary for it to be recognised by other States, so the effects of recognition by other States are purely declaratory. However, despite recognising the declarative nature of recognition, its effects should not be underestimated. Recognition of a new State dispels doubt by acknowledging that it is a new subject of international law. *A contrario sensu*, non-recognition consigns it to a kind of limbo that denies it access to the international community, which means that it lacks active and passive legitimacy in the international order, with all the restrictions that this entails. In this respect, the ILC at its 55th session declared that:

> While it may be concluded that the act of recognition of states is mainly declarative, it cannot be denied that non-recognition also has important legal ramifications. Indeed, non-recognition of an entity as a state affects the exercise of its rights under international law, such as, for example, rights deriving from the law concerning state immunity and the impossibility of being admitted to international organizations. Such a situation undoubtedly limits the international capacity of the state in practice[21].

Thus, despite the declaratory effect of recognition, the new entity will need the recognition of its peers, because it is precisely through this legal act that the new entity acquires a virtuality in the international sphere, which results in it effectively becoming a subject of law. Therefore, recognition, while not constituting the legal personality of the State, is necessary in the process of international consolidation of the new State. This reality is clearly demonstrated – to

21 Yearbook of the International Law Commission, 2003, vol. 2, no. 1, para. 92, p. 66.

take an extreme example – in the case of Somaliland, proclaimed an independent State on 18 May 1991 following the overthrow of Siad Barre, and which has all the elements necessary for accession to statehood – it has its own constitution, currency and government, holds periodic democratic elections, and is even more economically developed and politically stable than Somalia –, but which has not received any recognition. This situation makes it a kind of illusion in the international arena.

Similarly, the non-recognition – except by Turkey – of the TRNC, or the scant recognition of South Ossetia, Abkhazia or Transnistria are clear proof of the important role that recognition plays in being able to act as a State, since none of these entities plays any role in the field of international relations. That is, they do not deploy their supposed statehood.

Therefore, recognition is not a mere formality, as the legal situation of the new State is not the same before and after recognition.

However, there is also an opposing interpretation of the value of recognition; namely, that proceeding to recognise as a State an entity in which the necessary constitutive elements of statehood do not yet converge is ineffective. This shows that recognition does not create the State. An example in this respect would be the Sahrawi Arab Democratic Republic, proclaimed as a State on 27 February 1976 and recognised by more than 80 States, and even admitted as a Member State of an international organisation – the African Union – in 2002, but which cannot yet be considered a State in the international sphere due to its not having the necessary constitutive elements, in particular that relating to territory.

The specific case of Kosovo is also especially remarkable in this regard. This entity has accumulated 112 recognitions, which are also proof of the lack of constitutive effect produced by the act of recognition, because, in spite of them, Kosovo cannot be considered to have attained statehood as of today, insofar as it does not yet have all the constitutive elements required by international law; in particular, it lacks the necessary independence and effectiveness that should permeate the governmental element. Despite the already mentioned three-figure tally of recognitions, many of the States that gave their recognition refused, on 9 November 2015, to admit Kosovo as a Member State of UNESCO, which failed to achieve the necessary 95 votes in favour of its admission – the requirement for being a State (UN member or not) set out in Article II of UNESCO's Constitution was not met.

In the case of Kosovo, what is even more relevant is the fact that *several States have withdrawn their recognition of Kosovo* as a State – among them, Ghana and Nauru in November 2019, and Sierra Leone in March 2020, via an official note from their respective Ministries of Foreign Affairs[22]. In the case of Nauru,

22 The other States that reportedly have withdrawn their recognition of Kosovo are Burundi, Central African Republic, Comoros, Dominica, Grenada, Guinea Bissau, Lesotho, Madagascar, Nauru, Palau, Papua New Guinea, Solomon Islands, Suriname and Togo.

the note indicates that its decision to recognise Kosovo's independence was premature and contrary to Security Council resolution 1244[23]. This circumstance is extremely important, not only because it entails the withdrawal itself, but because recognition, being an act of one State that affects 'another' State, is irrevocable under the principle of estoppel. In accordance with this principle, which takes its inspiration from the Roman aphorism *venire contra factum proprio*, States are bound by their own acts, so that they cannot act against them if in doing so they infringe the rights or claims of another State. It would only be possible to revoke[24] such an act if it has not produced any legal effect (as if it had never happened), or has not affected another State, or if the acting State has the consent of the affected State. Both of these conditions seem to converge in the case of Kosovo, since no legal effects have been produced and no other State has been affected, insofar as Kosovo does not yet meet the requirements of international law to be considered as such. Hence, withdrawal or revocation is perfectly feasible, and estoppel does not apply. Furthermore, since the declaration of independence is illegal because it violates norms of *jus cogens*, any recognition thereof should be withdrawn.

Given this state of affairs, it is evident that the constitutive and declarative theories are deficient. Therefore, an eclectic model seems to impose itself, bringing together as it does both academic positions, neither of which is entirely convincing in isolation. According to this model, the act of recognition comprises two phases: in the first phase the recognition would have a constitutive scope (it determines the existence of the essential factors required for there to be a State); and in the second phase it is declarative, since it limits itself to pointing out the existence of this situation.

As far back as the middle of the last century, Lauterpacht expressed his view in terms of combining aspects of both theories, accepting the hypothesis that "recognition is a momentous, decisive and indispensable function of ascertaining and declaring the existence of the requisite elements of statehood with a constitutive effect for the commencement of the international rights and duties of the entity in questions", and attributing a duty of recognition to mitigate extreme cases of denial of reality[25].

It should be concluded that an entity's status as a State is, in principle, independent of recognition, although our assessments suggest – to paraphrase

23 https://es.news-front.info/2019/11/23/la-independencia-de-kosovo-continua-disminuyendo-otro-pais-retiro-el-reconocimiento-del-cuasi-estado/.

24 It should be remembered that recognition is a unilateral legal act. According to point 10 of the Guiding Principles applicable to unilateral declarations of States capable of creating legal obligations (adopted by the Commission in 2006, A/61/10), a unilateral declaration cannot be revoked arbitrarily. In determining arbitrariness, account should be taken of whether the declaration relates to revocation, the conduct of the subjects concerned, and whether there has been a fundamental change of circumstances. In line with the latter, unlike the recognition of States, the *recognition of Governments* is an essentially revocable act, especially in the face of unconstitutional changes.

25 Lauterpacht. *Recognition*..., op. cit., p. 51.

Crawford[26] – that the differences between the declarative and constitutive theories in practice are actually not as pronounced as they seem. Recognition of States thus brings together both positions insofar as it is declarative of an existing factual reality, but also constitutive in that it is necessary for the new State to participate in the international order. Therefore, we can conclude that the two theories complement each other to a certain degree[27].

Conditions of validity and legality: a duo that limits the discretionary nature of the act of recognising new States

As noted earlier, the act of recognition is a unilateral and discretionary act whose implementation depends – at least in principle – on the State's sovereign autonomy, since international law does not impose any obligation to recognise, and so refusing to recognise a new State does not constitute an internationally wrongful act. This means that each State must decide freely whether and when to recognise.

However, it is clear that discretion should not be synonymous with arbitrariness. That is why there are limitations imposed by the international legal order itself. We must bear in mind, as Kelsen[28] pointed out, that: "A State violates International Law and thus infringes upon the rights of other States if it recognizes as a State a community which does not fulfil the requirements of International Law".

In this regard, once a State makes the decision – basically political – to recognise a new State, it must bear in mind that in order to perform such an act, a number of conditions required by international law need to be met in relation to the entity it intends to recognise, and these conditions will operate as a limit on that discretion. As Sánchez Rodríguez points out[29], they are divided into conditions of validity and conditions of legality of the act of recognition.

The conditions of validity refer to compliance with the formal and material requirements imposed by the international system. With regard to the former, since we are dealing with a unilateral legal act, it must be carried out by a person with the capacity to bind the State internationally; namely, by a Head of State or Government or by a Minister for Foreign Affairs. It must also be clear that the State has a subjective intention to recognise the new entity as such.

As regards the material content of the act[30], it is clear that the situation to be recognised must exist in order for the act to produce the legal effects that

26 Crawford. *The Creation of States…* 2nd ed., op. cit., p. 28.
27 A position we also find in Nicholson, Rowan and Thomas D. Grant. "Theories of State Recognition". *Routledge Handbook of State Recognition*, edited by Gëzim Visoka, John Doyle and Edward Newman. New York: Routledge, 2019, pp. 25–37.
28 Kelsen, Hans. *Principles of International Law*. Rinehart, 1952, p. 70.
29 In González Campos et al. *Curso de Derecho Internacional…*, op. cit., pp. 512–513.
30 Although the act of recognition may be considered declaratory, it undoubtedly has important legal effects. The State undertakes to consider as such an existing factual

recognition entails, because insofar as the object of recognition does not exist, such recognition produces no effect. This connects us with the moment in time at which the act must take place, which is none other than the moment as from when the existence of the constituent elements of the State as required by international law – territory, population and government –, endowed with the necessary independence and effectiveness, is established. If the entity aspiring to statehood does not meet those criteria, it does not exist as a State and therefore cannot be recognised as such. The International Law Association (ILA) made this clear in its 2014 Final Report, affirming that State practice supports non-recognition "where the bases of statehood are not met by the aspiring state"[31].

In practice, however, it is sometimes the case that recognition is granted to an entity that is still in the process of formation – *in statu nascendi*. In other words, it does not meet the requirements imposed by international law. This has happened relatively often in the context of decolonisation, with the aim of supporting the struggle of liberation movements against administrative powers reluctant to grant independence on the basis of the principle of self-determination[32] – as was the case with Guinea-Bissau, among others. This eventuality connects us with premature recognition.

There is no doubt that premature recognitions clearly fall within the framework of validity; for as long as the object of recognition does not exist, recognition does not produce any effect – as is the case with the Sahrawi Arab Democratic Republic. Moreover, there is a broad academic majority that also holds that such recognition could be an unlawful act[33]. We fully share this view insofar as such recognition may involve *interference in matters which are essentially within the domestic jurisdiction of the predecessor State* from which the applicant for statehood emerges, as occurs in cases of secession; this entails a violation of the international norm that protects this fundamental principle. This has been, moreover, the response of States affected by such premature recognitions; for example, by England in relation to France's recognition[34] of the US declaration of independence in 1778 (which prompted the declaration of war), and by Colombia in relation to US recognition of Panama in 1903. In these cases, both States' justification for recognition was to 'accelerate' the process of statehood that was

or legal situation and to respect its legal consequences, so that it is obliged not to act against it in the future. This being so, the legal effects of recognition are mainly translated into enforceability. The State accepts certain legal facts which it admits are effective vis-à-vis itself. This, in turn, raises the question of their corresponding enforceability on the part of the recipient.

31 www.ila-hq.org/en/committees/draft-committee-reports-washington-2014.cfm, p. 26.

32 www.ila-hq.org/en/committees/draft-committee-reports-washington-2014.cfm, p. 26.

33 Among others, González Campos et. al., op. cit., p. 513; and Remiro Brotons et al., op. cit., p. 54.

34 In fact, France was the only state to recognise the independence of the United States before England accepted it. The rest did not recognise US independence until that acceptance took place.

already underway and irremediable[35]. This did not prevent them from recognising the illegality of their act of recognition, as occurred with the United States, which subsequently accepted responsibility for this act and paid Colombia compensation[36]. These observations can easily be extrapolated to the case of Kosovo, insofar as in the absence of an effective and independent government it still does not meet the material requirements for accession to statehood. Consequently, the more than one hundred recognitions received can be classed as premature and, therefore, as interference within the domestic jurisdiction of Serbia.

But we must not forget that in accession to statehood, besides effective compliance with the material requirements there is also the criterion of legality, i.e. respect for the fundamental principles of international law on the part of the aspiring State, which is something that we need to bear in mind in the case of Catalonia.

This being the case, any act of recognition requires that the recognised situation be lawful in order for it to be considered not only valid but also legal. That is why, in addition to the conditions of validity referred to on p. 197, there is also a condition of legality in the recognition of States, which is that the new State emerges in accordance with international law; more specifically, with the peremptory norms of international law. Thus, each State must decide freely whether and when to recognise, but with the logical limit of compliance with the requirements imposed by international law on the part of the entities subject to recognition. In the words of Chaumont, there is no room for the manufacture of States by foreign powers through an act that constitutes an intervention contrary to peremptory norms[37]. Consequently, entities whose statehood has been acquired in violation of the fundamental principles of international law and its consequent peremptory norms cannot be recognised. This is fully applicable in the case of a declaration of independence of Catalonia that is not made with the consent of the Spanish State, because it would be violating, among others, the principles of territorial integrity, self-determination of peoples and non-interference in the internal affairs of Spain.

This leads us to assess the existence of an obligation not to recognise new States that have arisen illegally, which obviously limits the discretion that accompanies the act of recognition, since recognising entities that do not

35 It should be noted that the two cases referred to predate the existence of the principle of self-determination of colonial peoples, and they occurred at a time when colonies were considered part of the territory of the colonial power. Following the advent of that principle, non-self-governing territories had an autonomous existence and were not part of the territory of the State administering them. For this reason, their independence cannot be regarded as a case of secession, but rather of decolonisation, without breaking the territorial integrity of the administering state.

36 Jiménez de Aréchaga, Eduardo. *Derecho Internacional Público*, vol. 2. Fundación Cultura Universitaria, 1995, p. 23.

37 Chaumont, Charles. "Cours général de droit international public". *Recueil des Cours*, vol. 129, 1970, p. 431.

comply with the law constitutes a violation of the principle that prohibits abuse of the law.

The international obligation not to recognise those who fail to respect legality in accession to statehood which should be met by States and international organisations in relation to Catalonia and other secessionist entities

We have already indicated that each State can decide freely to recognise or not recognise a situation. But this 'power' of non-recognition has nothing to do with the 'obligation' not to recognise certain unlawful situations that international law imposes today, thereby limiting the discretionary nature of the act of recognition. This means that, when the new situation generated in the international order is lawful, recognition or non-recognition by existing States is free and discretionary. However, when we are faced with a new situation that alters the international order and which has arisen in violation of international law or, more specifically, the fundamental rules of the international legal order, then recognition is no longer free and discretionary, since international law imposes on States and international organisations the obligation not to recognise the situation that has arisen in such a way. This is fully applicable to the case of State recognition that concerns us.

Many scholars affirm the existence of such an obligation not to recognise unlawfully created entities as States. According to Becker, "it is widely accepted that there exists a legal duty not to recognize as a state an entity which claims statehood on the basis of acts which are illegal"[38].

Menon further states that: "A state violates international law and thus infringes upon the rights of other states if it recognizes as a state a community which does not fulfil the requirements of international law"[39].

After a thorough and updated analysis of the right of secession in the light of Kosovo, Efevwerhan concludes that:

> The study has found that the international community would be opposed [to secession] if it is in violation of rules erga omnes or jus cogens in international law, such as self-determination, discrimination and the unlawful use of force, human and humanitarian rights. In the above circumstances, there is a collective duty of non-recognition of any entity created therefrom[40].

38 Becker, Tal. *International Recognition of a Unilaterally Declared Palestinian State*. Legal and Policy Dilemmas, Jerusalem Centre for Public Affairs (www.jcpa.org/art/becker1.htm).

39 Menon, Palat K. *The Law of Recognition in International Law: Basic Principles*. New York: Edwin Mellen Press Ltd, 1994, p. 28.

40 Efevwerhan, David. *Secession and the Lessons from Kosovo. New Dimensions in the Law of Secession*. Berlin: LAP Lambert Academic Publishing, 2010, p. 374.

It goes without saying that we are referring to the existence of an autonomous obligation of non-recognition, i.e. irrespective of the fact that it is determined by a Security Council Resolution acting within the framework of Chapter VII of the UN Charter, which urges States not to recognise. This case – which we will refer to later on – provides no cause for debate, since all the Member States of the United Nations have the obligation to comply with these resolutions, according to Article 25 of the Charter.

However, we should not lose sight of the fact that when the Security Council demands that States not recognise a situation that it describes as illegal, what it is doing is applying the rules that already exist in international law; in other words, it is not seeking to impose on States legal standards that are not previously binding on them. Centralised intervention by the Security Council is therefore of enormous practical importance, as it dispels any possible doubt about the illegality of the act and coordinates non-recognition efforts. It has therefore played a key role in the emergence of the customary norm in question.

Refutation of arguments against the existence of an obligation of non-recognition

In the face of sustained affirmation of the existence of a duty to not recognise situations created in violation of the peremptory norms of international law – including secessionist declarations – three arguments are usually invoked to deny its existence, which we will refute as appropriate[41].

The *first* argument refers to the *very structure of international law.* According to this argument, it is impossible to impose an obligation of non-recognition on a society that lacks a centralised authority capable of objectively qualifying a situation as internationally unlawful, and it is up to each subject to make such a qualification individually. Therefore, the obligation of non-recognition would be absurd, since there is no objective rule that legal subjects must obey[42]. This argument is the same as that once put forward against the existence of *jus cogens* norms, a legal category whose existence is not questioned today.

Therefore, it can be argued that this structural argument is in fact circular, since it draws a conceptual wall around the supposed structure of international law to prevent the entry of any rule that might entail a modification of that structure. In a large number of cases, various international bodies – such as the Security Council and the General Assembly of the United Nations – have made these 'centralised' qualifications, affirming the nullity and/or invalidity of unilateral proclamations of independence of secessionist entities and calling for them not to be recognised as States.

It should also be borne in mind that the eminently – albeit not totally – decentralised nature of the international community does not exempt States

41 See, in this regard, Christakis. "The State as a 'Primary Fact'...", op. cit., pp. 130–140.

42 Verhoeven. op. cit., p. 38.

from the obligation to eliminate the consequences of a "serious breach of an obligation arising under peremptory norms of general international law", as regulated by Articles 40 and 41 of the 2001 ILC Draft on Responsibility of States for Internationally Wrongful Acts[43], without subjecting it to the existence of a centralised institutional procedure. This has been reaffirmed by the ICJ in its 2004 *Advisory Opinion on the Wall on Palestinian Territory*. As Judge Winiarski maintains in this regard: "l'absence de procédure organisée ne supprime pas la nullité; la thèse: pas de nullité sans instance, n'est pas fondée"[44].

The *second* denial of the existence of the obligation of non-recognition is based on the argument of *ineffectiveness*. Its detractors claim that the doctrine of non-recognition has grown aware of an evident weakness in the facts. It is powerless to effectively combat burgeoning illegalities and is absolutely ineffective[45]. It is hard to comprehend how a rule that is incapable of combating the effectiveness of an unlawful situation can succeed in rejecting it; all it does is create unnameable legal fictions that bear no relation to reality.

Two responses can be given to counter this argument. First, it strikes us as paradoxical to propose the trivialisation of a reaction to the violation of a rule of law simply because that reaction is not always sufficient to restore legality. If firefighters are unable to put out a fire, the logical reaction is not to abolish the fire brigade but to strengthen it. As Chen pointed out in 1951:

> The doctrine of non-recognition, which postulates the responsibility of every State for the maintenance of the legal order, signifies the conviction of the States that the law exists. The failure of its application in any particular instance is strong argument that greater, and not less, collectivization

43 Article 40. Application of this chapter:

> 1. This chapter applies to the international responsibility which is entailed by a serious breach by a State of an obligation arising under a peremptory norm of general international law.
> 2. A breach of such an obligation is serious if it involves a gross or systematic failure by the responsible State to fulfil the obligation.
> Article 41. Particular consequences of a serious breach of an obligation under this chapter
> 1. States shall cooperate to bring to an end through lawful means any serious breach within the meaning of article 40.
> 2. No State shall recognize as lawful a situation created by a serious breach within the meaning of article 40, nor render aid or assistance in maintaining that situation.
> 3. This article is without prejudice to the other consequences referred to in this Part and to such further consequences that a breach to which this chapter applies may entail under international law.

44 Dissenting opinion in the Advisory Opinion of 13 July 1954 on the Effect of Awards of Compensation made by the United Nations Administrative Tribunal (ICJ Report, 1954, p. 65).

45 Verhoeven. op. cit., p. 38.

> and strengthening of the authority of international law is a needed for the peaceful enjoyment of life in the world. To advocate the view that, because in the past the international society has been too weak to enforce its will upon law-breakers, so law-breaking in future shall receive immediate acknowledgment of the society is a policy of despair and a condemnation of international society to a perpetual state of anarchy[46].

Furthermore, beyond theoretical considerations, a review of international practice hardly confirms the ineffectiveness of the obligation not to recognise wrongful situations created in violation of peremptory norms. Manchukuo did not survive, Southern Rhodesia did not prosper, the Bantustans have evaporated, Kuwait has not been annexed, the Turkish Republic of Northern Cyprus is not a State and has not been recognised (except by its sponsor State, Turkey); and neither have South Ossetia, Abkhazia, Transnistria and Nagorno-Karabakh. Bangladesh, the only example of successful secession, was only recognised when Pakistan abandoned its intention to recover it – the theory of eventual success. Meanwhile, Israel's occupied territories continue to maintain that status without any recognition validating their illegality. Therefore, far from being 'perfectly ineffective', the obligation of non-recognition is undoubtedly useful for responding to the unlawful situation and constitutes a real '*pied de nez*' for its effectiveness[47].

The *third* argument against the existence of the obligation not to recognise is based on an alleged *lack of positivity*. Here we find reasserted the argument put forward by Australia in the East Timor case, according to which there is no automatic obligation of non-recognition in international law. Only a Security Council resolution can impose such an obligation[48]. The ICJ did not take a position on this matter because it declared itself not competent to deal with the matter; obviously, this cannot be interpreted as a denial on its part of the existence of this obligation.

In the absence of a positive law text on this subject, as well as a judicial pronouncement, it is international practice – which we shall now discuss – that can demonstrate the existence of this obligation, which will be of a customary nature.

International practice supporting the existence of an obligation not to recognise entities arising in violation of international law

In our view, an examination of practice and, therefore, of the *opinio iuris* of States leaves little doubt as to the existence in general international law of the

46 Chen, Ti-Chiang. *The International Law of Recognition*. London: Frederick A. Praeger, 1951, p. 443.
47 Christakis. "The State as a 'Primary Fact'...", op. cit., p. 134.
48 *Australian Government Counter-Memorial*, chapter 2, sec. I, para. 350–359, pp. 157–161.

obligation not to recognise aspiring States that violate international law. Moreover, the number of different instruments asserting the existence of the principle has grown steadily. All of which shows us that this obligation should be fulfilled by States, independently of any mandatory Security Council resolution.

The list of *international texts* that generally include the obligation of non-recognition, both in the universal and the regional setting, is long. It begins with the famous Stimson Doctrine, which emerged in the 1930s, following the proclamation of Manchukuo as a State (1931), due to the efforts of the US Secretary of State to mobilise opposition to its recognition. This doctrine holds that "A foreign state's unlawful intervention -in that case, Japan's invasion of the northern Chinese province of Manchuria in violation of the 1928 Kellogg-Briand Pact of Paris- cannot be allowed to yield a successful secession"[49].

The principle was quickly taken up in various diplomatic instruments in the Americas, such as the Treaty of Non-Aggression and Conciliation signed in Rio de Janeiro on 10 October 1933; Article 11 of the Montevideo Convention on the Rights and Duties of States of 1933; the Lima Declaration of 22 December 1938; the preamble to the Havana Convention of 30 July 1940 on the Provisional Administration of European Possessions; or Article 17 of the OAS Charter, confirmed by Article 20 of the Protocol of Buenos Aires of 27 February 1967.

In the European framework, the proclamation of the principle came later but was equally forceful. It has been enshrined in texts as diverse as the Helsinki Final Act of 1975 (principle IV), the EEC Declaration in relation to the "Guidelines on the recognition of new States in Eastern Europe and the USSR" of 16 December 1991, and the aforementioned opinion of the Arbitration Commission of the European Peace Conference in Yugoslavia.

At the universal level, it should be noted that the UNGA has had occasion to affirm this principle repeatedly in such important resolutions as Resolution 2625 (XXV) of 24 October 1970, 3314 (XXIX) of 14 December 1974, 36/103 of 9 December 1981, or 42/22 of 18 November 1987.

The ILC, at its first meeting in 1949, noted in Article 11 of the draft Declaration on the Rights and Duties of States that "every State has the duty to refrain from recognizing any territorial acquisition made by another State in violation" of the principle of the prohibition of use of force. Fifty years later, in its draft articles on the responsibility of states for internationally wrongful acts, the ILC considered that this obligation of non-recognition concerned any situation created by "a serious breach of an obligation arising from a peremptory norm" (Articles 40 and 41).

We can see that none of these texts makes the application of the obligation of non-recognition subordinate to a resolution of the United Nations Security

49 Today this doctrine would be fully applicable to cases of secessions with a 'sponsor' State (which is why they have not failed since the outset): Abkhazia, South Ossetia and Transnistria, sponsored by Russia; Nagorno-Karabakh by Armenia; and the TRNC by Turkey.

Council or to another centralised finding of the wrongful act. On the contrary, most of the texts referred to speak of a real 'duty' of States in this field, individualised and independent of any collective reaction.

This is, as the ILC has pointed out, the "minimum reaction required from states to serious violations" of fundamental rules of international law[50].

Similarly, *State practice* confirms the existence of this obligation in general international law. Prior to 1945, this principle had been applied in relation to Manchukuo; in the Chaco War between Bolivia and Paraguay by the declaration of American States of 3 August 1932; as well as in the Leticia Incident between Colombia and Peru by the resolution of the Council of the League of Nations of 18 March 1933; and following the annexation of Ethiopia by Italy in 1935.

In contemporary international law, the duty of non-recognition has been applied in practice on numerous occasions. Let us look at some relevant milestones:

- The secession of Southern Rhodesia from the British Crown, proclaimed on 11 November 1965 by the Government of Ian Smith, was considered to be in violation of the right of peoples to self-determination, which led, as we have seen, to UN bodies calling for non-recognition on the part of all States.
- The termination of South Africa's mandate in Namibia in 1966 led both the General Assembly and the Security Council of the United Nations to urge all States to refrain from any relationship with South Africa in order not to recognise South African authority over the territory of Namibia.
- The creation of the Bantustans by South Africa, beginning with Transkei in 1976, was met with various resolutions of the General Assembly and the Security Council calling for their non-recognition.
- It is the secession of the TRNC that has led to a more widespread and uniform practice in relation to this duty. The aforementioned Security Council resolutions were followed by statements from many other international bodies and organisations that reacted in a similar way by affirming the 'illegality' or 'nullity' of the proclamation of independence of the TRNC and supporting the principle of non-recognition. Such was the case of the Final Communiqué of the Commonwealth Summit Conference held in New Delhi in November 1983, at which the Heads of Government denounced the declaration of independence as legally invalid and reiterated the call for its non-recognition and immediate annulment. Resolution (83) 13 of the Committee of Ministers of the Council of Europe also considered the Declaration of Independence legally invalid. As did the Declaration of the European Commission of 16 November 1982, which rejected the declaration and stressed that the government of the

50 ILC. "Commentary by the Commission on Article 41". Fifty-third meeting, A/56/10 (2001), p. 311.

Republic of Cyprus is the sole legal representative and the only one recognised by the European Community.

- In this respect, even the ECHR has ruled against Turkey in several judgments, stating that "the international community does not consider the TRNC as a state under international law and that the Republic of Cyprus constitutes the only legitimate government of Cyprus"[51].
- And looking at the most recent events both in Iraq with regard to Kurdistan, and in Spain with regard to Catalonia, the reaction of the international community has been absolutely unequivocal and consistent with the principle of non-recognition. There have been numerous official declarations from State representatives as well as from representatives of international organisations affirming the duty to refuse to recognise the alleged secessionist entity. This has happened, as we have already indicated, in the case of the Declaration of Independence of the Catalan Parliament, both the one suspended on 10 October 2017 and the one taken up again on 27 October. There has been a generalised practice of rejecting it and stating that it would never be recognised as a State.

We also find numerous government statements affirming the existence of this duty. Such is the case of the aforementioned Stimson Doctrine, undoubtedly a turning point in this regard. Another important political statement was the Welles Declaration, in 1940, in which then Secretary of State Sumner Welles stated, in response to the Soviet annexation of Estonia, Latvia and Lithuania, that "the people of the United States [were] opposed to predatory activities, no matter whether they are carried out by the use of force or the threat of force and to the intervention in the domestic affairs of another state"[52].

The United States expressly includes this obligation of non-recognition in the Restatement (Third) of the Foreign Relations Law of the United States in the following terms:

> A state has an obligation not to recognize or treat as a state an entity that has attained the qualifications for statehood as a result of a threat or use of armed force in violation of the United Nations Charter[53].

The statements made by several of the 11 States that made up the Study Group on Recognition/Non-Recognition of ILA are very clear in this regard. As stated in its 2014 Final Report, a number of these States strongly affirmed that an obligation of non-recognition does exist when a secessionist entity violates the territorial integrity of the State, uses armed force or violates any other

51 Case of *Loizidou v Turkey* (merits), Judgment of 18 December 1996, para. 44. Likewise, *Cyprus v Turkey*, Judgment of 10 May 2001, para. 90.

52 Costelloe. op. cit., p. 196.

53 https://books.google.es/books/about/Restatement_of_the_Law_Third.html?id=7QY3AQAAIAAJ&redir_esc=y.

peremptory norm of general international law, or when such an obligation is established by the Security Council – this is the view of Austria, Cyprus, Greece, Israel, South Africa and the United States[54].

Finally, we can refer to *judicial practice* in this area. In this regard, together with the aforementioned jurisprudence of the ECHR in relation to the TRNC, we find that the ICJ has been very clear and eloquent in formulating and affirming the existence of this obligation of non-recognition. On the one hand, in its advisory opinion of 21 June 1971 on the "Namibia exception", the Court noted:

> that States Members of the United Nations are under obligation to recognize the illegality of South Africa's presence in Namibia and the invalidity of its acts on behalf of or concerning Namibia, and to refrain from any acts and in particular any dealings with the Government of South Africa implying recognition of the legality of, or lending support or assistance to, such presence and administration[55].

More recently, the ICJ has had occasion to express its views on this matter in its *Opinion of 9 July 2004 on Legal Consequences of the Construction of a Wall in the Occupied Palestinian Territory*[56]. In this Advisory Opinion, citing Article 41 of the ILC's Draft Articles on the Responsibility of States for Internationally Wrongful Acts, the Court again proclaimed the duty not to recognise unlawful situations. Although the Court's position was broader than that of Article 41 itself, insofar as it referred to the obligation of non-recognition not in relation to peremptory norms, but to the breach of obligations *erga omnes*, which increased exponentially the number of cases covered by that obligation. Moreover, the Court rightly attributed that obligation not only to States but also to the General Assembly and the Security Council. This is wholly consistent with the provisions of Article 45 of the ILC's Draft Articles on the Responsibility of International Organizations (2011), which is identical to Article 41.

The Court concluded in this regard:

> All States are under an obligation not to recognize the illegal situation resulting from the construction of the wall and not to render aid or assistance in maintaining the situation created by such construction; all States parties to the Fourth Geneva Convention relative to the Protection of Civilian Persons in Time of War of 12 August 1949 have in addition the obligation. While rejecting the United Nations Charter and international

54 According to this Report, only the United Kingdom and Australia clearly stated their opposition to the existence of such an obligation (www.ila-hq.org/en/committees/draft-committee-reports-washington-2014.cfm, p. 6).

55 ICJ Reports, 1971, p. 58, para. 133.

56 ICJ Reports, 2004, para. 155–159.

> law, to ensure compliance by Israel with international humanitarian law as embodied in that Convention: (…)
>
> The United Nations, and especially the General Assembly and the Security Council, should consider what further action is required to bring to an end the illegal situation resulting from the construction of the Wall and the associated regime, taking due account of the present Advisory Opinion[57].

Similarly, we also find references to the existence of this duty in arbitration practice. Particularly telling is the arbitral decision of 17 February 1997, concerning the *Brcko Region Dispute* (*Sprska Republic v Federation of Bosnia and Herzegovina*), which considers the doctrine of non-recognition to be part of positive law and therefore applicable to the case submitted to the arbitral tribunal[58].

For its part, the Arbitration Commission of the International Conference on the Former Yugoslavia noted in its Opinion No. 10 of 4 July 1992 that the discretionary nature of State recognition is limited by respect for the peremptory norms of general international law, particularly those prohibiting use of force and those guaranteeing the rights of minorities[59].

In light of all this, that is, of international practice in the matter – including what happened regarding the declaration of independence of Catalonia in 2017 –, it can be concluded that there are more than enough arguments to maintain that in contemporary international law there exists an obligation not to recognise a secessionist entity according to the parameters of legality referred to earlier. We understand that its existence is beyond doubt[60].

The serious breach of a peremptory norm of general international law as a basis for the obligation of non-recognition

As we have been saying, the obligation not to recognise an entity as a State is based on the fact that it has unilaterally proclaimed itself a State in violation of a peremptory norm of general international law. This means, therefore, that the criterion of legality necessary for accession to statehood has not been met.

As Grant points out, if it were permissible to recognise an entity as a State when it has not respected the norms of *jus cogens*, "the aspiration of

57 Ibid., para. 163.
58 ILM, vol. 36 (2), 1997, para. 77 and 78.
59 *RGDIP*, 1993, p. 595.
60 The same conclusion was reached by the IHLADI Institute in the Resolution adopted at its session held in Lima, Peru, in December 2016, within the framework of its Third Commission "The creation of States in contemporary international law in cases of secession: effectiveness/legality": "6. States and international organizations should not recognize unilateral declarations of independence contrary to international law" (http://ihladi.net).

international law to regulate matters traditionally reserved to sovereign states is frustrated"[61].

The idea is that a State cannot exist and, therefore, cannot be recognised as a subject of law when its birth results from acts, conduct or situations contrary to the peremptory norms of general international law; in particular, those relating to the prohibition of use of force, the safeguarding of human rights and the self-determination of peoples, and even the territorial integrity of the State.

Reference is bound to be made to the aforementioned Article 41 of the 2001 ILC Draft Articles on Responsibility of States for Internationally Wrongful Acts, which provided that no state shall recognise as lawful a situation created by a serious breach of a peremptory norm of general international law, nor render aid or assistance in maintaining that situation.

The ILC explained in its comments that this is the obligation of the international community as a whole not to collectively recognise the legitimacy of situations directly resulting from serious violations of peremptory norms. The obligation applies to the 'situations' created, and so it not only refers to formal recognition but also prohibits any act involving such recognition. In the ILC's view, the existence of this obligation of non-recognition is supported by the practice and decisions of the ICJ; it has also been applied by the ECHR, as we had occasion to confirm in the preceding section. Not only that, it can also be seen in the practice of the Security Council when it establishes the obligation not to recognise secessionist entities in the event of a breach of fundamental rules of international law.

In this respect, the only doubt concerns identifying which peremptory norms are at stake. Given the lack of a positive law text that expressly includes them, this is a cloudy issue which has generated a perennial debate, and on which there is no unanimity. Nevertheless, there is no doubt about the *jus cogens* nature of the prohibition of use of armed force, as well as the self-determination of peoples, and some of the human rights directly linked to the right to life, generally thought of as the 'hard core': prohibition of genocide, apartheid, forced disappearance, torture, etc.

In this context, however, we find that there is no unanimity as to whether respect for the territorial integrity of the State is a *jus cogens* norm. In our opinion it is, not least because it forms an indissoluble part of the first of the fundamental principles set out in the UN Charter: the sovereign equality of States. This is also the ultimate foundation on which the whole structure of international law is built. Not for nothing does Tomuschat describe the sovereign equality and territorial integrity of the State as the fundamental rule of international law[62]. To deny its peremptory nature is to deny the basis of our system, since, as Carrillo Salcedo says, it forms part of that legal minimum that the international community requires for its survival as such[63]. This author considers it has a peremptory character.

61 Grant. *The Recognition of States…*, op. cit., p. 213.
62 Tomuschat. "International Law…", op. cit., p. 13.
63 Carrillo Salcedo. *Soberanía del Estado…*, op. cit., pp. 214–215.

Furthermore, there are references that support this conclusion, as in certain international texts such as the Helsinki Final Act of 1975 or the OAU Charter. Similarly, when the ILC was preparing the draft articles on the law of treaties, its commentaries on Article 53 cited the sovereign equality of States – which, as we know, implies their territorial integrity – as an example of a *jus cogens* norm.

But, above all, international practice confirms this. Undoubtedly, the most recurrent argument used by all States and international organisations to deny recognition to a secessionist entity and maintain that it is illegal and void, is that it is contrary to the territorial integrity of the parent State. Especially categorical in this respect is the written statement made by Russia in the proceedings leading to the ICJ's advisory opinion on Kosovo's declaration of independence, which cites Pellet when stating that the principle of territorial integrity "has acquired the character of a universal and peremptory norm"[64].

Secessionist peoples, groups or movements are obliged to respect territorial integrity, insofar as international law establishes it, two clear examples being Resolutions 1514 (XV) and 2625 (XXV) of the United Nations General Assembly, among others.

Consequently, if accession to statehood occurs in violation of one or more of these peremptory norms, there will be an obligation for all States not to recognise such a situation as lawful; that is, an obligation not to recognise the aspiring entity as a State.

Should recognition already have taken place, States have the *duty to revoke* it, because otherwise they would be committing an internationally wrongful act in violating this obligation of non-recognition. This is because recognition of fundamental illegalities is always subject to revocation[65]. This has been stated by Alexander Orakhelashvili in relation to the recognition of Kosovo: "Any recognition of the independence of Kosovo is an internationally wrongful act and generates the obligation to withdraw it"[66].

We have already mentioned the revocations of recognition that have occurred in relation to Kosovo. We should point out that retracting recognition of secessionist entities is nothing new. This has already happened, for example, with Abkhazia and South Ossetia, which were recognised by Tuvalu and Vanuatu, a recognition subsequently retracted by both. This reinforces our approach regarding the duty to revoke recognition of secessionist entities as States, as their declaration of independence violates *jus cogens* norms and, consequently, the obligation not to recognise exists. Maintaining such recognition would constitute an internationally wrongful act.

64 Written statement of 16 April 2009. Similar statements were made by Estonia, Finland and Ireland.

65 Brownlie, Ian. *International Law and the Use of Force*. Oxford: Oxford University Press, 1963, p. 421.

66 Orakhelashvili, Alexander. "Statehood, Recognition and the United Nations System: A Unilateral Declaration of Independence in Kosovo". *Max Planck Yearbook of United Nations Law*, vol. 12, 2008, p. 31.

It is therefore the case that *jus cogens* transforms non-recognition into a more effective principle deriving from the concept of objective illegality, and its object is determined not by subjective determinations but by peremptory norms[67].

The obligation of non-recognition of secessionist entities included within the principle of non-intervention in matters which are essentially within the domestic jurisdiction of the parent State

Aside from the applicant entity violating a peremptory norm in this process of accession to statehood – which is the basis of the international community's obligation not to recognise it as a State – we must also bear in mind that the obligation not to recognise that entity as a State arises insofar as it comes under the auspices of a specific peremptory norm, namely, the obligation of non-intervention in matters which are essentially within the domestic jurisdiction of the parent State, as set forth in Article 2(7) of the UN Charter.

As we have established, it is commonly accepted that international law does not regulate the right of secession[68], that the existence or not of a right of secession is a matter of domestic law and not of international law. If this is the case, if the right to secede is a matter of domestic law and domestic law does not recognise it and, despite this, an entity makes a declaration of independence, it is more than obvious that if a third State recognises this entity as a State, it is acting against one of the fundamental principles of international law: *the prohibition of interference in the domestic affairs of another State*; in this case, the State whose unity is at stake[69]. Not surprisingly, non-intervention in matters which are essentially within the domestic jurisdiction of the parent State and territorial integrity are two closely related principles.

In this respect, Resolution 2625 (XXV) considers any attack against the personality of the State or against some of its elements as contrary to the principle of non-intervention, and there is no doubt that consenting to a secession is an attack against the State and against one of its fundamental elements, namely, its territory. For its part, the ICJ, in *the case concerning military and paramilitary activities in and against Nicaragua (fond)*, holds that the prohibited

67 Orakhelashvili. *Peremptory Norms*..., op. cit., p.380. Rozakis, Christos L. *The Concept of Jus Cogens in the Law of Treaties*. Oxford: North Holland Publishing Co., 1976, p. 27.

68 As Corten points out, it does not regulate it because it is not intended to regulate this situation; it simply ignores it. See Corten. "Commentaire de l'article 52"..., op. cit., p. 1867 ff.

69 This is the idea behind the so-called Hallstein Doctrine established between 1955 and 1969, by virtue of which the Federal Republic of Germany broke off diplomatic relations with any State that recognised the German Democratic Republic. Similar to this is the 'one China' approach adopted by the People's Republic of China in relation to the Republic of China (Taiwan).

intervention must concern matters on which the principle of State sovereignty allows each State to decide freely (para. 205).

Given that international law does not regulate the right of secession, it is clear that this is a matter on which the State can decide freely – whether to grant it or not –, that is, it is essentially a domestic competence[70].

In this regard, the Declaration on the Inadmissibility of Intervention and Interference in the Internal Affairs of States, adopted by the UNGA in 1981 (Resolution 36/103), expressly includes the prohibition of such recognitions by incorporating into this norm of non-interference:

> f) The duty of every State to refrain from the promotion, encouragement or support, direct or indirect, of rebellious or secessionist activities within other States, under any pretext whatsoever, or any action which seeks to disrupt the unity or to undermine or subvert the political order of other States.

In this respect, State practice manifests itself in the same sense. Many States have expressly stated on numerous occasions that recognising secessionist entities as States constitutes interference in the affairs of the parent State. There is even internal practice that expressly reflects this situation, such as the aforementioned Restatement (Third) of the Foreign Relations Law of the United States, which establishes that premature recognition of a secessionist entity is a violation of the territorial integrity of the sovereign State in question and that treating such an unqualified entity as a State "is an improper interference in the internal affairs of the parent State and may rise to being a violation of the Charter of the United Nations"[71].

In this case, therefore, the obligation of non-recognition arises because it would be included in the obligation not to intervene in matters which are essentially within the domestic jurisdiction of the parent State, whereby recognising secession – as would happen in the case of Catalonia – violates the latter obligation and, consequently, the recognising State would be committing an internationally wrongful act.

Moreover, according to a fairly widespread view, non-intervention in matters which are essentially within the domestic jurisdiction of any State has the status of a *jus cogens* norm. Given the major significance of a secession for the territorial integrity of the State in which it occurs, it is our understanding that there is nothing to prevent the act of recognition from being qualified as a serious breach. That being the case, recognition of a secessionist entity as a State could even be covered by Article 40 of the 2001 ILC Draft Articles on

70 Pellet, Alain. "Quel avenir pour le droit des peuples à disposer d'eux-mêmes?". In *El Derecho internacional en un mundo en transformación. Liber Amicorum en Homenaje al profesor Eduardo Jiménez de Aréchaga.* Montevideo, 1994, p. 262.

71 Comments d and f to section 202. See reference at www.ila-hq.org/en/committees/draft-committee-reports-washington-2014.cfm, p. 6.

Responsibility of States for Internationally Wrongful Acts. This would entail obligations for other States, under the provisions of the aforementioned Article 41.

And given that recognition is a unilateral legal act, as provided for in Principle 8 of the 2006 ILC Guiding Principles on Unilateral Declarations of States, such an act *would be void* for being in conflict with a peremptory norm of general international law and, consequently, would have no legal effects.

Specifying the content of the obligation of non-recognition

The international obligation of non-recognition exists, but we must specify its content. As Christakis points out, it is necessary to demonstrate that "l'Empereur n'est pas nu"[72]; in other words, that it is not a hollow shell.

There is a lack of precise wording as regards the effects of this obligation. No general theory has been formulated.

We could say, paraphrasing St. Augustine's thought on time, "what is the obligation of non-recognition? If no one asks me, I know. But if I want to explain it to someone who asks me, I don't know…".

In order to cast light over this dark terrain, there is no other solution but to examine international practice, in particular that of States, and thereby clarify the content of this legal obligation. In short, we could say that the obligation not to recognise a situation arising in violation of international legality – such as a declaration of independence of a secessionist entity – comprises the following parameters.

The first thing we should bear in mind is that the obligation not to recognise does not simply establish a symbolic behaviour for States. It imposes, first and foremost, a *real duty to isolate* either the new regime that has emerged from the unlawful act (Rhodesia, Bantustan, TRNC, Sprska Republic, Abkhazia, etc.) or the *de facto* authority illegally exercised by a pre-existing regime over a territory (Namibia, Crimea, etc.).

Not to recognise is to refuse to render any kind of assistance to the perpetrator of a serious violation of domestic and international law; that is, to refuse to be an accomplice to such a violation. What matters is not so much that non-recognition means escaping the punishment that complicity would entail. The point is, above all, that in a system where sanctions are inadequate, this is the way to react and punish the perpetrator of the illegal act. To this extent, it is easy to conceive of the existence of an obligation not to recognise, since it expresses nothing but the condemnation of all forms of complicity in violation of the law.

Third States are thus under an *obligation not to do* anything that could be interpreted as an implicit recognition of the claim or status established by

72 Christakis. "The State as a 'Primary Fact'…", op. cit., p. 144.

violation of a peremptory norm of international law. More specifically, this translates into a number of obligations to abstain or *not to do*, which are as follows:

Obligation not to establish treaty relations with the illegal authority

This first dimension of the obligation of non-recognition is contained in the aforementioned note addressed on 7 January 1932 by US Secretary of State Stimson to the Japanese and Chinese Governments in connection with Manchukuo. This declaration was taken up almost literally by the Resolution on this crisis, adopted on 11 March 1932 by the General Assembly of the League of Nations, which imposed an obligation of non-recognition, subsequently detailed by the Circular of 7 June 1933 of the Advisory Committee on the Non-Recognition of Manchukuo, which specified the technical arrangements for its implementation[73].

In the case of Rhodesia, no State or international organisation concluded any treaty whatsoever with the Government led by Ian Smith. Even the International Telecommunication Union decided, in 1966, to refuse to accept any instrument of ratification or accession submitted to it by or on behalf of that illegal regime[74].

In its 1971 Advisory Opinion on Namibia, the ICJ ruled that States should not enter into treaty relations with the Government of South Africa if they intended to do so on behalf of Namibia. This obligation extended to previously signed treaties, pursuant to Article 64 of the 1969 Vienna Convention on the Law of Treaties[75].

Obligation not to establish diplomatic relations: neither to accredit nor to receive diplomatic missions

This second dimension of the obligation of non-recognition is also constantly confirmed by practice. It concerns the prohibition on establishing diplomatic relations with illegally created regimes insofar as such relations can be considered a recognition of such regimes.

Thus, in the case of Rhodesia, for example, all States respected the Security Council's appeal not to establish any diplomatic relations with the illegal authority (Resolution 217 (1965)). The ICJ also noted in its Opinion on Namibia that States should refrain from accrediting South African diplomatic missions or special missions whose jurisdiction extends to the territory of Namibia (para. 123). Likewise, all states heeded the call of the United Nations General Assembly not to establish diplomatic relations with any of the Bantustans. As has also occurred with the TRNC, South Ossetia or Abkhazia, with the exception of their respective sponsor States.

73 Text reproduced in *RGDIP*, 1933, pp. 358–363.
74 Nations Unies, *Annuaire Juridique*, 1966, p. 176.
75 ICJ Reports, 1971, para. 122.

Obligation to refuse the illegal entity's admission to and participation in an international organisation

This third dimension is closely linked to the previous one and is also confirmed by practice, which dates back to 1933 when the Advisory Committee on the Non-Recognition of Manchukuo invited States not only to refuse the admission of Manchukuo to any international organisation, but also to take all useful measures to prevent the participation of representatives of Manchukuo in any international association not created by an international treaty.

None of the secessionist entities aspiring to statehood has been admitted as a member of the UN or of any other international organisation; and none has ever participated or is currently participating in any international association. Only Kosovo has been admitted as a member of the IMF and the World Bank – international institutions – but, contrastingly, it has been refused admission to any international organisation despite having applied for membership, as we have already pointed out.

Of great significance in relation to this point is the practice concerning the TRNC, since not only has it not been admitted to any international organisation, but it has also been prevented from participating in any of the bodies of these organisations. Of particular relevance is Resolution 1376 of the Parliamentary Assembly of the Council of Europe, of 29 April 2004, whereby it decided to involve representatives of the Turkish Cypriot community in the work of the Assembly and its committees, though not as members of the TRNC but instead as members of the delegation of the Republic of Cyprus[76]. The Parliamentary Assembly even refused to grant TRNC observer status. Another important event which confirms the rejection of any recognition of the TRNC is the European Union's refusal to participate in a planned joint forum between the EU and the Islamic Conference, which was to have taken place on 4–5 October 2004 in Istanbul. The justification given by the EU was based on the fact that Turkey had announced the participation of Turkish Cypriots as representatives of the 'Turkish Cypriot State'.

Obligation to refuse to establish economic, commercial or other relations with the illegal authority

In the various Security Council resolutions relating to Namibia, the Bantustans or the TRNC cited earlier, we have found that the Council calls upon States to refrain from entering into not only diplomatic but all types of relations with such entities. It is in this frame of reference that we situate economic, commercial or any other kind of relations, which reaffirm the determination not to recognise.

76 A decision following the Annan Plan proposal on the reunification of Cyprus.

In this context, in relation to the TRNC, the Court of Justice of the European Union declared in its Judgment of 5 July 1994 that the authorities of the EU Member States could not authorise the import of goods and agricultural products from the occupied part of Cyprus unless they were duly accompanied by the necessary certificates issued by the authorities of the Republic of Cyprus[77]. This position was upheld in subsequent Judgments dated 4 July 2000[78] and 30 September 2003[79].

Obligation to refuse to recognise any legal effect of constitutional, legislative or administrative acts carried out by the illegal regime

Finally, international practice offers us examples both of international organisations and of international and domestic jurisdictions that have refused to recognise any legal effect of the acts of any illegal authority that could strengthen its illegal regime; even going so far as to declare them null and void: Israel, Southern Rhodesia, Namibia, Bantustan, TRNC, Iraq in Kuwait, etc.

We might even recall how the ECHR, in its Judgment of 18 December 1996 in the case of *Loizidou v Turkey* (merits), refused to recognise the TRNC as a State and to attribute legal value to the provisions of its Constitution of 7 May 1985[80].

All these dimensions of the obligation of non-recognition are different manifestations of a duty not to do anything that could, in one way or another, validate a void title and create rights in favour of an illegal entity.

Thus, we should bear in mind that an anti-legal situation – such as a secessionist entity's declaration of independence – could ultimately be 'legalised' by being recognised, not by one or more States individually, but by all other pre-existing States in general. In other words, it could lead to the validation of the illegal act of secession, pursuant to the maxim *ex iniuria oritur ius*.

77 Case C-432/92. Reference for a preliminary ruling by the House of Lords by order of that court of 20 May 1998 in the case of *Regina v Minister of Agriculture, Fisheries and Food, ex parte: S. P. Anastasiou (Pissouri) Ltd and Others*. Interveners: Cypfruvex (UK) Ltd and Cyprus Fruit and Vegetable.

78 Case C-219/98. Reference for a preliminary ruling from the House of Lords: *Regina v Minister of Agriculture, Fisheries and Food, ex parte: S. P. Anastasiou (Pissouri) Ltd and Others* ('Directive 77/93/EEC - Issue of phytosanitary certificates by third countries').

79 Case C-140/02. Reference for a preliminary ruling from the House of Lords: *Regina, on the application of S.P. Anastasiou (Pissouri) Ltd and Others v Minister of Agriculture, Fisheries and Food*. Interveners: Cypfruvex (UK) Ltd and Cypfruvex Fruit and Vegetable (Cypfruvex) Enterprises Ltd. (Approximation of laws – Plant health protection – Directive 77/93/EEC – Introduction into the Community of plants originating in third countries and subject to special requirements – Special requirements which cannot be fulfilled at places other than the place of origin – Affixing of an appropriate origin marking to the packaging of the plants – Official statement that the plants originate in an area considered to be free from the harmful organism in question).

80 Para. 44 and para. 56.

The decisive value of collective and institutional non-recognition. A brake on the statehood aspirations of secessionist entities that Catalonia should consider before continuing to pursue its goal

As we have seen, non-recognition has an evidently crucial role in responding to the illegality of a unilateral declaration of secessionist independence, *collective* and *institutional non-recognition* being much more important and effective in this condemnation of illegality; that is, the generalised absence of any recognition whatsoever.

It is vitally important for non-recognition to be regarded not as an isolated decision of a small minority – whose timeliness and effectiveness could be called into question – but as the result of a decision by the international community as a whole; in other words, as a kind of 'sanction' for the violation that such a secessionist declaration entails. Rozakis, a member of the European Commission on Human Rights, discussed at length the question of the sanctioning nature of non-recognition in his dissenting opinion on the Commission's report in the case of *Chrysostomos and Papachrysostomou v Turkey*, stating that:

> The non-existence of this entity (i.e. the TRNC) is the result of a decision of the international community not to attribute the quality of statehood to the northern part of the island. This attitude of the international community is manifested [...] by the resolution of the same world organization [the United Nations] calling upon the States of the international community to negate the existence of the northern part of Cyprus as a separate international entity [...] the non-recognition, proposed here by the Security Council, amounts virtually to a sanction inflicted by the international community against the primary illegality of the use of force to attain the political purpose of secession of the northern part of Cyprus from the Republic [...] In other words, the concept of non-recognition is used here [...] to prevent the attribution of statehood to an illegal entity[81].

In relation to collective non-recognition, non-recognition by international organisations, i.e. *institutional non-recognition*, is most effective in invalidating the legal effects of a secessionist entity's declaration of independence. This manifests itself in two ways: as an obligation *per se* not to recognise, and as a rejection of the entity's admission as a member of the international organisation.

Thus, non-recognition by international organisations constitutes 'the essential legal weapon' to combat serious violations of fundamental principles of international law. These organisations have acquired a decisive and almost guardian-like role in the interpretation of international legality.

81 Report of 8 July 1993, pp. 43–44.

This is particularly true of the United Nations. There is no doubt that, at present, the United Nations is becoming the collective judge of the statehood of secessionist entities; whether it be negatively through non-recognition of statehood, both by refusing membership and adopting a resolution that obliges its members not to recognise the entity as a State, which in turn means denying that entity international legal personality; or positively by granting its admission as a Member State. Dugard puts it as follows:

> Recognition by the United Nations has both a positive and a negative side, for the United Nations may both create a State and deny a State... may order the non-recognition of an entity that aspires to statehood and thereby effectively deny it international legal personality[82].

Consequently, institutional recognition or non-recognition plays a key role in the success or failure of the secession of a territory from the parent State.

The institutional obligation not to recognise

Of vital legal significance is the adoption of a decision by a body of an international organisation urging its Member States not to recognise a secessionist entity as a State. This is so insofar as the decision creates a legal and international obligation not to recognise such an entity. International practice in recent years offers recurrent situations in this regard. Both the Security Council and, on occasion, the General Assembly of the United Nations have adopted various resolutions in cases of secession urging UN members not to recognise secessionist entities as States.

As illustrative examples, we can cite the Security Council's categorical position on the non-recognition of Southern Rhodesia, to which we have referred throughout this book. Resolutions 216 and 217 (1965) uphold the "illegality and invalidity under international law" of the declaration of independence of the territory controlled by the white minority (Declaration of 11 November 1965), which they qualify as an "act of rebellion" by an illegal authority. The second of the aforementioned resolutions, moreover, urges all states not to recognise that illegal authority and not to maintain diplomatic or any other kind of relations with it. As a result, a policy of non-recognition was also initiated, reflected in particular in Council Resolution 277 (1977).

In the case of Namibia, the position of the UN was similar. Following Security Council Resolutions 269 (1969) and 276 (1970), which described South Africa's presence in that territory as "an illegal act, a usurpation of power and a foreign occupation of a territory", a procedure was initiated to eliminate the situation of illegality. In this regard, the first decision adopted in Resolution

82 Dugard, John. "The Secession of States and Their Recognition in the Wake of Kosovo". *Recueil des Cours*, vol. 357, 2011, p. 69.

283 (1970) of 29 July was also to urge all Member States to sever any relationship involving recognition of South Africa's authority over the territory of Namibia.

A similar initiative can be found regarding the Bantustans of South Africa (Transkei, Bophuthatswana, Venda and Ciskei). The Security Council, following the position previously adopted by the General Assembly in its Resolutions 3411 (XXV) and 31/6 of 1976, carried out an inflexible decision of non-recognition, as reflected in Resolutions 402 (1976) and 407 (1977), which call upon all States to avoid any form of recognition of any Bantustan. Resolution 402 (1976) of December 22 expressly:

1 *Endorses* General Assembly resolution 31/6 A which, inter alia, calls upon all Governments to deny any form of recognition to the so-called independent Transkei and to refrain from having any dealings with the so-called independent Transkei or other bantustans.
2 *Commends* the Government of Lesotho for its decision not to recognize the so-called independence of the Transkei.

However, undoubtedly the strongest position we find relates to the declaration of independence of the TRNC on 15 November 1983, which arose from a military occupation of that territory supported by the Turkish Government. The Security Council immediately denounced any attempt at secession, considering the proclamation of independence as "legally invalid", as stated in Resolution 541 (1983) of 18 November, where it:

6 *Calls* upon all States to respect the sovereignty, independence, territorial integrity and non-alignment of the Republic of Cyprus;
7 *Calls* upon all States not to recognize any Cypriot State other than the Republic of Cyprus.

A few months later, in response to the exchange of ambassadors between the TRNC and Turkey (the only State in the world to have recognised the secession), the Security Council, in its Resolution 550 (1984):

2 *Condemns* all secessionist actions, including the purported exchange of ambassadors between Turkey and the Turkish Cypriot leadership, declares them illegal and invalid and calls for their immediate withdrawal;
3 *Reiterates* the call upon all States not to recognize the purported State of the "Turkish Republic of Northern Cyprus" set up by secessionist acts and calls upon them not to facilitate or in any way assist the aforesaid secessionist entity;
4 *Calls* upon all States to respect the sovereignty, independence, territorial integrity, unity and non-alignment of the Republic of Cyprus.

Since these Security Council resolutions were adopted under Chapter VII of the UN Charter, they are binding on all UN Member States, in accordance with Article 25 of the Charter[83].

This means that they not only constitute UN non-recognition, but also create an *international legal obligation of non-recognition* for all UN Member States.

Refusal of admission as a Member State: the main weapon against the statehood aspirations of secessionist entities

In addition to the importance of an institutional resolution establishing the duty not to recognise, we should also bear in mind that international organisations play a decisive role in the normal functioning of a State in the framework of international relations, both for the State itself and for its citizens and enterprises.

Therefore, the failure to achieve Member State status in some international organisations means that it is completely impossible for the aspiring state to perform the most basic actions beyond its borders, thus condemning it to isolation and internal confinement. From a positive point of view of accession to statehood, although the United Nations cannot itself confer recognition, achieving UN membership has become the main symbol of general acceptance of statehood in contemporary international law. UN membership has come to be regarded as the "gold standard" of international legitimacy[84]. For the entity in question, it acts as a kind of imprimatur of statehood, because once a State has become a member of the UN, its statehood is no longer in question.

A contrario sensu, in view of this reality, within the framework of this response to, or 'sanctioning' of, the violation of legality that a secessionist entity's unilateral declaration of independence entails, refusal to admit it as a member of the UN is crucial.

However, not only the UN as such plays a fundamental role. In practice, its specialised agencies, by denying a secessionist entity admission as a member, are equally decisive, if not even more so. For if this happens, the secessionist entity will be unable to carry out any action at international level. No matter how much it claims to be a State, its capacity to engage in international relations is reduced to nothing. A few examples of this will suffice to show the importance of institutional non-recognition.

The Universal Postal Union (UPU) is a specialised agency of the UN which aims to strengthen the organisation and improve its postal services, to help provide technical postal assistance requested by its Member States, and to promote international cooperation in postal matters. The UPU sets tariffs, maximum and minimum weight and size limits, as well as conditions for the

83 Article 25: "The Members of the United Nations agree to accept and carry out the decisions of the Security Council in accordance with the present Charter".

84 Keating, Joshua. "How to Start Your Own Country in Four Easy Steps". *Foreign Policy*, February 2008.

acceptance of correspondence, and establishes regulations applicable to correspondence, and to objects whose transportation requires special care, such as infectious and radioactive substances.

These being its competences, it follows that if a State is not a member of this international organisation it cannot carry out postal communications anywhere in the world. In other words, neither the alleged State, nor its citizens, nor its enterprises, nor the population within the territory under its control, can send letters, parcels, get money orders, etc.

The International Telecommunication Union (ITU) is the UN's specialised agency responsible for regulating international telecommunications between different public authorities and operating companies. Among other functions, the ITU develops standards that facilitate the efficient interconnection of national communication infrastructures with global networks, allowing a seamless exchange of information, be it data, faxes or telephone calls, from anywhere in the world. It promotes the development of new applications such as internet, e-mail and multimedia services. It manages the sharing of the radio frequency spectrum and satellite orbits, limited natural resources used by a wide range of devices including mobile phones, radios and televisions, satellite communication systems, air and sea navigation safety systems, as well as wireless computer systems.

If a State is not a member of the ITU, it cannot, among other things, have its own international telephone code, making it impossible for anyone located there to perform such everyday actions as making or receiving an international call, or to rely on internet connection networks.

The International Civil Aviation Organization (ICAO) is a UN agency created in 1944 by the Chicago Convention on International Civil Aviation to study the problems of international civil aviation and to promote the only regulations and standards in global aviation. The ICAO is also responsible for standardising certain functions necessary for the activities of airlines, such as the Aeronautical Message Handling System (AMHS). This makes it a standardisation association. Each country must have access to Aeronautical Information Publications (AIP), which include essential information for air navigation based on the standards defined by the ICAO. These publications must be updated by each country every 28 days and, in addition, must include definitive regulations on airports and airspace. According to the ICAO, temporary air navigation hazards must be published using NOTAMs (Notices to Airmen). It is also responsible for the standardisation of machine-readable passports through the use of automatic readers at airports around the world.

If a State is not a member of the ICAO, not only can it not participate in the development of standards that regulate civil air navigation, but also its airspace is blocked because it is not subject to the common rules adopted within the framework of the ICAO. This may even mean that aircraft will not be able to enter or leave the airports of a self-proclaimed secessionist State, because the other existing States will bring all air navigation with it to a standstill. This has been the case with the TRNC, which has no air navigation for this very reason.

More recently in the same context, since the unilateral proclamation of independence by the Republic of Kurdistan on 25 September 2017, not only has Iraq suspended all flights to and from this separatist region, but so have many other States. Thus, the Federal Aviation Administration of the United States has prohibited US carriers (especially Delta and United Airlines, which covered that route) and commercial operators from flying over that territory. More specifically, the following airlines have since suspended flights over the territory and to the capital of Kurdistan: British Airways, Turkish Airlines, Lufthansa and its subsidiaries Austrian Airlines and Swiss, Etihad, Emirates, Air France, KLM and Virgin Atlantic.

Similarly, various aeronautical experts have stated that "no airline will fly over the pirate skies of the republic of Puigdemont. The ICAO does not assign rules to imaginary countries"[85]. Their conclusion is that there would be no flights in Catalonia. This is an important real warning that Catalan separatists should bear in mind.

The International Organization for Standardization (ISO) promotes the use of proprietary, industrial and commercial standards worldwide. The use of standards facilitates the creation of products and services that are safe, reliable and of high quality. Allowing direct comparison of products from different manufacturers makes it easier for new companies to enter new markets and assist in the development of global trade on a fair basis. Standards also serve to protect consumers and end users of products and services by ensuring that certified products conform to internationally standardised minimum requirements.

Unless you become a member of this organisation, you cannot have an ISO code, which, as we know, is the one used, among others, to issue passports, send goods, obtain internet domains, etc. The first consequence of not having an ISO code is that people who have the 'nationality' of a State that is not a member of this organisation are stuck there, because they do not have a passport that incorporates this code, and the same applies to any goods produced there.

In view of these examples, the conclusion is more than evident: the secessionist entity will have proclaimed itself independent, but neither it nor its inhabitants nor its business enterprises will be able to communicate – by telephone, by post, online, etc. – or move freely or work around the world if it does not become a member of the appropriate specialised agencies of the United Nations. This is why we advocate the effectiveness of institutional non-recognition.

But this is not only the case with the United Nations system. The same could be said to apply to regional organisations, which is particularly important in the European setting in relation to the European Union.

85 www.larazon.es/economia/aeropuertos-sin-reconocimiento-internacional-no-hay-espacio-aereo-BE16653301.

And while they may not be so important, it is also worth thinking about sports competitions and their respective organising bodies: International Olympic Committee, FIFA, UEFA, FIBA, FIA, etc. Although these are private entities, international practice shows that they maintain a consistency with respect to the positions held by the respective governments that participate in them. Moreover, it could reasonably be argued that the postponement caused by a collective and institutional non-recognition and the parent State's opposition to secession would very likely make it impossible for the 'athletes' attached to these self-proclaimed States to leave their respective territories, due to them being refused permission to enter or pass through the territory of other States. Obviously, deciding which individuals may enter or pass through (whether it be by air, land or sea) the territory of a State falls within the remit of its territorial powers, and it makes this decision with absolute discretion under the principle of sovereignty vested in it, as we have seen Iraq do in response to the unilateral proclamation of independence of Kurdistan. Not to mention any air blockade that other States may impose, preventing their airlines from making flights to and from the territory of secessionist entities, as often happens in international practice as a collective response to these illegal declarations.

Without any of this, it is evident that secessionist entities are bound, sooner or later, to perish or subsist in a permanent state of ostracism and international isolation. Hence the effectiveness of institutional non-recognition. Proof of this are the numerous failures of secessionist entities that eventually returned to their initial territorial integrity, such as Katanga, Biafra and, more recently, Kurdistan, which, one month after its proclamation of independence on 25 September 2017 and the international community's reaction against it, announced that it would be suspended.

One solution to this precarious situation that some unrecognised secessionist entities have used – including Abkhazia, South Ossetia and the TRNC – is to carry out all these actions through their sponsor – Russia and Turkey, respectively – that *is* a Member State of all these international organisations. In this way, the ISO codes, postal codes or internet networks of the sponsor States are used within the territory of these secessionist entities, which converts them into genuine "puppets" of those States. The alternative is clear in the future of illegal secessions: either live in international ostracism or be another State's "rag doll".

Catalonia should take note of these lessons before dragging its population into another secessionist adventure with dire consequences. And the Catalan people should also know what serious consequences would result from a secession without the approval of Spain and, consequently, of the international community. Furthermore, this warning would be equally valid for any other entity seeking a secession that is neither agreed upon nor admitted by the parent State.

Conclusions

The Catalan secessionist process from an international perspective

The secessionist challenge posed in Catalonia in recent years is not merely a proposal made by an elite, or an unfulfilled wish of a part of Catalan society represented to a greater or lesser extent by its political representatives, as is the case, for example, in Corsica or in the Flemish Region of Belgium. On the contrary, it is an aspiration which is defended on an ideological level and has already given rise to concrete and significant events. Indeed, since 2012, various resolutions issued by the Parliament of Catalonia have been reviewed and declared null and void by the Spanish Constitutional Court for contravening prevailing domestic law. The referendum held in 2014 was also declared illegal and its direct sponsors were convicted for their part in it. And the laws that provided for the subsequent 2017 referendum, as well as the 'consultation' and the subsequent declaration of independence, were also challenged and had important criminal and even constitutional consequences, resulting in the temporary suspension of Catalan autonomy.

All these acts have been ineffective to date, due to the forceful response of the Spanish State Government, police forces, courts of justice and the Constitutional Court, among other national institutions.

The Catalan secessionist project is clearly a matter of great significance for Spain as a whole. It has set the political agenda since 2014 just as it had done previously, at least from 2006, the year in which – after the partial rejection of the Statute of Autonomy approved by the regional parliament – nationalist pretensions start to become secessionist aspirations. In international terms, this issue does not really gain traction – beyond the occasional reference to nationalist claims, largely due to precedents from the first third of the twentieth century – until it is 'Europeanised' through foreign news media denunciation of policing methods during the 2017 referendum, and reports on the procedural and parliamentary escapades involving secessionist leaders on the run from Spanish justice in Germany, the United Kingdom, Switzerland, Belgium, as well as in the institutions of the European Union.

Since the process began in 2006, with varying degrees of repercussion abroad, it has become one of the more high-profile secessionist and separatist phenomena of recent years, which include the following: the separation of Montenegro (2006); the unilateral declaration of independence of the

DOI: 10.4324/9781003200772-6

Provisional Institutions of Self-Government of Kosovo (2008) and the subsequent ICJ Advisory Opinion (2010); the independence of South Sudan (2011); the Scottish independence referendum (2014); the conflict in Eastern Ukraine and the secession of Crimea (2014); the Iraqi Kurdistan referendum (2017); and the referendum on the island of Bougainville (2019). Catalan pro-independence propaganda and the news media have compared these events – as well as earlier ones such as the Supreme Court of Canada's decision on Quebec (1998), the independence of East Timor (2002), and even the independence of Slovenia (1991) – to the secessionist dynamic in Catalonia.

The study of secessionist processes carried out in this monograph covers very different aspects of the phenomenon, including concept, characteristics, distinction between secession and separation (with consent), types, political arguments, alleged legal bases, elements of statehood and ascertainment thereof, the importance of effectiveness, the effects of secession, respect for international law and international recognition, among others. This wide-ranging subject has been studied across four chapters, the first two focusing on peoples and the last two on States, although all of them are chiefly concerned with accession to statehood through secession.

Our analysis of international texts and international practice, together with that of other scholars, allows us to make some conclusive points about the legal consideration of the phenomenon of secession and also about the specific case of Catalonia's pretensions and the events that have taken place there.

State creation through secession consists of the effective separation of a territory and its population from a State, without the disappearance of the latter and without its consent thereto, colonial situations of course being a different matter. As for whether the scenario in Catalonia fits the proposed concept of secession, the answer could be affirmative in the sense that some of the political parties[1] and a part of Catalan society do want to separate the four Catalan provinces (Barcelona, Tarragona, Gerona and Lerida) that constitute the Autonomous Community of Catalonia from the Kingdom of Spain. And they appear to want to do so without the consent of this State's institutions – which represent the rest of its population – and while disregarding the ordinary and constitutional law issued by the Spanish Parliament, with the intention of forming a new State.

The declaration of independence and the so-called 'rules of disconnection' issued by the Catalan Parliament (Referendum and Transition Laws) and the

1 Political parties promoting independence in the regional parliament obtained 47.80% of the vote and 53.33% of the seats (72 out of 135) in the 2015 regional elections, and 47.50% of the vote and 54.81% of the seats (74 out of 135) in 2017. In the 2019 general election, they obtained 42.92% of the vote. In the surveys carried out by the *Centre d'Estudis d'Opinió*, a body of the Autonomous Government of Catalonia, support for independence was 42% (although 78.3% said they were in favour of holding a referendum to decide), according to the barometer of 31 July 2020, consulted on 27 September 2020 at http://ceo.gencat.cat/ca/barometre/detall/index.html?id=7688.

autonomous Government (execution decrees) prove the unilateral nature of the process. The essential difference with respect to Scotland's bid for independence is that the Catalan Government has neither made a proposal in the State parliament nor entered into talks with the Spanish Government. The task of convincing politicians and understanding public opinion carried out over many years of institutional loyalty by Scotland's devolved institutions has not been replicated in the relations between Catalonia's institutions and those of the Spanish State, nor with regard to general public opinion in Catalonia or Spain. In the latter respect, there is a huge difference between the Catalan independence proposal and those put forward in other parts of Europe. In Slovenia, Croatia and Lithuania, as well as in Transnistria and South Ossetia, there has been very broad social support for independence. In contrast, with less than 50% support for independence in Catalonia, 88% voted for independence in the 1991 referendum in Slovenia (with a 93.2% turnout), while 93% of Lithuanians did likewise in their referendum held the same year (with a turnout of 84.7%). In our opinion, this is due to two factors: first, the evident absence of a substantial majority demand for secession from Spain (which makes it similar to Scotland and Quebec); and second, the lack of equivalence between the independence option and ethnic identity, which differentiates it from the Baltic, Yugoslav and Caucasian secessions.

It also differs from other consensual 'separatist' experiences in which the Supreme Court of Canada was consulted on this issue by the Canadian Government. The Supreme Court's response was unequivocal in confirming there is no right of self-determination in Canada's constitutional order and in denying the existence of a situation of human rights violation that might justify a disputed remedial secession, despite certain passages being somewhat contradictory as regards its existence in international law. Nevertheless, the Supreme Court recommended that the parliamentary institutions regulate the separation, for which purpose it also proposed the criteria they should employ to ensure its clarity and effects. The consequence was the federal agreement to pass the 2000 Clarity Act. In the case of Catalonia, the work of Spain's Constitutional Court has consisted mainly in annulling the regional institutions' acts and regulations for contravening the law. However, in its judgments it has denied the competence of the regional bodies to legislate on self-determination and has based itself, even literally, on the Canadian Supreme Court's verdict to justify remedial secession, in our opinion without any foundation. Such legislative power rests with the Spanish Parliament, yet no proposal has been put forward nor debate initiated in either of its two houses by the pro-independence political parties or by any of the other parties in favour of holding a referendum, such as those on the far left of the political spectrum and the nationalist parties – on both left and right – of other Spanish regions.

As for what type of secessionist process we are dealing with, this is a proposed secession. We cannot consider it a thwarted secession because at no point has effective government been exercised exclusively by the Catalan institutions with the genuine absence of Spanish State institutions. With regard to the events of October 2017, it is particularly striking that the declaration of independence issued by the Catalan Parliament on 27 October 2017 was valid for its own authors for only a few minutes, given that the Catalan Government subsequently suspended it (along with some 40 decrees already prepared for this purpose in application of the Transition Law), claiming that the new State had structural and financial deficiencies as well as insufficient international recognition. In fact, it was a unilateral declaration of independence in two acts: on 10 October the regional president, Carles Puigdemont, proclaimed it in a speech, following the result of the referendum held on 1 October, but suspended it pending the Spanish Government's acceptance. As this was not forthcoming, the Senate proceedings for suspending autonomy being initiated instead, the Catalan president declared independence again, in parliament on 27 October, but without observing the formalities laid down in its regulations, the Catalan Government's own legal counsel already having warned of the declaration's illegality.

If we compare this declaration of independence with other recent examples, it does not follow the model of the Baltic republics in that it went ahead without waiting for international backing and the favourable – albeit resigned – opinion of the parent State, although there were also two declarations by the respective Baltic parliaments. In Estonia, independence was declared first on 8 May 1990, for domestic consumption only and with no response from Moscow or any international repercussions, and then a second time – nearly six months after the referendum on 3 March – on 20 August 1991, which led to its effective secession, with recognition received from Brussels on 28 August and from the USSR on 6 September. The Catalan declarations were made on 10 and 27 October 2017. On the first occasion, the President of the Catalan Government said he was expecting a response from the international community and the Spanish State. The second declaration, however, was made prematurely, as there was no favourable international reaction, and the State institutions did not abandon the administration in Catalonia. On the contrary, the support for Spain's territorial integrity expressed by the then European Council President, Donald Tusk, and the then President of the European Parliament, Antonio Tajani, was bolstered by the Governments of countries such as Australia, Brazil, Germany, the United States, Italy, France, the United Kingdom, Russia, Argentina, Mexico, Morocco, Azerbaijan, Portugal, Switzerland, Poland, Canada, Indonesia and Colombia. The only State that declared itself in favour of Catalan independence was Venezuela.

Nor does it resemble those made by the Caucasian entities, which led to their *de facto* separation, or by the Serbian entities, which allowed them to become *de facto* entities only temporarily. The reason for the difference is obvious: Catalonia has had no likeminded State to support and sustain its independence, be it permanent or temporary, like Russia in South Ossetia, Turkey in the TRNC, Armenia in Nagorno-Karabakh, or Serbia in Croatian Krajina. But then nor is it similar to other cases of thwarted secessions, such as Chechnya or Tamil Eelam, because in Catalonia there has been no effective exclusive administration by its institutions, which has only been possible in cases of international practice (except for the case of Somaliland, albeit in a 'failed state' context) owing to armed confrontation with State authorities and forces.

Various political arguments have been put forward by Catalan secessionism. First, ethnic identity, although rather than resorting to this term it prefers to claim an inherent right of the Catalan people, as is, to decide its political future exclusively and without any limitation. This alleged right of peoples to be States on the ground of being ethnically distinct communities does not exist in the international legal order. In any case, defending this argument raises the difficulties inherent in identifying the 'people' as well as problems specific to this particular case. International law has usually relied on a concept of 'people' that includes objective elements (distinctness in terms of race, culture, language, economy, society, history, geography, etc.) and subjective elements (community consciousness, defence of own identity, etc.). However, in our opinion – reflected in the report of the Special Rapporteur on minority issues, issued on 15 July 2019 – the concept should be restricted to the objective elements, because of the difficulty in verifying the subjective elements and the ease with which they can be manipulated. In other words, distinctness would suffice.

In the case of Catalonia, resorting to subjective elements would automatically reduce the Catalan people to the percentage that supports the defence of its own culture and has a Catalan community consciousness, whatever that percentage may be. Yet using objective elements hardly points to an objective and relevant distinctness beyond language. Of course, this does not mean that there are no specific social customs, economic characteristics, political institutions, etc., but rather that they are not sufficiently relevant under international law for this community to be considered as a people. According to the statistics provided by the Catalan institutions, only 36% consider Catalan to be the 'language of identification'. The greatest difficulty posed by this minority percentage and the dispersion it reflects is that, from the perspective of international law, a people must have a territorial connection or rootedness in order to pass the stage of non-discrimination granted to 'non-territorial minorities' and seek statehood.

Second, the recovery of lost statehood has been cited as sufficient cause, although certainly not in exclusive or very strong terms. In international law there is no such right unless we are talking about acquiring territory through the use of armed force, which has been universally prohibited since the UN Charter of 1945. Catalan secessionism has constructed a History of Catalonia which sidesteps the voluntary nature of the dynastic and territorial union of the County of Barcelona (and other possessions) and the Kingdom of Aragon, as well as between the Crown of Aragon and the Kingdom of Castile (and other possessions). With the same ulterior motives, it confuses the different episodes of internal confrontations – from the seventeenth to the twentieth century – between central governments and social sectors or even local authorities with international armed conflicts and, therefore, with a conquest by force. This is certainly not the only recent case, however, as this type of argument has also been used, in a more or less similar way, by Estonia and Slovenia.

Third, the right to self-determination has been claimed on the basis of historical grievances suffered by the Catalan people: loss of statehood in the sixteenth century, loss of its institutions in the seventeenth century, loss of its own personality in the complex Hispanic Monarchy of the early eighteenth century, and culminating in the fiscal balance, investments and even the amendment of the Statute of Autonomy in 2006. This too lacks a basis in international law, yet it is routinely cited by nationalist movements. Thus, the economic imbalance in the inter-territorial compensation fund was one of the arguments used by Slovenian independence supporters in 1991, which found great favour domestically but was given short shrift internationally. In contrast, Lithuania's evocation of being forcibly stripped of its sovereignty by the USSR in 1940 caused an emotional alignment between international public opinion and its independence movement in 1990.

And fourth, as far as arguments of a political nature are concerned, the ones outlined previously have been summed up in a single argument: the strength of the majority will of the Catalan people. However, nothing in current international law allows a group that forms part of a State to form a State of its own by the simple expression of its will. On the contrary, the international legal order considers that the State has discretionary power to administer its territory and its population, with very clearly defined limitations and all of them within the framework of fundamental human rights. And this 'right to decide', to use the terminology of Catalan nationalism, is neither provided for in any international law nor enshrined as a common human right, let alone as a fundamental human right. As the 1920 report on the Åland Islands states, "positive International Law does not recognize the right of national groups, as such, to separate themselves from the State of which they form part by the simple expression of a wish". And a century later this remains equally applicable, for as Kohen maintains, "neither human rights nor an emergent principle of democratic governance can be invoked to impose on a State the obligation to negotiate its partition"[2].

Moreover, the international order includes and especially protects, because of their structural nature, the principles of sovereign equality, territorial integrity and non-intervention in internal affairs, which inspire its laws and guarantee peaceful coexistence among States.

Although the issues it deals with are more domestic than international, it is important to remember that the Supreme Court of Canada, in its 1998 decision, considered that legitimacy should not be equated with sovereign will or majority rule in isolation. The will of the people must be expressed within the framework of established procedures and with the possibility of judicial review. In his analysis of this issue, Buchanan states that:

2 Kohen. "Introduction", op. cit., p. 18.

> decision making has its proper place. Since a unilateral right to amend the constitution is not among the rights specified for provincial governments, a fortiori there is no right, under the constitution, for the people of Quebec to make this decision by majority vote or in any other way. Proponents of the simple democratic argument might attempt to deflect this objection by claiming that the putative democratic right is not a legal right under the constitution but rather a moral right that follows from the principle of democracy, understood as a fundamental value that underlies majoritarian procedures at both[3].

Following the same line of argument, Spain's Constitutional Court, in its Ruling of 2 December 2015 concerning Resolution 1/XI, of 9 November 2015, of the Parliament of Catalonia, states that:

> Resolution 1/XI seeks, in short, to base itself on a principle of democratic legitimacy of the Parliament of Catalonia, the formulation and consequences of which are in absolute contradiction with the 1978 Constitution and the Statute of Autonomy of Catalonia. This subverts not only the postulates of the rule of law, based on full submission to the law, but also the very democratic legitimacy of the Parliament of Catalonia, which is recognised and protected by the Constitution. In the social and democratic State governed by the rule of law established by the 1978 Constitution, democratic legitimacy and constitutional legality cannot be set against each other to the detriment of the latter: the legitimacy of a public authority's action or policy consists basically of its conformity with the Constitution and the legal order[4].

As far as international law is concerned, Catalonia is obviously not a colony of Spain inasmuch as it does not meet the requirements established in UNGA Resolution 1541 (XV), of 15 December 1960, there being neither a geographical separation ('saltwater rule') nor a situation of subordination in which

3 Buchanan. "The Quebec Secession Issue…", op. cit., p. 244.

4 These same constitutional arguments, discrediting the theory of the majority will of the people, were expressed in the German Constitutional Court's Order of 16 December 2016, in response to an appeal lodged by a citizen claiming the possibility of a referendum on self-determination in Bavaria. The Court considers that in the Federal Republic of Germany, which is a nation-State based on the constituent power of the German people, the States do not own the Constitution, and therefore there is no room under the Constitution for individual States to attempt to secede. As echoed in the title of an article by Ragone, Sabrina. "Los Länder no son señores de la Constitución: el Tribunal Constitucional Federal Alemán sobre el referéndum separatista bávaro". *Teoría y realidad constitucional*, vol. 41, 2018, pp. 407–418, especially p. 417, referring to the Italian Constitutional Court's annulment, in 2015, of the Veneto Law that provided for a self-determination referendum, "regional autonomy cannot be qualified as sovereignty and regional institutions cannot be assimilated to national representative bodies".

its inhabitants have fewer rights. Consequently, it lacks the legitimacy to avail itself of the right of self-determination of peoples as recognised in the UN system and specifically in UNGA Resolution 1514 (XV) of 14 December 1960.

Between 1945 and 1970, no UN text relating to the legal regime of external self-determination of peoples was drawn up with express reference to ethnic minorities or with the intention of extending it beyond situations of colonial domination or subjugation by force. Only in one paragraph of UNGA Resolution 2625 (XXV) of 24 October 1970 are there a few lines declaring an exception to the territorial integrity of States in the event of discrimination against their nationals in political representations on the grounds of "race, creed or colour". This paragraph is contained in a resolution of the UNGA, which only has recommendatory powers in this matter, and so for it to be considered binding, it must be either reproduced in a conventional norm (which has yet to happen) or recognised as a peremptory norm in ICJ jurisprudence (which has not happened either), or generated as an international custom, with this *opinio juris* being perpetuated in other documents or declarations (it has only been reiterated in the 1993 Vienna Declaration of the Human Rights Summit) and there also being a confirmatory general practice.

The legal scholarship that defends the validity of remedial secession is, in our opinion, more voluntarist than realistic. Even though it may seem legitimate to promote the right of a minority to secede on the basis of a serious, massive and systematic violation of its fundamental human rights (life, physical integrity, personality, etc.)[5], proof of the aforementioned confirmatory general practice is required before it can acquire the status of an international norm. And in our view, international practice prior to 1970 is the opposite if we take into account the immediate precedent of Biafra (1967–1970), where the brutal repression of the Ibos did not result in the international community's support for their secessionist claims; or the independence of Panama (1903), Finland (1918) and Mongolia (1921), achieved in contexts very different from those of these serious human rights violations. Moreover, in a similar case, such as Ireland (1922), this was not the argument used. This confirms that Resolution 2625 did not declare an existing custom.

Nor does subsequent practice demonstrate any repeated, general and uniform application of what was declared in 1970. Although there are cases of discrimination and even of genocidal repression – as in Eritrea (1993), East Timor (2002) and South Sudan (2011) – this was neither alleged as a basis for their secessionist claims nor put forward as a reason why they should be recognised by the international community. The Eritreans based their claim on a breach of

5 Although, as Kohen warns, "Introduction", op. cit., p. 11, a temporary situation of human rights violation cannot be resolved with a radical and definitive solution such as secession. In this remedial secession there is no balance between the structural principles of respect for the territorial integrity of States and the protection of fundamental human rights.

the agreed federal scheme, the Timorese on their frustrated decolonisation. Only the South Sudanese alleged an insufferable discriminatory repression and the international community reacted positively, but only for reasons of regional security. There are no discriminatory situations in any of the other cases of eventual success: Slovenia, Croatia, Bosnia and Herzegovina, Macedonia and the Baltic republics. But even in the Baltic cases, the argument used was the recovery of statehood lost in 1940, not the situation of their peoples or citizens in the USSR. What, therefore, was the international community's reason for accepting these secessions? In the Yugoslav case, effectiveness, and in the Baltic case, effectiveness and the parent State's recognition. Why is such recognition not required in the Yugoslav cases? Because there is no parent State, the existing State having been dissolved.

Neither in *de facto* secessions nor in thwarted ones is there a refusal based on failure to comply with the 'safeguard clause' of Resolution 2625. Discrimination or repression against the Serbs of Krajina, the Chechens or the Tamils has not resulted in support from the international community. In a situation similar to Eritrea's, the secession of the Turkish Cypriot community has been condemned, because even though it achieved effectiveness for a time, there was no acceptance by the parent State. That is the reality: the principles of State sovereignty and territorial integrity prevailed over other possible considerations.

Therefore, remedial secession is not currently valid, but even if it were to exist in the future, the situation in Catalonia would still have to be vastly different. At present there is no discrimination in political representative bodies against Spanish nationals hailing from that region on the grounds of their race, colour or creed, which are the literal terms of Resolution 2625. Nor is there any discrimination on the basis of their culture, language or legal residence, or even for identifying as separatists, since the political participation of all options is permitted, including those that seek to destroy the unity and integrity of the State. This is indisputable. Furthermore, there can be no doubt that all the provisions of the regulations and guidelines of the UN (Article 27 of the ICCPR of 1966) and of the Council of Europe concerning the protection of minority rights (Charter for Minority Languages of 1992 and Framework Convention for the Protection of Minorities of 1995) are being complied with, both in the exercise of distinctness and in terms of non-discrimination, and there is even internal autonomy, as recommended by the Council of Europe.

Perhaps this situation of normality explains the lack of support, and not only of formal recognitions, in the international community. It is clear that in Spain there is no discrimination on the basis of territory of origin or language of identification (there are barely any more differences between Galicians, Asturians, Basques, Navarrese, Aragonese, Catalans, etc.). Nor is there any economic, legal or institutional mistreatment involving subordination, exploitation or alienation, and there is no situation of serious violation of human rights anywhere on Spanish territory. The humanitarian situation in Catalonia is not comparable to that of Kurdistan during the regime of Saddam Hussein, South Sudan under Omar el-Bashir, or Eritrea under Mengistu Haile Mariam. Nor is it comparable to Soviet domination of Estonia, Latvia or Lithuania, or to Indonesia's domination of East Timor. There is no humanitarian reason to support the claims of the Catalan secessionist groups, and nor is there any regional security reason, as there is no long-term armed conflict in Spain (unlike in South Sudan or Eritrea). Nor is there an internal political confrontation that threatens the dissolution of Spain, as there was in the former Yugoslavia. And if we ask ourselves, finally, why it has not received the backing of dozens of countries, unlike Kosovo, we can point out that Catalonia has not been subjected to systematic repression with the intention of expelling the Catalans from their territory, as occurred in the 1990s with the Kosovo Albanians, that it has not been *de facto* separated from its State by the UN, and that it does not have an administration run by this international organisation.

Having set out these conclusions concerning the non-existence of a secession right for minority peoples, we will now present those relating to the requirements they should meet in order to attain statehood.

The 1933 Montevideo Convention establishes certain criteria that reflect international practice regarding the constituent elements of the State, at least in relation to population, territory and organised government. In this respect there is absolute unanimity among experts, although the fourth conventional condition concerning international capacity tends to be considered more as a consequence of statehood. In addition, there is increasing demand for a further criterion: legality in the formation process. Necessary independence, added by various scholars such as Crawford, is particularly relevant in relation to secessionist processes, as their completion requires the absence not only of parent State administration, but also of dependence on other States, as occurs with *de facto* entities (Transnistria, Nagorno-Karabakh, etc.). It is independence that brings to this context the importance of effectiveness, as it is precisely the establishment of an effective, lasting and exclusive government over a population and a territory that allows the emergence of a new State to be affirmed.

It is the lack of effectiveness, both in the governmental and institutional apparatus in relation to a population and a territory with independence in respect of other international subjects, which means we have not been able to consider Catalonia – at any point in the secessionist process that Spain is being forced to withstand – as a State, or as having any prospects of becoming one. Although it has a specific population and a defined territory, the governing powers it exercises over them are those conferred by the Spanish State in accordance with the autonomous regime laid down in the 1978 Constitution, that is, inasmuch as the *Generalitat* of Catalonia is part of the Public Administration of Spain. The powers that it exercises – in healthcare or education, for example – are not its own but are conferred by the Spanish State, and are reversible, as demonstrated in October 2017 by the triggering of Article 155 of the Constitution to temporarily prevent the regional institutions from exercising these powers after they had failed to observe this fundamental rule. In any case, these are the competences of decentralised bodies of the State Administration (as in the Länder of Germany or the federal states of the USA), not those of sovereign States, such as defence and foreign affairs, and especially – within the latter – participation in international organisations, due to their effects on everyday life (communications, transport, movement of persons, exchange of goods, etc.).

These considerations should be taken into account in the event of any future declaration of independence not suspended as in October 2017. A simple declaration of political will is not enough: there must be effectiveness in the exercise not only of local competences but of real State powers, including – at another level – economic viability. The declaration of independence does not in itself grant statehood to a group and the territory on which it is settled.

It is also necessary to emphasise that this condition of effectiveness in exclusive government is completed in international practice by the tacit or express approval (with formal recognition) of the parent State. Undoubtedly, this is out of respect for the sovereignty of other States, but it is also as a matter of efficacy, since the parent State's renunciation entails peaceful continuity and the consolidation of the secession. This recognition was granted in the cases of Finland, Mongolia, Ireland, Bangladesh, Estonia, Latvia, Lithuania, Eritrea, East Timor and South Sudan, but it was not required in the States that emerged from the dissolution of Yugoslavia because, as mentioned previously, there was no longer a parent State. On the contrary, there is no such acceptance in what we call *de facto* entities (TRNC, Abkhazia, etc.) or in the cases of thwarted secession (Chechnya, Anjouan, etc.). For this reason, legal scholarship is increasingly receptive to including this circumstance as a requirement for 'eventual success', modulating or determining the necessary effectiveness. Moreover, UN practice is unanimous in terms of not granting member status until the parent State has given its recognition.

The Spanish State's actions described in this study (annulment of the laws, declarations and referendum calls issued by the Catalan regional institutions, criminal prosecution of those responsible, and temporary suspension of autonomy), represent its clear and unequivocal denial of this attempted secession. State institutions' rejection is a major obstacle – in accordance with existing practice – to international recognition of independence, when there are signs of effective government.

There are singular cases in which State entities have been recognised without such acceptance by the parent State, such as the Caucasian entities recognised by Russia or Armenia to the detriment of the territorial integrity of Georgia and Azerbaijan, respectively. But we consider them to belong to a special category because they are recognised only by their sponsor States (and the odd ally, or even each other), and because their proven dependence on them, if not their outright illegality due to the use of force and interference in internal affairs, has prevented their general recognition and admission to the UN. Catalonia does not have a sponsor, so it would not even qualify for this rather unusual category.

There are also cases in which territorial entities have been recognised as States prematurely, in the sense that they still do not have effective and exclusive government, as in the case of Kosovo. Here, the absence or imperfection of the constituent elements of the State – prerequisites for recognition – as a result of State competences (in foreign affairs, for instance) being exercised by the UN Special Representative prevents it from existing as such. It cannot be said that Catalonia is in this peculiar situation, as there has been no UN-approved *de facto* separation as in Kosovo. Nor can the humanitarian situation of the Kosovo Albanians in 1999 be equated with that of the Catalans in 2017.

Along with this classical position on State creation as regards effectiveness in the ascertainment of elements (*ex factis jus oritur*), another more comprehensive position emerges from the general international order as a whole, which includes considering legality (*ex iniuria ius non oritur*), as defended by scholars such as Crawford, Tancredi and Wallace-Bruce, among others, and upheld in different reports and resolutions of international organisations or scientific associations, such as the ILC or the IHLADI, respectively. This is a requirement arising from the necessary overall and balanced understanding of the structural principles of international law and its peremptory norms. It is also a matter of consistency, because just as the creation of a State through use of force (TRNC) or in a manner contrary to the self-determination of peoples (Southern Rhodesia) is not allowed, the same should go for any violation of another structural principle, namely respect for the sovereignty and territorial integrity of States, except with the consent of the injured party (which would be 'separation' and not 'secession'). In our view, this applies in particular to the behaviour of third States, which should not support such secessionist processes. This is demonstrated by the examples cited and, more recently, by the UN Security Council resolutions concerning the Sprska Republic and Krajina, the aforementioned Caucasian entities, and the secession of Crimea; as well as the resolutions adopted by regional bodies such as the African Commission on Human and Peoples' Rights (Katanga 1994 and Cameroon 2009) and the arguments given by numerous governments for not recognising self-proclaimed entities such as South Ossetia or Kosovo (including in the proceedings before the ICJ).

Fully accepting these considerations, a unilateral declaration of independence, such as the one made by some Catalan MPs in 2017, should be deemed – in accordance with international law – unlawful and invalid, since, at the very least, it contravenes the peremptory norm that demands due respect for a State's territorial integrity. This generates an obligation *erga omnes* by virtue of which international subjects should refrain from giving recognition and from supporting, favouring or sustaining a situation, also unlawful as a consequence, arising from such a unilateral declaration. This is the rationale that led the Governments of France, Germany and the United Kingdom, among others, and, as mentioned earlier, the European institutions to react in the way they did to the Catalan secessionists' unilateral declaration of independence.

In relation to recognition, we believe that an eclectic position on this legal concept is more in keeping with international practice, since we consider that there is a certain complementarity between the constitutive and declarative theories. Although recognition does not make a State, it does produce important legal effects. Similarly, we consider that the margin of discretion inherent in the political and declarative nature of the act of recognition is not synonymous with arbitrariness. Just as premature acts – such as US recognition of Panama in 1903 – are unlawful, there is also an obligation not to recognise when so urged by the UN Security Council (the international body responsible for peacekeeping), because a violation of international law has been ascertained, as in the aforementioned cases. Indeed, this international practice whereby a Security Council resolution imposes this obligation of non-recognition is not only widespread – not least in the field of secession – but has been consistently reflected in international texts, especially in the context of the prohibition of use of force (OAS Charter of 1948, Helsinki Act of 1975, etc.); as well as in ICJ jurisprudence – as in the advisory opinions on Namibia (1971) and the wall in occupied Palestinian territory (2004) – and in arbitral practice (as in the Brcko dispute between the Sprska Republic and Bosnia and Herzegovina, settled in 1997).

In the aforementioned cases, and also with respect to Catalonia's past actions and any it may take in the future, the obligation of non-recognition arises from the obligation of international subjects not to interfere in the internal affairs of States. It is firmly based in international law, particularly in this specific area of secession in UNGA Resolution 36/103 of 1981, which states that:

> the duty of States to refrain from the promotion, encouragement or support, direct or indirect, of rebellious or secessionist activities within other States, under any pretext whatsoever, or any action which seeks to disrupt the unity or to undermine or subvert the political order of other States.

This obligation includes not entering into treaty or diplomatic relations with the secessionist authority, refusing its admission to and participation in international organisations, not establishing economic ties or any other type of relationship, and rejecting any legal effect of acts carried out by or arising from the secessionist entity.

It is particularly important that the international community, when faced with a secession attempt such as that which occurred in Catalonia and bearing in mind its international illegality, ensures institutional non-recognition of the entity in question, i.e. that it not be accepted, assisted or engaged with, and, of course, that it not be allowed to join international organisations. We should not forget that membership of organisations not only represents a very important endorsement of the regularisation of the international relations of secessionist entities, but also enables businesses and individuals to perform numerous everyday activities. To these ends, it is especially necessary to be a member of the Universal Postal Union, the International Telecommunications Union, the International Civil Aviation Organization and the International Organization for Standardization, among others. Without institutional recognition, the viability of a self-proclaimed State of Catalonia will be very limited.

Finally, we should add that the 'separatist' (not 'secessionist') experiences of Quebec and Scotland can teach us some interesting lessons with a view to regulating the right of self-determination in Spain, should the need ever arise. As a prerequisite of lawfulness, it would have to be recognised in the legal system of the State, as it is the concern of its whole population; a matter which must be regulated in accordance with established procedures and which must count on judicial guarantees based on the rule of law. According to Canadian and British provisions, a referendum on self-determination must be carried out with a census that includes all nationals residing on the territory and, according to other experiences, also those living elsewhere in the State and abroad who have a special connection with the territory (for example, last place of residence if they have emigrated, or if they are public-sector employees posted to other parts of the State or abroad). Furthermore, the referendum must pose a clear question, asking only about the independence of the territory. The process must have the procedural guarantees proper to any electoral event: a campaign conducted under conditions of institutional impartiality and of freedom and equality of means among the parties defending the various options; a referendum carried out by independent electoral bodies with standard electoral supervision and, ultimately, by courts of justice; and a significant turnout and support for independence beyond a simple majority, as has been required in the referendums held on the islands of Bougainville and Nevis.

There are two additional questions that will need to be determined by agreement between the parties – but following pre-established rules – if effective separation is achieved. The first should be definitive boundary delimitation, given that self-determination applies – as was established in the Scottish case – to each of the territorial areas consulted in a referendum, so that only those with that significant turnout and support for independence will accede to it (provided that, at the same time, territorial contiguity and viability are ensured). And the second is guaranteeing respect for the rights of the resultant minorities, as it is necessary – being a requirement of the international order – that the rights of those who do not share the objective distinctness (in language, for example, but also in territorial origin) or national mobilisation (due to not being pro-independence) be protected under the terms laid down in the universal and regional human rights systems, i.e. preserving their exercise of distinctness and non-discrimination. In this respect, there should be no repeat of the following undesirable outcomes in other cases of separations or secessions, especially in the early years of independence: prohibition of the Cyrillic alphabet in Moldovan schools; nationality denied to Eritreans who were civil servants of the State of Ethiopia, or to Estonians who do not speak the national language; entry to the civil service denied to Latvians who cannot demonstrate knowledge of the national language, etc. And the same goes for abusive practices, such as differing population delimitation of electoral districts to the detriment of areas inhabited by minorities, as occurred in Macedonia.

The secession proposal supported by those in favour of Catalan independence since 2014, and especially in September and October 2017, can find no refuge in the current international legal system, neither in terms of their rationale for creating a new State without Spain's consent, nor with a view to their possibly gaining international recognition from other States and international organisations. International practice supports this view, both with regard to successfully completed secessions and in relation to thwarted or unaccepted secessions (*de facto* entities). Non-colonial peoples are not entitled to external self-determination, and there is no right of remedial secession on the ground of violation of the human rights of ethnic minorities.

If Catalonia wants to become a State, effective and exclusive government on its territory must be ascertained. But far more importantly, it must be ascertained lawfully, both by the 'people' concerned and by the other States and organisations of the international community. Which means respecting the sovereignty and territorial integrity of the Spanish State, as well as fulfilling the obligation not to interfere in its internal affairs.

Bibliography

Abi-Saab, George. "Cours général de droit international public". *Recueil des Cours*, vol. 207, 1987, pp. 9–463.

Abi-Saab, Georges and Michell Virally. *Les Résolutions dans la formation du droit international du développement.* Genève: Librairie Droz, 1971.

Acosta Sánchez, Miguel A. "Kosovo: ¿una (nueva) piedra en el zapato de la política exterior de la UE?". *Revista de Derecho Comunitario Europeo*, vol. 31, 2008, pp. 773–804.

Ahmed, Dirdeiry M. *Boundaries and Secession in Africa and International Law: Challenging Uti Possidetis.* Cambridge: Cambridge University Press, 2015.

Alonso de Antonio, Ángel L. "La cuestión lingüística en la Sentencia del Tribunal Constitucional sobre el Estatuto de Autonomía de Cataluña". *Teoría y Realidad Constitucional UNED*, vol. 27, 2011, pp. 449–460.

Álvarez Ortega, Miguel. "El castellano en las aulas catalanas: claves de una incómoda recurrencia". *Revista de Estudios Políticos*, vol. 169, 2015, pp. 267–298.

Álvarez Vélez, M. Isabel. "Cataluña, las consultas populares y el referéndum: comentario a la STC 51/2017, de 10 de mayo 2017". *Teoría y Realidad Constitucional*, vol. 41, 2018, pp. 435–446.

Anderson, Glen. "Unilateral Non-Colonial Secession and the Use of Force: Effect on Claims to Statehood in International Law". *Connecticut Journal of International Law*, vol. 28, no. 2, Spring 2013, pp. 197–242.

Anderson, Glen. "A Post-Millennial Inquiry into the United Nations Law of Self-Determination: A Right to Unilateral Non-Colonial Secession". *Vanderbilt Journal of Transnational Law*, vol. 49, no. 5, 2016, pp. 1183–1254.

Andrés Sáenz de Santamaría, Paz. "La libre determinación de los pueblos en la nueva sociedad internacional". *Cursos Euromediterráneos Bancaja de Derecho Internacional*, vol. 1, 1997, pp. 113–204.

Anzilotti, Dionisio. *Corso di Diritto Internazionale* (vol. I). Roma: Athenaeum, 1928.

Arangio-Ruiz, Caetano. "The Normative Role of the General Assembly of the United Nations and the Declaration of Principles of Friendly Relations". *Recueil de Cours*, vol. 137, no. 3, 1972, pp. 419–742.

Ariel Bonfanti, Fernando. "Estado Islámico: Amenaza para el mundo o el surgimiento de un nuevo Estado". *Revista Geográfica Digital IGUNNE Facultad de Humanidades*, vol. 25, 2016.

Arp, Björn. "The ICJ Advisory Opinion on the Accordance with International Law of the Unilateral Declaration of Independence in Respect of Kosovo and the International Protection of Minorities". *German Law Journal*, vol. 11, 2010, pp. 847–866.

Badía Martí, Ana. *La participación de la ONU en procesos electorales*. Madrid: McGraw Hill, 1998.

Bar Cendón, Antonio. "El proceso independentista de Cataluña y la doctrina jurisprudencial: una visión sistemática". *Teoría y realidad constitucional*, vol. 37, 2016, pp. 187–220.

Barboza, Julio. *Derecho internacional público*. Buenos Aires: Zavalía, 2001.

Baty, Thomas. *The Canons of International Law*. London: J. Murray, 1930.

Bayefsky, Anne. *Self-Determination in International Law: Quebec and Lessons Learned*. The Hague: Kluwer, 2000.

Becker, Tal. *International Recognition of a Unilaterally Declared Palestinian State*. Legal and Policy Dilemmas, Jerusalem Centre for Public Affairs (www.jcpa.org/art/becker1.htm).

Bellew, Chelsea Elizabeth. "Secession in International Law: Could ISIS Become a Legally Recognized State?". *Ohio Northern University Law Review*, vol. 42, no. 1, 2015, pp. 239–266.

Bienvenu, Pierre. "Secession by Constitutional Means: The Decision of the Supreme Court of Canada in the Quebec Secession Reference". *Hamline Journal of Public Law & Policy*, vol. 23, no. 1, Fall 2001, pp. 185–254.

Bolton, Grace and Gezim Visoka. "Recognizing Kosovo's Independence: Remedial Secession or Earned Sovereignty?". *South East European Studies at Oxford Occasional Paper*, vol. 11/10, October 2010.

Borgen, Christopher J. "From Kosovo to Catalonia: Separatism and Integration in Europe". *Goettingen Journal of International Law*, vol. 2, no. 3, 2010, pp. 997–1033.

Borgen, Christopher J. "The Language of Law and the Practice of Politics: Great Powers and the Rhetoric of Self-Determination in the Cases of Kosovo and South Ossetia". *Chicago Journal of International Law*, vol. 10, no. 1, Summer 2009, pp. 1–33.

Bossuyt, Marc J. *Guide to the 'travaux préparatoires' of the International Covenant on Civil and Political Rights*. The Hague: Nijhoff, 1987.

Brewer, Evan M. "To Break Free from Tyranny and Oppression: Proposing a Model for a Remedial Right to Secession in the Wake of the Kosovo Advisory Opinion". *Vanderbilt Journal of Transnational Law*, vol. 45, no. 1, January 2012, pp. 245–292.

Brilmayer, Lea. "Secession and Self-Determination: A Territorial Interpretation". *Yale Journal of International Law*, vol. 16, no. 1, Winter 1991, pp. 177–202.

Brownlie, Ian. *International Law and the Use of Force*. Oxford: Oxford University Press, 1963.

Brownlie, Ian. *Principles of Public International Law*. 7th ed., Oxford: Clarendon Press, 1998.

Buchanan, Allen. *Secession: The Morality of Political Divorce from Fort Sumpter to Lithuania and Quebec*. Boulder: Westview Press, 1991.

Buchanan, Allen. "Theories of Secession". *Philosophy & Public Affairs*, 1997, pp. 30–61.

Buchanan, Allen. "The Quebec Secession Issue: Democracy, Minority Rights, and the Rule of Law". *Nomos*, vol. 45, 2003, pp. 238–271.

Buchheit, Lee C. *Secession*. New Haven: Yale University Press, 1978.

Burri, Thomas. "Secession in the CIS: Causes, Consequences and Emerging Principles". In *Self-Determination and Secession in International Law*, edited by Christian Walter and others. Oxford: Oxford University Press, 2014, pp. 138–154.

Burri, Thomas. "The Kosovo Opinion and Secession: The Sounds of Silence and Missing Links". *German Law Journal*, vol. 11, 2010, pp. 881–890.

Caballero Huayllani, Julio César. *Teoria de la nulidad del acto juridico*. www.monografias.com/trabajos88/nulidad-del-acto-jurdico/nulidad-del-acto-jurdico.shtml#efectosdea#ixzz4OwkuRQCL.

Calonge Velázquez, Antonio. "El derecho de secesión en Canadá: una regulación jurídica completa y un problema sin resolver". *Revista de Derecho de la Unión Europea*, 2013, pp. 107–124.

Cançado Trindade, Augusto Antonio. "International Law for Humankind: Towards a New Ius gentium. General Course on Public International Law". *Recueil des Cours*, vol. 316, 2005, pp. 1–304.

Caris, Charles and Samuel Reynolds. "ISIS Governance in Syria". *Institute for the Study of War*, July 2014.

Carpentier, Chantal. "Principe Mythique des Nationalités: Tentative de Dénonciation d'un Prétendu Principe". *Revue Belge de Droit International*, vol. 25, no. 2, 1992, pp. 351–389.

Carrillo Salcedo, Juan Antonio. *Soberanía del Estado y Derecho Internacional*. Madrid: Tecnos, 1976.

Carrillo Salcedo, Juan Antonio. "Sobre el pretendido derecho a decidir en Derecho internacional contemporáneo". *El Cronista del Estado Social y Democrático de Derecho*, vol. 33, 2012, pp. 20–22.

Cassese, Antonio. *Self-Determination of Peoples: A Legal Reappraisal*. New York: Cambridge University Press, 1995.

Castellino, Joshua. *International Law and Self-Determination*. The Hague: Nijhoff, 2000.

Cavaré, Louis. *Le Droit International Public Positif*. Paris: Pedone, 1962.

Charpentier, Jean. *La reconnaissance internationale et l'évolution du Droit des gens*. Paris: Pedone, 1956.

Chaumont, Charles. "Cours général de droit international public". *Recueil des Cours*, vol. 129, 1970, pp. 335–527.

Chemillier-Gendreau, Monique. "A propos de l'effectivité en Droit International". *Revue Belge du Droit International*, vol. 11, 1975, pp. 38–46.

Chen, Ti-Chiang. *The International Law of Recognition*. London: Frederick A. Praeger, 1951.

Christakis, Theodore. *Le droit à l'autodétermination en dehors des situations de décolonisation*. Paris: La Documentation Française, 1999.

Christakis, Theodore. "The State as a 'Primary Fact': Some Thoughts on the Principle of Effectiveness". In *Secession. International Law Perspectives*, edited by Marcelo G. Kohen. Cambridge: Cambridge University Press, 2006.

Christie, Emily. "Accordance with International Law of the Unilateral Declaration of Independence in Respect of Kosovo, ICJ Advisory Opinion 22 July 2010, General List No. [4]". *Australian International Law Journal*, vol. 17, no. 1, 2010, pp. 205–212.

Christopher, Anthony J. "Secession and South Sudan: An African precedent for the future?". *South African Geographical Journal*, vol. 93, no. 2, 2011, pp. 125–132.

Clark, Donald and Robert Williamson. *Self Determination. International Perspectives*. Basingstoke: Macmillan Press, 1996.

Combacau, Jean and Serge Sur. *Droit international public*. Paris: Montchrestien, 8th ed., 2008.

Corten, Olivier. "Commentaire de l'article 52". In *Les Conventions de Vienne sur le droit des traités. Commentary Article by Article*, edited by Olivier Corten and Pierre Klein. Bruxelles: Bruylant, 2006, pp. 1867–1900.

Costelloe, Daniel. *Legal Consequences of Peremptory Norms in International Law*. Cambridge: Cambridge Studies in International and Comparative Law, 2017.

Couveinhes-Matsumoto, Florian. *L'effectivité en droit international*. Bruxelles: Bruylant, 2014.

Crawford, James. "The Criteria for Statehood in International Law". *BYIL*, 1977, pp. 93–182.

Crawford, James. *The Creation of States in International Law*. 1st ed., Oxford: Oxford University Press, 1979.

Crawford, James. "La pratique des États et le droit international relativement à la sécession unilatérale". *Cour Suprême du Canada*, no. 25508, 1997.

Crawford, James. *State Practice and International Law in Relation to Unilateral Secession: Report*. Canada: Department of Justice, 1997. Consulted in https://is.muni.cz/el/1422/jaro2006/MP803Z/um/1393966/INTERNATIONAL_LAW_AND_UNILATERAL_SECESSION.pdf?lang=en

Crawford, James. *The Creation of States in International Law*. 2nd ed., Oxford: Oxford University Press, 2006.

Critescu, Aureliu. "*Le droit à la autodétermination: développement historique et actuel sur la base des instruments des Nations Unies*". UN Doc E/CN.4/Sub.2/404/Rev.1, N.Y.: UN, 1981.

Cullen, Anthony and Steven Wheatley. "The Human Rights of Individuals in De Facto Regimes under the European Convention on Human Rights". *Human Rights Law Review*, vol. 13, no. 4, 2013, pp. 691–728.

Czaplinski, Wladyslaw. "Ius Cogens and the Law of Treaties". In *The Fundamental Rules of the International Legal Order. Ius Cogens and Obligations Erga Omnes*, edited by Charles Tomuschat and Jean-Marc Thouvenin. Leiden/Boston: Martinus Nijhoff Publishers, 2006.

Dalle Mulle, Emmanuel and Ivan Serrano. "Between a Principled and a Consequentialist Logic: Theory and Practice of Secession in Catalonia and Scotland". *Nations and Nationalism*, vol. 25, no. 2, 2019.

Day, Joel. "The Remedial Right of Secession in International Law". *Potentia*, vol. 4, 2012, pp. 19–33.

Degan, Vladimir Djuro. "Création et disparition de l'État (à la lumière du démembrement de trois fédérations multiethiques en Europe)". *Recueil des Cours*, vol. 279, 2007.

Dersso, Solomon. "The African Human Rights System and the Issue of Minorities in Africa". *African Journal of International and Comparative Law*, vol. 20, no. 1, 2012, pp. 42–69.

Díaz Barrado, Castor. "La protección de las minorías en el seno del Consejo de Europa". *Anuario de la Facultad de Derecho, Universidad de Extremadura*, vol. 17, 1999, pp. 125–170.

Díez de Velasco, Manuel. *Instituciones de Derecho internacional Público*. Madrid: Tecnos, 2009.

Dinstein, Yoram. "Is There a Right to Secede". *American Society of International Law Proceedings*, vol. 90, 1996, pp. 299–303.

Dugard, John. "The Secession of States and Their Recognition in the Wake of Kosovo". *Recueil des Cours*, vol. 357, 2011.

Dugard, John, and David Raic. "The Role of Recognition in the Law and Practice of Secession". *Secession. International Law Perspectives*, edited by Marcelo Kohen. Cambridge: Cambridge University Press, 2006, pp. 94–137.

Dupuy, Pierre-Marie. "L'unité de l'ordre juridique international: Cours général de droit international public". *Recueil des Cours*, vol. 297, 2002, pp. 9–489.

Eastwood, Lawrence S. "Secession: State Practice and International Law after the Dissolution of the Soviet Union and Yugoslavia". *Duke Journal Comparative & International Law*, vol. 3, no. 2, 1993, pp. 299–350.

Efevwerhan, David. *Secession and the Lessons from Kosovo. New Dimensions in the Law of Secession.* Berlin: LAP Lambert Academic Publishing, 2010.

Hortal, Cervell, María José and Césareo Gutiérrez Espada (eds) *El Estado Islámico (DAESH), ¿aprenderemos la lección?* Valencia: Tirant, 2018.

Emerson, Rupert. "Self-Determination". *American Journal of International Law*, vol. 65, no. 3, 1971, pp. 459–475.

Erlich, Haggai. *The Struggle over Eritrea, 1962–1978: War and Revolution in the Horn of Africa.* Stanford: Hoover Institution Press of Stanford University, 1983.

Escobar Hernández, Concepción. "La posición del Reino de España en el procedimiento consultivo: una aproximación general". *Revista Española de Derecho Internacional*, vol. 63, no. 1, 2011, pp. 11–27.

Eudes, Marie. "Retour sur une réussite passée inaperçue: L'Accord de Belfast et la nouvelle lecture du droit à l'autodétermination". *Revue générale de droit international public*, vol. 110, no. 3, 2006, pp. 631–646.

Ezetah, Chinedu Reginald. "International Law of Self-Determination and the Ogoni Question: Mirroring Africa's Post-Colonial Dilemma". *Loyola of Los Angeles International and Comparative Law Journal*, vol. 19, August1997, pp. 811–856.

Fernández de Casadevante, Carlos. "El derecho de autodeterminación: una lectura desde España". *Revista Electrónica Cordobesa de Derecho Internacional Público*, vol. 1, 2018.

Fiore, Pasquale. *International Law Codified and Its Legal Sanction or the Legal Organization of the Society State.* New York: Baker, 1918.

Fisher, Steven R. "Towards Never Again: Searching for a Right to Remedial Secession under Extant International Law". *Buffalo Human Rights Law Review*, vol. 22, 2015–2016, pp. 261–296.

Fox, Gregory. "Eritrea". In *Self-Determination and Secession in International Law*, edited by Christian Walter et al., Oxford: Oxford University Press, 2014, pp. 273–291.

García Pedraz, Fernando. *Consecuencias económicas de una eventual secesión de Cataluña sobre Cataluña.* Madrid: Facultad de Ciencias Económicas y Empresariales. ICADE, 2015.

Gilbert, Geoff. "The Legal Protection Accorded to Minority Groups in Europe", *Netherlands Yearbook of International Law*, vol. 23, 1992, pp. 67–104.

Gjidara, Marc. "Cadres juridiques été règles applicables aux problèmes européens de minorités". *Annuaire Français de Droit International*, vol. 37, no. 1, 1991, pp. 349–386.

González Campos, Julio D., Luis Ignacio Sánchez Rodríguez and Paz Andrés Sáenz de Santa María. *Curso de Derecho Internacional Público.* Madrid: Civitas, 2008.

Goodwin, Morag. "From Province to Protectorate to State? Speculation on the Impact of Kosovo's Genesis upon the Doctrines of International Law". *German Law Journal*, 2007, vol. 8, no. 1, pp. 1–20.

Grant, Thomas D. *The Recognition of States: Law and Practice in Debate and Evolution.* Westport: Praeger, 1999.

Grant, Thomas. "Defining Statehood: The Montevideo Convention and its Discontents". *Columbia Journal of Transnational Law*, vol. 37, 1998–1999, pp. 403–458.

Gros Espiell, Héctor. "En torno al derecho a la libre determinación de los pueblos". *Anuario de Derecho Internacional*, vol. 3, 1976, pp. 49–74.

Grotius, Hugo. *De Iure Belli ac Pacis.* 1646.

Guibernau, Montserrat. "Prospects for an Independent Catalonia". *International Journal of Politics, Culture and Society*, vol. 27, 2014, pp. 5–23.

Guilhaudis, Jean François. *Le droit des peuples à disposer d'eux-mêmes.* Grenoble: Presses Universitaires, 1976.

Gutiérrez Espada, Cesáreo and Romualdo Bermejo García. "*Kosovo de nuevo: apuntes críticos sobre su declaración de independencia, su constitución y otras reflexiones*". Real Instituto Elcano, Working Document no. 41, 2008.
Gutiérrez Espada, Cesáreo and Romualdo Bermejo García. "*De la opinión consultiva de las Corte Internacional de Justicia, de 22 de julio de 2010, sobre Kosovo*". Real Instituto Elcano, Working Document no. 35, 2010.
Gutiérrez Espada, Cesáreo and Romualdo Bermejo García. "El derecho de libre determinación de los pueblos no coloniales a la luz del Derecho internacional". In *La autodeterminación a debate*, edited by J.J. Solozábal. Madrid: Edit. P. Iglesias, 2014, pp. 93–108.
Hannum, Hurst. "Rethinking Self-Determination". *Virginia Journal of International Law*, vol. 34, 1993, pp. 19–25.
Hannum, Hurst. "The Specter of Secession: Responding to Claims for Ethnic Self-Determination". *Foreign Affairs*, vol. 77, no. 2, 1998, pp. 13–18.
Helgesen, Jan E. "Protecting Minorities in the Conference on Security and Co-operation in Europe (CSCE) Process". *International Journal on Group Rights*, vol. 2, no. 1, 1994, pp. 7–34.
Heraclides, Alexis. *The Self-Determination of Minorities in International Politics*. New York: Routledge, 1991.
Higgins, Rosalyn. *Problems and Process: International Law and How We Use It*. Oxford: Clarendon Press, 1994.
Holsti, Kalavi J. *Taming the Sovereigns: Institutional Change in International Politics*. Cambridge: Cambridge University Press, 2004.
Horowitz, Donald L. *Ethnic Groups in Conflict*. Los Angeles: University of California Press, Updated Edition, 2000.
Howard, Rhoda E. *Human Rights in Commonwealth Africa*. Totowa, NJ: Rowman and Littlefield, 1986.
Hoyle, P.A. "The Eritrean National Identity: A Case Study". *North Carolina Journal of International Law and Commercial Regulation*, vol. 24, 1998, pp. 381–416.
Humphrey, John P. *Human Rights and the United Nations. A Great Adventure*. New York: Transnational Pub., 1984.
Islam, M. Rafiqul. "Secession Crisis in Papua New Guinea: The Proclaimed Republic of Bougainville in International Law". *University of Hawaii Law Review*, vol. 13, no. 2, 1991, pp. 453–476.
Jellinek, Georg. *Allgemeine Staatslehr*. Berlin: Verlag von O. Haring, 1905.
Jennings, Robert Yewdall. "Nullity and Effectiveness". In *Cambridge Essays in International Law Essays in Honour of Lord McNair*. London: Stevens & Sons, 1965.
Jiménez de Aréchaga, Eduardo. *Derecho Internacional Público*, vol. 2, Montevideo: Fundación Cultura Universitaria, 1995.
Johnson, C. Don. "Toward Self-Determination – A Reappraisal as Reflected in the Declaration on Friendly Relations". *Georgia Journal of International and Comparative Law*, vol. 3, no. 1, 1973, pp. 145–163.
Kamenu, Onyeonoro S. "Secession and the Right of Self-Determination: An OAU Dilemma". *Journal of Modern African Studies*, vol. 12, 1974, pp. 355–376.
Keating, Joshua. "How to Start Your Own Country in Four Easy Steps". *Foreign Policy*, February 2008.
Kelsen, Hans. "The Pure Theory of Law and Analytical Jurisprudence". *Harvard Law Review*, vol. 55, 1941–1942, pp. 44–70.
Kelsen, Hans. *Principles of International Law*. New York: Rinehart, 1952.

Kibble, Steve. "Somaliland: Surviving Without Recognition". *International Relations*, vol. 15, no. 5, 2001, pp. 5–25.

Kohen, Marcelo G. "La création d'états en droit international contemporain". *Cursos Euromediterráneos Bancaja de Derecho Internacional*, vol. 6, 2002, pp. 543–636.

Kohen, Marcelo G. "Introduction". *Secession. International Law Perspectives*, edited by Kohen. Cambridge: Cambridge University Press, 2006, pp. 1–20.

Kooijmans, P.H. "Tolerance, Sovereignty and Self-Determination". *Netherlands International Law Review*, vol. 43, 1996, pp. 211–217.

Koskenniemi, Martti. "National Self-Determination Today: Problems of Legal Theory and Practice". *The International and Comparative Law Quarterly*, vol. 43, no. 2, 1994, pp. 241–269.

Kreijen, Gerard. *State Failure, Sovereignty and Effectiveness*. Leiden: Martinus Nijhoff, 2004.

Kreyenbroek, Philip G. and Stefan Sperl (eds.). *The Kurds. A Contemporary Overview*. New York: Routledge, 1992.

Kumbaro, Dajena. *The Kosovo Crisis in an International Law Perspective: Self-Determination. Territorial Integrity and the NATO Intervention*. NATO Report, 2001.

Lagerwall, Anne. *Le principe ex injuria jus non oritur en droit international*. Bruexelles: Bruylant, 2016.

Lauterpacht, Hersch. *Recognition in International Law*. Cambridge: Cambridge University Press, 1947.

Lauterpacht, Hersch. *Oppenheim, International Law: A Treatise*. London, New York, Toronto: Longmans, Green, and Co., 8th ed., 1955.

Lirola Delgado, Isabel. "El ejercicio de las relaciones exteriores de Kosovo por la UNMIK. ¿Una nueva manera de crear un "frankenstein" en Derecho Internacional?". *Revista Académica de Relaciones Internacionales*, vol. 10, 2009.

Liszt, Franz von. *Das Völkerrecht: Systematisch Dargestellt*. Berlin: Häring, 1904.

Lokosang, Laila. *South Sudan: The Case for Independence & Learning from Mistakes*. Bloomington, IN: Xlibris, 2010.

López Basaguren, Alberto. "Escocia: el referéndum sobre la independencia y la propuesta de reforma de la Devolution". *Revista Española de Derecho Constitucional*, vol. 104, 2015, pp. 135–147.

López Martín, Ana Gemma. *El territorio estatal en discusión: la prueba del título*. Madrid: McGraw Hill, 1999.

López Martín, Ana G. *Derecho internacional público*. Madrid: Dilex, 5th ed., 2019.

López Martín, Ana G. and José Antonio Perea Unceta. "Los efectos en los derechos humanos de las secesiones de Estados y entidades no aceptadas por la comunidad internacional". *Foro, Nueva Época*, vol. 21, no. 1, 2018, pp. 57–91.

López Martín, Ana G. and José Antonio Perea Unceta. *Creación de Estados, secesión y reconocimiento*. Valencia: Tirant lo Blanch, 2018.

Mansergh, Nicholas. "Ireland: The Republic Outside the Commonwealth". *International Affairs*, vol. 28, no. 3, 1952, pp. 277–291.

Mariño Menéndez, Fernando. "Naciones Unidas y el derecho de autodeterminación". In *Balance y perspectivas de las Naciones Unidas en el cincuentenario de su creación*. Madrid: Universidad Carlos III, 1996.

Martínez Jiménez, Aitor. *El derecho de autodeterminación de los pueblos en el siglo XXI*. Pamplona: Aranzadi, 2015.

McCorquodale, Robert. "Self-Determination: A Human Rights Approach". *International and Comparative Law Quarterly*, vol. 43, no. 4, 1994, pp. 857–885.

McIntosh, Simeon. "The St. Kitts-Nevis Question: Secession or Constitutional Reform?". *Caribbean Law Review*, vol. 7, 1997, pp. 419–463.
Menon, Palat K. *The Law of Recognition in International Law: Basic Principles*. New York: Edwin Mellen Press Ltd, 1994.
Miaja de la Muela, Adolfo. "El principio de efectividad en Derecho internacional". In *Cursos de Derecho internacional de Vitoria 1957*. Valladolid, Spain: Universidad de Valladolid, 1958.
Miaja de la Muela, Adolfo. "Nuevas realidades y teorías sobre la efectividad en Derecho internacional". *ADI*, vol. 3, 1976, pp.3–47.
Miguel Bárcena, Josu de. "El proceso soberanista ante el Tribunal Constitucional". *Revista Española de Derecho Constitucional*, vol. 113, 2018, pp. 133–166.
Murswiek, Dietrich. "The Issue of a Right of Secession Reconsidered". In *Modern Law of Self-Determination*, edited by Christian Tomuschat. Dordrecht: Nijhoff, 1993, pp. 21–39.
Musgrave, Thomas D. *Self-Determination and National Minorities*. New York: Oxford University Press, 2000.
Mustafa, Zubeida. "The Principle of Self-Determination in International Law". *The International Lawyer*, vol. 5, no. 3, 1971, pp. 479–487.
Nanda, Ved P. "Self-Determination under International Law: Validity of Claims to Secede". *Case Western Journal of International Law*, vol. 13, no. 2, 1981, pp. 257–280.
Nayar, M.G. Kaladharan. "Self-Determination Beyond the Colonial Context: Biafra in Retrospect". *Texas International Law Journal*, vol. 10, 1975, pp. 321–346.
Nicholson, Rowan and Thomas D. Grant. "Theories of State Recognition". In *Routledge Handbook of State Recognition*, edited by Visoka Gëzim, John Doyle and Edward Newman. New York: Routledge, 2019.
Noronha, Kimberly M. "Refugees and National Identity: National Identity and Eritrean Refugees in the Sudan". Available at SSRN: https://ssrn.com/abstract=1026847, 2004.
Oeter, Stefan. "Secession, Territorial Integrity and the Role of the Security Council". In *Kosovo and International Law: The ICJ Advisory Opinion of 22 July 2010*, edited by Peter Hilpold. Leiden: Nijhoff, 2012, pp. 109–138.
Oeter, Stefan. "The Role of Recognition and Non-Recognition with Regard to Secession". *Self-Determination and Secession in International Law*, edited by Christian Walter and others. Oxford: Oxford University Press, 2014, pp. 51–74.
Ofuatey-Kodjoe, W. *The Principle of Self-Determination in International Law*. New York: Nellen, 1977.
Okoronkwo, Pius L. "Self-Determination and the Legality of Biafra's Secession under International Law". *Loyola of Los Angeles International and Comparative Law Review*, vol. 25, no. 1, Winter 2002, pp. 63–116.
Onguergouz, Fatsah. *The African Charter on Human and Peoples' Rights: A Comprehensive Agenda for Human Rights and Sustainable Democracy in Africa*. The Hague: Kluwer Law International, 2003.
Oppenheim, Lassa. *International Law: A Treatise. Vol. I. - Peace*. New Jersey: The Lawbook Exchange. Clark, 3rd ed., 1920.
Oraison, André. "L'obligation n de non-reconnaissance de l'État d'Anjouan: les problèmes posés par la nouvelle balkanisation de la République fédérale islamique des Comores". *Annuaire des pays de l'océan Indien*, vol. 15, 1997, pp. 143–164.
Orakhelashvili, Alexander. "Statehood, Recognition and the United Nations System: A Unilateral Declaration of Independence in Kosovo". *Max Planck Yearbook of United Nations Law*, vol. 12, 2008, pp. 1–44.

Orakhelashvili, Alexander. *Peremptory Norms in International Law*. Oxford: Oxford University Press, 2006.

Oskam, Jeroen. "A New State in Europe? Scenarios for Catalan Self-Determination". *Futures*, vol. 64, 2014, pp. 51–60.

Pagliari, Arturo S. *Curso de Derecho internacional público*. Córdoba: Advocatus, 2nd ed., 2013.

Palmisano, Giuseppe. *Nazioni Unite e autodeterminazione interna*. Milano: Giuffrè, 1997.

Pavkovic, Aleksandar and Peter Radan. *Creating New States. Theory and Practice of Secession*. Aldershot: Ashgate, 2007.

Pegg, Scott. *International Society and the De Facto State*. Aldershot: Ashgate, 1998.

Pellet, Alain. "The Opinions of the Badinter Arbitration Committee. A Second Breath for the Self-Determination of Peoples". *European Journal of International Law*, vol. 3, January1992, pp. 178–185.

Pellet, Alain. "Quel avenir pour le droit des peuples à disposer d'eux-mêmes?" In *El Derecho internacional en un mundo en transformación. Liber Amicorum en Homenaje al profesor Eduardo Jiménez de Aréchaga*. Montevideo: Fundación de Cultura Universitaria, 1994.

Pentassuglia, Gaetano. *Minorities in International Law. An Introductory Study*. Strasbourg: Council of Europe Publishing, 2002.

Perea Unceta, José Antonio. *La actuación de las Naciones Unidas en el conflicto de la Antigua Yugoslavia*. Madrid: UCM, 2000.

Perea Unceta, José Antonio. "Los derechos de las minorías nacionales en las entidades secesionadas no reconocidas: jurisdicción del Tribunal Europeo de Derechos Humanos y atribución de la responsabilidad en su efectiva protección". In *Las minorías en el contexto actual*, edited by Ana G. López Martín and Carmen Otero García-Castrillón. Madrid: Dykinson, 2020, pp. 27–57.

Peters, Anne. "Statehood after 1989: 'Effectivités' between Legality and Virtuality". *Proceedings of the European Society of International Law*, vol. 3, 2010, pp. 1–13.

Peters, Anne. "The Principle of Uti Possidetis Iuris: How Relevant is it for Issues of Secession?". In *Self-Determination and Secession in International Law*, edited by Christian Walter et al., Oxford: Oxford University Press, 2014, pp. 95–137.

Pierce, Anne Rice. *Woodrow Wilson and Harry Truman: Mission and Power in American Foreign Policy*. Westport: Praeger, 2003.

Pomerance, Michla. *Self-Determination in Law and Practice: The New Doctrine of the United Nations*. The Hague: Nijhoff, 1982.

Pomerance, Michla. "The Badinter Commission: The Use and Misuse of the International Court of Justice's Jurisprudence". *Michigan Journal of International Law*, vol. 20, no. 1, 1998, pp. 31–58.

Pons Rafols, Xavier. "Sentencia del Tribunal Constitucional (Pleno) 42/2014, de 25 de marzo de 2014". *Revista de Derecho Internacional*, vol. 2, 2014, pp. 201–210.

Pons Rafols, Xavier. *Cataluña: Derecho a decidir y Derecho internacional*. Madrid: Reus, 2015.

Quane, Helen. "The United Nations and the Evolving Right to Self-Determination". *International & Comparative Law Q.*, vol. 47, 1998, pp. 537–572.

Quel López, F. Javier. "La práctica reciente en materia de reconocimiento de Estados: Problemas en presencia". In *Cursos de Derecho Internacional de Vitoria-Gasteiz*, Madrid: Tecnos, 1994, pp. 39–82.

Quivooij, Romain. "The Islamic State". *Policy Report*, 2015.

Radan, Peter. "Post-Secession International Borders: A Critical Analysis of the Opinions of the Badinter Arbitration Commission". *Melbourne University Law Review*, vol. 24, no. 1, 2000, pp. 50–76.

Radan, Peter. "Secession: A Word in Search of Meaning". In *On the Way to Statehood: Secession and Globalisation*, edited by Aleksandar Pavkovic and Peter Radan. Aldershot: Ashgate, 2008, pp. 17–31.

Ragone, Sabrina. "Los Länder no son señores de la Constitución: el Tribunal Constitucional Federal Alemán sobre el referéndum separatista bávaro". *Teoría y realidad constitucional*, vol. 41, 2018, pp. 407–418.

Redslob, Robert. "Le principe des nationalités". *Recueils des Courses de l'Académie de Droit International*, The Hague, vol. 37, no. 3, 1931, pp. 1–82.

Remiro Brotons, Antonio et al. *Derecho internacional*. Madrid: McGraw Hill, 1997.

Richter, Dagmar. "Illegal States?". In *Unrecognised Subjects in International Law*, edited by Władysław Czapliński and Agata Kleczkowska. Warsaw: Scholar Publishing House Ltd., 2019, pp. 19–57.

Ridao, Joan. *El dret a decidir. La consulta sobre el futur politic de Catalunya*. Barcelona: Institut d'Estudis Autonòmics, 2014.

Rigo Sureda, Andrés. *The Evolution of the Right of Self-Determination*. Leyden: Sijthoff, 1973.

Roben, Volker. "The ICJ Advisory Opinion on the Unilateral Declaration of Independence in Respect of Kosovo: Rules or Principles". *Goettingen Journal of International Law*, vol. 2, no. 3, 2010, pp. 1063–1086.

Roch, François. "Réflexions sur l'évolution de la positivité du droit des peuples à disposer d'eux-mêmes en dehors des situations de décolonisation". *Revue québécoise de droit international*, vol. 15, no. 1, 2002, pp. 33–100.

Rodríguez Villena, Alejandro. "Análisis de la situación de la minoría grecochipriota en la República Turca de Norte de Chipre desde el Derecho internacional". In *Las minorías en el contexto actual*, edited by Ana G. López Martín and Carmen Otero García-Castrillón. Madrid: Dykinson, 2020, pp. 59–72.

Roethke, Peter, "The Right to Secede Under International Law: The Case of Somaliland". *Journal of Modern African Studies*, 2006, pp. 35–47.

Rosenstock, Robert. "The Declaration of Principles of International Law Concerning Friendly Relations: A Survey". *American Journal of International Law*, vol. 65, no. 5, 1971, pp. 713–735.

Roth, Brad. "Secession, Coups and the International Rule of Law: Assessing the Decline of the Effective Control Doctrine". *Melbourne Journal of International Law*, vol. 11, 2010, pp. 1–47.

Rousseau, Charles. *Droit international public*. Paris: Dalloz, 1974.

Rozakis, Christos L. *The Concept of Jus Cogens in the Law of Treaties*. Oxford: North Holland Publishing Co., 1976.

Ruiz Fabri, Hélène. "Genèse et disparition de l'État à l'époque contemporaine". *Annuaire Français de Droit International*, vol. 38, 1992, pp. 153–178.

Rupen, Robert A. "Notes on Outer Mongolia Since 1945". *Pacific Affairs*, vol. 28, no. 1, 1995, pp. 71–79.

Ryngaert, Cedrick and Christine W. Griffioen. "The Relevance of the Right to Self-Determination in the Kosovo Matter: In Partial Response to the Agora Papers". *Chinese Journal of International Law*, vol. 8, no. 3, 2009, pp. 573–587.

Salmon, Jean. "L'État dans le droit international d'aujourd'hui". *Recueil des Cours*, vol. 347, 2010, pp. 9–78.

Salvioli, Grabiele. "L'effettività in Diritto internazionale". *Rivista trimestrale di Diritto Pubblico*, 1953, pp. 271–280.

Saxena, J.N. *Self-Determination: From Biafra to Bangla Desh*. Delhi: University of Delhi, 1978.

Scelle, George. *Précis de Droit des Gens: Principes et Systématique*. Paris: Dalloz, 1932.

Seara Vázquez, Modesto. *Derecho internacional público*. Mexico: Editorial Porrua, 1991.

Premdas, Ralphe, W.R. de A. Samarasinghe and Alan Anderson (eds.). *Secessionist Movements in Comparative Perspective*. London: Bloomsbury, 1993.

Servitja, Xavier. "El Estado Islámico y la organización administrativa del Califato a nivel provincial". *Revista de Estudios en Seguridad Internacional*, vol. 18, 2015.

Shaw, Malcolm. *International Law*. Cambridge: Cambridge University Press, 8th ed., 2017.

Smouts, Marie-Claude. "Décolonisation et sécession: double morale à l'ONU?". *Revue Française de Science Politique*, vol. 22, no. 4, 1972, pp. 832–846.

Sorenson, John. "Opposition, Exile and Identity: The Eritrean Case". *Journal of Refugee Studies*, vol. 3, no. 4, 1990, pp. 298–319.

Sornarajah, M. "Internal Colonialism and Humanitarian Intervention". *Georgia Journal of International and Comparative Law*, vol. 11, 1981, pp. 45–77.

Soroeta Liceras, Juan. "La opinión consultiva de la Corte Internacional de Justicia sobre Kosovo de 22 de julio de 2010". *Revista Electrónica de Estudios Internacionales*, vol. 25, 2013.

Souleimanov, Emil Aslan, Eduard Abrahamyan and Huseyn, Aliyev. "Unrecognized States as a Means of Coercive Diplomacy? Assessing the Role of Abkhazia and South Ossetia in Russia's Foreign Policy in the South Caucasus". *Southeast European and Black Sea Studies*, vol. 18, no. 1, 2018, pp. 73–86.

Stavenhagen, Rodolfo. *Los pueblos indígenas y sus derechos*. México: UNESCO, 2007.

Sterio, Milena. *Secession in International Law: A New Framework*. Cheltenham: Elgar, 2018.

Stokke, Kristian. "Building the Tamil Eelam State: Emerging State Institutions and Forms of Governance in LTTE-Controlled Areas in Sri Lanka". *Third World Quarterly*, vol. 27, no. 6, 2006, pp. 1021–1040.

Summers, James. "Kosovo". In *Self-Determination and Secession in International Law*, edited by Christian Walter et al. Oxford: Oxford University Press, 2014, pp. 235–253.

Summers, James. *People and International Law – How Nationalism and Self-Determination Shape a Contemporary Law of Nations*. Leiden: Martinus Nijhoff, 2007.

Suzuki, Eisuke. "Self-Determination and World Public Order: Community Response to Territorial Separation". *Virginia Journal of International Law*, vol. 16, 1976, pp. 799–864.

Taki, H. "Effectiveness". In *Max Planck Encyclopedia of Public International Law*, vol. III. Oxford: Oxford Public International Law, 2010, para. 10

Talmon, Stefan. *La non-reconnaissance collective des États illégaux*. Cours et travaux no 9. Paris: Université Pantheon-Assas, 2007.

Tancredi, Antonello. "A Normative 'Due Process' in the Creation of States Through Secession". In *Secession. International Law Perspectives*, edited by Marcelo G. Kohen. Cambridge: Cambridge University Press, 2006.

Tancredi, Antonello. *La secessione nel diritto internazionale*. Padova: Cedam, 2006.

Thornberry, Patrick. *International Law and the Rights of Minorities*. Oxford: Clarendon Press, 1991.

Tomuschat, Christian. "Self-Determination in a Post-Colonial World". In *Modern Law of Self-Determination*. Dordrecht: Nijhoff, 1993, pp. 1–19.

Tomuschat, Christian. "International Law: Ensuring the Survival of Mankind on the Eve of a New Century. General Course on Public International Law". *Recueil des Cours*, vol. 281, 2001, pp. 9–438.

Tomuschat, Christian. "The Status of the 'Islamic State' under International Law". *Die Friedens-Warte*, vol. 90, no. 3–4, 2015, pp. 223–244.

Touscoz, Jean. *Le principe d'effectivité dans l'ordre international*. Paris: Librairie générale de droit et de jurisprudence, 1964.

Tunkin, Grigory Ivanovich. *Theory of International Law*. Cambridge, MA: Harvard University Press, 1974.

Umozurike, U. Orji. *Self-Determination in International Law*. Hamden: Archdon Books, 1972.

Van Den Driest, Simone F. *Remedial Secession: A Right to External Self-Determination as a Remedy to Serious Injustices*. Antwerp: Intersentia, 2013.

Vashakmadze, Mindia and Matthias Lippold. "Nothing but a Road towards Secession – The International Court of Justice's Advisory Opinion on Accordance with International Law of the Unilateral Declaration of Independence in Respect of Kosovo". *Goettingen Journal of International Law*, vol. 2, no. 2, 2010, pp. 646–647.

Vattel, Emer de. *Le Droit des Gens*. 1758.

Verdross, Alfred. *Derecho internacional público* (translated by Antonio Truyol Serra). Madrid: Aguilar, 1957.

Verhoeven, Joe. "La reconnaissance internationale: Déclin ou renouveau?" *AFDI*, vol. 29, no. 9, 1993, pp. 7–40.

Vidmar, Jure. "South Sudan and the International Legal Framework Governing the Emergence and Delimitation of New States". *Texas International Law Journal*, vol. 47, no. 3, Summer 2012, pp. 541–560.

Vidmar, Jure. "The Annexation of Crimea and the Boundaries of the Will of the People". *German Law Journal*, vol. 16, 2015, pp. 365–383.

Virally, Michael. "Panorama du droit international contemporain. Cours général de droit international public". *Recueil des Cours*, vol. 183, no. 5, 1983, pp. 13–382.

Visoka, Gëzim, John Doyle and Edward Newman. *Routledge Handbook of State Recognition*. New York: Routledge, 2019.

Vitoria, Francisco. *De Indis ac de Iure Belli Relectiones*. Ed. Simon. 1696.

Wallace-Bruce, Nii Lante. *Claims to Statehood in International Law*. New York: Carlton Press, 1994.

Walter, Christian. *Self-Determination and Secession in International Law*, edited by Ch. Walter, Anetje Von Ungern-Sternberg and Kavus Abushov. Oxford: Oxford University Press, 2014.

Weiss, Gordon. *The Cage: The Fight for Sri Lanka and the Last Days of the Tamil Tigers*. New York: Bellevue Literary Press, 2012.

Welhengama, Gnanapala and Nirmala Pillay. *The Rise of Tamil Separatism in Sri Lanka: From Communalism to Secession*. New York: Routledge, 2014.

Weller, Marc. *The Rights of Minorities in Europe*. Oxford: Oxford University Press, 2005.

Weller, Marc. *Escaping the Self-Determination Trap*. Leiden: Nijhoff, 2008.

Wilson, Gary. "Self-Determination, Recognition and the Problem of Kosovo". *Netherlands International Law Review*, vol. 56, no. 3, 2009, pp. 455–481.

Wood, John R. "Secession: A Comparative Analytical Framework". *Canadian Journal of Political Science*, vol. 14, 1981, pp. 109–135.

Wright, Jane. "The OSCE and the Protection of Minority Rights". *Human Rights Quarterly*, vol. 18, no. 1, 1996, pp. 190–205.

Xanthaki, Alexandra. *Indigenous Rights and United Nations Standards. Self-Determination, Culture and Land*. New York: Cambridge University Press, 2007.

Yakemtchouk, Romain. "Les républiques baltes en droit international. Echec d'une annexion opérée en violation du droit des gens". *Annuaire Français de Droit International*, vol. 37, 1991, pp. 259–289.

Appendix

Year	*New State*	*Parent State*	*Form*
2011	South Sudan	Sudan	**secession**
2006	Montenegro	Serbia and Montenegro	separation
2002	East Timor	Indonesia	**secession**
2000	Tuvalu	United Kingdom	decolonisation
1999	Kiribati	United Kingdom	decolonisation
	Nauru	Australia	decolonisation
	Tonga	United Kingdom	decolonisation
1994	Palau	USA	decolonisation
1993	Andorra	Spain/France	former protectorate
	Czech Republic	Czechoslovakia	separation: dissolution
	Slovakia	Czechoslovakia	separation: dissolution
	Eritrea	Ethiopia	**secession**
1992	Bosnia and Herzegovina	Yugoslavia	**secession**
	Serbia and Montenegro	Yugoslavia	separation: dissolution
1991	Ukraine	USSR	separation
	Belarus	USSR	separation
	Moldova	USSR	separation
	Georgia	USSR	separation
	Armenia	USSR	separation
	Azerbaijan	USSR	separation

Year	*New State*	*Parent State*	*Form*
	Uzbekistan	USSR	separation
	Kazakhstan	USSR	separation
	Turkmenistan	USSR	separation
	Tajikistan	USSR	separation
	Kyrgyzstan	USSR	separation
	Estonia	USSR	**secession**
	Latvia	USSR	**secession**
	Lithuania	USSR	**secession**
	Marshall Islands	USA	decolonisation
	Micronesia	USA	decolonisation
1991	Slovenia	Yugoslavia	**secession**
	Croatia	Yugoslavia	**secession**
	Macedonia	Yugoslavia	**secession**
1990	Namibia	South Africa	decolonisation
	Yemen	North and South Yemen	union
1984	Brunei	United Kingdom	former protectorate
1983	Saint Kitts and Nevis	United Kingdom	decolonisation
1981	Antigua and Barbuda	United Kingdom	decolonisation
1981	Belize	United Kingdom	decolonisation
1980	Vanuatu	UK/France	decolonisation
1979	Saint Vincent and the Grenadines	United Kingdom	decolonisation
1979	Saint Lucia	United Kingdom	decolonisation
1978	Dominica	United Kingdom	decolonisation
1978	Solomon Islands	United Kingdom	decolonisation
1977	Djibouti	France	decolonisation
1976	Seychelles	United Kingdom	decolonisation
1975	Angola	Portugal	decolonisation
1975	Cape Verde	Portugal	decolonisation
1975	Comoros	Francia	decolonisation
1975	Mozambique	Portugal	decolonisation

Year	*New State*	*Parent State*	*Form*	
1975	Papua New Guinea	Australia	decolonisation	
1975	São Tomé and Príncipe	Portugal	decolonisation	
1975	Surinam	Netherlands	decolonisation	
1974	Granada	United Kingdom	decolonisation	
1973	Guinea-Bissau	Portugal	decolonisation	
1973	Bahamas	United Kingdom	decolonisation	
1971	Bahrain	United Kingdom	former protectorate	
1971	UAE	United Kingdom	former protectorate	
1971	Oman	United Kingdom	former protectorate	
1971	Qatar	United Kingdom	former protectorate	
1971	Bangladesh	Pakistan	**secession**	
1970	Fiji	United Kingdom	decolonisation	
1968	Equatorial Guinea	Spain	decolonisation	
1968	Mauritius	United Kingdom	decolonisation	
1968	Swaziland	United Kingdom	former protectorate	
1967	South Yemen	United Kingdom	decolonisation	until 1990
1966	Barbados	United Kingdom	decolonisation	
1966	Botswana	United Kingdom	decolonisation	
1966	Guyana	Netherlands	decolonisation	
1966	Lesotho	United Kingdom	former protectorate	
1965	Rhodesia – Zimbabwe (1979)	United Kingdom	decolonisation	
1965	Gambia	United Kingdom	decolonisation	
1965	Maldives	United Kingdom	decolonisation	
1965	Singapore	Malaysia	separation	
1964	Malawi	United Kingdom	former protectorate	
1964	Malta	United Kingdom	decolonisation	
1964	Tanzania	Tanganyika and Zanzibar	union	

Year	*New State*	*Parent State*	*Form*	
1963	Kenya	United Kingdom	decolonisation	
1963	Zanzibar	United Kingdom	former protectorate	
1962	Samoa	New Zealand	decolonisation	
1962	Algeria	France	decolonisation	
1962	Burundi	Belgium	decolonisation	until 1964
1962	Jamaica	United Kingdom	decolonisation	
1962	Rwanda	Belgium	decolonisation	
1962	Trinidad and Tobago	United Kingdom	decolonisation	
1962	Uganda	United Kingdom	decolonisation	
1961	Kuwait	United Kingdom	former protectorate	
1961	Egypt	UAR	separation: dissolution	
1961	Syria	UAR	separation: dissolution	
1961	Mauritania	France	decolonisation	
1961	Sierra Leone	United Kingdom	decolonisation	
1961	Tanganyika	United Kingdom	decolonisation	until 1964
1960	Upper Volta – Burkina Faso (1984)	France	decolonisation	
1960	Cameroon	France/UK	decolonisation	
1960	Central African Republic	France	decolonisation	
1960	Chad	France	decolonisation	
1960	Congo	France	decolonisation	
1960	Zaire – DR Congo (1997)	Belgium	decolonisation	
1960	Nigeria	United Kingdom	decolonisation	
1960	Madagascar	France	decolonisation	
1960	Senegal	Mali Federation	separation: dissolution	
1960	Mali	Mali Federation	separation: dissolution	
1960	Somalia	UK/Italy	decolonisation	

Year	New State	Parent State	Form	
1960	Togo	France	decolonisation	
1960	Cyprus	United Kingdom	decolonisation	
1960	Ivory Coast	France	decolonisation	
1960	Dahomey – Benin (1974)	France	decolonisation	
1960	Gabon	France	decolonisation	
1960	Niger	France	decolonisation	
1959	Mali Federation	France	decolonisation-separation	until 1960
1958	Guinea	France	decolonisation-separation	
1958	United Arab Republic (UAR)	Egypt and Syria	union	until 1961
1957	Malaysia	United Kingdom	decolonisation-separation	
1957	Ghana	United Kingdom	decolonisation-separation	
1956	Morocco	France/Spain	former protectorate	
1956	Sudan	UK/Egypt	former protectorate	
1956	Tunisia	France	decolonisation	
1955	Cambodia	France	former protectorate	
1954	Vietnam	France	decolonisation-secession	
1953	Laos	France	decolonisation-separation	
1949	Indonesia	Netherlands	decolonisation-secession	
1949	German Democratic Republic	Germany		until 1990
1948	Israel	United Kingdom	former mandate	
1948	Ceylon – Sri Lanka (1991)	United Kingdom	decolonisation-separation	
1948	Burma	United Kingdom	decolonisation-separation	
1948	South Korea	Japan/UN	decolonisation-separation	
1948	North Korea	Japan/UN	decolonisation-separation	

Year	*New State*	*Parent State*	*Form*	
1947	Pakistan	United Kingdom	decolonisation-secession	
1947	India	United Kingdom	decolonisation-secession	
1947	Libya	Italy	decolonisation-separation	
1946	Jordan	United Kingdom	former mandate	
1946	The Philippines	USA	decolonisation-separation	
1945	Syria	France	former mandate	
1944	Iceland	Denmark	separation	
1943	Lebanon	France	former mandate	
1932	Iraq	United Kingdom	former mandate	
1923	Egypt	United Kingdom	former protectorate	
1922	Ireland	United Kingdom	**secession**	
1921	Mongolia	China	**secession**	
1919	Afghanistan	United Kingdom	former protectorate	
1918	Hungary	Austria-Hungary	separation	
1918	North Yemen	Ottoman Empire	**secession**	until 1990
1918	Czechoslovakia	Austria-Hungary	**secession**	until 1992
1918	Yugoslavia	Serbia and others	union/secession	until 1992
1918	Poland	Russia/Germany/ Austria-Hungary	**secession**	until 1940
1918	Estonia	Russia	**secession**	until 1940
1918	Latvia	Russia	**secession**	until 1940
1918	Lithuania	Russia	**secession**	until 1940
1917	Finland	USSR	**secession**	
1912	Albania	Ottoman Empire	**secession**	
1910	South Africa	United Kingdom	decolonisation-separation	
1908	Bulgaria	Ottoman Empire	**secession**	
1903	Panama	Colombia	**secession**	

Year	*New State*	*Parent State*	*Form*	
1902	Cuba	USA	former protectorate	
1901	Australia	United Kingdom	decolonisation-separation	
1882	Serbia	Ottoman Empire	**secession**	until 1918
1878	Montenegro	Ottoman Empire	**secession**	until 1918
1877	Romania	Ottoman Empire	**secession**	

Index